M

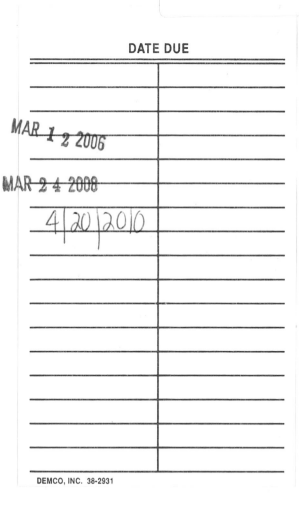

DATE DUE

MAR 1 2 2006	
MAR 2 4 2008	
4/20/2010	

DEMCO, INC. 38-2931

MAR 2 4 2004

THE FOURTH R

JOAN DELFATTORE

The Fourth R

Conflicts Over Religion in America's Public Schools

YALE UNIVERSITY PRESS   NEW HAVEN & LONDON

Designed by Rebecca Gibb. Set in Scala type by Ink, Inc. Printed in the United States of America by R. R. Donnelley.

Library of Congress Cataloguing-in-Publication Data
DelFattore, Joan, 1946–
The Fourth R : conflicts over religion in America's public schools / Joan DelFattore.
    p.   cm.
Includes bibliographic references and index.
ISBN 0-300-10217-8 (cloth : alk. paper)
1. Religion in the public schools—United States. I. Title.
LC111.D43 2004
379.2'8—dc22
2003017364

A catalogue record for this book is available from the British Library.

The paper in this book meets the guidelines for permanence and durability of the Committee on Production Guidelines for Book Longevity of the Council on Library Resources.

10 9 8 7 6 5 4 3 2 1

Dedicated with love to the memory of my father and aunt,
A. Richard Del Fattore (1921–1993) and sister M. Angelica
Del Fattore, O.P. (1929–2002)

Contents

Acknowledgments

This study benefited greatly from the generous financial support of the Spencer Foundation and the University of Delaware's Center for Advanced Study and General University Research Program. The research time and travel opportunities thus provided were invaluable.

I am also grateful to the many people who took time out of their sometimes frenetic schedules to be interviewed for this book. The information and insights they offered have made this study far richer than it would otherwise have been. Some of them—notably Elliot Mincberg, Deanna Duby, and Judith Schaeffer of People for the American Way; Brent Walker of the Baptist Joint Committee on Public Affairs; Barry Lynn, Steven Green, and G. Robert Boston of Americans United for Separation of Church and State; Kimberlee Colby of the Christian Legal Society; James Henderson of the American Center for Law and Justice; and Forest Montgomery of the National Association of Evangelicals —also gave me access to legal briefs, depositions, legislative and lobbying materials, and other published documents. Though a matter of public record, such items would have been difficult if not impossible to track down elsewhere, particularly with respect to events that took place some time ago. While it would be unrealistic to expect all these highly disparate thinkers—some of whom have moved on to new positions—to agree with everything in this book, I hope that they will find it at least reasonably balanced. It says much for their own commitment to open debate that their help was never made conditional on my viewpoint.

Special thanks are due to the members of Delaware's congressional delegation for giving me numerous opportunities to get out of the ivory tower for a close-up look at real politics. Senator William V. Roth (R), Senator Joseph R.

Biden, Jr. (D), and Representative Michael N. Castle (R) allowed me to accompany them to various events and patiently answered many questions, most beginning with "Why ...?" and some consisting entirely of "*Why?*" As a long-time member and former chairperson of the Senate Judiciary Committee, through which passed much of the legislation discussed in this book, Senator Biden spent additional hours sharing memories and reflections about the people, issues, and dynamics underlying that process. All this is greatly appreciated, as is the kindness shown to me by Senator Thomas R. Carper (D) and his staff during a summer fellowship in his office shortly after this book was completed—in preparation for the next one.

Last but by no means least, I am indebted to Robert M. O'Neil of the Thomas Jefferson Center for Protection of Free Expression and the University of Virginia School of Law, and to the other scholars who read the manuscript and made excellent suggestions. The same is true of editors Gladys Topkis, Erin Carter, and Nancy Moore Brochin, together with the many other people at Yale University Press who worked hard to bring this publication to fruition.

Whatever good qualities may be found in this book owe much to the thoughtfulness and expertise of the people mentioned here. Any mistakes are my own.

1

Crucible

Crucible: a vessel of a very refractory material ... used for melting
and calcining a substance that requires a high degree of heat; a
severe test; a place or situation in which concentrated forces interact
to cause or influence change or development.

—*Merriam Webster's Collegiate Dictionary*

In a *B.C.* comic strip, a child says that God must not be very smart because
"He's been kicked out of every school in the country." When another *B.C.*
child sneezes in school, he and his teacher have to go outside so the teacher
can say "God bless you." In another comic strip, *The Wizard of Id,* Sir Rodney
reports a small boy to the king for trying to smuggle a Bible into school in his
shoulder holster. A teenager in the comic strip *Kudzu* earns As for not bringing weapons to school, not smoking, and not using drugs, but he gets an F in
"Not Praying." Bumper stickers, talk shows, political speeches, and late-night
comedy monologues all spread the same message: God has been kicked out of
the public schools, and the mere mention of religion will bring the Supreme
Court swooping down like the Monty Python version of the Spanish Inquisition. Such assertions, which many Americans accept as common knowledge,
are catchy, emotionally compelling, and wildly misleading.

GETTING DOWN TO SPECIFICS
Consider three recent incidents involving religion in the public schools.

- A devout Christian student organizes and leads a prayer meeting in the
  school's lobby before class each morning. Approximately thirty-five students voluntarily join him in reading the Bible and praying before going to
  their homerooms.
- Sixth-graders are upset because a classmate has died, and their teacher tells

them that they need fear nothing because Jesus will save them. She lays her hands on their heads and prays for them.

- A first-grade teacher allows students to read aloud from books they bring from home. When one little boy comes in with *The Beginner's Bible,* the teacher has him read from it to her alone, not to the whole class.

Many Americans might assume that the first two examples are unlawful because they involve a connection between religion and public education, whereas the teacher in the third example either acted correctly or should have rejected the Bible reading altogether. In reality, the situation is more complex than that. Beginning in the early 1960s, the Supreme Court has repeatedly struck down *government-sponsored* religious observances, such as state-mandated Bible reading and prayer, while upholding the right of individual students to engage in religious speech on their own initiative.

Based on this distinction between the actions of school officials and those of students, the Court's decisions pose no obstacle to the first situation described above, in which a before-school prayer circle was organized by a student named Ben Strong at Heath High School in Paducah, Kentucky. This circle received national attention under tragic circumstances in December 1997, when some of its members were gunned down by a schoolmate who was subsequently subdued by Strong. According to newspaper accounts, the prayer circle was operated entirely by students and took place when they were not in class and were free to talk about any subject of their choice. There was no indication that any student was coerced to participate or that teachers or administrators were involved. If all this is true, then school officials would have no obligation— and, indeed, no right—to act as "prayer police," permitting students to talk about sports, music, politics, and other secular subjects but silencing any mention of religion. Such discrimination with regard to the students' private speech would represent hostility toward religion, not the governmental neutrality mandated by the Constitution.

By contrast, the second example presented here involves a teacher-initiated, teacher-run religious exercise that clearly conflicts with the Supreme Court decisions discussed throughout this book. At the center of the controversy was Mildred Rosario, a substitute teacher at Intermediate School 74 in the Bronx, who described herself as a born-again Pentecostal Christian. Her purpose, she later explained, was to console her grieving students by giving them hope in Jesus following the drowning death of their classmate. Although the impromptu prayer service she conducted in June 1998 took place during class time, she felt that she had adequately protected her students' religious liberty by telling them that if they preferred not to pray they could work on the computers in the back of the room or read a book. No one did so, but one student, a Jehovah's Witness, later complained that she had been uncomfortable with the prayers but had felt constrained to stay in her seat. Rosario was fired over the protests of political figures, such as Speaker of the House Newt Gingrich (R-Georgia) and Mayor Rudolph Giuliani, who called for the return of religion and morality to the crime-wracked public schools.

By far the most difficult of the three examples is the last, which combines student initiative with the actions of school officials. It arose in Medford Township, New Jersey, where first-grade teacher Grace Oliva rewarded proficient readers by allowing them to bring their favorite books from home to read aloud in class. Among the students thus selected was Zachary Hood, who brought in a children's version of the Bible and proposed to read the story of Jacob and Esau. When Oliva prevented him from reading it to the other students, his mother, Carol Hood, filed suit. The federal district court dismissed the complaint, saying among other things that if Oliva had allowed Zachary to read a Bible story to the class, her six-year-old students might well have formed the impression that she approved of it as a religious text—an impression that might have been strengthened had she said something like "Very good" at the end of the reading. A three-judge panel of the Court of Appeals for the Third Circuit upheld this decision, but when all fourteen Third Circuit judges subsequently reviewed it, they tied. This outcome, which had the effect of sustaining the earlier ruling, illustrates the difficulty of balancing a student's right to express religious views against the school's obligation to avoid endorsing or hindering the beliefs of either the speaker or the listeners.[1]

Not surprisingly, much of the current debate over prayer in public schools involves gray-area situations of this kind, in which the overlapping actions of students and school officials give rise to substantial disagreement about where the lines should be drawn with respect to religious activity. In a case discussed in Chapter Thirteen, for instance, a high school principal suggested to student council members that they could have daily prayers if they asked to do so, whereupon they made the request. Do those prayers qualify as student-initiated, or were they the result of the principal's action? In a similar case, the parents of young children wished to have them participate in before-school-prayer services run by older students. Is it lawful for teachers to escort them as a group? As these examples suggest, the current standard for dealing with religion in the public schools, which might be summarized as "Student-Run

Prayer Good; School-Run Prayer Bad," is by no means as clear-cut as it might appear. Moreover, transcending concerns about its application to specific situations is the larger question of whether, if it could be carried out perfectly in practice, this standard would be the best one to use.

In order to assess the present approach to school prayer in an informed way, it is essential to understand why and how it came to be what it is. As its complexity and uncertainties suggest, it was not conceived in ivory-tower serenity as a sort of Platonic ideal of religion in the public schools. Rather, it represents the outcome of more than a century of raucous push-and-pull among warring interests and viewpoints whose adherents have fought each other in the courts, in the legislatures, and sometimes in the streets. Diverse though their immediate catalysts have been, these disputes have tended to converge into a gradual movement, always uneven and to this day incomplete, from a highly majoritarian view of school prayer toward an increasing deference to individual choice. At the majoritarian end of this continuum lie the nineteenth- and early twentieth-century events discussed in the next few chapters, in which schoolchildren were routinely beaten and expelled for refusing to read the King James Bible. At the individualist end of the continuum or, more accurately, at the point we have presently reached in an ongoing process, is the widespread assumption that private choice is the gold standard in matters of religion, whereas the faintest hint of encouragement or inhibition by state or school officials is sufficient at least to raise questions. This book is, in the simplest terms, a map of the social, political, and legal road that American public schools have traveled in their journey from *there* to *here*.

STARTING POINT

Most of the historical context for this study is provided in Chapters Two and Three, which deal with the earliest controversies over religious expression in American public schools—and the most violent. A particularly noteworthy example is an 1844 dispute between Catholics and Protestants in which more than twenty people were killed, including an unlucky bystander whose head was shot off by a stray cannonball. These chapters attempt to convey the tone and intensity of such conflicts as recorded in nineteenth-century newspapers and public debates as well as in earlier scholarship. They do not claim to break new ground; rather, they strive to inform some readers and remind others of the school-prayer practices prevailing in this country prior to the Civil War, together with the sometimes bloody controversies they engendered.

Dramatic as the street fights of the nineteenth century were, they could not be sustained in the face of opposition to religious violence by the majority of Americans of all faiths. By the early twentieth century, conflicts over religion in the public schools took the form of state court proceedings, several of which are discussed in Chapter Four. Although the rulings of the various state courts were far from unanimous, they suggested a trend toward rejecting government-enforced majoritarian religious exercises, at least in some parts of the country. Then, as Chapters Five and Six explain, this standard abruptly became the law of the land when the Supreme Court handed down a series of landmark decisions declaring that religion in the public schools, previously regulated solely by state law, is subject to the U.S. Constitution and federal law. State-sponsored religious instruction and devotional exercises, once considered sacrosanct and untouchable, were now forbidden throughout the country.

These Supreme Court decisions of the 1950s and 1960s, which represent the first of two watersheds in the treatment of religious expression in American public schools, also mark the transition from the background chapters of this book to its main subject: the evolution of thought on religion in the public schools since it became a federal matter. From this point on, the book is based almost entirely on court documents, including not only decisions but also depositions, affidavits, exhibits, and transcripts of hearings and trials; congressional materials, including the *Congressional Record,* transcripts of congressional hearings, and "Dear Colleague" letters exchanged among members of Congress; lobbying letters and talking points prepared by advocacy groups for use with members of Congress, together with newsletters and appeals for funds; and news reports. In addition, the chapters dealing with relatively recent events incorporate material from interviews with members of Congress, parties and attorneys in lawsuits, advocacy-group lawyers and lobbyists, and other participants in the contemporary school-prayer debate. Their firsthand recollections, often humorous or poignant, add a sense of immediacy and a human-interest dimension to documentary material that might otherwise seem more academic than real.

Following the discussion of the Supreme Court's early school-prayer decisions in Chapters Five and Six, the next three chapters deal with attempts to restore traditional public-school devotionals either through a constitutional amendment or by limiting the power of the federal courts to decide school-prayer cases. Since school prayer was highly popular, then as now, it seemed at first as if those efforts must succeed. Nevertheless, a schism soon developed between people who favored a return to the precise situation that had existed before the Supreme Court's rulings and those who thought that some adjustments were in order. In particular, many religious people drew back from endorsing any proposal that would once again allow students to be penalized for declining to participate in majoritarian religious practices, and some of them even questioned whether the state should be in the business of prescribing prayers at all. Consequently, no proposed constitutional amendment attracted enough votes to pass either House of Congress—a result attributable in no small part to the persistence of dedicated traditionalists who fought for a greater degree of majoritarian rule in religious matters than the Vietnam-era public was prepared to accept. The same was true of proposals to curb the power of the federal courts to decide cases dealing with certain hot-button topics, including school prayer. Even if Congress has the authority to bring about this result, which is far from being a settled question, such proposals are too far from the median of American thought to garner the necessary support.

In the course of discussing reactions to the Supreme Court's early school-prayer rulings, these chapters also introduce the book's detailed treatment of the crucial role played by advocacy groups in the debate over religious expression in the public schools. Such organizations, which have been active in this matter since the early nineteenth century, came to prominence when attorneys from the American Civil Liberties Union, the American Jewish Congress, and other groups filed the federal lawsuits that led to the nationwide banning of state-sponsored religious exercises. Their success was one of the factors that inspired the establishment of similar advocacy groups, such as People for the American Way, as well as opposing organizations, such as the Moral Majority, Concerned Women for America, and the American Center for Law and Justice. (Descriptions of advocacy groups active in the school-prayer debate appear in the Appendix.) Because of the prohibitively high financial cost of school-prayer litigation, these groups collectively serve as unofficial gatekeepers to the federal courts, as few private citizens can afford to initiate such cases without their support. They also conduct highly sophisticated lobbying campaigns based on grassroots activism as well as interactions with members of Congress and their staffs. Combining these two spheres of activity, the advocacy groups discussed from Chapter Seven onward coordinate a highly effective interplay between litigation and legislation, often using the court cases in which they participate as the justification for proposed new laws, and vice versa.

THINKING OUTSIDE THE BOX

By the early 1980s, many Americans had reached adulthood without ever having experienced traditional school prayer, and ideas for bringing religion into
the schools without reverting to earlier practices began to gain in popularity.
The most obvious of these alternatives, discussed in Chapter Ten, was to institute moments of silence allowing each child to pray—or not—as he or she
saw fit, free from the influence of school authorities or classmates. Obviously,
moments of silence have in them more of the individualistic than of the collective, and several states permit or mandate their use in the public schools
because of the privacy and individual choice they afford. Nevertheless, their
very noninvasiveness also makes them controversial. To advocates of state-
endorsed majoritarian devotionals, whatever prayers may be said in silence
lack the social and moral value inherent in common religious exercises affirming
the students' membership in a community that is partially defined by its distinctive form of worship. Seeking nothing short of a return to state-sponsored
majoritarian devotionals, they view moments of silence as particularly insidious for precisely the reasons that make them so attractive to others.

This tension between individualistic and majoritarian aims also arose in
conjunction with proposals made in the 1970s and 1980s to allow students to
engage in vocal prayer on their own initiative. Rather than seeking a return to
state-approved, school-run majoritarian worship, proponents of what became
known as "equal access" focused on the right of individual students to pray
aloud with a minimum of involvement by school officials. This search for a
means of accommodating religious expression by the students themselves led
to the second watershed in the generations-old debate over religion in the
public schools: the establishment of equal access as the principle governing
religious expression in today's public schools.

The equal-access movement takes its name from its contention that students should be equally free to engage in either religious or secular speech
during noninstructional time, when they are at liberty to speak as they choose.
This emphasis on the students' personal rights to freedom of speech and religion, as contrasted with the school officials' constitutional obligation to be
neutral toward religion, is the model that governs the real-life examples presented at the beginning of this chapter. Underlying it are three assertions that
have revolutionized the way in which American courts and legislative bodies
think about school prayer:

- The government may neither endorse nor inhibit religion, but this mandatory neutrality does not extend to private citizens merely because they are in a government building or engaged in a government-run activity, such as public education.
- Religious expression by private citizens, including public-school students, should fall under the same rules that govern other forms of free speech.
- Excluding student-initiated prayer during times when students are free to talk about other topics of their choice places religious speech at a disadvantage relative to secular speech. This not only violates the students' right to free speech but also represents governmental hostility, not the required neutrality, toward religion.

Building on earlier events discussed in previous chapters, Chapters Eleven and Twelve explain the process by which equal access emerged as the dominant approach to prayer in the public schools of the late twentieth and early twenty-first centuries, including the passage of the Equal Access Act of 1984 and court decisions interpreting both the law itself and the underlying equal-access concept. Specific examples of the ways in which this new paradigm is being applied appear in Chapter Thirteen, which deals with lawsuits over religious activities during the regular school day; and in Chapter Fourteen, which treats cases involving other school-sponsored events, such as graduation ceremonies and football games. Since these lawsuits arose in part because of confusion over the precise application of equal-access principles, the U.S. Department of Education has joined several advocacy groups in attempting to elucidate them insofar as possible in their present stage of development. These efforts are discussed in Chapter Fifteen, together with additional examples of the impact of equal access on today's public schools.

By no means should this emphasis on clarifying the practical ramifications of equal access be taken to mean that it has become so well-established in principle that advocates of state-prescribed communal school prayer have simply folded their tents and stolen away. Among the most convincing evidence to the contrary is the fact that a congressional vote on a constitutional amendment to restore government-run prayer took place as recently as 1998, and attempts to deprive the federal courts of jurisdiction over school prayer have never entirely ceased. Indeed, it is fair to say that the underlying viewpoints and dynamics of the struggle over religion in the public schools have remained remarkably consistent over time; it is the players who change, not the game itself. To be sure, today's public schools are so secular that someone from the nineteenth century would hardly recognize them—and would almost certainly be appalled in the bargain. But that reflects which side tends to win school-prayer battles, not what the various sides think and how they operate. Far from discouraging advocates of majoritarian school prayer, the secularization of public education and the concomitant growth of individualism in religious matters have energized even as they have marginalized.

It is also important to note that the trend toward excluding religious speech from the public schools has by no means moved in a straight line. For one thing, despite the Supreme Court's rulings, school officials in some parts of the country have never ceased to sponsor religious activities, so that several of the most recent lawsuits discussed in this book resemble the school-prayer cases of half a century earlier. More significantly, the policies of law-abiding schools have become friendlier toward religion as a result of the student-centered approach described in this chapter. Consequently, although religion is far less prevalent in public schools today than in 1880, it is somewhat more so than in 1980. Finally, the public response to the 1999 Columbine school shootings and the September 11 attacks demonstrated beyond any doubt that the impulse to conflate majoritarian religious belief with patriotism, and to promote it in the public schools as an element of Americanism, cannot be dismissed as a thing of the past. Under these circumstances, it would be understating the truth to suggest that previous generations of controversy merely cast their shadow over the current struggle to define what would constitute a fair and balanced treatment of religion in the public schools. Despite all the changes that have taken place in the way this issue is handled, the convictions that animated even the earliest disputants remain alive and well today, as do modern versions of the strategies they used and the dynamics underlying the conflicts in which they engaged. It is thus no exaggeration to say that this book is, in part, the story of how the past lives in the present.

PARAMETERS

As this brief overview suggests, this study is fundamentally interdisciplinary, approaching religion in public education from the perspective of law, politics, and history. Naturally, its intended audience includes scholars, practitioners, and students in all these fields, but it also invites the public at large to participate in an informed discussion of religious freedom in America's public schools. Of course this is a matter of concern to those directly affected by it, but the way in which it is handled—not only *what* is decided, but *how* it is decided—also reflects and helps to shape the society in which we all live. In an effort to make this material accessible to the widest possible audience, the book includes brief explanations of legal procedures, political processes, and terminology with which some readers may already be familiar. Similarly, while most legislative battles and court cases are summarized more or less concisely, a few are depicted in more detail to convey not only factual material but also a sense of what such events look like and how the political and legal processes actually work.

A word about the scope of the book is also in order. By now it is clear that its subject matter—the evolution of religious expression in the public schools, including both state-sponsored and privately initiated practices—is philo-sophically challenging as well as historically complex. It is also more or less closely connected to numerous other issues, such as religiously motivated challenges to instructional materials, the shaping of public-school districts to accommodate religious sects, and the after-hours use of public-school build-ings by nonschool religious groups. But each of these topics, while not unre-lated to prayer in the public schools, involves its own set of historical events and legal precedents, many of which are tangential to the present study. Given the realities of space and time, what this book offers is an in-depth treatment of religious speech *in* the public school program, not a broader survey of the many links to be found between religion *and* public education in general. For the same reason, the book deals with the question of tax funding for religious schools only as it relates to disputes over prayer in public schools. Chapters Two through Four, for instance, mention numerous controversies of the nine-teenth and early twentieth centuries in which Catholics argued that the inclu-sion of state-sponsored Protestant practices in the public schools made the public funding of Catholic schools a matter of simple justice. This theme is revisited in later chapters because the Catholic Church, evangelical Christian groups, and conservative political organizations continue to associate pro-posed school-prayer initiatives with broader changes in the relationship between church and state—including permitting the public funding of reli-gious schools and other church-run activities. Beyond that, however, the story of the campaign for vouchers or other forms of public support for religious education involves federal laws and lawsuits dealing with educational funding policies that are intrinsically complicated and only marginally related to the main thrust of this book. Given the complexity of public-school prayer in and of itself, together with the large number of issues that would arguably come into play if the scope of the book were broadened, it is deemed preferable to do a thorough job of discussing religious expression in the public schools, reserving related but distinguishable matters for future studies.

Stating that this book concerns itself only with the ongoing national debate over religious expression in the public schools is not to suggest that the topic is treated as if it existed in a vacuum. Chapter Two, for instance, mentions economic and social factors that exacerbated religious tensions between nineteenth-century Protestants and Catholics, and Chapters Seven and Eight discuss the impact of court-ordered racial desegregation on public reaction to the Supreme Court's school-prayer decisions. Most significantly, the centuries-long debate over religion in the public schools goes to the heart of the interplay between two of the most sacred principles on which American culture is based: majority rule and individual rights. Every court, legislative body, school board, and public official who has ever attempted to resolve a dispute over specific school-prayer policies has had to grapple with the difficulty of balancing these competing claims. In religious matters, as in racial and ethnic concerns, the public schools serve as a flashpoint for tensions that inevitably arise when people of widely varied backgrounds and viewpoints try to get along in a free society.

Like it or not, the public-school system is one place where everyone's views have to be considered. No matter how strongly people may feel about the correctness of their own beliefs, no matter how frustrated they may become by what they perceive as the blindness and stubbornness of others, the curse and the blessing of the school-prayer debate is that it confronts participants with the reality that whatever rules apply to them also apply to everyone else. Individuals are free to believe that their religion is superior to all others or that religion in general is superstitious bunk, but the government must accord the same legal rights to believers of all stripes as well as to nonbelievers. If students are allowed to engage in religious speech, then all religious speech must be equally accommodated, as must speech on other topics. Despite arguments to the contrary by determined activists on both sides, it seems clear that neither governmental favoritism toward any religious orientation nor inhibition of the students' rights to free speech and free exercise of religion would be constitutional, politically feasible, or morally justifiable. While it would be highly overoptimistic to claim that these political and legal necessities have induced all participants in the school-prayer debate to seek broadly acceptable solutions that would accommodate others' convictions on the same basis as their own, at least it creates a forum in which this imperative must inescapably be faced.

2

The Past That Never Was

If history repeats itself, and the unexpected always happens, how incapable must Man be of learning from experience.

—*George Bernard Shaw*

Whenever I give public lectures dealing with school prayer, audience members who attended public schools before the 1960s are eager to share their personal recollections. Some of them describe noncontroversial prayers and Bible readings that created a warm, secure atmosphere while fostering the morality and discipline that marked the schools of that period. Others suggest that the students' behavior was characteristic of the time, and public schools that had no religious services were just as orderly as those that did have them. Many people observe that the prayers in most schools were Protestant, which was acceptable to some non-Protestants but not to all. Some remember feeling angry and embarrassed at having to leave the room during the prayers, while others complain that they never had the option of being excused. Of course, these conflicting accounts reflect each person's own perspectives and beliefs as well as wide variations in the way school prayer was handled—if it existed at all—in different states and school districts. A good example was provided by a retired corporate attorney named Tom, who took one of my graduate seminars. He remarked to the class that no one in his rural North Carolina high school had objected to the daily devotionals, and he said the same thing to his former classmates at their fiftieth reunion, which took place while the seminar was in progress. One of his former schoolmates unexpectedly erupted, saying angrily that as a Catholic he certainly *had* objected to the exclusive use of Protestant prayers, hymns, and Bible readings. Those practices, he fulminated, were clearly meant to suggest that Protestantism was the law of the land and that anything else was a deviation from the state-endorsed norm. The people at the reunion were taken aback, Tom later reported, because it had never crossed their minds that anyone might have resented the use of the once-ubiquitous King James Bible. "Hell," he concluded, "I never even knew the guy was Catholic."

The assumptions shared by most of those North Carolina alumni reflect the widespread belief that state-sponsored school prayer had been trouble-free for some 170 years before it was suddenly banned by a 1963 Supreme Court decision intended to appease a tiny anti-prayer minority. A prominent spokesman for this viewpoint was Senator Strom Thurmond (R–South Carolina), former chairperson of the Senate Judiciary Committee, who sponsored several pieces of legislation aimed at restoring school-run prayer. "Well, still, I say 170 years is a long time," he commented at a 1983 Judiciary Committee hearing, "and it is kind of strange that no one raised the point, no one tested it, no one went to the Supreme Court of the United States, and then, when the Supreme Court handed down their decision, everybody seems to feel, well, that is it" ("Voluntary School Prayer," p. 419). Nevertheless, the historical record clearly contradicts the implication that school-prayer disputes sprang up for the first time during the social unrest of the 1960s. Without doubt, the majority of Americans in any given period have favored school prayer, but reservations about it have been shared by significant numbers of people— believers and nonbelievers alike—for as long as public schools have existed.

BEGINNING AT THE BEGINNING

In *Pillars of the Republic* (1983), historian Carl Kaestle notes that when the United States emerged as an independent nation in the late eighteenth century, many of its schools reflected some form of sectarian religious belief even if they were not under the direct control of any church. Some of these early schools provided free education for the children of the poor, while others did not; and some religious faiths offered no schooling or provided it only in certain parts of the country. This approach to education worried social reformers, not because it included religious instruction but because it created uneven educational opportunities that depended on where people lived, what faith they professed, and how much money they had. Although it is commonly believed that post-Revolutionary Americans advocated widespread schooling either because of its economic benefits or because it was essential to maintaining a republican form of government, Kaestle suggests that religious motives were even more important. For one thing, he points out, the new nation was dominated by Protestants who were deeply committed to the belief that everyone should be able to read the Bible. In addition, education was seen as a means of promoting morality, which most Americans—then as now—associated with religious teachings. As a result, relatively few people of that period favored entirely secular schooling; to most educators, the question was not *whether* to promote religion but *whose* religion to promote.

This chapter and the two that follow focus on the Protestant-Catholic conflicts that dominated the educational scene after the late 1830s, but arguments over the furtherance of one Protestant denomination over another had begun much earlier. As an example, early nineteenth-century Massachusetts schools that received public funds tended to favor the politically dominant Congregationalist faith, to the increasingly vocal dismay of Unitarians and Episcopalians, among others. Similarly, the earliest attacks on the public funding of church-run schools in New York City were aimed primarily at Baptists and Methodists, not at Catholics. As this chapter demonstrates, the arrival of large numbers of Catholic immigrants eventually led most Protestants to unite in opposing all public funding for religious education, but even before that took place, rivalries among Protestant denominations had led educational reformers to seek a practical way of providing children of all faiths with at least a no-frills elementary education.

Not surprisingly, in view of all these factors, the approach that soon became dominant in many states was the establishment of schools deemed "nonsectarian" at the time, although by today's standards they would be better described as pan-Protestant. While carefully avoiding any discussion of issues that divided Protestant denominations, such as predestination and the proper form of Baptism, these schools had daily readings from the King James Bible, which was generally accepted by Protestants but not by Catholics or non-Christians, as well as Protestant hymns and recitations of the KJB version of the Lord's Prayer and the Ten Commandments. Although a few schools of this kind had existed earlier, they began to emerge as a major force in American education in the early decades of the nineteenth century.

Among the many scholarly works that deal with the rise of these so-called nonsectarian schools, William K. Dunn's *What Happened to Religious Education?* (1958) and James W. Fraser's *Between Church and State* (1999) provide particularly comprehensive treatments of the process by which, paradoxically, this attempt to minimize divisiveness in education became explosively controversial in its own right. In particular, both works include substantive discussions of one of the best-known exponents of nonsectarian public schools, Horace Mann of Massachusetts, who in 1837 became secretary of the first state board of education in America. Like the efforts of reformers elsewhere in the country, Mann's attempts to limit religious expression to what he considered nonsectarian practices drew fire for a variety of reasons. As noted earlier, Congregationalism had been the favored religion in many Massachusetts schools, and its adherents were outraged by the prospect of replacing it with what they saw as skeletal religious observances. Even some non-Congregationalists, hoping to preserve the possibility of state funding for their own schools, protested that the elimination of doctrinal religion would leave the schools essentially godless.

Attacking Mann's policies from a different standpoint were Catholics and some Protestants who viewed generic Protestantism as a distinct religious tradition, since it includes some faiths and excludes others. To them, promoting the common usages of Protestantism was not nonsectarian but merely majoritarian, and thus an inadequate means of providing equitable educational opportunities to people of all faiths. Nevertheless, their sense of inclusivity rarely extended beyond Christianity. Although Jewish organizations now vigorously oppose government-sponsored school prayer, and representatives of other non-Christian faiths are beginning to be heard, the controversies that took place in the nineteenth and early twentieth centuries were conducted primarily by Christians who, if they agreed on little else, shared the strong conviction that non-Christian beliefs did not deserve the same consideration as their own. In view of the all-but-universal assumption that the public schools should promote Christianity over any other belief system, it would be a gross oversimplification to view the debate over nonsectarianism as a conflict between people who wanted to accommodate all faiths and those who wanted to consider only their own religious tradition. In reality, with the exception of a few early advocates of entirely secular schooling, almost everyone wanted to draw a circle that included certain faiths and excluded others; the point of contention was how broadly that circle should be drawn.

FOLLOW THE MONEY

One of the earliest crises to erupt over the rise of "nonsectarian" schools pitted a fiery Catholic bishop, John Hughes, against New York City officials in an argument about money—an association of ideas that can still be seen in today's debates about government vouchers for religious schools. The importance of the financial element is reflected in the title of one of the earliest studies of this dispute, which remains the most comprehensive: Vincent P. Lannie's *Public Money and Parochial Education: Bishop Hughes, Governor Seward, and the New York School Controversy* (1968). This chapter is indebted to Lannie's work and to two later books that place this dispute in a broader historical context: Kaestle's *The Evolution of an Urban School System: New York City, 1750–1850* (1973), which shows how the Hughes controversy flowed from previous events; and Diane Ravitch's *The Great School Wars: New York City, 1805–1973. A History of the Public Schools as Battlefield of Social Change* (1974), which treats it as the starting point for an extended discussion of later conflicts surrounding the operation of public schools in that crowded, diverse, and constantly changing city.

To offer some insight into the intensity of the Hughes controversy and the personalities and beliefs of the people involved, this chapter quotes extensively from a public debate between Hughes and his opponents reported in several sources, notably William O. Bourne's *History of the Public School Society of the City of New York* (1870). There are also numerous excerpts from newspapers of the time, including both Catholic and anti-Catholic publications. Finally, some material on Hughes himself has been extracted from an 1866 biography by one of his secretaries, John Hassard, who had the use of the bishop's private papers as well as access to his friends and colleagues; from an 1892 biography by Reverend Henry Brann; and from a more recent (and less laudatory) biography by Richard Shaw (1977). As indicated earlier, neither this chapter nor the two that follow claim to reveal startling new information or insights regarding the events of the nineteenth and early twentieth centuries; in fact, it is difficult to cite any one specific source for much of this material because it is a matter of common knowledge among historians of the period. Rather, the purpose of these chapters is to present the thinking behind the early disputes, together with their tone and the nature of their key participants, as background for a later analysis of more recent school-prayer conflicts.

Bishop Hughes's long-running quarrel with New York officials began at a time when almost all the public funds allotted to education in the city were given to a private organization, the Public School Society (originally the Free School Society), whose extensive school system promoted generic Protestant beliefs. Hughes argued vehemently that New York's parochial schools should also receive tax support; as he explained in one of his many speeches, Catholics "feel it unjust and oppressive that while we educate our children, as well we contend as they would be at the public schools, we are denied our portion of the school fund, simply because we at the same time endeavor to train them up in principles of virtue and religion. This we feel to be unjust and unequal. For we pay taxes in proportion to our numbers, as other citizens [do].... Is it not, then, hard and unjust that such a man cannot have the benefit of education for his child without sacrificing the rights of his religion and con-science?" (Hassard, p. 231).

The fact that the Catholic schools were sectarian did not necessarily render them ineligible for tax support because such matters were, at that time, a mat-ter of local option; Supreme Court rulings to the contrary did not begin to appear until more than a century later. In New York City, the board of alder-men, known as the Common Council, had voluntarily chosen to support only what they considered nonsectarian schools, not only because of anti-Catholic sentiment but also because the powerful Public School Society disliked com-petition from any source. More than two decades before the Hughes contro-versy began, the PSS had persuaded the Common Council to rule against Baptist, Presbyterian, and Methodist schools that had laid claim to funds and students the PSS considered its own. The definition of nonsectarianism the council adopted at that time made public funding available to schools whose programs included religious practices common to more than one denomina-tion, such as generic Protestant prayers and readings from the King James Bible. Excluded from public support were schools that used texts and practices distinctive to a particular denomination.

Predictably, Hughes rejected the council's definition of nonsectarianism, maintaining that Protestantism as a whole is a belief system that is clearly dis-tinguishable from other religious traditions. If the council persisted in denying funds to Catholic schools on the basis of sectarianism, he maintained, it should also withhold funding from the PSS as long as Protestant observances took place in its schools. This assertion was a calculated risk because the last thing the bishop wanted was the exclusion of Bible reading and prayer from all pub-licly funded schools. Apart from its moral and spiritual implications, such an action would have eliminated his best arguments for securing public funds for Catholic schools. His aim was to use the threat of either defunding the PSS schools or terminating their popular religious practices as political leverage to wring financial support for Catholic schools out of reluctant city officials.

In addition to—and arguably in conflict with—his assertion that the PSS schools were promoting Protestantism, Hughes accused them of being secu-lar and even atheistic. Paraphrasing a Hughes speech quoted by both Hassard and Brann, Lannie attempts to reconcile these two elements of the bishop's perspective, which was common among Catholic leaders of the period. "According to Hughes," Lannie states, "there could be no Christianity without sectarianism, for if Roman Catholicism, Methodism, Episcopalianism, Pres-byterianism, Lutheranism, et al. were removed from the schools, then Christianity would cease to exist in them. Sectarianism and Christianity were one and the same; the one could not exist without the other. In Hughes's mind, no other alternative was possible" (p. 54). Not surprisingly, the bishop's opponents accused him of inconsistency for asserting that what they considered nonsectarian practices rendered the schools at once Protestant and wholly devoid of any religion. More broadly, his willingness to jeopardize the well-loved PSS devotionals in order to achieve his own goals inevitably provoked a backlash of anti-Catholic feeling. In his opponents' view, his behavior proved what they had believed all along: that the Catholic Church was a devious, equivocating, untruthful enemy of God's word as presented in the KJB, and thus a threat to freedom, democracy, morality, and Americanism.

Underlying this controversy over school funds was the political power newly wielded by the rapidly growing population of Irish Catholic immigrants, whose arrival was changing the ethnic profile of the city. Because of the long and bitter history of religious conflict in their homeland, the Irish men and women flooding into New York were predisposed to be suspicious of Protestant state officials, including the PSS. In the Ireland they had left, laws had been enacted to prevent the Catholic majority from voting, attending universities, being teachers or lawyers, or owning more than a specified amount of land. Although these laws were not always enforced, they came into play during times of turmoil, and their mere existence was enough to make the Irish immigrants highly skeptical of the claim that Protestant rule meant individual liberty, democracy, and justice for all. Nor were their experiences entirely different in this country, where some states had anti-Catholic religious tests for elected officials, and Catholic chaplains were sometimes barred from administering the rites of the Church in public hospitals. In such circumstances, it is neither surprising nor unique that a population of largely uneducated, poor, and politically unsophisticated people looked to its religious leaders to further its interests in an unfamiliar and hostile environment. This, in turn, increased the political power of Church officials, who were able to influence significant numbers of votes. It was this factor, more than any other, that made it impossible for city and state officials to ignore Hughes's arguments about public funding for Catholic schools.

Apart from their general anti-Catholic sentiments, some nineteenth-century New Yorkers were specifically concerned about the growth of a separate Catholic school system because they saw it as an obstacle to the assimilation of the newcomers into the mainstream culture. Whereas Hughes emphasized the need to protect Irish Catholic children from the shabby treatment they received in the public schools, including the ridicule of their ethnicity and religion, his opponents focused on what they saw as the Church's desire to keep its flock isolated, indoctrinated, and obedient. Indeed, many of the measures Hughes advocated to protect his religious followers from the insults, exploitation, and general hostility of the surrounding Protestant culture also served to insulate them from outside influences that might dilute their ethnic and religious identity, expose them to new ideas that clashed with their existing beliefs, or tempt them to stray from their culture and from the authority of the Church. Many of Hughes's arguments in favor of Catholic education emphasized the preservation of New York's Irish Catholic community as a distinct population, educating its children in schools whose main purpose was to inculcate Catholic doctrine. He was unabashedly jealous of the authority he exercised over most of the city's Catholic residents, and his writings and public speeches provide a solid basis for Shaw's blunt assertion that he "had little use for any Catholic whom he could not control" (p. 3). Naturally, this attitude fed the widespread fear that a large American Catholic population, divided from its Protestant neighbors and subservient to the bishops and the pope, could undermine the democratic foundations of this country and turn it into the kind of theocracy the Founders had been determined to avoid. PSS officials, convinced that it was not the public-school system but the immigrants' attitude that required change, accused Hughes of poisoning his followers' minds against Protestants in general and the PSS in particular in order to keep them ignorant, isolated, and subject to his authority.

Although the suspicion with which many Protestant New Yorkers viewed the Irish Catholic newcomers grew partially out of religious differences, it also reflected financial interests and cultural conflicts. According to Ravitch (1974),

> There were jobs for the Irish in New York, but they were at the
> lowest level of the social and economic ladder.... Living as they did
> in the most abject poverty, the Irish overwhelmed the city's few
> and inadequate public relief institutions.... The Irish were
> different from native Americans: they dressed differently, spoke
> differently, drank too much, brawled too openly, and stuck
> together.... Then too the Irish were blamed for the very condi-
> tions of which they were the victims, just as later immigrants
> would be. They were accused of importing poverty, filth, and vice
> from Europe. American workers held them responsible for flood-
> ing the labor market and depressing wages. Many natives consid-

ered the Irish a drunken, ignorant people given to petty criminal-
ity. (p. 29)

Interesting discussions of the multifaceted nature of the conflict between the
Irish newcomers and earlier residents of the city can also be found in the Pulitzer
Prize–winning *Gotham* (1999), by Edwin G. Burrows and Mike Wallace, and
in Herbert Asbury's *The Gangs of New York* (1927), which inspired a Martin
Scorsese film of the same title.

In view of all these factors, it is not surprising that public support was largely
on the side of the PSS in its struggle to preserve its own nondenominational
Protestant practices while denying public funding to Catholic schools. Moreover, many people honestly did not understand what conceivable objection
there could be to religious exercises that, to them, seemed entirely harmless
and wholesome. They saw no reason for excusing children from reading the
KJB or reciting the Protestant version of the Lord's Prayer merely because these
practices contradicted the religion the children were taught at home; rather,
they viewed such devotionals as a religiously neutral and effective way to unite
all schoolchildren in a common culture and to integrate immigrants into the
American mainstream. As this suggests, there was a great deal of resistance to
acknowledging that Catholic texts and beliefs deserved the same consideration
as those of Protestantism, and anything having to do with Irish identity or culture was despised. Ironically, the gross insensitivity with which Irish Catholics
were treated in the public schools fueled the very attitude that the school officials
deplored: the determination to maintain separate schools in which Irish
Catholic children would not be exposed to derision and ridicule and have their
beliefs denigrated. As Shaw remarked, "The frustrating element of the whole
debate was that neither side seemed capable of understanding the limits of
their own prejudice or of properly addressing the prejudice of the other....
What the arguments did present was a potpourri of the religious antagonisms
between native and new-immigrant America" (p. 147).

At first, Hughes and other Catholic leaders tried to advance their cause by
clarifying why they objected to religious exercises that seemed so unifying and
"American" to many Protestants. Not only did the Catholic Church reject the
King James translation, they explained, but it also forbade its members from
drawing their own conclusions about the meaning of the Scriptures. The
Church defines itself as the only true interpreter of the Bible, and the Catholic
translation, known as the Douay Version, includes footnotes and commentary
giving the Church's explanation of certain texts. Contrary to the prevalent

Protestant belief that reading the Bible "without note or comment" represents religious neutrality because each reader draws his or her own meaning from the text, the bishops saw it as hostile to the Church's assertion that even adults, let alone children, are incompetent to interpret the Bible for themselves.

Hughes and his fellow bishops soon found that their explanations merely made the situation worse. Many Americans, strongly loyal to the KJB, became resentful when what they regarded as a foreign church rejected it. They saw no significant doctrinal differences between the King James and Douay Versions, and the Church's determination to tell its members how to interpret the Bible reinforced its image as an arrogant, European-controlled, un-American dictatorship. Hughes and his allies finally resorted to asking whether the religious freedom of which America's Protestants proudly boasted applied to all faiths or only to those the majority found acceptable. At bottom, of course, the real issue was not scriptural translation or even theology, but the clash between America's long-established Protestant identity and the assertion that such a fundamentally different system as Catholicism merited equal treatment.

The emergence of the King James Bible as the central symbol of this conflict was inevitable. From the time it first appeared in the early seventeenth century, it has functioned as the icon of Protestantism: the embodiment of the defiance that the early Protestants hurled into the teeth of the Catholic Church. This sense of hostility was neither inferential nor subtle; the original dedication, omitted from modern printings but still used in Hughes's time, refers to the pope as "that man of Sinne" (*English Bible*, p. 3), and the original preface denies the legitimacy of the Catholic Church and accuses it of hiding the truths of Scripture from the common people. While conceding that Church officials had approved a few English translations of the Bible, the preface asserts that those translations were deliberately rendered so obscure that the average reader could not understand them. Moreover, it states, the translations approved by the Church were made available only to Catholics of proven loyalty, described as "such as are, if not frozen in the dregs, yet sowred with the leaven of their superstition" (p. 17). Not unreasonably, nineteenth-century Catholics, many of whom had fled countries in which bitter religious wars had raged for centuries, would not allow school officials to hand their children *that* book and teach them that it was *the* Word of God. The PSS and its supporters were equally adamant that the continued freedom of this nation depended on teaching future generations to accept the KJB and all it stood for, including— and especially—the rejection of papal authority.

THIS IS *MY* COUNTRY

Hughes and other Catholic bishops tried to reassure wary Protestants that although the Church itself is a hierarchical institution, Catholic citizens were perfectly capable of distinguishing between the authoritarian structure of their church and the republican framework of their country. In the bishops' view, there was no contradiction between fidelity to the Church's teachings in matters of religion and wholehearted participation in the civil government's democratic political practices. Nevertheless, many nineteenth-century New Yorkers did not see how anyone could adhere to the Catholic Church and still be thoroughly American. To them, Catholicism was foreign and, in New York at that time, largely Irish. Indeed, a survey of newspaper stories dealing with Hughes's request for public funds shows that the words "immigrant," "Catholic," "Irish," "foreigner," and "alien" were employed interchangeably as well as contemptuously.

Negative attitudes toward the newcomers were particularly intense within a political movement known as nativism, which is the subject of Ray Allen Billington's classic study, *The Protestant Crusade, 1800–1860: A Study of the Origins of American Nativism* (1938). As Billington explains, to nativists who viewed the immigrants as "a Rome-directed group of papal serfs, bent on the planned destruction of the United States" (p. 127), it was essential for the public schools to Americanize their children by inculcating Protestant principles that would make them patriotic Americans rather than lackeys of the pope. From that perspective, the enforced reading of the KJB in the schools appeared to be nothing more than an act of self-defense on the part of the native-born population. It was therefore inevitable that Hughes's attack on the popular religious practices of the PSS schools, coupled with his determination to keep Catholic children in a separate school system—funded with taxpayers' money, no less—would raise nativist hackles.

WHAT HAPPENED TO HUGHES'S REQUEST FOR FUNDS?

Many of the PSS trustees were avowed nativists, as were the editors of several newspapers, notably the *New York Observer*. Together, the PSS and the nativist press fanned public animosity toward Hughes's proposal. The bishop presented his views in public meetings and in his own newspaper, the *Freeman's Journal,* whose title was intended as a refutation of the claim that the Catholic Church was the enemy of personal liberty. In autumn 1840, the Common Council attempted to resolve the matter by holding a two-day public debate on Hughes's petition. According to the *Observer,* the hall was so crowded that the council members and speakers could barely squeeze in. The PSS was represented by two of its trustees, Theodore Sedgwick and Hiram Ketchum, both of whom were nativists and lawyers. Several Protestant clergymen also spoke in support of the PSS. Bishop Hughes had arranged to have a Catholic lawyer assist him in upholding the Church's side of the controversy, but according to Hassard's eyewitness account, "the gentleman to whom the cause was intrusted was prevented by the bursting of a blood-vessel from attending the debate; so Bishop Hughes had to fight the battle alone" (p. 234).

In response to Hughes's lengthy plea on behalf of the Catholic schools, Ketchum and Sedgwick presented what they considered compelling historical, cultural, and civic reasons for having all schoolchildren read the KJB and no other. According to Ketchum, "The institutions of liberty and the altars of piety have sprung up in the path of that translated Bible; and wherever that translated Bible has gone, popular institutions have risen. All those glorious principles, which here in this country are so conspicuous, have come from that Bible; and wherever that translated Bible has been kept from the hands of the laity, there has been darkness and despotism." "I want those children so brought up," he added, "that, when they become men, they shall have pure American feelings" (Bourne, pp. 246, 247). Sedgwick agreed. According the *Observer*, he told the council that "The Bible without note or comment inculcating [moral] sentiments had always spread virtue and peace, but it was the notes and comments of the Roman Catholic version inculcating transubstantiation, fasts, penances, etc., that had laid the world in blood and ashes" (November 7, 1840, p. 178).

Clergymen supporting the PSS echoed its claim that Catholicism represented a threat to American democracy. A Presbyterian minister, having acknowledged that he would have opposed the petition for school funds even if it had come from a Protestant church, added, "I do view it with more alarm on account of the source from which it comes," since "any man who looks at the history of the Catholic Church... [which] continues to be almost uniformly the enemy of liberty, will look upon this application with suspicion and fear. I do so not only as an American, but as a Christian, as a Protestant, and as a Presbyterian." In response to Hughes's allegation that the PSS school system "leads to infidelity," he said, "[L]et no man think it strange that I should prefer even infidelity to Catholicism. Even a mind as acute as Voltaire's, came to the conclusion that if there was no alternative between infidelity and the dogmas of the catholic church, he should prefer infidelity. I would choose, Sir, in similar circumstances to be an infidel to-morrow" (*Important and Interest-*

ing Debate on the Claim of the Catholics to a Portion of the Common School Fund [1840], p. 39). Similar sentiments were expressed in a memorandum submitted to the Common Council by a Methodist group. "We are sorry," it said in part, "that the reading of the Bible in the public schools, without note or commentary, is offensive to them; but we cannot allow the Holy Scripture to be accompanied with *their* notes and commentaries, and to be put into the hands of the children who may hereafter be the rulers and legislators of our beloved country; because, among other bad things taught in these commentaries, is to be found the lawfulness of murdering heretics, and the unqualified submission, in all matters of conscience, to the Roman Catholic Church" (Bourne, p. 200). The *Observer* elaborated on this theme, praising "the principles of universal toleration, which are so sacredly cherished in this country, (and we would add in every other free country where the Bishop's religion is not in the ascendancy)" (November 7, 1840, p. 178).

AND IN THE OTHER CORNER

Hughes had several opportunities to rebut his opponents and did so for three or four hours at a time. A skilled debater, he gave such a performance that even the *Observer* was moved to pay him a backhanded compliment: "No one could hear him without painful regret that such powers of mind, such varied and extensive learning, and such apparent sincerity of purpose were trammelled with a false system of religion" (November 7, 1840, p. 178). In addition to denying the PSS's claim that its schools were nonsectarian, Hughes reviled it as a greedy monopoly eager to keep all the school money in its grasp, thus denying Catholic children a publicly funded education within their own faith. "I believe," he declared, "if some of these gentlemen, who consider themselves now as eminent Christians, had lived at the period when Lazarus lay languishing at the gate of the rich man, petitioning for the crumbs that fell from the table, they would have sent their remonstrance against his petition" (Bourne, p. 223).

In response to the Methodists' memorandum to the council, which included a litany of horrors that the Catholic Church had allegedly perpetrated over the centuries, the bishop conceded some of the charges but challenged others. He added that Methodism had dark chapters of its own, although it was a very young religion in comparison with Catholicism. It had, he said, "fewer crimes" but also "fewer virtues to boast of. And, in its career of a hundred years, it has done as little for mankind as any other denomination" (Bourne, p. 212). Later, when a Methodist speaker kept asking barbed questions, Hughes taunted him by observing, "I am now not surprised at his say-ing so often that he would 'like to know,' for a little more knowledge would be of great advantage to him" (p. 293). He also denied that the Catholic version of the Bible called for the burning of heretics, offering to wager $1,000 to be used for good works if his foes could prove their contention. In reply, a Methodist minister, Reverend Thomas E. Bond, triumphantly observed that "our Church is old enough to teach us the sinfulness of betting!" (p. 257). Hughes retorted that he thought the Bible also said something about not bearing false witness against one's neighbor.

In addition to responding to his opponents, Hughes went on the offensive, claiming that anti-Catholicism pervaded the instructional materials used in PSS schools. The trustees indignantly protested that he had rejected their ear-lier invitation to have diocesan officials review those materials and remove anything offensive. He was unwilling to help improve the PSS curriculum, they alleged, because his real purpose was to get money for Catholic schools. On the contrary, he retorted, accepting their offer would merely have bur-dened the Catholic Church with the unpopular role of censor without reduc-ing the underlying anti-Catholicism of the schools. The trustees must have been either hopelessly anti-Catholic or singularly obtuse, he added, if they could not see for themselves that some of their materials were biased.

To support his charge of anti-Catholicism, Hughes cited a history textbook that described the Protestant leader John Huss as a "'zealous reformer from popery, who... was bold and persevering; but at length, trusting himself to the deceitful Catholics, he was by them brought to trial, condemned as a heretic, and burnt at the stake'" (Bourne, p. 192). Similarly, *A System of Universal Geog-raphy* stated, "'Superstition prevails not only at Rome but in all the states of the Church. The inhabitants observe scrupulously all the ceremonies of religion omitting nothing connected with form or etiquette, although apparently desti-tute of true devotion. Confession is a practice which all follow more from cus-tom than from christian humility, and rather to lull the conscience than to correct vice'" (Shaw, p. 141). Furthermore, he said, several PSS school libraries housed a book called *The Irish Heart,* which featured a character named Phe-lim McGee. "'When Phelim had laid up a good stock of sins,'" he read aloud, "'he now and then went over to Killarney, of a Sabbath morning, and got *"relaaf by confissing* them out o' the way," as he used to express it, and sealed up his soul with a *wafer....* [Later he] returned quite invigorated for the perpetration of new offences'" (Bourne, p. 251). *The Irish Heart* went on to say, "'The emi-gration from Ireland to America, of annually increasing numbers, extremely needy and in many cases drunken and depraved, has become a subject for grave and fearful reflection.... [S]hould the materials of this oppressive influx continue to be the same, instead of an asylum our country might be appropriately styled the common sewer of Ireland'" (Shaw, p. 142).

Hughes's final example was a Temperance Society tract that, he alleged, was part of the library collection in PSS schools. The tract stated,

> For when drunkenness shall have been done away, and, with it, that just relative proportion of all indolence, ignorance, crime, misery, and superstition, of which it is the putative parent, then truly a much smaller portion of mankind may be expected to follow the dark lantern of the Romish religion. That religion is most likely to find professors among the frivolous and the wicked, which, by a species of ecclesiastical legerdemain, can persuade the sinner that he is going to heaven, when he is going directly to hell. By a refined and complicated system of Jesuitry and prelatical juggling, the papal see has obtained its present extensive influence throughout the world. (Bourne, p. 251)

The PSS trustees protested angrily that that tract had already been taken out of the school libraries, and Hughes knew it. Hughes then took them to task for having allowed such a libelous book to find its way into their schools in the first place.

When the debate finally ended, the Common Council did what any self-respecting government body would do today: it appointed a committee to study the matter. Following a delay of several months and much prodding from Hughes, the committee presented its report. It recommended against funding the Catholic schools because, it said, the PSS schools were nonsectarian and the Catholic schools sectarian. It also recommended removing some of the more blatantly anti-Catholic books in the hope that more immigrant children might then attend the public schools. Friends of the PSS rejoiced when the council accepted the committee's recommendations by a vote of 15–1, but nativist leaders sounded a note of caution: Hughes was not a man to give up easily. "The price of liberty," warned the *Observer*, "is sleepless vigilance, when a power so crafty, so far-reaching is seeking to win or drive the people of this country into its deadly toils" (January 16, 1841, p. 10).

ALTERNATE METHODS OF CAT-SKINNING

As the *Observer* had feared, exactly a month after the council's vote, the bishop gave a speech to a large assembly of Catholics. "We must not fold our arms and rest," he adjured them. "We must take measures. I trust that no such defeat as we have experienced—the defeat of justice by authority—will make you give up your principles" (Hassard, p. 240). The initiative Hughes had in mind was an attempt to go over the heads of the city officials by petitioning the state legislature to change the way state education funds were distributed. The state provided a great deal of the money that supported New York City schools, and state law gave the Common Council a free hand to allocate those funds as it saw fit. Hughes wanted the state legislature to revise that policy in a way that would make it more difficult for the council to deny funding to sectarian schools. The petition was referred to the New York secretary of state, John Spencer, and urged on by Governor William Seward (later appointed U.S. secretary of state by President Abraham Lincoln), he crafted a proposal to break the power of the PSS and distribute state education funding more widely across the city's schools. This legislation seemed on the point of passing the state senate when the vote was abruptly postponed, perhaps in part because of an inflammatory newspaper story about a popular Catholic priest, William Hogan, who had been excommunicated twenty years earlier for defying the church hierarchy. The story included a horrifying formula of excommunication that had allegedly been pronounced against Hogan, although in reality it was a fictional parody taken from Laurence Sterne's novel *Tristram Shandy*. A PSS supporter distributed copies to the senate, and this was widely credited with causing the postponement.

A disappointed Hughes blamed the failure on Democratic politicians who, he alleged, took Irish Catholic support for granted without giving Catholic interests a high enough priority. "You have often voted for others," he told a Catholic audience shortly before the election of 1841, "and they did not vote for you" (Brann, p. 82). Determined to demonstrate the political power of the Catholic community, he held a mass meeting four days before election day. While supporting ten of the thirteen Democrats running for election to the state assembly, he proposed write-in candidates for the other three assembly seats. It was understood that none of the write-in candidates would win; the point was to show what would happen to the three disfavored Democrats if the Catholics in their respective districts voted for someone else.

Naturally, this maneuver provided a public relations bonanza for nativists who claimed that Catholic political power was a threat to democracy and could lead to the takeover of America by the Vatican. "If [Hughes's action] does not convince the American people that the Romish church is seeking political power," exclaimed the *Observer*, "we shall begin to despair of the Republic" (November 6, 1841, p. 178). As the *Observer* recounted the meeting at which Hughes proposed his slate of candidates, "[S]o that the poor Papists might feel the full force of the danger they would incur by daring to disobey his authority, he called to his aid the terror of his ghostly office, and declared it a SIN to vote for any candidate that was opposed to their claims." According to the newspaper, he then ordered "his trembling followers to go to the polls and put *that* ticket into the ballot boxes" (November 6, 1841, p. 178). Hughes's secretary, Hassard, told a very different story. In his version of the meeting, the bishop repeatedly asked his audience whether they would unite, whether they would get out on election day and cast a vote for their children's future, whether they would take their rightful place as Americans, and so forth. According to Hassard, "The cheers and shouts, the stamping of feet, the waving of hats and handkerchiefs, were such as even an Irish assemblage in its most enthusiastic moments seldom gives way to" (pp. 245–46). Handbills were also posted in Catholic neighborhoods saying such things as "'Catholics Arouse! To the Rescue! Irishmen to your posts!! The friends of an equal distribution of the School Fund, are called upon to rally!'" (Billington, p. 161, n. 42).

On election day, Hughes's write-in candidates received only a small proportion of the total vote, leading some opponents to claim that he had suffered a humiliating defeat. Nevertheless, the three disfavored Democratic candidates lost to their Whig opponents by fewer than the number of votes cast for the write-in contenders. Assuming that most if not all of those voters were Catholics who would otherwise have supported the Democrats, the bishop had made his point. When the New York City delegates to the state legislature set off for Albany that winter, they were determined that something was going to have to be done about what they called "the school issue."

With Seward's continued encouragement, the state legislature once again began considering the reorganization of New York City's educational system. Fittingly, this delicate political task was led by William Maclay, a Democratic assemblyman, whose ability to skate on thin political ice was convincingly demonstrated when he won endorsements from both Hughes and the nativist American Protestant Union. Emphasizing not religion but the PSS's monopoly on school funds and its failure to appeal to large numbers of the city's poorest residents, Maclay's committee endorsed a plan to replace the citywide school system with local boards that would make their own decisions about which schools to fund and through what mechanism. Before reporting this proposal to the full assembly, Chairman Maclay sent it to Hughes for his review. That information was leaked to the nativist press, setting off a furor. To the *Christian Intelligencer,* as quoted in the *Catholic Herald,* Hughes's participation was a "'humiliating and alarming fact.'" "'A foreign Popish priest is permitted to control the legislature of New York!'" the paper exclaimed, adding, "'To propitiating the influence of the Popish priesthood at the polls, the best system of Common School instruction in the land is to be destroyed— a host of salaried officers created—and POPERY nursed at the public charge! Yield to it this power, and will it stop here? Who that knows its spirit—who that reads its history, believes it? WILL NOT PROTESTANTS AWAKE? If not— when shorn, bound and tortured, let them not complain.'" The *Catholic Herald* retorted, "[W]e would but ask is Protestantism in this free country to have the exclusive advantage of public nursing, and that too at the expense of the followers of that very POPERY to their own exclusion and insult, and are we to regard Protestantism as a State religion par excellence?" (April 7, 1842, p. 109).

In the end, the state legislature passed a compromise bill that established local school boards as well as a citywide board of education while prohibiting the allocation of state funds to schools in which "any religious sectarian doctrine or tenet shall be taught, inculcated, or practiced" (Bourne, p. 524). The legislature thus denied to Hughes and his allies what they most wanted— financial support for Catholic schools—but it broke the PSS's monopoly on public funding and established powerful neighborhood boards, some of which would undoubtedly be dominated by Catholics. When Governor Seward signed this bill into law, outraged nativists demonstrated their displeasure by rioting in the streets and breaking windows and furniture in Hughes's house. "[F]ortunately for the mob," Brann remarked without apparent irony, "the bishop was out of town" (p. 86).

LOCAL OPTION

Inevitably, the prohibition on funding sectarian schools, intended to prevent the use of public money for Catholic education, also perpetuated the argument over whether generic Protestantism can be considered sectarian. This question came to a head in the city's ethnically diverse Fourth Ward, an extremely poor area of lower Manhattan plagued by gangs that, according to Asbury, "were so far beyond the pale that not even the politicians dared protect them" (p. 95). The school trustees of the Fourth Ward did nothing to improve their district's image in the eyes of more affluent and conventional New Yorkers when they declared that not only Protestantism but Christianity itself is sectarian. In a memorandum to the New York City Board of Education, the trustees proposed to remove from the schools the KJB and other popular works that promoted religious themes. Their rationale for recommending this action, radically broad-minded by the standards of the time, was based on the conviction that equal treatment should be accorded to all religious beliefs, including the Jews' denial of the divinity of Jesus and the Universalists' objection to traditional Christian teachings about heaven and hell.

A select committee appointed to examine this memorandum was horrified by its assertion "that [the Fourth Ward trustees] do not see any good reason why the religious opinions of the Jews should not be regarded with the same favor of those of Christians." To the committee, this was "a most extraordinary and untenable position" because "if carried out, [it] would justify the Mahometans, the Chinese or Pagans, on their coming among us, to object to our whole system of public instruction, because it interfered with their monstrous, absurd, and unintelligible dogmas and superstitions. Even the Jews... cannot have the same privileges as those who embrace the Christian religion.... [Christianity is] in various ways incorporated and interwoven with our political systems, and recognized as the predominant religion of our State" (*Report of the Select Committee of the Board of Education*, 1843, p. 7). As to the justice of taxing religious minorities to support schools that opposed their beliefs, the committee found it "a sufficient answer that these institutions were established before they came; they are such as the majority of the people deemed most effectual for their government and conducive to their happiness" (p. 8). This emphasis on majority rule was also reflected in the committee's definition of the term "sectarian" to denote any belief system that "departs from, or holds tenets different from the established or prevailing religion of a state or Kingdom" (p. 11). Since Protestantism was undeniably the "prevailing religion" of New York, they concluded that only religions that differed from it could be deemed sectarian and thus excluded from publicly funded schools.

Negative as the committee report was, it paled by comparison with the fulminations of the nativist press. "Every week witnesses the progress of the enemy," the *Observer* thundered in response to the trustees' proposals. "Having hitherto been successful in their demands, the Roman Catholics are becoming more bold, and being now joined by the Universalists and Jews, will probably soon extirpate the last vestige of moral instruction from our public schools." The newly appointed superintendent of schools, a prominent nativist named William Stone, received correspondingly high praise for "denounc[ing] the communication as the most audacious document ever thrown in the teeth of an intelligent public" (July 22, 1843). Emphatically denying that the KJB and the other challenged books were sectarian, Stone alleged that "'a large number of most respectable and intelligent Jews'" were willing to have their children read the New Testament because of the moral principles it inculcates. Many Jews, he added, also recognized that "'they have enjoyed civil rights only in countries where there is a free circulation of the Bible'" (December 23, 1843, p. 202). Stone's remark referred to the ongoing persecution of Jews in Catholic countries, such as Poland, which nativists often mentioned to discourage unity between Catholics and Jews in America.

Shortly afterward, the New York state legislature passed new legislation to say that nothing in the school reorganization statute was meant to "'authorize the board of education to exclude the Holy Scriptures without note or comment, or any selections therefrom, from any of the schools provided for by this act; but it shall not be competent for said board of education to decide what version, if any, of the Holy Scriptures without note or comment, shall be used in any of the said schools'" (Bourne, p. 280). Since the Douay translation of the Bible includes the Catholic Church's interpretations of scriptural passages, this was found to be the kind of "note or comment" forbidden by the new law, which meant that only Protestant versions of the Bible could be used in the public schools. Nevertheless, the PSS and its supporters paid a high price for their victory over the Catholic Church. Burdened by increasing debt and dwindling income, the PSS soon went out of existence as an independent entity.

3

Religion as a Team Sport

Fanaticism consists in redoubling your efforts when you have forgotten your aim.

—*George Santayana*

Contentious as the New York City controversy undoubtedly was, it was essentially a war of words punctuated by a few fistfights and some minor property damage. Unfortunately, the same cannot be said of a dispute that erupted at about the same time over Bible-reading in the Philadelphia public schools. Churches, homes, and businesses were destroyed by mobs, and the rioting became so bad that peacekeeping troops were encamped in the city for weeks. Countless people were injured, and more than twenty lost their lives. Understandably, these events are often used to refute the claim that religion in the public schools did not cause any serious problems until the 1960s.

This violent episode in Philadelphia history is analyzed at length in Michael Feldberg's *The Philadelphia Riots of 1844: A Study of Ethnic Conflict* (1975), which is by far the best single source. Information is also drawn from the works by Billington, Dunn, Hassard, and Shaw mentioned earlier, as well as from *History of Philadelphia, 1609–1884* (1884), by J. Thomas Scharf and Thompson Westcott; *Encyclopedia of Philadelphia* (1931), by Joseph Jackson; and *Philadelphia: A History of the City and Its People* (1912), by Ellis P. Oberholtzer. Material on the Catholic diocese of Philadelphia comes from Joseph Kirlin's *Catholicity in Philadelphia* (1909), John O'Shea's *The Two Kenricks* (1904), and John G. Shea's *A History of the Catholic Church within the Limits of the United States* (1892). Information and quotations are also taken from newspapers, pamphlets, and other materials published at the time of the 1844 riots.

THE BISHOP AND THE SCHOOL BOARD

The Philadelphia dispute grew out of a policy enacted by the city school board to prevent school personnel from inculcating the distinctive tenets of any particular denomination. It was preceded by a rationale stating,

> That as all sects contribute in the payment of taxes to the support of Public Schools, the introduction of any religious or sectarian forms as a part of the discipline of the Schools, must have a tendency to impair the rights of some—and that whilst this Board is convinced of the utter impossibility of adopting a system of religious instruction that should meet the approbation of all religious societies, they are equally satisfied no injury may result to the pupils from confining the instruction in our schools to the ordinary branches of elementary education; inasmuch as ample facilities for religious improvement are presented for the choice of parents or guardians, in Sabbath Schools, and other establishments for that purpose, which are organized and supported by various religious communities. (Kirlin, pp. 311–12)

Although this rationale appeared to be leading up to the elimination of all religion from the public schools, the policy itself contained a loophole: "'RESOLVED: That this Board cannot but consider the introduction or use of any religious exercises, books, or lessons into the Public Schools, *which have not been adopted by the Board,* as contrary to law; and the use of any such religious exercises, books, or lessons, is hereby directed to be discontinued'" (p. 312; emphasis added). Because of the italicized clause, the policy did not ban religion altogether but merely allowed the city school board, rather than local officials, to decide which religious texts and observances would be permitted.

Shortly after enacting this policy, the all-Protestant board mandated the daily reading of the King James Bible by all public-school students. The Catholic bishop of Philadelphia, Francis Patrick Kenrick, responded with a letter saying that although he had no objection to Protestant students reading the KJB, Catholic students could not in good conscience do so. He asked the board either to allow Catholics to use the Douay Bible or to excuse them from Bible-reading altogether. He also asked that they be exempted from other religious observances, such as reciting the Lord's Prayer. "'It is not consistent with the laws and discipline of the Catholic Church,'" he explained, "'for their members to unite in religious exercises with those who are not of her communion. We offer up prayers and supplications to God for all men; we embrace all in the sincerity of Christian affection; but we confine the marks of religious brotherhood to those who are of the household of the faith'" (p. 313). (The Catholic Church no longer forbids interdenominational worship.)

The board assured Kenrick that no student would be forced to read the KJB, but before long Catholic parents were again protesting that their children were being humiliated, beaten, suspended, and expelled for refusing to do so. Accusations couched in the florid style of nineteenth-century journalism appeared in the Catholic press, such as the story of a little girl who

> had to submit to corporal punishment, before her companions, with a spiritual lecture from the Teacher.... The child returned to her parents, exhibiting the marks of violence inflicted upon her.... It will not do to affirm, "that no one is compelled to read the Protestant Bible." This is sheer cant. The children are called up in class to read it, and disobedience is a punishable offence. The poor children know it, and fear to refuse. Hence, they are compelled to violate their conscience, lest they be subject to the punishment inflicted by the pious Teacher, for refusing to read the blessed word of God. (*Catholic Herald,* May 12, 1842, p. 149)

A week later, the *Herald* recounted a scene that allegedly took place in the same classroom when another child refused to read the Bible.

> "Why do you grow pale?" asked the gentle hearted inquisitor. "I'm delicate ma'am, and afraid of being whipped," answered the child. "And would you bear a whipping rather than read the Bible" asked Miss M. "Yes, ma'am," sobbed out the young martyr. "Sit down you little fool," rejoined the Teacher, and the poor trembling child sat down with all the merit, but without the punishment of martyrdom. (May 19, 1842, p. 157)

In spring 1844, Bishop Kenrick joined frustrated Catholic parents in making a formal complaint to the school board. They renewed their request to allow Catholic children to use the Douay Version, but the board refused to countenance the use of any translation that included the Church's explanatory notes. As the New York state legislature had done a few years earlier, it tried to compromise by permitting students to use "any particular version of the

Bible, without note or comment" (Dunn, p. 271). In the board's view, this policy established a neutral standard under which any denomination was free to produce its own unannotated translation of the Bible for use in the schools. Catholics, of course, reviled it as "a virtual adoption of the Protestant principle, that the Bible without note or comment is the rule of faith, and it was consequently the assumption of a sectarian bias for public education" (*Catholic Herald*, March 7, 1844, p. 76).

While refusing to allow Catholic students to use the Douay translation, the board tried to placate the Catholic community by establishing heavy penalties for school personnel who forced unwilling children to read the KJB. This concession infuriated Philadelphia nativists, who, like their brethren in New York City, felt that immigrant children could not be properly Americanized unless they learned to revere the KJB as the source of liberty and morality. In their view, the board's opt-out policy represented nothing less than a governmental blessing on Catholic contempt for all that was most sacred to true Americans, and they warned that growing Catholic political power would ultimately overthrow democracy and place the nation under Vatican rule.

No doubt this dispute would have become heated under any circumstances, but there are few problems that a political campaign cannot make worse. As the election of 1844 approached, the nativists, organized into the Native American Party, tried to broaden their base of support by accusing Kenrick of seeking to ban the Bible from the schools. He replied in an open letter published in several newspapers: "'Catholics have not asked that the Bible be excluded from the Public Schools,'" he wrote. "'They have merely desired for their children the liberty of using the Catholic Version in case the reading of the Bible be prescribed by the Controllers or Directors of the Schools'" (Kirlin, p. 315).

THE BATTLE OF NANNY GOAT MARKET

As the campaign progressed, nativists held large anti-Catholic rallies in Irish neighborhoods, whose residents hurled insults and rocks at the speakers and on one occasion silenced them by destroying the platform on which they were standing. Nativists retaliated by vandalizing Irish property, and it was only a matter of time before serious violence broke out. Inevitability became reality on May 6, when approximately two thousand nativists attended a rally in Kensington, then a northern suburb of Philadelphia with a large Irish population. A heavy rain began to fall, and when the nativists sought shelter at the nearby Nanny Goat Market, shots were exchanged with the Irish inhabitants. The first man to die, eighteen-year-old George Schiffler, was venerated for years afterward as a nativist hero and martyr. The rioters spilled into the streets, where Kensington residents fired from windows and rooftops. Armed reinforcements from a neighboring Protestant area came to the aid of the nativists, who smashed the windows and doors of the buildings from which the Catholics were firing. After about an hour of this, Philadelphia's sheriff, Morton McMichael, managed to quell the disturbance.

The next day's issue of the nativist periodical *Native American* was a call to arms. "'The bloody hand of the Pope has stretched itself forth to our destruction,'" it thundered. "'We now call on our fellow-citizens, who regard free institutions, whether they be native or adopted, to arm. Our liberties are now to be fought for; let us not be slack in our preparations'" (Billington, p. 225). The same sentiment was echoed in placards summoning nativists to a mass meeting behind Independence Hall. "'LET EVERY MAN COME PREPARED TO DEFEND HIMSELF,'" they proclaimed (Oberholtzer, p. 293).

Impelled by impassioned speeches at the rally, approximately three thousand nativists marched to Kensington carrying a tattered American flag that had allegedly been trampled underfoot by Irish Catholics. According to a pamphlet printed shortly afterward, they found the Kensingtonians "in a dreadful state of excitement, and even women and boys joined in the affray, some of the women actually throwing missiles.... Many of the women who were not engaged with weapons, incited the men to vigorous action, pointing out where they could operate with more effect, and cheering them on and rallying them to a renewal of the conflict whenever their spirits fell or they were compelled to retreat. As in most other riots which we have noticed in our city and county, small and half-grown boys formed no inconsiderable portion of the combatants on both sides, and contended with the most sanguinary spirit" (*Full and Complete Account*, 1844). For their part, the nativists burned whole blocks of homes and businesses, including the Nanny Goat Market. Alarmed Protestant residents, seeking to protect their property from the mob, displayed American flags, hand-painted nativist messages, and clippings from nativist publications. After about an hour, the militia came to the aid of Sheriff McMichael and his beleaguered deputies, and the situation was brought under control. Four nativists and an Irishman had been shot dead, and a charred body, presumably Irish, was found in one of the burned-out buildings.

Bishop Kenrick promptly called on Catholics who had committed acts of violence to repent and set an example of patience and pacifism. "I earnestly conjure you all," he wrote, "to avoid all occasion of excitement, and to shun all public places of assemblage, and to do nothing that may exasperate. Follow peace with all men, and have that CHARITY without which no man can see GOD" (*Catholic Herald,* May 9, 1844, p. 149). He closed the churches and forbade public worship "'until it can be resumed with safety, and we can enjoy our constitutional right to worship God according to the dictates of our conscience'" (O'Shea, p. 52). When priests were pelted with rocks, he advised them to abandon their clerical garb, and he instructed pastors to surrender their keys to the sheriff and leave the protection of church property to him. By behaving in this fashion, he predicted, Catholics would improve both their spiritual and material welfare because the moderate Protestants who made up the majority of the population would reject nativist violence and rally in defense of religious liberty.

The fighting resumed on the morning after the riot, when nativists returned to Kensington ostensibly to search for armed Irish partisans but in reality to set fire to the houses that were still standing. They also burned St. Michael's Church, whose pastor had obeyed the bishop's order to turn over the keys to the militia commander. On that occasion, as on many others, Catholics accused the militia not only of indifference to the fate of Catholic property but of complicity in its destruction. City officials did try to intervene when nativists attacked St. Augustine's Church in an affluent neighborhood near what is now the historic center of Philadelphia; indeed, the mayor was knocked unconscious by a rock as he tried to disperse the mob. The firemen, however, were less obliging. According to a nineteenth-century account,

> somebody had entered the church and kindled a fire, the light of which was soon seen. No efforts were made to quench the flames. They increased in brightness as pew led the fire to pew, the galleries caught, and at length the flames broke forth from the roof and the windows in front, and finally the steeple was on fire, and as the cross which crowned the height yielded to the flames and fell in, plaudits arose with savage exultation from many in the streets. The firemen who were upon the ground did not attempt to play upon the church, but devoted themselves to saving the adjoining property. The flames were resistless and they left nothing unconsumed,—nothing but the blackened walls, and there in the morning, through the broken windows over what had been the high altar, were seen as plainly as they had existed on the previous day, the remarkable words, "THE LORD SEETH." (Scharf and Westcott, pp. 666–67)

The burning of St. Augustine's had the unintended effect of energizing affluent Philadelphia Protestants who suddenly found their own neighborhoods in danger. They were led by a well-known lawyer, Horace Binney, who was called upon by his associates to take charge of the situation. According to a biography written by his son, Binney later recalled that "'I replied to [a friend] that I would not go, that the men in authority were the men to take the responsibility of the proper measures.... To this he rejoined that I *must* go... that the authorities had been in session during the night, and instead of doing anything, appeared to be stupefied'" (Binney, p. 236). At a rally attended by thousands of Philadelphians, Binney and other prominent residents advised each neighborhood to organize a citizens' watch with "the legal right, for the protection of property and life, to resist and to defeat the mob by the use of any degree of force that was necessary for this purpose" (p. 238). Citizen guards began patrolling that evening, identified by white muslin hatbands bearing the words "peace police" (Scharf and Westcott, p. 667).

To supplement the neighborhood watches, peacekeeping units were formed by civic and professional organizations, including the prestigious Philadelphia Bar Association. Approximately sixty lawyers, law students, and clerks patrolled for five nights under the command of Colonel John Swift; and in contravention of the common belief that regimenting lawyers is akin to herding squirrels, "Colonel Swift, we are told, has spoken of their discipline and order in the highest terms" ("Praiseworthy," [Philadelphia] *Legal Intelligencer*, May 15, 1844, p. 2). A month later, an essay in the *Pennsylvania Law Journal* reflected the mood of the time in its celebration of the bar association's contribution. "It is a matter of some congratulation," it stated,

> that the Philadelphia bar, at the time of the late emergency, was
> so fully buckled up to the occasion, as to resolve to go through the
> duty that might be prescribed, without much regard to those
> technicalities by which the profession so often suffers itself to be
> hampered in extreme cases. That gentlemen of all ages—from
> the jurist who has retired from the clash of courts to the quiet of
> chambers, to the student who has yet to look before him at the
> epoch of the first speech,—that all classes of a profession, to say
> the least, the most sedentary, and the least acquainted with gymnastics, should have hurried together at the first call, and for five
> long nights should have carried muskets and undergone drill,—
> is a thing most creditable.... If no glory was won, for ultimately

whatever personal disarrangements took place, were occasioned
rather from the awkwardness of allies than the malice of foes,—
at least good feeling was extended. ("The Late George Gordon
Riots, and the Law Concerning Them," June 1844, p. 334n)

THE CHURCH MILITANT

Shortly after order was restored, nativists in New York City proposed to demonstrate solidarity with those in Philadelphia by holding a rally in City Hall Park.
The American flag that had allegedly been trampled by Irish Catholics in Kensington was to be carried aloft, and there was open talk of fanning out from the
park to attack nearby churches. Nevertheless, while rowdy nativists rejoiced in
the prospect of disorder, more responsible Native American Party leaders
wanted to postpone the rally "until the country gets calm and tranquil" (*New
York Herald*, May 9, 1844). The fight to defend the Bible, as the nativists characterized it, had increased the party's popularity in Philadelphia, but newspapers
elsewhere in the country were taking a negative view of the violence. With a
national election approaching, party leaders feared that additional riots would
be more of a liability than an asset. Nevertheless, the plans for the rally—and
the threats to Catholic churches—continued, at least for a time.

It is hardly necessary to say that Bishop Hughes's reaction to all this was
nothing like Bishop Kenrick's. In his view, a mob was nothing more than an
assemblage of cowards, and the best way to prevent violence was to intimidate
them into backing down. He therefore summoned approximately twenty-five
hundred Catholic men, saw to it that they were armed, divided them among
the threatened churches, and issued a public statement that was the nineteenth-century equivalent of "Go ahead. Make my day." Confronted by the
inevitable accusation that he was fomenting violence, he retorted that, to the
contrary, he had taken the most volatile elements of the Catholic community
off the streets and placed them under supervision in the churches. As long as
the churches remained unmolested, he said, the situation would be more
peaceful than it would have been otherwise; but if the nativists carried out
their threat, then Catholics could not be blamed for defending their property.

In principle, Hughes agreed with Kenrick that the key to winning the dispute was to enlist the support of mainstream Protestants, but his method of
doing so differed dramatically from the pacifism of his Philadelphia colleague. It did not escape his notice that public involvement in putting down
the Philadelphia riots had escalated as soon as affluent Protestant neighborhoods were drawn into the fray, so in addition to warning that Catholics were

prepared to defend their own property, he predicted that if provoked by nativist attacks they would burn Protestant property throughout the city. He was careful not to condone violence, but he described it as inevitable and indicated that he could do nothing to prevent it. His well-known influence over the Catholic community rendered this statement less than convincing to some skeptical New Yorkers, but Hughes made it plain that he did not plan to follow Kenrick's example. Before numerous witnesses, he told Mayor Robert Morris that "'If a single Catholic Church is burned in New York, the city will become a second Moscow.'" During an invasion by Napoleon's troops about thirty years earlier, Moscow had been burned to the ground; Hughes used the image as a modern speaker might allude to the devastation of Dresden or Beirut. It was particularly apposite, however, because many of those fires had been set by the Muscovites themselves. When the mayor asked whether Hughes seriously thought that Catholic churches would be burned, the bishop replied, "'No, sir; but I am afraid that some of yours will be burned. We can protect our own. I come to warn you for your own good'" (Shaw, p. 197). If, as Hughes stated, his purpose was to attract public attention, there can be no doubt of his success.

Despite Mayor Morris's participation in the discussions with Hughes, the real center of power in the city was the mayor-elect, James Harper, who had run for office on the Native American Party ticket. While committed to the nativist cause, Harper took Hughes at his word and was understandably reluctant to become mayor of a burned-out city. He also realized that the national reaction to the Philadelphia riots was dimming his party's hopes of winning governorships and congressional seats in the upcoming election. Accordingly, he used his influence to help persuade the organizers of the rally to cancel it, which they did with some reluctance. Hughes, of course, was elated. "'We knew the nature of a mob,'" he crowed, "'especially a mob of church-burners, convent-sackers, and grave-robbers; that with it a firm front is the best peacemaker, and that to let it know that, be the authorities as supine as they pleased, the scenes of Philadelphia could not be renewed with impunity in New York, would do more for order than all the twaddle that could be poured out by all the papers in the country.'" Writing in the *Freeman's Journal*, he described Catholics who disapproved of his methods as "'generally good, cautious souls, who believe in stealing through the world more submissively than suits a freeman,'" while those who supported him were "'men who feel no consciousness of inferiority to any portion of their fellow-citizens, but who are, in every sense of the word, thoroughly American'" (Hassard, p. 277).

FIREWORKS IN PHILADELPHIA

After a lull of several weeks, violence returned to Philadelphia in the wake of a Fourth of July parade in which approximately five thousand nativists marched, carrying anti-Catholic banners and pictures of fallen comrades. The next day, a nativist crowd collected at St. Philip Neri Church, where guns had been stored after the May riots. Some of the guns were surrendered, but when nativist leaders searched the church and found additional weapons, the sheriff called in the militia to avert possible violence. The next night, the militia attempted to clear nearby side streets with bayonets, whereupon the nativists hurled bricks. The commander ordered his men to fire their cannons, but a former congressman, Charles Naylor, threw himself in front of the guns. He was arrested and confined in the church basement.

The next day, Naylor's supporters went down to the nearby docks, unbolted a cannon from one of the ships moored there, and pulled it up the hilly streets to the church. They called for the release of Naylor and the removal of an Irish militia company stationed at the church. When their demands were not met, they loaded the cannon with nuts, bolts, broken glass, nails, chains, and other shrapnel and fired it at the church. More cannons were brought up from the docks, but after a second barrage the nativist leaders offered to restore order if both Naylor and the Irish militia were removed. This was done, and nativists occupied the church. Soon afterward, other nativists who had been left outside smashed down the doors with a battering ram and milled around the sanctuary without doing serious damage. The militia commander, returning with additional troops, tried to clear the church and the streets, resulting in bloody fighting that brought death and injury to combatants and noncombatants alike. Perhaps the most bizarre event was the death of an unidentified German man who, leaning out of the attic window of a nearby house, was decapitated by a stray cannon ball. Feeling that the militia was causing more unrest than it was quelling, the governor withdrew the troops from that area but left them quartered elsewhere in the city for several weeks. As one eyewitness observed early in August, "Since that time the city has worn in some measure the aspect of a military encampment" (*Catholic Herald,* August 1, 1844, p. 243).

Grand juries appointed to examine the events of May and July laid the blame for the disturbances squarely on the Irish Catholic population. According to the May jury, which included two nativist leaders, the troubles were attributable to

the efforts of a portion of the community to exclude the Bible
from the public schools. Those efforts in some measure gave rise
to the formation of a new party, which called and held public
meetings in the district of Kensington, in the peaceful exercise of
the sacred rights and privileges guaranteed to every citizen by the
Constitution and laws of our State and country. These meetings
were rudely disturbed and fired upon by a band of lawless, irre-
sponsible men, some of whom had resided in the country only
for a short period. This outrage, causing the death of a number of
our unoffending citizens, led to immediate retaliation, and was
followed up by subsequent acts of aggression, and in violation
and open defiance of all law. (Scharf and Westcott, p. 668)

In a pamphlet addressed to the citizens of Philadelphia, a committee of
prominent Catholics angrily denied "that one party were rioters and the other
the assailed" (*Address of the Catholic Lay Citizens*, 1844, p. 3). They accused the
grand jury of having taken testimony only from nativists and challenged the
assertion that Catholics had sought to exclude the Bible from the public
schools. In reality, they said, Catholics "limited their request to the liberty of
using their own version, and did not in any way interfere with the use of the
Protestant version by such as chose to adopt it.... [E]specially in the city to
which William Penn gave the name and impress of brotherly love, we pre-
sume it is unnecessary to put forward any plea in support of the constitutional
and legal right to have our religious predilections respected" (p. 6). They also
criticized "the soft tones and delicate phrases in which the Grand Jury has
hinted at the burning of two churches" and other Catholic property, including
"the letters and papers, and picture of George Washington, preserved with
religious care in the Church of St. Augustine, of which he was one of the earliest benefactors.—The Grand Jury complaisantly alludes to all these as 'acts of
retaliation.' Retaliation against whom?" (p. 9). In the writers' view, the majority of Catholics had done nothing to justify the nativist violence that the jury
was so willing to excuse.

To bolster its assertion that Catholics had not sought the removal of the
Bible from the public schools, the *Address* called upon Protestant members of
the city school board "to state ... whether [Catholics] have asked for the exclusion of the Bible ... [or] interfered with the use of the Protestant version of the
Scriptures by Protestant children" (p. 10). Seven Protestant board members
responded that no such actions had ever been taken. Apparently unpersuaded

by all this, the judge who oversaw a grand jury convened after the July rioting stated that "[T]he wholesale slaughter...was the natural result of [the Catholics'] unnatural position" of opposition to the Bible (*Catholic Herald*, July 11, 1844). Nevertheless, a court eventually ordered the city to pay $33,468.98 in compensation for St. Michael's Church and $47,433.87 for St. Augustine's. According to Kirlin, the reason for the odd sums was that the twelve jurors who heard the case could not agree on the award, so they added up the amounts each of them proposed and divided the total by twelve.

TAR AND FEATHERS FOR THE JESUIT

Although the violence of the Philadelphia riots was not repeated on the same scale anywhere else, Protestants and Catholics throughout the country continued to disagree about Bible-reading and prayer in the public schools. In 1852, the American Catholic bishops took a hard stand on the matter at their First Plenary Council, chaired by Bishop Kenrick in his new role as archbishop of Baltimore and apostolic delegate. A report submitted by a committee of bishops stated, "'And when Catholics object to [Protestant practices], they are immediately held up to public execration as enemies of the Bible and of free institutions.... Melancholy experience has shown the consequences of all this. Catholic children exposed to insidious, if not open attacks on their religious principles and practices, *become ashamed of their faith....* it is morally impossible, [that] their faith should not be weakened and their feelings warped'" (Dunn, p. 217). Accordingly, the council adopted a resolution reminding Catholics that their children were forbidden to read the KJB. This precept was far from new, of course, but the council's action caused some bishops to enforce it more vigorously, thus increasing the incidence of controversies.

The first major dispute to arise from the bishops' ruling was initiated by a Jesuit priest, John Bapst, who had been sent from a seminary in Switzerland to minister to the Abnaki tribe in rural Maine. As recounted in the *History of the Archdiocese of Boston in the Various Stages of Its Development, 1604 to 1943*, Vol. II (1944), by Robert H. Lord, John E. Sexton, and Edward T. Harrington, Bapst resided in the small town of Ellsworth, where he told the Catholic children that the bishops had forbidden the reading of the KJB. Two of his young parishioners subsequently refused to participate in Bible-reading and were expelled, despite the priest's appeal to the school committee on their behalf. According to Bapst, one of the committee members declared, "We are determined to protestantize the Catholic children; they shall read the Protestant Bible or be dismissed from the schools; and should we find them loafing around the wharves, we will clap them into jail" (Lord et al., p. 673). Shortly after the expulsions, two members of the school committee visited each classroom and ordered the children to read aloud from the KJB. Those who refused were dismissed, and Bapst established a school for them in a disused chapel.

Two years later, the dispute took a new turn when one of Bapst's parishioners, Lawrence Donohoe, told his daughter, Bridget, not to read the KJB in class. She was expelled, but instead of sending her to Bapst's school, Donohoe enrolled her in a private school and sued the State of Maine for reimbursement. Her lawyer, identified in court documents only by his surname, Rowe, took a stand that was highly unusual at the time: he tried to convince an American court that the majority does not rule in matters of religion. "[A]s protestants regard instruction in protestant christianity as the most essential branch of education," he explained,

> therefore if the majority of the school be protestants, the committee may enforce such a system of instruction upon all; and Mahomedans, catholics, or Mormons may follow their example if they get the power. "The greatest good of the greatest number." This tyrannical doctrine of pure democracy, we generally hear only from the lips of demagogues. Lawyers and statesmen have usually supposed that one great object of a written constitution was to do away with a principle so obviously unjust, and to substitute for it, the equal good of all. (*Donohoe v. Richards,* 38 Me. 379 [1854], p. 387)

He went on to assert that the KJB is sectarian, and requiring Catholics to read it violated their religious freedom and impermissibly involved the school committee in a theological dispute.

Rowe had a watertight case by today's standards, but in 1854 his argument was too radical to consider. The court declared that the KJB was nonsectarian and that the Catholics' request to use their own translation was a ruse intended to further their aim of removing the Bible from the public schools. If Bridget could not read the KJB, the court reasoned, then no one could read it aloud in her presence, and oral Bible-reading would thus be eliminated. The court also found that her freedom of religion had not been violated and indeed was not even at issue. In the court's view, the case was not about religious liberty but about the authority of the school committee to expel students who disobeyed the rules:

No scholar can escape or evade such requirement when made by
the committee, under the plea that his *conscience* will not allow
the reading of such book. Nor can the ordinance be nullified,
because the church of which the scholar is a member, hold, and
have so instructed its members, that it is a *sin* to read the book
prescribed. A law is not unconstitutional, because it may prohibit
what one may *conscientiously* think right, or require what he may
conscientiously think wrong. A requirement by the superintend-
ing school committee, that the *Protestant version* of the Bible shall
be read in the public schools of their town, by the scholars who
are able to read, is in violation of no constitutional provision, and
is binding upon all the members of the schools, although composed of diverse *religious sects.* (p. 380)

The court concluded that the Donohoe family, not the school committee, was
seeking special treatment for a particular religion. "[Bridget's] claim to be
exempted from a general regulation of the school rests entirely on her religious belief," the court found, "and is to the extent that the choice of reading
books shall be in *entire subordination to her faith, and because it is her faith*"
(p. 406). If Catholics did not want to read the KJB, the court observed, their
remedy was not to supersede the school committee but to elect members who
would accede to their wishes.

Naturally, Donohoe's lawsuit enraged Ellsworth's nativist population, and
most of their hostility was directed at the foreign Catholic priest who had
started all the trouble. While the case was in progress, The *Ellsworth Herald*
ran an advertisement saying, "1000 MEN WANTED. To Protestant laborers
everywhere, we say, Come to Ellsworth and come quickly! for your services
may be needed in more ways than one" (Lord et al., p. 674). Fearing violence,
Bapst's superiors reassigned him to Bangor and told him to stay away from
Ellsworth, and shortly afterward the old chapel that housed the Catholic
school was bombed. Some citizens denounced this action at a town meeting,
but the nativists took over and passed a resolution saying:

Whereas, we have good reason to believe that we are indebted to
one John Bapst, S.J., Catholic Priest, for the luxury of the present
law suit now enjoyed by the school committee of Ellsworth,
therefore Resolved, That should the said Bapst be found again
upon Ellsworth soil, we manifest our gratitude for his kindly

interference with our fine schools, and attempt to banish the
Bible therefrom, by procuring for him, and trying on an entire
new suit of clothes such as cannot be found in the shops of any
tailor and that when thus apparelled, he be presented with a fine
ticket to leave Ellsworth upon the first railroad operation that may
go into effect. (Lord et al., p. 675)

The point of this heavy-handed humor was that they wanted to coat Bapst with
hot tar, roll him in feathers, and ride him out of town on a rail.

The nativists' wish came true a few months later when Bapst, traveling
near Ellsworth, stopped overnight to hear confessions and say Mass. A mob
surrounded the house where he was staying, whereupon he heroically surrendered himself (Catholic version) or was dragged sniveling from his hiding
place (nativist version). Either way, he was stripped, tarred, feathered, and carried to the wharf on a rail. When Catholics found him about an hour later, a
prominent Protestant resident offered sanctuary in his home. Bapst's protec-
tor and other Protestant citizens demanded retribution against his assailants,
whose identity was known, but a grand jury refused to indict them.

A ROSE BY ANY OTHER NAME

While Bapst was struggling with school officials in Maine, a more wide-rang-
ing controversy was brewing in neighboring Massachusetts, which was experiencing an influx of Irish Catholic immigrants. Nativists, worried that the
newcomers might become sufficiently powerful to gain public funding for
Catholic schools, proposed an amendment to the state constitution that would
prohibit the use of tax money for sectarian education. As Hughes had done in
New York more than a decade earlier, Massachusetts Catholics retorted that
such a provision would also cut off support to schools that used the KJB. The
amendment was ratified by popular vote in 1855, and despite the complaints
of Catholics, it had no effect on Bible-reading in the public schools.

The governor of Massachusetts and several of its legislators belonged to the
Know-Nothing Party, which had evolved from the Native American Party. Like
their nativist counterparts in Philadelphia and New York, they believed that
the KJB should be read by all schoolchildren because it held the key to democracy and Americanism. Accordingly, in addition to denying funds to Catholic
schools, they enacted truancy laws compelling students who could not afford
private-school tuition to attend public schools, where they would be required
to read the KJB. This attempt to ensure the inculcation of Protestant princi-

ples was compromised, however, by the willingness of many public-school teachers to work out unofficial arrangements for their Catholic students. Most commonly, they read the Bible aloud but did not ask the children to do so, thus reducing the students' role to one of passive listening. Similarly, when classes recited the Lord's Prayer in unison, some teachers looked the other way if Catholics did not participate or used their own wording. They did the same with regard to recitations of the KJB translation of the Ten Commandments, and it was this practice that roused the ire of nativist officials.

By any objective standard, there is little difference between the Protestant and Catholic versions of the Commandments. In both, the First Commandment forbids the worship of false gods, but Catholics omit the explicit prohibition against graven images that makes up the Protestant Second Commandment. As a result, the Catholic version is one commandment ahead of the Protestant most of the way through. In the Catholic version, for instance, the Seventh Commandment is "Thou shalt not steal," which is the Protestant Eighth Commandment. Nevertheless, the Catholic version has ten commandments, not nine, because it splits the Protestant Tenth Commandment in two. The Protestant "Thou shalt not covet thy neighbor's house, thou shalt not covet thy neighbor's wife, nor his manservant, nor his maidservant, nor his ox, nor his ass, nor any thing that is thy neighbor's" thus becomes "Thou shalt not covet thy neighbor's wife" and "Thou shalt not covet thy neighbor's goods." There are also a few differences in the wording of some commandments, with the Catholic version generally the shorter of the two. Since society would be much improved if people refrained from stealing, lying, coveting, and so forth, it might not seem to matter whether those precepts are numbered 7, 8, 9, or $22^{1}/_{4}$. As with the exclusive use of the KJB, however, the real issue was not accuracy but power. To be sure, nativists regarded the omission of the KJB Second Commandment as proof that Catholics blasphemously worshipped statues of the Virgin Mary and the saints, but their chief objection to allowing schoolchildren to recite the Catholic version was that it would suggest official sanction of what they saw as a perversion of Scripture. The substance of either version had little to do with it; the main point was symbolism, not content, and from that perspective the choice of Protestant or Catholic made all the difference in the world.

The intense feelings associated with different versions of the Ten Commandments led to a particularly ugly confrontation in the all-male Eliot School in Boston, where most of the students were Catholic. Early in 1859, the chairman of the school committee, a Know-Nothing named Micah Dyer, discovered that Catholic boys were remaining silent during the weekly group recitation of the Commandments. Indeed, some teachers were going so far as to allow them to recite the Douay Version. Dyer demanded that each boy, individually, recite the King James Version of the Decalogue every Monday morning. An eleven-year-old named Thomas Wall refused to do so, and the parish priest told the other boys to follow Thomas's example. Accordingly, when the recitation began the next Monday, he and approximately two-thirds of his schoolmates refused to participate until the vice-principal, McLaurin Cooke, caned Thomas so severely that he complied.

The Walls sued Cooke for assault, and the decision of the Boston Police Court includes a vivid account of the event. Thomas, it seems, refused to obey Cooke's order on the grounds that his father "had told him for his life not to [recite the Commandments], and that his priest had also told him not to say them, and that on the Sunday previous to the 14th the priest (Father Wiget), while addressing nine hundred children of St. Mary's Church, of whom Wall was one, told them not to be cowards to their religion, and not to read or repeat the Commandments in school, that if they did he would read their names from the altar." When school officials determined that Thomas was "one of, if not the principal actor" in "a concerted plan of action" to defy them, Cooke beat him "with a rattan stick, some three feet in length, and three-eighths of an inch thick, by whipping upon his hands. From the time when the punishment commenced to the time when it ended, repeated inquiries were made of Wall if he would comply with the requirements of the school. Some thirty minutes time was occupied in the whole," including a few intervals when Cooke left the room. "The blows," said the court, "were not given in quick succession, but with deliberation. . . . The master ceased to punish when Wall submitted to the requirements of the school." "Wall's hands were swollen," the decision added, and "he was taken to the sink by the defendant twice, and his hands held in water. The physician who saw his hands in the afternoon of Monday, and prescribed for them, after describing their appearance, says that he did not think the injury very severe; that at the time he thought he would recover from it in twenty-four hours" (*Report of the Trial of McLaurin F. Cooke*, 1859, pp. 81, 82).

Like the court in the Donohoe case in Maine, the Boston Police Court reasoned that if the Catholics prevailed, then "at any time when one pupil can be found in each public school in the Commonwealth with conscientious scruples against reading the Bible, or hearing it read, the Bible may be banished from them, and so the matter of education may be taken from the State government and placed in the hands of a few children" (p. 83). The court also

found that the KJB is a nonsectarian source of generally accepted moral teachings and that the central issue in the case was not religious liberty but school
discipline. According to the decision, neither Thomas's father nor his priest
had any authority in the matter, because "By sending his child to school [the
parent] surrenders so much of his parental rights over the child as would, if
exercised, conflict with the reasonable rules and regulations of the school"
(p. 84). Based on this reasoning, the court found that Cooke's action had been
justified. "The mind and the will of Wall," the decision stated,

> had been prepared for insubordination and revolt by his father
> and the priest. . . . The extent of the punishment was left as it were
> to his own choice. From the first blow that fell upon his hand
> from the master's rattan, to the last that was given, it was in his
> power to make every one the last. He was punished for insubor-
> dination, and a determination to stand out against the lawful
> commands of the school. Every blow given was for a continued
> resistance and a new offence. The offence and the punishment
> went hand in hand together. The punishment ceased when the
> offence ceased. (p. 86)

A similar case in Shirley, Massachusetts, reached the same result a few
years later. In that situation, a teacher named Leonard Spalding severely beat
John and Mary Hehir for refusing to read the KJB. When their parents complained to the school committee, Spalding beat them again. Their mother
tried to discuss the matter with him, and in her presence he beat both of them
once more, using a heavy stick. He was sent for trial to the county court, but a
grand jury refused to indict him.

A ROCK AND A HARD PLACE
The bishop of Boston, John Fitzpatrick, viewed the Wall case with alarm
because he had been trying desperately to avoid a confrontation over religion
in the public schools. Catholic schools were few and far between in some
areas of Massachusetts, and with all hope of public funding dashed by the new
amendment to the state constitution, he did not intend to build more. Since
the new law requiring children to attend school included severe penalties for
noncompliance, any controversy that might keep Catholics out of the public
schools had the potential to cause serious problems. Discussions of his struggles with this dilemma, together with excerpts from his writings, appear in

Lord, Sexton, and Harrington, and in *Fitzpatrick's Boston, 1846–1866* (1984), by Thomas H. O'Connor.

On March 15, 1859, Fitzpatrick wrote a lengthy entry in his *Memoranda* expressing his concern that children who left the public schools might be convicted of truancy and

> sent to a penal institution at Westboro College the reform school.
> There they may be kept until 21 years old cut off from all catholic
> instruction. At the same time it is impossible to open catholic
> schools. To buy lots and erect buildings for this purpose would
> cost at least half a million of dollars, and then the annual
> expenses for the support of such schools would be, at lowest esti-
> mate 30 or 40 thousand dollars.... No redress can be expected by
> petition to the authorities for the state is ruled by a vast majority
> of persecuting bigots who, a few years ago, were bound by oath,
> as members of the know-nothing party, to oppress Catholics. The
> very laws alluded to were framed, no doubt, for the express pur-
> pose of corrupting the faith of Catholic children. The only alter-
> native at present seems to be that the children, under open
> protest, submit to the tyranny exercised over them, but at the
> same time to loathe and detest its enactments. This very sense of
> unjust oppression may, with God's grace, strengthen them in
> their attachment to the faith. (Lord et al., pp. 595–96)

Accordingly, Fitzpatrick told the Catholic children of his diocese to do whatever was necessary to remain in the public schools. He then sent a letter to the School Committee of Boston protesting that "The law as administered holds forth the Protestant version to the Catholic child and says, 'receive this as the Bible.' The Catholic child answers, 'I cannot so receive it.' The law, as adminis-tered, says, 'you must, or else you must be scourged, and finally banished from the school'" (p. 597). He also tried to clarify the objections the Church had at that time to interfaith worship. Protestants of different denominations often prayed together, he noted, "and in so doing they give and receive mutual satis-faction, mutual edification. The Catholic cannot act in this manner. He cannot present himself before the Divine presence in what would be for him a merely simulated union of prayer and adoration. His Church expressly forbids him to do so. She considers indifference in matters of religion, indifference as to the distinction of positive doctrines in faith, as a great evil which promiscuous worship would tend to spread more widely and increase" (p. 598). The bishop concluded by explaining that he had hitherto remained silent on these issues because whenever Catholics tried to address them, "It has been represented that the design was to eliminate and practically annihilate the Bible. This has never been true; and yet this has always been believed, and a rallying cry, 'To the rescue of the Bible!' has resounded on every side. Angry passions have been roused, violent acts have been committed, and, almost invariably, the last condition of things has been worse than the first" (p. 599).

Dyer persuaded the school committee to ignore Fitzpatrick's letter, but a month later one of its members, a Protestant pastor, proposed that only the teacher, not the students, should be required to read the Bible aloud. Dyer, arguing that Fitzpatrick's surrender had made any such compromise unnecessary, led the opposition and won by one vote. The following fall, a priest was elected as the first Catholic member of the school committee, and the pastor's proposal was reintroduced and passed. A bill that would allow dissenting students throughout Massachusetts to be excused from religious activities was defeated by Know-Nothings in the state legislature, but a subsequent attempt succeeded in 1864.

4

Off the Streets and Into the Courts

There is a tendency on the part of majorities to equate their own
beliefs with the natural order of things.... [A] message affirming a
religious principle of a majority faith may be understood by the
members of that religion to be a simple and non-controversial statement of the truth and not an endorsement of a contested issue of
faith. To my mind such statements are still unconstitutional
endorsements.

—*Alan Brownstein*

Although the beatings, riots, and shows of force that marked early school-
prayer disputes were often successful in the short term, they carried the seeds
of their own destruction. True to Bishop Francis Patrick Kenrick's prediction,
most Americans were repelled by violent attempts to repress disfavored beliefs,
and by the last third of the nineteenth century physical aggression had been
almost entirely replaced by lawsuits testing the limits of majority and minority
religious rights. Unlike earlier disputes, in which dissenters had been careful
to disclaim any hostility toward Bible-reading and prayer in the public schools,
many post–Civil War lawsuits called for the elimination of religious exercises
rather than the mere excusal of dissenting students. Nor were such measures
advocated exclusively by members of minority faiths. As the nation's population grew more diverse, an increasing number of Protestants came to feel that
the only truly equitable solution would be to exclude all religion, including
pan-Protestantism, from publicly funded schools. One of the clearest statements
of this viewpoint was offered by a Presbyterian preacher and scholar, Samuel
Thayer Spear, who observed in *Religion and the State* (1876) that Protestant
supporters of school prayer "*substantially ask for themselves in respect to the public schools what they deny to Catholics*" by approving Protestant, but not Catholic,
practices in publicly funded schools. "King James's version is all very well for

them," Spear wrote, "since they are agreed in accepting it; but it is not so for these other parties, who are taxed in common with them for the support of public schools, and who under our theory of government have just as many and just as sacred rights as they have in these schools" (p. 41).

As Spear's remarks suggest, and as the controversies discussed in the rest of this book demonstrate, the Protestant-versus-Catholic configuration of many nineteenth-century disputes gradually gave way to coalitions of like-minded people of varied religious persuasions, including non-Christians as well as Catholics and Protestants. To be sure, several of the lawsuits presented in this chapter were filed by Catholics in opposition to Protestant practices, but over time there has been a marked trend toward a form of activism in which members of different faiths join together to support or oppose a particular policy.

THE STATE OF THE CASE

Unlike today's school-prayer lawsuits, most of which are heard in federal courts, the nineteenth- and early twentieth-century cases discussed in this chapter were decided by state courts. For reasons explained below, the federal government did not become involved with religion in the public schools until the mid-twentieth century. Before then, each state could adopt any policies it wished, and disputes were adjudicated in the state's own courts. The result was a wide variation in the way school-prayer practices evolved in different states. According to the Congressional Research Service, immediately prior to the Supreme Court's landmark school-prayer decisions in the early 1960s, religious observances were required in the public schools of Alabama, Arkansas, Delaware, Florida, Georgia, Idaho, Kentucky, Maine, Massachusetts, New Jersey, Pennsylvania, Tennessee, and the District of Columbia. They were forbidden in Alaska, Arizona, California, Illinois, Louisiana, Nebraska, Washington, Wisconsin, and Wyoming, while the rest of the states left decisions about school prayer to local districts (*Congressional Record,* March 5, 1984, p. 4321). It is no coincidence that most of the states that forbade school prayer are in the midwestern and western parts of the country, since a post–Civil War federal law required the constitutions of newly admitted states to ban the use of public funds for sectarian education—a regulation that many older states had voluntarily adopted. The original intent of such policies was to prevent tax funding of Catholic schools, and, as the previous chapters explain, at first they had no effect on public-school prayer. By the late nineteenth century, however, some state courts and attorneys general were interpreting them to exclude all religious exercises from publicly funded schools.

Like Horace Mann's effort to reduce religious divisiveness by removing denominational instruction from the public schools, attempts to achieve the same end through the elimination of pan-Protestant worship turned out to be at least as contentious as the religious exercises themselves. Indeed, a disproportionate amount of school-prayer litigation took place not in states that had school prayer but in those that banned it, since lawsuits were filed not only by people who wanted religious exercises in the schools, but also by those who sought to restrain school officials from sponsoring them in defiance of state law. Regardless of the specific facts of each case, they all wrestled with the same fundamental conflict: some people argued that the absence of traditional school prayer would violate their religious rights, while others maintained that *their* freedom of conscience would be compromised by its inclusion. Courts were asked either to determine whose views took precedence or to balance competing claims so that everyone's interests would be protected, at least to some extent.

One possible solution to this dilemma had been suggested in earlier generations by Catholics, such as the parents of Bridget Donohoe and Thomas Wall, who had sought to have their children excused from religious observances in the public schools. Although such requests met with little success at the time, the resistance of school officials began to weaken as the non-Protestant population grew larger, more powerful, and better integrated into the American mainstream. Amid increasingly numerous and intense challenges to traditional school prayer, some state authorities and school boards began to look favorably on opt-out arrangements that might pacify religious minorities and allow popular religious practices to continue.

Ironically, the same social changes that made opt-out policies more attractive to school officials led some school-prayer opponents to reject them as inadequate. In the early to mid-nineteenth century, beleaguered religious minorities, many of whom were newly arrived immigrants, would have been delighted to see their children excused from Protestant prayers and Bible-reading. By the end of the century, however, their more confident and better established descendants did not hesitate to demand equal treatment for non-Protestant faiths. As they saw it, the state was giving primacy to Protestantism by presenting it as the quintessentially American faith, and excusing some students from participation did nothing to lessen that effect.

School-prayer lawsuits of the late nineteenth and early twentieth centuries also reflected an evolution of thought regarding the relationship between majority rule and individual freedom of conscience. In the disputes discussed in Chapters Two and Three, few people denied the school authorities' right to prescribe majoritarian religious observances, and the notion that participation should be a personal choice was widely viewed as antisocial, unpatriotic, and a threat to authority and social order. Even those who asked for students to be excused usually took pains to disclaim any disrespect toward majoritarian religious practices. As the turn of the century approached, however, the assertion that freedom of conscience resides in the individual and is not subject to rules imposed by the majority became more prevalent. In the view of some plaintiffs in the lawsuits discussed in this chapter, the very notion of granting permission for nonparticipation in prayer was inconsistent with the belief that each person is inherently free to make his or her own choices in that regard. The majority's votes unquestionably give it the power to enact regulations and then decide whether to grant exemptions; what was in dispute was its right to do so where religion is concerned.

A SAMPLING OF CASES

Space does not permit a discussion of all the state-court cases that addressed these issues prior to the Supreme Court's intervention in the early 1960s, but five examples may serve to establish a historical context for the Court's rulings. The earliest of these lawsuits, decided in 1872, was filed by Protestants who challenged a school board policy excluding all religious exercises from the public schools. In the other four cases, decided between 1890 and 1927, Catholics and, in some instances, allies of other faiths objected to the continuing use of the KJB and Protestant prayers and hymns. The cases are presented in chronological order, although some of the earlier decisions were closer to today's jurisprudence than were some later ones; the development of ideas, like other forms of evolution, seldom moves in a straight line. Unless otherwise indicated, the information provided about these cases is drawn from the courts' decisions. Discussions of additional cases from this period can be found in *Separation of Church and State in the United States* (1948), by Alvin W. Johnson and Frank H. Yost; and in Donald Boles's *The Bible, Religion, and the Public Schools* (1961).

Although each of the cases mentioned here was decided on the basis of a particular state's constitution, laws, and legal precedents, they addressed some common themes, notably the problem of defining the term "nonsectarian." In the lawsuits discussed in the previous chapter, the courts invariably ruled that reading the KJB, reciting its translations of the Lord's Prayer and the Ten Commandments, and singing Protestant hymns were nonsectarian activities. By the end of the nineteenth century, however, such practices were often classified as sectarian, and the courts then had to decide whether forcing dissenters to participate violated their religious rights. When almost all the courts that considered this issue ruled that it did, they were called upon to determine whether school officials could retain such observances as long as unwilling students were excused. As these five cases illustrate, that turned out to be an extremely difficult question to answer.

Example One: School Prayer in a Minor Chord

The dispute that led to *Cincinnati v. Minor* began when the Cincinnati school board proposed to give public funds to both public and parochial schools on the condition that no religious exercises could take place in any of them. Anti-Catholic forces, alleging a plot to ban the Bible from the public schools, prevented that policy from being enacted. The archbishop of Cincinnati, John Purcell, then pressed for unconditional public funding of Catholic schools. When the school board said that it would not support sectarian education, he protested that the KJB was still being read in the public schools. His opponents retorted that the policy of denying public funds to sectarian education pertained only to church-run schools, not to Bible-reading in the public schools.

Up to that point, the Cincinnati dispute resembled the earlier controversies in New York and Philadelphia discussed in Chapters Two and Three. In Cincinnati, however, it was not only Catholics but also Jews, Unitarians, Universalists, and Quakers who expressed reservations about the religious practices of the public schools. When Purcell confronted the school board, the leaders of those other groups were right beside him—a decidedly mixed blessing from the bishop's point of view. While broad-based opposition to the reading of the KJB strengthened his contention that the practice was sectarian, it undermined his claim that religious equity could be achieved simply by supporting two sets of schools: one Protestant, one Catholic. As different religious groups introduced a multiplicity of viewpoints and priorities into the debate, clear-cut answers became harder to find, and school officials were drawn to a solution that neither the Catholic Church nor the Protestant majority wanted: the elimination of all religious elements from public education.

The school board rejected Purcell's request for funds, but it agreed that greater religious parity was needed in the public schools. Having considered several options, such as an opt-out policy and the use of varied religious texts, the board decided that there was no way to have religious observances in publicly funded schools without engendering divisiveness and inequality among people of different faiths. Accordingly, it enacted a resolution saying, "[R]eligious instruction and the reading of religious books, including the Holy Bible, are prohibited in the common schools of Cincinnati, it being the true object and intent of this rule to allow the children of the parents of all sects and opinions, in matters of faith and worship, to enjoy alike the benefit of the common-school fund" (*Board of Education of Cincinnati v. Minor*, 23 Ohio St. 211 [1872], p. 211). This outcome dismayed Purcell, to whom "benefit of the common-school fund" meant support for Catholic schools, but he took no further action. Other Cincinnatians urged the board to restore devotionals to the public schools, and when it refused to do so, thirty-seven Protestants filed suit. They maintained that Christianity represents the heritage of this nation, is essential to good citizenship and moral character, and cannot lawfully be excluded from the schools. The Superior Court of Cincinnati agreed, ordering the school board to reinstate daily prayer and Bible-reading. The Supreme Court of Ohio reversed this ruling on the ground that the relevant issue was not religion but the power of education officials to control the public-school program. As Chapter Three illustrates, earlier courts had used this argument to justify retaining mandatory religious practices, and the Ohio court felt that the same logic should apply when a board wanted to terminate the prayers. In its view, the same authority that had allowed the Cincinnati board to sponsor religious observances in the past also permitted it to exclude them, and either way the courts had no business to intrude.

Having found that decisions about school prayer rested with local school boards, the court expressed its nonbinding agreement with the Cincinnati board's belief that majorities have no moral right to rule in matters of religion. "True Christianity," the decision stated, "never shields itself behind majorities" (p. 247). Moreover, "To teach the doctrines of infidelity, and thereby teach that Christianity is false, is one thing; and to give no instructions on the subject is quite another thing. The only fair and impartial method, where serious objection is made, is to let each sect give its own instructions, elsewhere than in the state schools, where of necessity all are to meet; and to put disputed doctrines of religion among other subjects of instruction, for there are many others, which can more conveniently, satisfactorily, and safely be taught elsewhere" (p. 253).

Example Two: My Way or the Highway
Despite the Cincinnati board's legal victory, its decision to terminate an existing school-prayer policy was not widely imitated. More commonly, if officials accommodated dissenters at all, they did so by allowing those children to be

excused. The underlying rationale—that no parent could reasonably complain if other people's children read the Bible—enjoyed wide acceptance, but not everyone agreed with it, and disputes involving opt-out policies began to make their way into the courts. Among the earliest of these cases was *Weiss v. District Board*, filed by six Catholic parents in Edgerton, Wisconsin, who objected to the school-sponsored reading of the KJB. Although the board offered to excuse their children, they sought to end what they considered the illegal promotion of Protestantism by public officials. The Wisconsin state constitution prohibits sectarian instruction in publicly funded schools, and the plaintiffs interpreted this provision as a ban on any activity that conflicts with one or more faiths. The board replied that the school's practices were not sectarian, but terminating them in order to conform to Catholic teachings *would* be sectarian and would thereby violate the very provision of the state constitution on which the plaintiffs were relying. And even if the court disagreed with that argument, the board alleged, the plaintiffs would still have no basis for a lawsuit because their children did not have to participate in the Bible-reading.

The Wisconsin Supreme Court ruled that because the practice of reading the KJB without note or comment is unacceptable to some faiths, its inclusion in tax-funded schools violated the state constitution. Moreover, the court found, the school officials' willingness to excuse individual students did not render school sponsorship of religious observances permissible. As the decision explained, "When, as in this case, a small minority of the pupils in the public schools is excluded, for any cause, from a stated school exercise, particularly when such cause is apparent hostility to the Bible which a majority of the pupils have been taught to revere, from that moment the excluded pupil loses caste with his fellows, and is liable to be regarded with aversion and subjected to reproach and insult. But it is a sufficient refutation of the argument that the [opt-out policy] tends to destroy the equality of the pupils which the constitution seeks to establish and protect, and puts a portion of them to serious disadvantage in many ways with respect to the others" (*State ex rel. Weiss et al. v. District Board of School District No. Eight of the City of Edgerton*, 76 Wisconsin 177 [1890], pp. 199–200).

Example Three: Some of the People Some of the Time
Among the many decisions that differed from *Weiss* was *Pfeiffer v. Board of Education*, filed by a Catholic father who felt that his son should not have to leave the room to avoid the school-sponsored reading of the KJB. In his view, this opt-out procedure branded the boy as a second-class citizen in the eyes of his

classmates and, more significantly, in the eyes of government officials whose choice of that particular religious text was an endorsement of Protestantism. Since the Michigan state constitution contained the familiar ban on religious instruction in tax-funded schools, the arguments in *Pfeiffer* were almost identical to those in *Weiss,* but the outcomes could not have been more different. In an 1898 decision, the *Pfeiffer* court ruled that the KJB is nonsectarian and that the state constitution prohibited tax funding of parochial schools but not prayer in public schools. The court also chided Pfeiffer for intolerance for seeking to compel all students to refrain from an activity of which he did not approve, even though his own son was not compelled to participate. As long as the boy was excused from the Bible-reading, the decision stated, his family had no basis for a lawsuit.

Example Four: Ring in the New
By the turn of the twentieth century, opt-out policies had become such a well-established factor in school-prayer cases that the courts sometimes considered them over the objections of both sides. In *Ring v. Board of Education of District 24,* for instance, Catholic parents sought to terminate public-school devotionals by invoking a provision of the Illinois state constitution that forbade discrimination on the basis of religion. They opposed the establishment of an opt-out policy on the ground that sponsoring Protestant practices was inherently discriminatory and would remain so even if some students were excused. The school board, maintaining that Bible-reading, prayer, and hymn-singing were nondiscriminatory activities that promoted morality and good citizenship, felt that such exercises should not be made optional because their purpose was to unite the entire school and to promote common moral values in all students.

The Illinois Supreme Court found that the challenged activities did indeed violate the state constitution because they were "the ordinary forms of worship usually practiced by Protestant Christian denominations" (*Ring v. Board of Education of District 24,* 245 Illinois 334 [1910], p. 338). In response to the school board's claim that the religious exercises were nondiscriminatory because they were accepted by most residents of the district, the court observed, "The majority of [Illinois citizens] adhere to one or another of the Protestant denominations. But the law knows no distinction between the Christian and the Pagan, the Protestant and the Catholic. All are citizens. Their civil rights are precisely equal. The law cannot see religious differences, because the constitution has definitely and completely excluded religion from the law's contemplation in considering men's rights. There can be no distinction based on religion" (p. 349). This ringing emphasis on total religious equality led to the inescapable conclusion that even if the plaintiffs or the school board had sought an opt-out provision, such a policy would not have made state-sponsored religious activities acceptable. To the contrary, the decision stated, "If the instruction or exercise is such that certain of the pupils must be excused from it because it is hostile to their or their parents' religious belief, then such instruction or exercise is sectarian and forbidden by the [state] constitution" (p. 351).

Example Five: Like It or Not

In contrast with *Ring*, some courts were so convinced of the efficacy of opt-out policies that they mandated them over the objections of both the plaintiffs and the defendants. In *Vollmar v. Stanley*, for instance, a Colorado school board discovered that Catholic children were leaving their classrooms to avoid reading the KJB. The board subsequently required all students to be present for the Bible-reading, and the Vollmar family sued. They had not challenged the unofficial opt-out arrangement, but in their lawsuit they sought nothing less than the exclusion of Protestant practices from the public schools. Rejecting the Vollmars' contention that a practice is sectarian if it contradicts the beliefs of any faith, the Supreme Court of Colorado defined sectarianism in terms of distinctions among Christian denominations. Without explicitly affirming that Christianity means Protestantism, its 1927 decision stated that the KJB was not rendered sectarian by the fact that Catholics did not accept it. Nevertheless, the court ordered the school officials to adopt an opt-out policy because even nonsectarian practices might be religious enough to conflict with the Vollmars' parental right to control their own children's upbringing. The board appealed, arguing that the court had no authority to impose an opt-out policy when neither party had requested one, but the decision was upheld.

As these five cases illustrate, long before the U.S. Supreme Court began ruling on school prayer, state courts throughout the country had soundly rejected the once-prevalent notion that public schools have the right to impose majoritarian religious practices on all students. Beyond that, several courts had declared that school officials may not sponsor such observances even if dissenters are excused. To be sure, attitudes toward state-sponsored school prayer were not changing at the same rate or in the same way in all states, and there were serious disagreements about the extent to which opt-out policies protect minority rights. Nevertheless, the Supreme Court's rulings were nowhere near so unprecedented as its critics sometimes claim. Those decisions were novel in that they applied federal norms to the states, but the foundation for the Court's approach to school prayer per se had been laid by several state courts long before the federal judiciary came into the picture.

HERE COME THE (FEDERAL) JUDGE

The reason for the federal courts' absence from early school-prayer disputes can be found in the opening words of the First Amendment to the Constitution: "Congress shall make no law respecting an establishment of religion [the Establishment Clause], or prohibiting the free exercise thereof" [the Free Exercise Clause]. When that provision was ratified in 1791, it meant exactly what it said: *Congress* could not establish a national church or interfere with anyone's free exercise of religion. Each state, however, could regulate religious practice in any way it liked, even to the extent of creating official state churches or expressing a preference for Protestantism or Christianity over other faiths. Delaware's 1776 state constitution, for instance, required officeholders to profess belief in the Holy Trinity and in the divine inspiration of the Old and New Testaments, while in some states only Protestants could hold certain offices. The states themselves later disestablished their official churches and repealed religious requirements for public office, but many of them continued to permit or even mandate religious exercises in the public schools. As a result, school prayer was squarely in the center of the controversy that arose when the federal courts began to assert authority over the states with regard to religion.

The starting point for federal intervention in religious matters was the ratification of the Fourteenth Amendment in 1868. At first glance, this amendment does not appear to have anything to do with school prayer; indeed, it does not explicitly mention religion at all. It does, however, include the following declaration: "No State shall make or enforce any law which shall abridge the privileges or immunities of citizens of the United States; nor shall any State deprive any person of life, liberty, or property, without due process of law; nor deny to any person within its jurisdiction the equal protection of the laws." Since the mid-twentieth century, the Supreme Court has interpreted this language to mean that the states, like the federal government, must respect the fundamental liberties protected by the U.S. Constitution, including free exercise of religion and freedom from government establishments of religion. In consequence, the states are no longer at liberty, as they once were, to enforce policies either favoring or disfavoring any or all religious beliefs.

The Court laid out this principle in several decisions, notably *Cantwell v. Connecticut* and *Everson v. Board of Education of Ewing Township*. In *Cantwell*, the Court found in favor of Jehovah's Witnesses who had been arrested for distributing anti-Catholic literature in a Catholic neighborhood and for playing a recording describing a book entitled "Enemies," which included a diatribe against the Catholic faith. According to the Court, the Witnesses' conduct had been orderly and lawful, and they could not be punished solely for disseminating beliefs that some listeners found offensive. Most significant was the Court's explicit declaration that "The fundamental concept of liberty embodied in [the Fourteenth] Amendment embraces the liberties guaranteed by the First Amendment. The First Amendment declares that Congress shall make no law respecting an establishment of religion or prohibiting the free exercise thereof. The Fourteenth Amendment has rendered the legislatures of the states as incompetent as Congress to enact such laws" (*Cantwell v. Connecticut*, 310 U.S. 296; 60 S. Ct. 900 [1940], p. 903).

The Court provided a more detailed explanation of this point in *Everson*, which dealt with transportation subsidies for parochial-school children. The dispute arose in Ewing Township, New Jersey, where most students took public buses to school. The school board reimbursed parents for those fares regardless of which school their children attended, and a taxpayer challenged the use of public funds for transportation to religious schools. The Court ruled that offering free public transportation to all schoolchildren is comparable to making police, fire, and emergency medical services available wherever they are needed. Nevertheless, although the Court upheld this particular practice, it reiterated that the First Amendment's religion clauses apply to the states as well as to Congress:

> The "establishment of religion" clause of the First Amendment means at least this: Neither a state nor the Federal Government can set up a church. Neither can pass laws which aid one religion, aid all religions, or prefer one religion over another. Neither can force nor influence a person to go to or to remain away from church against his will or force him to profess a belief or disbelief in any religion. No person can be punished for entertaining or professing religious beliefs or disbeliefs, for church attendance or non-attendance. No tax in any amount, large or small, can be levied to support any religious activities or institutions, whatever they may be called, or whatever form they may adopt to teach or practice religion. (pp. 511–12)

Detailed discussions of the significance of this decision may be found in *Everson Revisited* (1997), a collection of essays edited by Jo Renée Formicola and Hubert Morken; and in Donald Boles's *The Two Swords: Commentaries and Cases in Religion and Education* (1967), which also covers other school-prayer decisions from the 1950s and 1960s.

The notion that the Fourteenth Amendment causes the First Amendment to apply to the states, known as "incorporation theory," set off a controversy that continues to rage today. As a matter of history, there can be no doubt that when the Fourteenth Amendment was ratified in the wake of the Civil War, it was directed toward racial equity rather than religious freedom. What is in dispute is whether its plain language justifies the Court's interpreting it to include religion, and whether the results of doing so are good or bad. Opponents of incorporation theory see it as a politically motivated attempt to justify federal intrusion into matters that had long been under state control, including not only religion but also such issues as racial segregation and women's rights. Since state laws tend to reflect the majority's wishes, opponents of incorporation theory also accuse the Court of disenfranchising the majority in order to privilege minorities. In their view, incorporation theory must be reversed if states' rights—and, by extension, majority rule—are to be safe from federal interference. By contrast, supporters of incorporation theory focus not on the balance of power between federal and state governments but on the protection of individual rights from infringement by any level of government. In their view, even if the framers of the Fourteenth Amendment did not have religion in mind, its wording amply justifies the Supreme Court's conclusion that the states must respect all fundamental human liberties, including religious freedom. This interpretation is not unfair to majorities, they assert, because majorities have no legitimate right to use their voting power to promulgate state laws prejudicial to minorities. And while conceding that majoritarian dominance in religious matters was considered legal throughout most of American history, they deny that majorities are entitled to violate minority rights indefinitely merely because they got away with it in earlier generations.

Objections notwithstanding, since the mid-twentieth century incorporation theory has been the law of the land, and its effects on school-prayer cases are evident throughout the rest of this book. Among other things, plaintiffs in school-prayer cases now have the choice of filing their complaints in either federal or state court, and no matter which court hears the case, its decision must take into account the U.S. Constitution and federal laws as well as state constitutions and state statutes. Moreover, regardless of whether a lawsuit goes through state or federal courts, its outcome can be appealed to the U.S. Supreme Court. This is particularly significant because the Supreme Court is the only court whose decisions are binding throughout the country, so the possibility of bringing cases there carries with it the potential to affect school-prayer practices nationwide.

CHAMPAIGN COCKTAIL

The first case regarding religion in the public schools to reach the Supreme Court dealt with a program of religious instruction in the public schools of Champaign, Illinois. It began when a committee of Protestant, Catholic, and Jewish clergy asked the school board for permission to offer religious instruction in public-school classrooms during school hours. The board agreed, and the parents of students in the fourth through ninth grades were asked to sign permission slips indicating whether they wanted their children to participate and, if so, in what religion. The vast majority of students attended the religion classes, which were held for one hour a week. Nonparticipants were supposed to continue with their regular studies.

The clergy committee provided religion teachers at no cost to the district, but public-school officials had the authority to reject any proposed instructor, monitor student attendance, and supervise the classes. They could even decide which religions would be allowed to participate, and their exclusion of the Jehovah's Witnesses led to allegations of religious discrimination. The Jewish community also became dissatisfied with the program when their rabbi had to stop offering classes because separating the Jewish children from the Christian majority had led to a spate of anti-Semitic slurs. Moreover, students who did not wish to take any religion class said that they were criticized by teachers and classmates and, instead of being given alternate instruction, were made to sit in the hallway as if they were being punished.

When disgruntled parents received no satisfaction from the school officials, one of them, Vashti McCollum, filed suit in the Illinois state courts. In a book entitled *One Woman's Fight* (1951), she later described herself as a humanist who belonged to no organized faith but was not hostile to religion. Nevertheless, she strongly believed that the First Amendment prevents public-school officials from overseeing any program of religious instruction. Even if the school officials had behaved with the utmost sensitivity, she maintained, they would have had no right to make religion classes part of the regular school day. The school board responded that it was merely accommodating the religious rights of those students who chose to attend religion classes, and no unwilling child was required to do so.

The Illinois state courts agreed with the board, but the U.S. Supreme Court saw the matter differently. According to the Court, "Pupils compelled by law to go to school for secular education are released in part from their legal duty upon the condition that they attend the religious classes. This is beyond all question a utilization of the tax-established and tax-supported public school system to aid religious groups to spread their faith. And it falls squarely under the ban of the First Amendment (made applicable to the States by the Fourteenth) as we interpreted it in *Everson v. Board of Education*" (*McCollum v. Board of Education of School District No. 71*, 333 U.S. 203; 68 S. Ct. 461 [1948], pp. 209–10). (For recent interviews with Vashti McCollum and her son James, now a lawyer admitted to the Supreme Court bar, see Robert Alley's *Without a Prayer*, 1996).

TESTING THE BOUNDS

The program struck down in *McCollum* took place in public-school classrooms during the school day, with the active participation of education officials. It was not clear, however, whether all those elements had to be present for religion classes to be found unconstitutional. Would it be acceptable, for instance, for school officials to excuse students from class so that they could attend religious instruction elsewhere? That question formed the basis of a lawsuit that arose in New York City, where the schools were dismissing students one hour early every Friday for the purpose of attending religion classes. School personnel checked parental permission slips and made sure that the excused students did indeed attend religion classes, but they did not decide which faiths could offer instruction, nor did they evaluate it in any way. True to New York's long history of religious dissent, parents who opposed these arrangements filed suit. Among other things, they felt that public-school officials should not monitor which students were receiving instruction in which faiths, and they claimed that nonparticipants received no meaningful alternate instruction. They also denied that released time was necessary to protect the religious rights of students who were free to attend religion classes on their own time. Most significantly, they asserted that school officials were deliberately encouraging attendance at religion classes by excusing students during the regular school day, so that "the weight and influence of the school is put behind a program for religious instruction" (*Zorach v. Clauson*, 343 U.S. 306; 72 S. Ct. 679 [1952], p. 309).

The New York state courts found the released-time arrangement constitutional because it required relatively little action on the part of school officials, and the U.S. Supreme Court agreed. Pointing out that parents are free to take their children out of school for medical appointments and the like, the Court declared that the released-time policy merely made it easier for them to exercise that right with regard to religion classes. Had the allegation that school officials were encouraging students to attend religion classes been proven, the decision cautioned, the outcome would have been different; but in light of the existing evidence, the Court found that the school officials were merely excusing children for religious instruction at their parents' request, which does not violate the First Amendment. "Government may not finance religious groups nor undertake religious instruction nor blend secular and sectarian education nor use secular institutions to force one or some religion on any person," the decision stated. "But it can close its doors or suspend its operations as to those who want to repair to their religious sanctuary for worship or instruction" (p. 314). As these excerpts suggest, the primary reason for the differing outcomes of *Zorach* and *McCollum* was the extent to which the religious activities in each case were initiated and run by private citizens rather than by school officials—a distinction that was to become increasingly important in resolving school-prayer controversies.

While *Zorach* was in progress, the Supreme Court heard arguments in a case entitled *Doremus v. Board of Education of Hawthorne,* which challenged a New Jersey Bible-reading statute. It was later dismissed because the student plaintiff had graduated from high school, and since the plaintiffs were no longer directly affected by the statute, they had no standing to continue the lawsuit. By then, however, it was clearly only a matter of time before the Court would return to the issue of state-sponsored religious exercises in the public schools.

5
Stalin and School Prayer

> The moment a mere numerical superiority by either states or voters in this country proceeds to ignore the needs and desires of the minority, and for their own selfish purpose or advancement, hamper or oppress that minority, or debar them in any way from equal privileges and equal rights—that moment will mark the failure of our constitutional system.
>
> —*Franklin Delano Roosevelt*

Ten years passed after the inconclusive termination of *Doremus v. Board* before the Supreme Court heard another school-prayer case, *Engel v. Vitale*. At issue was a new prayer composed at the behest of the New York State Board of Regents, which recommended its use in the public schools. Because of the unique facts of this case, the Court's ruling that the Regents' actions were unconstitutional did not affect traditional religious exercises such as Bible-reading and the Lord's Prayer. All the same, it marked the end of an era. For the first time in American history, the Supreme Court told state officials what they could and could not do with regard to prayer in the public schools, and from that time on the federal government has been a major player in the development of policies regarding religious expression in public education.

The immediate result was the termination of devotionals that local majorities and school officials would have preferred to retain, but over time the federal sword has proved to be double-edged. Although a return to state-sponsored school prayer would be very popular in some parts of the country, in other areas public sentiment and the preferences of school officials would tend to exclude all religion from the public schools. The application of a national standard thus interferes not only with school personnel who are determined to use their official positions to promote majoritarian religious beliefs, but also with those who would be happy to exclude all religion, including the constitutionally protected religious speech of the students as individuals, if they were still in a position to do so. The principle underlying both outcomes is the same: the state cannot interfere with religious freedom, which means that it can neither promote its own favored beliefs nor prevent individuals from exercising their personal religious rights.

GOD BLESS AMERICA

In its own way, *Engel* was as much a product of the cold war as were the novels of Ian Fleming and John le Carré. When the lawsuit was filed in 1958, the Communist Party had consolidated its hold on most of Eastern Europe and was exerting strong influence elsewhere. Both Soviet and American political rhetoric suggested that its goal was nothing short of world domination, and despite the Senate's condemnation of Senator Joseph McCarthy (R-Wisconsin) four years earlier, the fear of infiltration by Communist sympathizers remained strong.

To many Americans, the fundamental threat of Communism—and the best defense against it—was neither economic nor political but religious. The nineteenth-century assertion that the King James Bible was the foundation of democracy had become less prevalent, but there remained a widespread belief that the only reliable basis for personal and political liberty is faith in a Creator who has endowed humanity with certain rights. Since the Soviet Union was closely identified with atheism while most Americans considered themselves a religious people, belief in God came to symbolize the difference between democracy and totalitarianism. Atheism, which had never been popular, was considered close to treason, whereas public worship was seen as an affirmation of patriotism and love of freedom.

In these circumstances, it is not surprising that elected officials proposed a variety of measures designed to display and promote religious fervor. Notable among these was the addition of the words "under God" to the Pledge of Allegiance, and lest there be any doubt about the relevance of this action to the threat of Communism, a 1954 report by the House Judiciary Committee offered the following rationale: "Our American Government is founded on the concept of the individuality and the dignity of the human being. Underlying this concept is the belief that the human person is important because he was created by God and endowed by Him with certain inalienable rights which no civil authority may usurp. The inclusion of God in our pledge therefore would further acknowledge the dependence of our people and our Government upon the moral directions of the Creator. At the same time it would serve to deny the atheistic and materialistic concepts of communism with its attendant subservience of the individual" ("Amending the Pledge of Allegiance to the Flag of the United States," p. 2). For these reasons, the report asserted, a profession of faith in God should be an integral element of declaring loyalty to the United States.

In addition to differentiating between Communism and democracy, religion was widely seen as the best means of addressing the increase in crime, divorce, and social unrest that followed World War II. Although the 1940s and 1950s are often portrayed as the good old days when families were intact and doors were never locked, many people felt that pre-war values were rapidly eroding. Indeed, as William Fleming illustrates in *God in Our Public Schools* (1944), even before the war some Americans had begun deploring what they saw as a moral decline that cried out for a greater emphasis on school prayer. Accordingly, in the late 1940s and early 1950s, some state legislatures and school boards passed regulations requiring schools to have daily Bible-reading and prayer, often in conjunction with the Pledge. Many of these policies merely codified practices that had been going on for generations, but their supporters felt that making them official would affirm America's commitment to morality while also promoting patriotism. Several of the school-prayer measures challenged in Supreme Court cases, including *Engel*, dated from this post-war period.

CAMEL: A HORSE DESIGNED BY A COMMITTEE

Amid these political and social concerns, the New York State Board of Regents, which oversees public education in that state, appointed a committee of Protestant, Catholic, and Jewish clergy to compose a prayer. Mindful of New York's diverse population and its stormy history with regard to religion in the public schools, the Regents asked the committee to be sure that the prayer was devoid of sectarian doctrine and entirely inoffensive. The committee responded with a petition that became known as the Regents' Prayer: "'Almighty God, we acknowledge our dependence upon Thee, and we beg Thy blessings upon us, our parents, our teachers and our Country'" (*Engel v. Vitale*, 370 U.S. 421; 82 S. Ct. 1261 [1962], p. 1262).

The Regents distributed the prayer in a booklet entitled "Statement on Moral and Spiritual Training in the Schools" (1951), in which they urged but did not require local school officials to adopt it for daily use. To emphasize their commitment to avoiding religious divisiveness, they also exhorted teachers to be "'mindful always of the fundamental American doctrine of the separation of church and state, and careful at all times to avoid any and all sectarianism or religious instruction which advocates, teaches or prefers any religious creed. Formal religion is not to be injected into the public school'" (Brief of Respondents, pp. 10–11). The Regents later reiterated in court documents that the prayer was not intended to proselytize but to meet "the dire need, in these days of concentrated attacks by an atheistic way of life upon our world and in these times of rising juvenile delinquency, of crime increasing both numerically and in gravity of offense, with an ever-swelling number of criminals being counted in the younger age groups, of finding ways to pass on America's Moral and Spiritual Heritage to our youth through the public school system" (Brief of the Board of Regents, November 14, 1961, p. 14). As these quotations suggest, the Regents' justifications for recommending the prayer were essentially the same as those offered by nineteenth-century school officials to explain why students should read the KJB. Just as their predecessors had regarded generic Protestantism as a nonsectarian source of morality, a fundamental element of American heritage and identity, and the best defense against the threat of domination by a totalitarian foreign power—in that instance, the Vatican—so the Regents attributed the same qualities to a broader version of monotheism.

To the Regents, as to their nineteenth-century counterparts, the religious view they espoused appeared normative because it represented ideas that the vast majority of the population not only credited but held sacred. Nevertheless, the Regents' Prayer was not, as its advocates suggested, dogma-free. Rather, the beliefs it promoted were so widely shared that they did not appear to be doctrinal but were simply taken for granted, as the KJB had once been. Its assertions that there is one God, that God created the universe, and that God responds to petitionary prayer were not what the Regents deemed "formal religion," any more than the KJB was what earlier school authorities had considered sectarian. Yet the Regents' Prayer conflicts with deistic, polytheistic, nontheistic, and atheistic beliefs even more directly than the KJB differs from Catholicism. More fundamentally, the two major principles underlying the prescription of public-school devotionals were the same as they had always been: if a set of beliefs is shared by enough of the population, it is deemed to transcend doctrinal religion even if it conflicts with minority views; and the public schools should teach students that the nation's security and morality depend upon the widespread acceptance of majoritarian tenets. Indeed, the Regents' Prayer so overtly associated religion with Americanism that it raised concerns about "the propriety of assuming that the Deity, in dispensing blessings, can be induced to recognize the political boundaries of a specific country" (Brief Amici Curiae of the Synagogue Council of America and the National Community Relations Advisory Council, p. 10).[1]

While the Regents' claim that their prayer did not represent "formal religion" was harshly challenged by people who considered it sectarian, it was also attacked by those who felt that its very lack of doctrinal content placed it in competition with the religious tenets of more creedal faiths. By their standards, the Regents' Prayer was mealymouthed mush that hardly deserved the name of prayer. Including it in the public-school program was, in their view, a ploy meant to replace robust and sometimes contentious adherence to specific doctrines with a bland, lowest-common-denominator, one-size-fits-all, homogenized public-school religion or civic religion that government officials found conveniently noncontroversial. Clearly, these competing assertions that the Regents' Prayer included too much doctrine to be nonsectarian and too little to be meaningful represented a later stage of the same conflict that had bedeviled Horace Mann and other education leaders in the 1830s. When they replaced denominational religion with pan-Protestant practices, they were accused both of retaining too much sectarianism and, conversely, of sacrificing substance for the sake of inclusivity. More than a century later, the Board of Regents, feeling it necessary to take yet another step away from doctrinal religion in order to accommodate New York's steadily increasing religious diversity, eschewed pan-Protestant exercises in favor of generic monotheistic worship—and thereby became the target of exactly the same double-edged criticisms as Mann had received.

THE BALLOON GOES UP IN NEW HYDE PARK

In hindsight, it may appear that the Regents' Prayer was doomed from its inception because it neither embraced all religious beliefs nor satisfied people who wanted traditional Bible-based prayers. Nevertheless, it provoked more indifference than controversy until, seven years after it was first distributed, it was adopted by the school board in the Herricks District in northern New York State. Although the Regents had merely recommended the prayer, local boards had the authority to make it mandatory in their schools, and the Herricks board did so. School officials later claimed that dissenting students were excused on request, but no explicit opt-out policy existed until a court required the board to add one.

Within days, the new policy was challenged by Lawrence Roth, "a plastics-plant foreman with a passion for left-wing causes" (Joshua Hammer, "The Sly Dog at Fox," Newsweek, May 25, 1992, p. 63). On his instructions, his sons,

Joseph and Daniel, left their classrooms every morning to avoid the Regents' Prayer. Joseph, who later became chairman of the Twentieth Century Fox Film Corporation, recalled in newspaper and magazine interviews that his family's nonconformism had been criticized far more severely by adults than by other students. Daniel concurred. "'I definitely remember an antagonism from the teachers, no question about that. There were comments made,'" he said (Friendly and Elliott, 1984, pp. 119–20). Despite these tensions, no one tried to force Joseph and Daniel to participate in the religious exercises, but Roth was determined to stop what he considered the unconstitutional promotion of religion by school officials. On the advice of lawyers from the New York Civil Liberties Union, he placed an advertisement in a local newspaper, which turned up approximately fifty parents who objected to the prayer. Four of them eventually joined him in suing the school board in the New York state courts, with representation from the NYCLU. Their names were listed alphabetically beginning with a parent named Steven Engel, and the first-named defendant was board president William Vitale, so the case was entitled *Engel v. Vitale.*

Naturally, parents who favored the prayer were outraged by the lawsuit, and sixteen of them—seven Protestants, five Catholics, three Jews, and one unaffiliated—joined *Engel* as defendant-intervenors supporting the board. Roth himself was identified as an atheist, although there was some uncertainty about his beliefs. In a *New York Times* interview quoted in Mark Dudley's *Engel v. Vitale* (1995), he said, "'I would classify myself as a very religious person, but not a churchgoer. I have prayed myself, many times—not in a beseeching manner, but more in seeking guidance'" (p. 62). His fellow plaintiffs included two Jews, one Unitarian, and one member of the Society for Ethical Culture.

In view of the role Catholics had played in earlier disputes over prayer in the New York schools, there is some irony in the fact that the NYCLU assigned *Engel* to a Catholic attorney, William Butler, on the ground that Catholics were widely viewed as God-fearing members of the social mainstream. As Fred Friendly and Martha Elliott later reported in *The Constitution: That Delicate Balance* (1984), Butler was asked to take the case during a meeting of the NYCLU board, of which he was a member. "'[W]hen the case came up,'" he explained, "'they decided that the lawyer could not be a Jew [because of anti-Semitic prejudice against the NYCLU, which was viewed as being dominated by Jews]. He must be Catholic, that is, someone taking the attitude that he is DEFENDING prayer and religious freedom, not attacking it. And they looked down at the end of the table and saw a nice Irish-Catholic boy—William Butler'" (p. 118).

IF AT FIRST YOU DON'T SUCCEED

As was true of the cases discussed in Chapters Three and Four, the definition of nonsectarianism was crucial to the early stages of *Engel*. Reverting to the standard used in the Donohoe and Wall cases, the trial court found that because the Regents' Prayer reflected beliefs shared by several denominations, it was nonsectarian even if some people did not accept it. This being so, the court stated, there was nothing to stop school officials from using it to promote religious belief over disbelief as long as they avoided what the Regents described as "formal religion." Nevertheless, the court declined to endorse the early nineteenth-century belief that categorizing a religious practice as nonsectarian gives school officials the authority to compel participation by all students. As most state courts had done since the Civil War, the New York court ruled that the prayer could be recited in the schools only if dissenters were excused. Accordingly, the court upheld the board's policy on the condition that an explicit opt-out provision be added. The state Appellate Court affirmed this decision; as a concurring opinion observed, any embarrassment experienced by students who opted out of the prayer was "the price which every nonconformist must pay" (*Engel v. Vitale*, 206 N.Y.S. 2d 183 [1960], p. 192). The plaintiffs also lost in the highest court in the state, the Court of Appeals, which found that "Saying this simple prayer may be, according to the broadest possible dictionary definition, an act of 'religion,' but when the Founding Fathers prohibited an 'establishment of religion' they were referring to official adoption of, or favor to, one or more sects" (*Engel v. Vitale*, 10 N.Y.2d 174 [1961], p. 180). As this reference to the Founders suggests, the court relied heavily on its interpretation of the past to defend religious practices in the public schools.

Although arguments based on history had appeared in earlier decisions, it was in *Engel* that they took on the major role they continue to play today. "It is an indisputable and historically provable fact," the Court of Appeals declared, "that belief and trust in a Creator has always been regarded as an integral and inseparable part of the fabric of our fundamental institutions. It is not a matter of majority power or minority protection. Belief in a Supreme Being is as essential and permanent a feature of the American governmental system as is freedom of worship, equality under the law and due process of law. Like them it is an American absolute, an application of the natural law beliefs on which the Republic was founded and which in turn presuppose an Omnipotent Being" (pp. 181–82). Nevertheless, the Court of Appeals, like other twentieth-century courts that adopted this view of history, stopped short of allowing school officials to compel students to participate. By this time, it had become clear to all but the most intractable reactionaries that the days of mandatory school prayer were over, and the best outcome for which school-prayer advocates could realistically hope was the continuation of majoritarian religious exercises for those students who chose to engage in them. The demise of enforced universal participation, which marked the first major stage of the trend toward individual choice that now dominates discussions of school prayer, had for all practical purposes become an accomplished fact.

TRY, TRY AGAIN

Having lost their case in the New York state courts, the plaintiffs' only options were to surrender or to appeal to the U.S. Supreme Court. Unlike other courts, the Supreme Court can, with a few exceptions, decide which cases it chooses to hear, and it accepts only a small percentage of the appeals it receives. When *Engel* was among the cases selected, attorneys for both sides submitted written arguments, called briefs, to the Court.

The brief of the plaintiffs, now called petitioners, focused on two issues that had dominated school-prayer cases for more than a century: the definition of sectarianism and the ability of opt-out policies to protect minority rights. In their view, "nonsectarian" connotes "universal," not merely "majoritarian." "The Regents' Prayer is sectarian and denominational, since it includes a declaration of belief in the existence of God," their brief declared, "which is a belief not shared by several faiths in this country, including the Society for Ethical Culture, to which one petitioner belongs.... Moreover, [the trial court] found, as a fact, that the prayer is contrary to the religions of petitioners who have a religion and to the beliefs of petitioner who professes none" (Brief for Petitioners, p. 7). With respect to opt-out policies they wrote, "The same officials who teach children, and demand that the latter learn, that two plus two equals four and that 'c-a-t' spells 'cat' now say that there is a God, to Whom children should say a specified daily prayer, and from Whom children may ask, and expect to receive, blessings for themselves as well as others. Under these circumstances, petitioners respectfully submit, the effect on the children involved will be much the same whether they say the Regents Prayer, or remain silent while it is said, or even if they leave the classroom or the school building during its recitation" (p. 32).

The defendant school officials, now called respondents, chose to focus on the often-repeated assertion that it was not the continuation of public-school devotionals but their termination that would be coercive, since it would force all students to refrain from prayer, and school officials would have no choice but to promote atheism. (For similar arguments in earlier cases, see, for instance, *Donohoe v. Richards* in Chapter Three and *Pfeiffer v. Board of Education* in Chapter Four.) The school officials also elaborated at length on the historical and patriotic themes that had dominated the Court of Appeals decision, presenting school prayer as quintessentially American. As many school-prayer advocates would do in future cases, they quoted extensively from the speeches and writings of the Founders, emphasizing references to religion as the basis on which this nation was conceived. They also alluded to such matters as tax exemptions for churches, presidential declarations of national days of thanksgiving, government funding for military and prison chaplains, the opening of legislative sessions with prayer, the use of the Bible in administering oaths, the inclusion of "In God We Trust" on money and "under God" in the Pledge of Allegiance, and the opening of Supreme Court sessions with the words "God save the United States and this Honorable Court." Finally, they used the House of Representatives committee report on adding "under God" to the Pledge to support the implication that curtailing state-sponsored prayer would aid and abet Communism. "The Constitution of the United States," they wrote, "is incapable of being so interpreted as to require that the wall of separation of church and State become an iron curtain" (Brief of Respondents, p. 14).

SCHOOL PRAYER GOES TO WASHINGTON

The opening paragraphs of the Supreme Court's decision in *Engel* leave no doubt that the Court differed significantly from the New York school officials in its view of the relationship between American history and school prayer. "It is a matter of history," the decision stated, "that this very practice of establishing governmentally composed prayers for religious services was one of the reasons which caused many of our early colonists to leave England and seek religious freedom in America" (*Engel v. Vitale*, 370 U.S. 421; 82 S. Ct. 1261 [1962], p. 1264). The decision added that the Founders "knew, some of them from bitter personal experience, that one of the greatest dangers to the freedom of the individual to worship in his own way lay in the Government's placing its official stamp of approval upon one particular kind of prayer or one particular form of religious services" (p. 1266). "It is an unfortunate fact of history," the Court observed pointedly, "that when some of the very groups which had most strenuously opposed the established Church of England found themselves sufficiently in control of colonial governments in this country to write their own prayers into law, they passed laws making their own religion the official religion of their respective colonies" (p. 1265).

In addition to expressing the Court's interpretation of American history as it relates to the association between church and state, the decision in *Engel* included three important legal principles. First, it affirmed that school prayer is not the exclusive province of state laws and constitutions but is subject to the U.S. Constitution and federal law. Second, it addressed the decades-long debate over the efficacy of opt-out policies, ruling that state sponsorship of any religious exercise would be unconstitutional even if participation were entirely voluntary, and the Court did not concede that it was. "When the power, prestige, and financial support of government is placed behind a particular religious belief," the decision said, "the indirect coercive pressure upon religious minorities to conform to the prevailing officially approved religion is plain" (p. 1267). Third, the Court declined even to discuss whether the Regents' Prayer was sectarian or nonsectarian because that distinction made no difference. The salient point, in its view, was that the government may not support religious beliefs or prescribe religious exercises regardless of their level of generality or the percentage of the community that finds them acceptable. Nevertheless, the Court took pains to clarify that *Engel* did not ban from the public schools all references to religion. Students could go on reading historical documents and singing patriotic songs that mention God, and teachers remained free to teach about religion in a nonproselytizing manner. The Court also rejected the often-repeated charge that prohibiting state-sponsored prayer indicated a willingness to promote atheism. "It is neither sacrilegious nor antireligious," the decision stated, "to say that each separate government in this country should stay out of the business of writing or sanctioning official prayers and leave that purely religious function to the people themselves and to those the people choose to look to for religious guidance" (p. 1269).

The Court's distinction between permissible and impermissible religious preferences was either overlooked or ignored by some critics of *Engel*, who maintain to this day that the Court banned all mention of religion from the public schools, thus requiring school officials to engage in the active endorsement of atheism. In making this argument, they place great weight on a concurring opinion written by Justice William O. Douglas, who agreed with the majority decision but added that in his view, even the most modest expenditure of public funds for religious purposes is unconstitutional.[2] While conceding that the financial cost of the Regents' Prayer was minimal, he took the opportunity to call for the discontinuation of government-funded military and legislative chaplaincies, the deletion of references to God from the opening of court proceedings, and so forth. No other justice joined Douglas's concurrence, which went much further than the Court's opinion did. Nevertheless, although it has no legally binding force, it has played an important role in the political and public response to *Engel*. Inadvertently or deliberately, advocates of state-sponsored prayer quote Douglas's most inflammatory passages as if they represented the official ruling of the Court, thus supporting the contention that the Court's power must be curbed if God is not to be excluded from all aspects of public life.

Another separate opinion was filed by Justice Potter Stewart, the only member of the Court to vote against the majority. In his view, the children's right to engage in school prayer if they wished to do so should not be subordinated to concerns about who had written the Regents' Prayer or who had determined that it, rather than any other prayer, would be recited. Unlike his colleagues, he believed that the First Amendment prevented the government from promoting any particular religious denomination but not from supporting religion in general over nonbelief. He therefore concluded, "I cannot see how an 'official religion' is established by letting those who want to say a prayer say it. On the contrary, I think that to deny the wish of these school children to join in reciting this prayer is to deny them the opportunity of sharing in the spiritual heritage of our Nation" (pp. 1274–75). Stewart's views are discussed more fully in the next chapter, in conjunction with his dissent in another case.

THE SUIT HITS THE FAN

Justice Stewart may have been a minority of one on the Supreme Court, but he undoubtedly spoke for the majority in terms of public opinion. In vigorous attacks by religious, civic, and political leaders, *Engel* was denounced as a pro-Communist establishment of atheism in America's public schools. Although the decision painstakingly specified that what it was striking down was not prayer but the government's ability to *"prescribe by law* any particular form of prayer which is to be used as an *official* prayer in carrying on any program of *governmentally sponsored* religious activity" (p. 1266; emphasis added), its opponents insisted that the Court had thrown God out of the schools—a canard that persists to the present day.

Beginning on the morning after *Engel* was announced, several members of Congress took to the floor to decry the decision in language that occasionally verged on the abusive. A few examples of those post-*Engel* speeches may serve to illustrate the kind of overstatement that has characterized discussions of the Supreme Court's school-prayer decisions ever since.

Senator Herman Talmadge (D-Georgia): "[The ruling was] an outrageous edict which has numbed the conscience and shocked the highest sensibilities of the Nation. If it is not corrected, it will do incalculable damage to the fundamental faith in Almighty God which is the foundation upon which our civilization, our freedom, and our form of government rest" (*Congressional Record*, June 26, 1962, p. 11675).

Representative Horace Kornegay (D–North Carolina): "This decision should be disturbing to all God-fearing people in that it appears to foster and advance the cause of atheism. I am a sta[u]nch believer in the separation of church and State but not in the separation of God and government" (pp. 11719–20).

Senator James Eastland (D-Mississippi): "In the minds of little children not versed in the intricacies of law, [*Engel*] can well create the fixed impression that the act of praying to God is in itself unconstitutional wherever the prayer might be uttered" (June 29, 1962, p. 12235).

While the outcry against *Engel* undoubtedly reflected sincere concern about school prayer, it was also fueled by dissatisfaction with the Court's rulings in other cases. A few years earlier, the Court had struck down state and local policies permitting racial segregation in schools, hotels, restaurants, swimming pools, libraries, and other public facilities. Opponents of these decisions objected not only to desegregation but also to what they saw as federal usurpation of power that rightfully belonged to the states. To them, *Engel* provided yet another example of the Court's infuriating disregard for state sovereignty. Moreover, as a matter of practical politics, it was not feasible to muster nationwide support for a return to racial segregation; but if the Court could be discredited because of its allegedly anti-religious bias, that might contribute to a broad-based public demand for a curtailment of its power over the states. As University of Richmond professor Robert Alley (1994) noted, "While protesting desegregation often proved difficult to embrace in a nation where conscience had long been affected by the protests and the ringing words of Martin Luther King, Jr., this new issue might well place those [pro-segregation] politicians on a presumed high moral ground against a perceived secularistic trend in the Court" (p. 109).

The first member of Congress to link *Engel* with the Court's school-desegregation decision in *Brown v. Board of Education* (1954) was Senator Willis Robertson (D-Virginia), whose son Pat is a well-known television evangelist and political activist. "In 1954," Senator Robertson said, "the Supreme Court of the United States—a court for which, as a young lawyer in the early part of

the current century, I had unbounded admiration—not only reversed all previous decisions of all Federal and State courts on the subject of the operation
of segregated public schools, but, for purely psychological reasons, so interpreted the equal rights provision of the Fourteenth Amendment as to amend
the Constitution by judicial fiat" (*Congressional Record*, June 26, 1962, p. 11707).
The same, he asserted, was true of *Engel*. Shortly afterward, Senator Sam
Ervin (D–North Carolina) suggested that in *Engel* "the Supreme Court has
held that God is unconstitutional, and for that reason the public schools must
be segregated against Him" (p. 11709). A similar point was made more bluntly
by Representative George Andrews (D-Alabama), who said in a 1963 television interview that the Court had "put the Negroes in the schools—now they
put God out of the schools" (Friendly and Elliott, p. 109). The National Association for the Advancement of Colored People alluded to such remarks in a letter to the Senate Judiciary Committee: "It is the opinion of many who
attended the [NAACP] convention that a substantial part of the attack on the
U.S. Supreme Court, because of the prayer decision, is in reality a part of the
continuing effort to discredit our highest Court because of the 1954 school
desegregation decision" ("Prayers in Public Schools," p. 149).

Far from being deterred by the criticism they encountered, opponents of
Engel went on to use the association between school prayer and desegregation
to support the claim that the Supreme Court was pro-Communist. Civil rights
leaders like Martin Luther King, Jr., together with such integrationist organizations as the NAACP and the ACLU, were widely accused of having Communist sympathies, and the Court's desegregation decisions had been
condemned as a Communist-inspired attack on American institutions, social
order, and private property. The Court had also restrained government investi-
gations of suspected "reds" by ruling that Communists—real or alleged—
have the same legal rights as anyone else. Given the popular belief that
religion is the foundation of democracy, it took only a small leap of logic to
suggest that the alleged attack on prayer was yet another sign of a predilection
for atheistic Communism. Representative John Bell Williams (D-Mississippi),
for instance, claimed that he could "detect in [*Engel*] and other recent actions a
deliberate and carefully planned conspiracy to substitute materialism for spiritual values, and thus to communize America" (*Congressional Record*, June 26,
1962, p. 11734).

Members of Congress who accused the Court of Communist leanings did
not hesitate to suggest that it was metaphorically and perhaps literally guilty of
treason. According to Senator Talmadge, *Engel* had "dealt a blow to the faith of

every believer in a Supreme Being and it has given aid and comfort to the disciples of atheism by whatever name they may call themselves" (*Congressional Record*, June 26, 1962, p. 11675). Similarly, Representative Francis Walter (D-Pennsylvania), chairman of the House Committee on Un-American Activities, tied *Engel* to a Supreme Court decision reversing the conviction of an alleged Communist. To him, *Engel* was "just one more decision in line with the philosophy guiding the group of men sitting there as the Justices of our Court of last resort. They have been handing down similarly motivated decisions for a long while" (p. 11719). Perhaps the most colorful speech tying *Engel* to desegregation and Communism was given by Representative Lucius Mendel Rivers (D–South Carolina), who said,

> [T]he Court has now officially stated its disbelief in God Almighty. This, to me, represents the most serious blow that has ever been struck at the Constitution of the United States. I know of nothing in my lifetime that could give more aid and comfort to Moscow than this bold, malicious, atheistic, and sacrilegious twist of this unpredictable group of uncontrolled despots.... Never in my 22 years as a Member of this Congress have I witnessed such a complete breakdown of the moral makeup of this judicial body. Ninety percent of its time has been spent on the protection of Communists, Communist sympathizers, fellow travelers, and problems directly affecting the National Association for the Advancement of Colored People.... Mr. Chairman, this Court legislates—not adjudicates—with one eye on the Kremlin and the other eye on the headquarters of the NAACP. (p. 11732)

THE OTHER SIDE OF THE COIN

Leading the opposition to this flood of anti-Court sentiment was President John Fitzgerald Kennedy. "'In the efforts we're making to maintain our Constitutional principles, we will have to abide by what the Supreme Court says,'" he declared. "'We have a very easy remedy here, and that is to pray ourselves. We can pray a good deal more at home and attend our churches with fidelity and emphasize the true meaning of prayer in the lives of our children'" (Sherrow, 1992, p. 50). A few voices were also raised in Congress—albeit quietly— in the same cause. Senator Kenneth Keating (R–New York), having joined the early chorus against *Engel*, later expressed concern that the decision was being used "to heap abuse upon [the Court's] members or to undermine its status"

(*Congressional Record,* June 27, 1962, p. 11832). Senator Jacob Javits (R–New York) ventured the opinion that *Engel* was not so far-reaching as some of his colleagues had suggested. Far from precluding student prayer, he said, it merely forbade state endorsement of any particular form of worship. Similarly, Senator Philip Hart (D-Michigan) told an interviewer, "I don't want my children in a public school classroom to be exposed to someone else's religion or formula: so that I think the Supreme Court decision was right and proper" (Friendly and Elliott, p. 109).

The congressional response to *Engel* mirrored public reaction around the country, where calls for moderation were largely swamped by passionate anti-Court rhetoric, including highway billboards calling for the impeachment of the chief justice. Nevertheless, while some religious and political leaders continued to condemn the Court, others began to suggest that perhaps it was not the business of school officials to compose or prescribe prayers. Then, almost exactly a year after *Engel,* the Court struck down two state laws mandating Bible-reading in the public schools. This new decision, which responded in part to a lawsuit filed by the atheist leader Madalyn Murray O'Hair, immediately eclipsed *Engel* as the focal point of public and congressional wrath.

6

The Myth of Madalyn Murray O'Hair

The day that this country ceases to be free for irreligion it will cease
to be free for religion—except for the sect that can win political
power.

—*Justice Robert Jackson*

Among the many misconceptions that plague discussions of school prayer is
the widespread belief that a wild-eyed atheist named Madalyn Murray O'Hair
single-handedly—or single-footedly—kicked God out of the public schools. In
truth, by the time her case reached the Supreme Court so many other school-
prayer lawsuits were in progress that the outcome would almost certainly
have been the same without her. Indeed, the Court did not even hear her case
separately but joined it with a similar action filed by a Unitarian family in
Pennsylvania. All the same, her extravagant speech, open antagonism toward
religion, and association with the Communist Party caused her to be regarded
as the flesh-and-blood embodiment of hostility to prayer. As recently as 1999,
when she had been missing for four years, she was rumored to have "gone off
to die quietly so Christians wouldn't pray over her" (Katie Fairbank, "O'Hair
Allegedly Was Killed," [Wilmington, Delaware] *News Journal,* May 28, 1999,
p. A17). (In fact, she had been kidnapped and murdered by an employee who
stole her money; her remains were identified in March 2001.) The *Washington
Post* described her as "that vilified and idolized secularist war-horse" (Paul
Duggan, "The Root of All Evil," August 17, 1999, p. C1), and a lawyer who paid
$12,000 for her personal papers echoed her own belief that she was "the most
hated woman in America" (Associated Press, "Papers of Missing Atheist Go
for $12,000," [Wilmington, Delaware] *News Journal,* April 22, 1999, p. A18).

BIRTH OF A LEGEND

Madalyn Murray, who later remarried and became Madalyn Murray O'Hair, entered the history—and folklore—of church/state disputes in the fall of 1960. Her older son, William, was a seventh-grader in a Baltimore public school, and Murray demanded that he be excused from the daily prayers and Bible-reading. Their accounts of the basis for her protest differ: William, now a born-again Christian and a leading school-prayer advocate, claims that he was used as a tool of his mother's hostility toward religion, whereas Murray asserted that she went to the principal only because William asked her to do so.

When the principal refused to excuse William from the morning exercises, Murray unsuccessfully sought help from school officials and advocacy groups. William stopped going to school, and two weeks later a local newspaper reported the story after Murray wrote to the editor about it. William then returned to class accompanied by reporters, and for days the school administrators struggled to keep the journalists corralled and to prevent William from staging a demonstration. Meanwhile, Murray entertained the journalists with vivid language and anti-religious rhetoric, calling the principal "the Buxom Bitch," describing religion as organized insanity, and accusing the post office of stealing her mail. She also claimed that her neighbors had called the police about her barking dogs because the dogs were atheists. On the advice of the attorney general of Maryland, the Baltimore school board instituted an opt-out policy, but by then Murray was determined to eliminate religious exercises from the public-school program. Once again, she sought help from advocacy groups, but none of the organizations she approached was willing to represent her after an attorney provided by the American Civil Liberties Union, who had acted on her behalf during the early stages of the controversy, declined to continue doing so. Both then and in her later writings, she accused the ACLU of hostility toward atheists, since all its school-prayer cases included some religious plaintiffs. The ACLU responded that it had already filed so many lawsuits that were essentially the same as Murray's that her case would not have been a good use of its resources. Her former attorney also implied that she had proved to be a more colorful and impulsive client than lawyers prefer to have when they are trying to set precedents in constitutional law.

Having given up on the ACLU, Murray accepted the help of a lawyer who had ties to the Communist Party. She claimed to have met him through a Fuller Brush salesman, known only as "Bob," who, she said, had come to her door and identified himself as a Communist after reading news stories about her case. Murray had traveled to the Soviet Union and had allegedly tried to give up her U.S. citizenship and defect to Communism, but the true nature and extent of her Communist ties were never entirely clear. Nevertheless, they were widely discussed because, despite the popular linkage of Communism with school-prayer protests, she was the only plaintiff in any of the Supreme Court cases who was shown to have any such connections. The Communist issue was also raised in early news stories about William, whose history teacher had scolded him in front of the class for writing a pro-Soviet essay. His schoolmates subsequently called him a "Commie" and beat him up whenever they could catch him. Recalling these incidents in his 1995 book, *Let Us Pray*, he sided with his tormentors. "We lived in an ethnic working-class neighborhood," he wrote. "Many of our neighbors were Polish and Hungarian Catholics who had escaped the violence of Communist countries. Our family wanted to replace the democracy they had sought in America with the same godless totalitarianism that they had escaped from. Some had lost loved ones to Communist gulags. In my eagerness to please my mother and her Marxist friends, I was ignorant of the pain I caused my neighbors" (p. 19).

When it became known that Murray's lawyer had represented Communists, she first denied having been aware of it and then retracted that statement. The attorney bowed out, and she engaged Leonard Kerpelman, a Baltimore lawyer with no experience in constitutional law. She became his client because he was the only lawyer willing to represent her without charge, but her estimate of him was not high. "With him as our counsel," she later wrote, "it meant that we were *really* on our own" (O'Hair, 1989, p. 153). Kerpelman's opinion of her is not recorded.

The Murrays filed their lawsuit, *Murray v. Curlett*, in the Maryland state courts; the first-named defendant, John Curlett, was president of the Baltimore City school board. Their complaint challenged not only the practices at William's school but also a school board policy that, in conformity with Maryland state law, provided for "'the reading, without comment, of a chapter in the Holy Bible and/or the use of the Lord's Prayer. The Douay version may be used by those pupils who prefer it. Appropriate patriotic exercises should [also] be held as a part of the general opening exercise of the school or class'" (*Murray v. Curlett*, 228 Md. 239 [1962], pp. 241–42). The board responded with a short document called a "demurrer," asking the court to dismiss the case without a trial. The court did so, declaring that public schools may and should advance religion because failing to do so would establish atheism. Like many of the state court decisions discussed in Chapters Three and Four, this one asserted that sectarian practices would be impermissible but that the

Bible is nonsectarian. "The inference that the Holy Bible is either sectarian or partisan," the decision stated, "is a rather startling and novel thought." The court also found no merit to the Murrays' claim that believers and nonbelievers should be treated equally. In its view, the religious freedom of believers would be curtailed if religious exercises no longer took place in public schools, but "Just how the religious liberty of a person who has no religion can be endangered is by no means made clear" (*Murray v. Curlett,* unpublished opinion of the Superior Court of Baltimore City, April 27, 1961, p. 9). The decision also suggested that if nonbelief were accorded equal status with belief, some of America's most cherished traditions might be excluded from the public schools. "It is even possible," the court speculated, "that United States currency would not be accepted in school cafeterias because every bill and coin contains the familiar inscription, 'IN GOD WE TRUST'" (p. 17). When this ruling was upheld by Maryland's highest court, the Murrays turned to the U.S. Supreme Court.

The Supreme Court had handed down *Engel v. Vitale* shortly before agreeing to hear *Murray v. Curlett,* and the Murrays' brief followed the reasoning of that decision closely. They asserted that they had no objection to the use of religious texts in secular instruction, "including the Bible in all or any of its versions, when such material is presented and discussed as literature or history." What they opposed, they explained, was exactly what the Court had struck down in *Engel:* "favor for religion as opposed to non-religion, and... the conduct of religious teachings, whether such teachings be called sectarian or whether they be called non-sectarian" (Brief of the Petitioners, December 10, 1962, p. 9). In arguing that the recently adopted opt-out policy did not adequately resolve the dispute, they relied heavily on the Court's ruling that school-sponsored religious observances are unconstitutional even if dissenters are excused.

Engel was, of course, very bad news for the school officials, whose case had until then been based on the assertion that nonsectarianism and an opt-out policy were sufficient to render school-sponsored prayer constitutional. In an attempt to find new ground on which to stand, their brief alleged that the opening exercises in the Baltimore schools were not merely nonsectarian but entirely nonreligious. While conceding that the Bible and the Lord's Prayer are religious in origin, the brief contended that they "are not used in the challenged opening exercises as a form of religious instruction or as a religious service. Rather, these materials are utilized as a source of inspirational appeal to inculcate moral and ethical precepts of value in a salutary and sobering exercise with which to begin the school day" (Brief of Respondents, January 8, 1963, p. 4). Unable to find any comparable distinction between Maryland's opt-out policy and the one struck down in *Engel,* the school officials had little choice but to ask the Court to reconsider its ruling on that point.

THE OTHER SHOE DROPS

While the Murrays and the Baltimore school officials were preparing their briefs, the Supreme Court agreed to hear another school-prayer case, *Abington v. Schempp. Abington* was an ACLU-supported Pennsylvania lawsuit that O'Hair often mentioned when castigating the organization for declining to represent her. Although the background of *Abington* was considerably less dramatic than that of *Murray,* the two appeals raised the same issues, and the Supreme Court heard them together and handed down a single decision covering both. At issue in *Abington* was a 1949 Pennsylvania statute mandating that "'At least ten verses from the Holy Bible shall be read, or caused to be read, without comment, at the opening of each public school on each school day, by the teacher in charge.... If any school teacher, whose duty it shall be to read the Holy Bible, or cause it to be read, shall fail or omit so to do, said school teacher shall, upon charges preferred for such failure or omission, and proof of the same, before the board of school directors of the school district, be discharged'" (*Schempp v. Abington,* 177 F. Supp. 398 [1959], p. 399, n. 3). Although the statute did not mention the Lord's Prayer, Abington officials confirmed that it was recited as a matter of tradition throughout the district.

The oldest of the Schempps' three children, Ellory, was a junior at Abington High School when he concluded from his study of the Bill of Rights that the daily Bible-reading and prayer were unconstitutional. With his parents' approval, he stopped participating in the devotionals, and his homeroom teacher sent him to the vice-principal for refusing to rise for the Lord's Prayer. In a recent interview with Robert Alley, a prominent opponent of state-sponsored school prayer, Schempp recalled that the vice-principal was "flabbergasted by my behavior" (Alley, 1996, p. 94). The boy was referred to the guidance counselor, who, Schempp quipped, eventually concluded that he was sane and allowed him to spend homeroom period in her office each day. A new principal later rescinded that arrangement and required Ellory to participate in the prayers, but by then he had already contacted the ACLU. In February 1958, ACLU attorneys filed suit in federal court on behalf of the Schempp family, which included two younger children who would continue to attend the Abington public schools after Ellory graduated. On the advice of his lawyers, Ellory complied under protest with the requirement to take part in the morning exercises, as did the younger Schempp children.

The Abington school officials' refusal to establish an opt-out policy even after the lawsuit was filed was one of the few elements distinguishing the Schempp case from *Murray v. Curlett*, and it arose because they maintained all along that the exercises were not religious. They described the daily Bible-reading not as worship but as an educational exercise designed to familiarize students with a seminal text that has played a major role in American history, as well as influencing literature throughout the western world and promoting generally accepted moral norms. Since the Bible-reading was not being conducted as a religious exercise, they asserted, no student had any basis for demanding to be excused as a matter of religious freedom. The Schempps retorted that the state law's repeated references to the "Holy" Bible and the reverential manner in which the daily readings were conducted suggested otherwise. They challenged their opponents to provide another example of secular instruction that consisted of requiring all students to rise from their seats for the reading of archaic and complex language to children as young as six with no explanation or discussion. And where else in the curriculum, they inquired, did teachers face dismissal for failing to use exactly the same text and teaching method from the first grade through the senior year of high school? Further, the Schempps maintained, the Bible-reading was not only religious but sectarian. As Unitarians, they asserted that their beliefs conflicted with such biblical doctrines as the Immaculate Conception, the Trinity, the divinity of Christ, and the anthropomorphic nature of God. They also objected to stories of blood sacrifices, uncleanness, leprosy, and a vengeful Deity. And, they added, there could be no secular justification for demanding that all students stand to recite the Lord's Prayer every day. Accordingly, they sought not an opt-out policy but the removal of Bible-reading and the Lord's Prayer from the official school program.

Since the facts of the morning exercises were not in dispute, both sides relied heavily on expert witnesses to explain their significance. The Schempps' expert was a rabbi and scholar, Dr. Solomon Grayzel, who concentrated on making the point that the daily Bible-reading was both religious and sectarian. "I don't want to step on anybody's toes," he testified, "but the idea of God having a son is, from the viewpoint of Jewish faith, practically blasphemous" (trial transcript, August 5, 1958, p. 44). Similarly, he denied the school board's assertion that the readings took place without comment, since the KJB contains Christocentric chapter headings, epigraphs, and other explanatory material suggesting, among other things, that the primary purpose of the Hebrew scriptures/Old Testament is to foretell the coming of Jesus. He also asserted that Jewish students were harmed by the use of certain verses, notably the one in which the Jews cry out to Pontius Pilate, "His blood be upon us and upon our children." "And I submit to you," he testified, "that this verse, this excla-mation has been the cause of more anti-Jewish riots throughout the ages than anything else in history. And if you subject a Jewish child to listening to this sort of reading, which is not at all unlikely before ... Easter, I think he is being subjected to little short of torture" (p. 53). Indeed, he asserted, such passages do more harm when read without any clarification other than the KJB notes than they might do if accompanied by a cultural or historical explanation.

To counter Dr. Grayzel's remarks, Dr. Luther Allan Weigle, dean emeritus of Yale Divinity School, testified that neither the Bible nor the practice of read-ing it without comment is sectarian. The Bible, he argued, has "great value, it seems to me, to the perpetuation of those institutions and those practices which we ideally think of as the American way of life, because the Bible has entered vitally into the stream of American life" (p. 154). He added, "I see nothing in the Lord's Prayer that is sectarian. Everything in that prayer can be paralleled in Jewish literature, in the Holy Scriptures of the Jewish people" (p. 155). Nevertheless, when the Schempps' attorney asked him, "When you said 'non-sectarian,' did you mean as among the various Protestant sects?" he replied, "I meant among the various Christian bodies" (p. 161).

Weigle's Christocentric view of the Bible probably did not help the school officials' case, but it made little real difference because the main issue was not whether the Abington morning exercises were sectarian but whether they were in any way religious. And even that turned out to be a pointless distinction, since the federal district court that heard the case declared that public schools were prohibited not only from promoting sectarian tenets but also from advancing religion in general over nonbelief. While agreeing with the school officials that the secular use of the Bible as an instructional tool would be con-stitutional, it rejected their contention that such was the case here. "In our view," the decision stated, "inasmuch as the Bible deals with man's relationship to God and the Pennsylvania statute may require a daily reminder of that rela-tionship, that statute aids all religions. Inasmuch as the 'Holy Bible' is a Christ-ian document, the practice aids and prefers the Christian religion" (p. 405).

TRY, TRY AGAIN

At the time this decision was handed down, the Supreme Court had not yet ruled in *Engel* that opt-out provisions are insufficient to render state-spon-sored prayer constitutional. Consequently, the Pennsylvania school authorities thought that if they established a provision for excusing individual students, they might be able to preserve the morning devotionals even if the courts continued to deem them religious. Thus, the Pennsylvania statute was amended to say: "Any child shall be excused from such Bible reading, or attending such Bible reading, upon the written request of his parent or guardian" (*Schempp v. Abington,* 201 F. Supp. 815 [1962], p. 817). School officials then asked the court to reverse its ruling and dismiss the case on the ground that the opt-out policy had resolved the conflict between the Schempps and the school district. When the Schempps reiterated that what they wanted was not an opt-out policy but the termination of the religious exercises, the court ordered a new trial.

Ellory Schempp was in college when the second trial took place in 1961, but his siblings, Roger and Donna, were still in the Abington public schools. They had chosen not to take advantage of the new opt-out policy, and despite a barrage of objections from the school board's attorneys, their father was allowed to explain why. "We originally objected to our children being exposed to the reading of the King James version of the Bible," he testified, "which we felt was against our particular family's religious beliefs, and under those conditions we would have theoretically liked to have the children excused. But we felt that the penalty of having our children labelled as 'odd balls' before their teachers and classmates every day in the year was even less satisfactory than the other problem" (trial transcript, October 17, 1961, p. 214). Moreover, although there had been no suggestion that his family had Communist connections, Schempp worried about the popular perception that opponents of school prayer were atheists, and atheists were Communists. As he pointed out, children excused from the prayers would also miss the Pledge of Allegiance, thus further confusing the issue of exactly what they were dissenting from. The school board's lawyers tried to counter his testimony by arguing that a particular family's choice not to use the opt-out policy did not detract from its effectiveness in protecting the rights of dissenters, but the court was not persuaded. In its view, the morning exercises were school-sponsored religion, and the opt-out policy neither made that sponsorship constitutional nor eliminated coercion to participate.

Following its second loss in the district court, the school board turned to the U.S. Supreme Court, which agreed to hear an appeal. (The title of the case then changed from *Schempp v. Abington,* as it had been when the Schempps were suing the Abington board, to *Abington v. Schempp,* indicating that the board was now initiating the legal action.) By this time, the Supreme Court's decision in *Engel* had been announced, and in an effort to prevent that precedent from dooming their case, the school officials' attorneys raised a novel argument. In order to be truly neutral toward religion, they asserted, the courts must not change the way anything has been done in the past. "Does not the religious neutrality required by the First Amendment mean that neither the religious nor the nonreligious may use the government to improve their respective positions?" they asked. Pointing out that the Court had rejected attempts to add new religious exercises to public schools in *McCollum* and *Engel*, they asserted that neutrality required it to uphold the existing practices of the Pennsylvania schools. Otherwise, if courts could halt the introduction of new religious observances while removing the old ones, the result would not be religious neutrality but "a policy that required the government to remove from public life all of the admittedly existing religious leaven and in its place establish an absolute nonreligious state. Such a policy could not be considered by reasonable men to be anything other than one of hostility toward religion as a matter of law" (Brief for Appellants, January 4, 1963, p. 39). The Schempps retorted that whenever their opponents said that "the government" should be neutral in religious matters, they invariably meant only the judicial branch. "This is a curious and ingenious argument," their brief suggested. "Its initial fallacy is the equation of this Court with 'the government.' It blithely ignores the obvious fact that what [the Schempps] are complaining about is that 'the government' in the person of the legislature of Pennsylvania has not observed the 'neutrality towards religion' which [the school officials] so rightly commend. In such a situation to urge this Court to be 'neutral' by not interfering is to be oblivious to the very function of the judiciary and, because one branch of the government is induced to remain supine, the non-neutrality of the other is allowed to continue. This is neutrality with a vengeance!" (Brief for Appellees, February 1, 1963, p. 22).

SCHEMPP MEETS MURRAY

On February 27, 1963, the Supreme Court heard oral arguments in *Murray v. Curlett* and *Abington v. Schempp*. The first speaker was the Murrays' lawyer, Leonard Kerpelman, who denied his opponents' assertion that school prayer was acceptable as a matter of tradition. "Well I don't think, if Your Honors please, that we can repeal the Constitution by this particular means," he said. "A matter which is once unconstitutional does not become constitutional by being allowed to persist" (transcript of the oral argument in *Murray v. Curlett*, p. 4). The justices, as is their custom, interrupted frequently. Justice Potter Stewart, the lone dissenter in *Engel*, was particularly persistent in challenging Kerpelman about the rights of the students who wanted to pray and about the use of a demurrer instead of a trial in the Maryland courts. His point was that because no trial had taken place, there was no testimony or other evidence to show how the school had conducted the prayers and enforced the opt-out policy.

The school board's lawyer, an experienced advocate named Francis Burch, had an even worse time, albeit for different reasons. When he claimed that Bible-reading had a calming effect on the students, one of the justices said, "You could just give them tranquilizer pills, if that's—if that's the purpose" (p. 22). Later, in an effort to demonstrate that the Bible was not being read for religious reasons, Burch speculated that the people of Baltimore might be equally willing to have their children read the Koran, the Veda, or a Buddhist text. The Court's response appears in a parenthetical notation in the transcript: "[Laughter]." When Burch tried again to make that point, Justice Black cut in. "It seems to me," he observed, "like you'd do better if you'd face the issue. I don't know what's the answer to it, but how can you assert seriously or argue or ask us to consider seriously this is not a religious ceremony based on the Bible and the Lord's Prayer? Those who are strongest for it I doubt, would not hesitate to say that" (p. 27).

Following the oral argument in *Murray,* the Court heard from attorneys representing the Abington school board and the Schempps. The board's attorney, Philip Ward, disagreed with the Schempps' contention that the opt-out provision harmed dissenters by marking them as "different." On the contrary, he suggested, the policy was a celebration of individuality that contrasted with the bleak enforced orthodoxy of dictatorships. In response to one justice's suggestion that his advocacy of opt-out policies sounded like the separate-but-equal doctrine of racial segregation, he declared, "That's the glory of the country: they can be separate, they have the right to be separate. There are only two places where they would all be the same. One, of course, would be a totalitarian state where we couldn't be different; and two would be some sort of big togetherness state where we never did anything unless everybody wanted to do that very same thing" (transcript of the oral argument in *Abington v. Schempp,* p. 14). Shortly afterward, Justice Black asked Ward about the use of the Koran as a source of moral precepts, and Ward quipped, "The one thing I know about the Koran is it says that you should have no more than four wives." Using his joke as an illustration, he told Black that the Baltimore schools would not use the Koran "because we don't consider the Koran the supreme source of morality that we consider the Bible." "Why?" asked Black. Because, Ward said, it is better to use a familiar book that teaches morals of which everybody approves. Black said, "Everybody?" (pp. 19–20) and Ward conceded that he meant the majority, but he continued to maintain that the reason for using the Bible was not that it is a religious text.

The Schempps' attorney, Henry Sawyer, ridiculed Ward's claims about the Bible as a source of moral instruction by quoting several scriptural passages involving actions that would not be morally acceptable today. His main point, however, was not to critique the Bible but to argue that state-sponsored religious practices are unconstitutional. "The question is," he said, "is it a constitutional right, under the free exercise clause, to have the state conduct the prayer, or 'to pray,' in other words, under the aegis of the state? And I think clearly not. Even if the overwhelming majority so feel, I think it probably has nothing to do with the question of majorities" (p. 29). This mention of majorities led Justice Stewart to ask whether Bible-reading would be acceptable if the students themselves voted overwhelmingly to have it, and Sawyer's response reflected the distinction between government and private action that would later become a dominant element in school-prayer lawsuits. If, he said, the students in Stewart's hypothetical situation were acting entirely on their own, that would be fine; but if the Bible-reading were conducted over the public address system when the students were gathered for other school purposes, that would involve school sponsorship and would be unacceptable regardless of the majority vote. "But isn't it a gross interference with the free exercise of the religion," Stewart asked, "of those, in my imaginary case—those 98 percent of the student body who say our religious beliefs tell us that this is what we want to do?" "Well, they have a right to do it, Your Honor," Sawyer replied, "but they haven't got a right to get the state to help them" (p. 30). Later, the Court raised the question of America's religious heritage, and Sawyer responded with an impassioned speech. "I think tradition is not to be scoffed at," he said, "but let me say this very candidly: I think it is the final arrogance to talk constantly about the religious tradition in this country and equate it with this Bible. Sure, religious tradition. Whose religious tradition? It isn't any part of the religious tradition of a substantial number of Americans.... And it's just, to me, a little bit easy and I say arrogant to keep talking about our religious tradition. It suggests that the public schools, at least of Pennsylvania, are a kind of Protestant institution to which others are cordially invited" (p. 46).

DECISION

In an 8–1 decision, the Supreme Court found in favor of the Schempps and the Murrays. To Madalyn Murray's fury, the cases were listed in that order, and the decision is so commonly referred to as "Abington" that few nonlawyers realize that it also covered her case. She later alleged that although the Court had received her appeal first, given it a lower file number, and heard it first, "so great was the onus against [atheists] that in the historical recording of the case it was titled Abington School District vs. Schempp rather than to let the name of Atheists (Murray vs. Curlett) be reported out in any official United States legal reports!!" (O'Hair, p. 277).

The opinion, written by Justice Tom Clark, was based on an early version of a concept that was later expanded into the so-called *Lemon* test (see Chapter Fourteen). In determining whether a school prayer law is constitutional, Justice Clark wrote, "The test may be stated as follows: What are the purpose and the primary effect of the enactment? If either is the advancement or inhibition of religion then the enactment exceeds the scope of legislative power as circumscribed by the Constitution. That is to say that to withstand the strictures of the Establishment Clause there must be a secular legislative purpose and a primary effect that neither advances nor inhibits religion" (*Abington v. Schempp*, 374 U.S. 203; 83 S.Ct. 1560 [1963], p. 222). On the basis of that standard, the Court declared that the morning exercises in the public schools of Abington and Baltimore were unconstitutional because the advancement of religion was their primary purpose and effect. Moreover, far from improving the situation, the opt-out policies merely provided further evidence that the activities were religious.

In response to the argument that eliminating Bible-reading and the Lord's Prayer from the public schools would show hostility toward religion, the decision stated, "We agree of course that the State may not establish a 'religion of secularism' in the sense of affirmatively opposing or showing hostility to religion. . . . We do not agree, however, that this decision in any sense has that effect." The Court also clarified, as it had done in *Engel*, that "Nothing we have said here indicates that [literary or historical] study of the Bible or of religion, when presented objectively as part of a secular program of education, may not be effected consistently with the First Amendment. But the exercises here do not fall into those categories. They are religious exercises, required by the States in violation of the command of the First Amendment that the Government maintain strict neutrality, neither aiding nor opposing religion" (p. 225). Similarly, the Court rejected the school board's contention that terminating state-sponsored religious observances would violate the religious freedom of the majority. "[W]e cannot accept," the decision stated, "that the concept of neutrality, which does not permit a State to require a religious exercise even with the consent of the majority of those affected, collides with the majority's

right to free exercise of religion. While the Free Exercise Clause clearly prohibits the use of state action to deny the rights of free exercise to *anyone*, it has
never meant that a majority could use the machinery of the State to practice its
beliefs" (pp. 225–26).

As he had done in *Engel*, Justice William O. Douglas wrote a concurrence
arguing for the elimination of all government funding for religious purposes.
The lone dissent in *Abington*, as in *Engel*, was written by Justice Stewart, although
in this case he stopped short of saying definitively that the morning exercises
were constitutional. The reason for his indecision was that *Murray* and *Abington*, as presented to the Court, did not include what he considered adequate
factual information. Unlike his colleagues, Stewart thought that opt-out policies were capable of providing adequate protection for dissenters, but because
there was no evidence showing how they were applied in the Baltimore and
Abington schools, he did not declare outright that the practices of those schools
were acceptable. Instead, he stated as a general principle that the only obligation the government owes dissenters is "that of refraining from so structuring
the school environment as to put any kind of pressure on a child to participate
in those exercises; it is not that of providing an atmosphere in which children
are kept scrupulously insulated from any awareness that some of their fellows
may want to open the school day with prayer, or of the fact that there exist in
our pluralistic society differences of religious belief" (pp. 316–17). On the
other hand, "if the exercises were held during the school day, and no equally
desirable alternative were provided by the school authorities, the likelihood
that children might be under at least some psychological compulsion to participate would be great. . . . [But] I think we would err if we *assumed* such coercion in the absence of any evidence" (p. 318). Ideally, he suggested, religious
exercises might be held before or after school or when students were free to
engage in any one of several activities. More than twenty years later, after he
had retired from the Court, a version of that plan passed Congress overwhelmingly under the title of the Equal Access Act, which the Court subsequently upheld (see Chapters Eleven and Twelve).

GO THOU AND DO LIKEWISE

Naturally, *Abington* had a marked impact on other school-prayer cases making
their way through the courts. Notable among these was *Chamberlin v. Dade
County Board of Public Instruction*, which went through the Florida state courts
in conjunction with another case, *Resnick v. Dade County*. The plaintiffs were
agnostic, Jewish, and Unitarian parents who objected to such activities as

Bible-reading (with and without comment), the Lord's Prayer, after-hours Bible classes, religious films and symbols, holiday services, a religious census of the students, and religious tests for the employment and promotion of school personnel. They also sought to prevent the Gideons from distributing Bibles in the school and to remove a sign erected on the school lawn by a local church. Despite an opt-out policy covering some of these practices, the plaintiffs wanted all of them terminated.

The trial court upheld most of the disputed practices, including Bible reading and the Lord's Prayer. The Florida State Supreme Court affirmed this decision, declaring that the U.S. Supreme Court's distorted interpretations of the Constitution were undermining the rightful authority of the states and threatening the "long established and accepted customs of the vast majority of the American people" (*Chamberlin v. Dade County*, 143 So. 2d 21 [1962], p. 30). The Florida court also objected to what it saw as the misuse of the Constitution to bestow special privileges on minorities. *Chamberlin*, it contended, was "just another case in which the tender sensibilities of certain minorities are sought to be protected against the allegedly harsh laws and customs enacted and established by the more rugged pioneers of the Nation. In the instant case we are told that the primary objects of solicitude are the children of the plaintiffs, atheists, Unitarians and Jews, which children, although not required to be present at the time, will, so it is said, suffer some supposedly irreparable emotional stress if their classmates are permitted to hear the Bible read" (pp. 31–32). Indeed, the court found, the opt-out policy itself was evidence of special treatment for minorities, since students could not ordinarily pick and choose which parts of the state-approved school program they wished to attend. "The plaintiffs assume," said the court, "inferentially at least, that minorities enjoy a peculiar susceptibility to psychological and emotional trauma and compulsions and are entitled to some peculiar and fatherly protection against the strange ways of the ordinary American citizen. But such is not the case. The minority is entitled to enjoy the same privileges and the same justice as are enjoyed by people generally as an inherent right. The minority and the majority are both denied the privilege of disrupting the lives of others because of some hyper-sensitivity or fractious temperament" (p. 32).

Chamberlin was appealed to the U.S. Supreme Court, which vacated the decision of the Florida Supreme Court and sent the case back with instructions to reconsider it in light of *Abington*. The Florida court subsequently affirmed its earlier ruling on the ground that Florida's Bible-reading statute had the explicit secular purpose "'of good moral training, of a life of honorable thought and good citizenship.'" More significantly, the court declined to comply with *Abington* because it felt that "the establishment clause of the Constitution was never designed to prohibit the practices complained of" (*Chamberlin v. Dade County,* 171 So. 2d 535 [1965], pp. 537, 538). Once again, the plaintiffs appealed to the U.S. Supreme Court, which struck down Bible-reading and the recitation of the Lord's Prayer in the Florida schools but did not address the plaintiffs' other claims because they were not presented in a way that would allow a federal court to decide them.

Although the Supreme Court elected to make *Abington* rather than *Chamberlin* its test case on Bible-reading and prayer in the public schools, one of the issues raised by the Florida lawsuit deserves mention because of its relevance to later school-prayer controversies. The *Resnick* plaintiffs' attorney, Leo Pfeffer, was a renowned First Amendment litigator and scholar who had, among other things, written amici curiae briefs in *Engel* and *Abington* on behalf of the Synagogue Council of America and the National Community Relations Advisory Council. As a lead attorney in *Resnick,* he framed the case in terms of the Free Exercise Clause, whereas *Murray* and *Abington,* like most school-prayer lawsuits of that time, emphasized the Establishment Clause. This distinction is important because the Establishment Clause defines what the government can and cannot do: in particular, it cannot favor or disfavor any religious view. By contrast, the Free Exercise Clause focuses on the right of individuals, including students, to practice their religion as they see fit. In Pfeffer's view, prescribing certain religious observances for use in the public schools not only represented an establishment of religion by the government but also impinged on the students' personal right to free exercise of religion. Ironically, Pfeffer's approach had a great deal in common with that of Justice Potter Stewart, the only member of the Supreme Court who wanted to uphold state-sponsored prayer in *Engel* and *Abington* as long as dissenters were offered a sufficiently attractive way to opt out. Both Pfeffer and Stewart sought to emphasize not the school officials' behavior but the students' religious rights. The reason they disagreed so completely about whether state-sponsored school prayer is permissible is that Stewart discussed free exercise in terms of the right of the majority to have its prayers, whereas Pfeffer thought that the Free Exercise Clause was meant to protect religious minorities from state interference with their religious practices (as by trying to engage them in religious observances other than their own). Nevertheless, each of them maintained in his own way that school-prayer lawsuits should focus not on school officials but on students. Had the Supreme Court elected to decide *Chamber-*

lin/Resnick, with its emphasis on the Free Exercise Clause, rather than *Abington,* based primarily on the Establishment Clause, the case law regarding school prayer might well have evolved differently, or at least at a different rate of progression. As Chapters Eleven and Twelve demonstrate, the student-focused approach advocated in different ways by Pfeffer and Stewart eventually became the dominant model for resolving school-prayer disputes, although arguably later than it might otherwise have done.

SECOND GENERATION

As the Florida State Supreme Court's remarks suggested, some states and school districts were loathe to comply with *Abington,* and the inevitable result was more lawsuits. As an example, New Jersey Attorney General Arthur Sills sued two recalcitrant school boards in his state, one of which had also been sued a decade earlier in *Doremus v. Board of Education of Hawthorne,* a school-prayer case dismissed by the Supreme Court because the plaintiffs' child had graduated (see Chapter Four). The outcome of *Doremus* had left Hawthorne's religious practices intact, and despite the Supreme Court's subsequent ruling in *Abington,* the school board refused to terminate them. In *Sills v. Board of Education of Hawthorne,* both the Superior Court of New Jersey and the State Supreme Court ruled against the Hawthorne officials, who thereupon reluctantly complied.

In contrast to the Hawthorne board's open defiance of *Abington,* the school board in Netcong, New Jersey, tried a less direct approach. Over Sills's objections, it established morning exercises in which students read and reflected on the sections of the *Congressional Record* in which the prayers of the House and Senate chaplains are reported. When this stratagem was brought to the attention of Congress, Representative Richard Roudebush (R-Indiana) applauded "the ingenious idea of reading Chaplain prayers from the *Congressional Record* each day as a substitute for regular prayer services outlawed by the Supreme Court." Realizing that the chaplains' prayers might be difficult for younger students to understand, he and some of his colleagues began reading children's prayers into each week's *Record.* "I hope this plan catches on like wildfire," Roudebush said, "and that schools across the Nation will turn to the pages of the *Congressional Record* for a source of children's prayers inserted to provide a legal remedy to the tragic Supreme Court decision" (*Congressional Record,* October 2, 1969, p. 28284).

Bolstered by such support, the Netcong board defied Sills's order to terminate the readings, and he once again went to court. The dispute became so unpleasant that the trial court reproved pro-prayer activists for describing those who differed with them "as 'Anti-God,' 'Anti-Christ' or 'Communists.' Telegrams and letters were sent to the court... which clearly and depressingly set forth the temper of the community and the eagerness of certain 'citizens' to create division, diversion and prejudice" (*State Board of Education v. Board of Education of Netcong*, 108 N.J. Super. 564; 262 A. 2d 21 [1970], p. 571). Similarly, the court chastised the board for using "intemperate and unwarranted adjectives" to describe the Supreme Court, and it cited several early school-prayer decisions to refute the assertion that *Abington* was "a recently concocted, ultra-liberal construction of our Federal Constitution" (p. 580). Not surprisingly, the court also rejected the argument that reading what the Netcong board described as "remarks" from the *Congressional Record* was a secular exercise. In its view, "To call some of the beautiful prayers in the *Congressional Record* 'remarks' for a deceptive purpose is to peddle religion in a very cheap manner under an assumed name. This type of subterfuge is degrading to all religions" (p. 583). This decision was upheld by the New Jersey State Supreme Court, and when the U.S. Supreme Court declined to hear an appeal, Representative John Hunt (R–New Jersey) protested, "it is extremely difficult to comprehend how this innocuous exercise... violates the spirit of the Constitution. In my estimation, it is the denial of this right that is a gross distortion of the ideals and aspirations of our Founding Fathers" (*Congressional Record*, December 3, 1970, p. 39853).

THE OTHER WAY AROUND

Whereas both New Jersey cases were filed by state officials against local boards, in other instances it was the state authorities themselves who were sued for defying *Abington*. Such a lawsuit took place just across New Jersey's southern border, where the attorney general of Delaware, David Buckson, ordered school officials to ignore the Court's ruling. Delaware's two school-prayer statutes, adopted in 1953 to codify much older practices, required the reading of at least five Bible verses daily and forbade all religious exercises other than Bible-reading and the recitation of the Lord's Prayer. Teachers who failed to comply faced a twenty-five-dollar fine for the first offense (a substantial part of a week's salary in 1953) and the revocation of their teaching credentials for any subsequent offense. The Lord's Prayer, permitted but not required by law, was commonly recited following the Bible-reading. Although the statutes did not specify any particular version of the Bible, school officials stated that they purchased only the KJB and, as far as they knew, no other translation was used in the schools.

Attorney General Buckson told Delaware school officials to continue these practices after *Abington* because, he claimed, state laws took precedence over Supreme Court rulings. The president of the ACLU of Delaware, Irving Morris, retorted that unless Delaware had seceded from the Union, it was subject to the rulings of federal courts. He also told a reporter for the local newspaper that the ACLU-DE would provide legal representation to any parents who wanted to challenge Buckson's order. Morris later explained that the organization had been asked several times to file a school-prayer lawsuit but had declined to do so because its resources were stretched to the limit by a school-desegregation fight that was then raging. Nevertheless, he wrote in a magazine article, "I was not at all prepared to have the chief law enforcement officer in Delaware abandon the rule of law, which is the essence of the social compact. . . . Attorney General Buckson's opinion set an example for the people of the State of Delaware to follow, which, I thought, would have put us on the road to anarchy; I would have none of it" (Morris, 1986, p. 8). More prosaically, he acknowledged that the case was such an easy win that it required little effort. Indeed, the complaint he filed consisted of little more than a reference to *Abington*.

The plaintiffs on whose behalf Morris filed the lawsuit were W. Harry and Anne Johns of Dover and Garry and Mary DeYoung of Middletown. Each couple had children in the Delaware schools, and Mary DeYoung taught second grade at Middletown School No. 60. Nevertheless, Buckson denied that either family had standing to sue. As he framed the argument, Delaware's school-prayer laws could be challenged only if they promoted a religion with which the plaintiffs disagreed. The Johnses, he said, were Presbyterians who could hardly claim that reading the KJB and reciting the Lord's Prayer contradicted their religion. Garry and Mary De Young were agnostics, and Buckson argued that it is impossible to violate the religious convictions of people who do not know what their convictions are. Had he prevailed, the often-repeated accusation that anyone who opposes school prayer must be an atheist or at least a non-Christian would have become reality, since only those whose views were demonstrably incompatible with the Bible would have been able to challenge traditional public-school devotionals.

The lawsuit, *Johns v. Allen* (Robert Allen was the first-named member of the state school board), was heard by a three-judge panel of the federal district court headed by Chief Judge John Biggs, Jr., of the Court of Appeals for the

Third Circuit. Judge Biggs, who had presided over a similar panel in *Abington*, had written the decision that had subsequently been upheld by the Supreme Court. Delaware's school-prayer statutes were almost identical to the Pennsylvania law struck down in *Abington*, and Biggs, whom Morris described as "tall, autocratic, powerful" (p. 13), did not look favorably on Buckson's open defiance. Moreover, as Buckson pointed out with a laugh during an interview for this book, the opposing candidate he had defeated for the post of attorney general had been none other than John Biggs III. Obviously, Buckson knew that he had no chance of success; as he explained in the interview, he was hoping to run for governor and did not want to appear to be cooperating too tamely with a Supreme Court ruling that most Delawareans disliked. An interview with Morris elicited roughly the same idea from a different perspective: "What'd he have to lose? If he won, he was a miracle worker. If not, well, at least he would've put up a fight" (January 16, 1997). Other elected officials, from the governor on down, followed Buckson's lead in emphasizing that the threat to the popular religious exercises emanated from the federal courts, not from them. Since Delaware's schools were embroiled in an intensely controversial court-ordered program of racial desegregation, the federal judiciary was an easy target for public wrath.

At the trial, the Johnses echoed the sentiments expressed by a fellow Presbyterian, Samuel Thayer Spear, almost a century earlier (see Chapter Four). In Harry Johns's view, "[T]o establish that the King James version of the Bible is read in our schools surely must prejudice [children] to feel that this is the authorized Bible in the public schools, and I feel that is wrong." As a member of the Protestant majority, he said, "I feel I have a greater responsibility under the American concept of religious freedom to protect those who do not read my Bible at home or do not read any Bible." Anne Johns added that school prayer "is damaging to [children's] development as citizens of our country because we teach them to admire and respect certain ideals that our country stands for, like religious freedom and equality. But when they get to school they find out that priority is given to Protestants. And I think that this demonstrates a double standard in our attitude" (trial transcript, January 27, 1964, pp. 123, 130, 154). Mary DeYoung's testimony was similar to that of the Johnses, but Garry DeYoung proved to be a much more inflammatory witness. Among other things, he said that all Catholic nuns and priests are sexual perverts, and he testified at length about a book of iconoclastic, erotic poetry that he had published at his own expense. Morris later confessed that he had been unaware of his client's more exotic views and was horrified when a front-page story in the next day's newspaper left the impression that he himself shared them.

The trial was further enlivened by a celebrity witness, Episcopal Bishop James Pike of California, a well-known advocate of state-sponsored school prayer. He denied that Delaware's school-prayer laws favored Christianity because, he said, Jesus was "a first century rabbi" and the Lord's Prayer is "the summation of Jewish piety" (trial transcript, March 30, 1964, p. 250). He added that nothing in the Bible conflicts with Jewish beliefs when read without comment. "[H]earing what the New Testament says in a literary way about Jesus Christ," he said, "no Jew could say is not so, that is, the Bible does say it and it is part of the literature of our culture that these beautiful words have been written, and any Jew knows that" (p. 275). Similarly, he stated that the rights of agnostics and atheists were not being violated "because it is not being read devotionally; it is being read like five verses of Shakespeare" (p. 257).

Following the trial, the Middletown School Board announced that it would not renew Mary DeYoung's teaching contract for the following year. Morris offered to represent her in a suit against the school district, but she declined. The DeYoungs moved to another state, which forced them to withdraw from the case before the decision was issued. To no one's surprise, that decision, written by Judge Biggs, struck down Delaware's school-prayer laws not only because Bible-reading and the Lord's Prayer were religious but also because the exclusion of any other form of worship favored a particular religious tradition. Governor Elbert Carvel announced that the state would appeal to the Supreme Court, but Buckson dissuaded him because such an appeal would have been costly, time-consuming, and unsuccessful. Having made his points—political, personal, and legal—he told the school officials to obey the court's order. As Morris would have it, Delaware was back in the Union.

IN THE PUBLIC ARENA

In addition to generating a series of lawsuits, *Abington* unleashed a flood of public and political protest. Nevertheless, although this decision affected far more schools than did *Engel*, the reaction to it lacked the note of startled hysteria that had greeted the Court's first intervention in school-prayer matters. Among other things, the news media, which had helped to exaggerate the effect of *Engel*, was better prepared to deal with shades of meaning in *Abington*. University of Virginia law professor Robert O'Neil, who was Justice William Brennan's law clerk when *Abington* was decided, recalled seeing a headline saying, "Supreme Court Bans Devotional Use of the Bible in Schools." The qualifying term "Devotional," he felt, marked an improvement over the frenzied coverage of *Engel*, which had suggested that no mention of God was permitted in public schools (interview, December 10, 1999). Like the media, some religious leaders responded in a more measured way to *Abington* than they had to *Engel*. Among these was the dean of the Episcopal Cathedral in Chicago, who told a reporter for *Time* magazine, "'Unlike last year when I reacted emotionally, illogically, and non-intellectually, this decision doesn't disturb me'" (Fenwick, 1989, p. 139). Methodist Bishop John Wesley Lord also supported the Court, suggesting that the real tradition of religious freedom in America was better served by *Abington* than it would have been by the continuation of school prayer. "'We accept the declaration of the Court,'" he said, "'in full recognition of the historic spiritual value the decision seeks to preserve.'" Similarly, the 1963 assembly of the United Presbyterian Church declared, "Now that the Court has spoken, responsible Americans will abide by its decision in good grace'" (*Congressional Quarterly*, June 21, 1963, p. 1002).

Clearly, religious people who agreed with the Court were more outspoken and received more public attention after *Abington* than they had after *Engel*. Ironically but predictably, this indication that not all God-fearing Americans supported state-sponsored worship galvanized some school-prayer advocates into redoubling their efforts to make the Court's actions appear extreme. "'God pity our country,'" said evangelist Billy Graham, "'when we can no longer appeal to God for help'" (Beaney and Beiser, 1964/1993, p. 419). Similarly, Bishop Fulton J. Sheen, a popular television evangelist known for his anti-Communist rhetoric, offered the bewildering but emotionally stirring prediction that the Court's next anti-prayer decision "will be a repetition of article 124 of the Soviet Constitution, which reads: 'The Soviet Union recognizes freedom of religious worship and freedom of antireligious propaganda.' If a court says, 'Thou shalt not pray,' because it will offend the atheists, then is not the next step to give to the atheists rather than to God-fearing men the right to propaganda? The next decision logically will be that one which affirms that antiprayer and antireligion in school have the support of law in education. America has reached a critical hour where its citizens must once again hear the words that Washington spoke to his soldiers at Valley Forge: 'Put only Americans on guard tonight'" (*Congressional Record*, March 11, 1964, p. 5010).

Bishop Sheen's association of *Abington* with atheistic Communism was shared by several members of Congress and from there it was but a short step to the assertion that prayer is a fundamental right of American schoolchildren because this is a Christian nation. Senator Willis Robertson (D-Virginia), for instance, deploring what he saw as "disrespect for the Bible and for the fact that we are a Christian Nation," asserted that "the most inherent distinction between our representative democracy and communism is our belief in God and the acceptance of the Bible as His Holy Word" (*Congressional Record*, June 19, 1963, pp. 11143, 11145). Among the most often used to justify this Christian Nation position was a book by Justice Joseph Story, who was appointed to the Supreme Court in 1811. Although he was a child when the Constitution and the Bill of Rights were drafted, he was so close to the Framers' generation and such a prominent constitutional expert that his statements about their intentions are given great weight. Story wrote (1833/1987),

> Probably at the time of the adoption of the constitution, and of the [first] amendment to it ... the general, if not the universal, sentiment in America was, that Christianity ought to receive encouragement from the state, so far as it is not incompatible with the private rights of conscience, and the freedom of religious worship. An attempt to level all religions, and to make it a matter of state policy to hold all in utter indifference, would have created universal disapprobation, if not universal indignation.... The real object of the amendment was, not to countenance, much less to advance Mahometanism, or Judaism, or infidelity, by prostrating Christianity; but to exclude all rivalry among Christian sects, and to prevent any national ecclesiastical establishment, which should give to an hierarchy the exclusive patronage of the national government. (pp. 700–701)

Without necessarily challenging Story's analysis of the Framers' intent, foes of the Christian Nation theory vigorously denied that eighteenth-century social views should dominate current interpretations of the Constitution. As Justice Brennan observed in his concurring opinion in *Abington*, what the First Amendment protects is the concept of religious freedom, not the specific way in which it was put into practice two hundred years ago. By way of comparison, Christian Nation opponents noted that many Founders deemed "All men are created equal" compatible with slavery and with the denial of equal rights for women. Since then, they asserted, cultural evolution and the Fourteenth Amendment have caused the freedoms enjoyed by any demographic group to be shared by all, thus rendering the Founders' privileging of Christianity incompatible with the present-day understanding of religious freedom.

CIVIL DISOBEDIENCE

As the Christian Nation rhetoric suggests, pockets of determined resistance to *Abington* continued in some areas, led by fiery political officials. Governor George Wallace of Alabama, who had once blocked the entrance of the state university to impede court-ordered integration, announced, "I don't care what they say in Washington, we are going to keep right on praying and reading the Bible in the public schools of Alabama" (Alley, 1994, pp. 122–23). Similarly, Senator Olin Johnston (D–South Carolina) spoke out in favor of the kind of defiance exhibited by the Hawthorne and Netcong school districts in New Jersey and by the attorney general of Delaware. "Despite the Supreme Court ruling," he said, "I am urging schoolteachers and schools to continue the reading of the Bible and to continue praying in classrooms. There is no statutory provision to penalize the school officials for defying the Supreme Court. They can continue to pray and read the Bible in schools until a court injunction is issued in each individual and every case, restraining them from continuing the practice in defiance of the Supreme Court" (*Congressional Record*, June 19, 1963, p. 11090).

Amid all the political speeches and lawsuits, it was reasonable to ask whether most schools were in fact complying with the Supreme Court's ruling. Among those who sought to answer this question was education scholar H. Frank Way, Jr., who distributed a questionnaire to randomly selected teachers throughout the country. On the basis of their self-reports, he concluded that "with the exception of the South, the [religious] practices had largely disappeared in public elementary schools by the academic year 1964–65" (Way, 1968/1992, p. 457).[1] A different methodology led to quite different results in a case study of four midwestern communities reported in *The School Prayer Decisions: From Court Policy to Local Practice* (1971). Its authors, Kenneth M. Dolbeare and Phillip E. Hammond, used interviews, public records, and on-site observation to support their assertion that relatively little change took place in communities where public pressure to retain the status quo was strong. While a few school officials openly defied the Court, they noted, far more found ways to engage in inaction, denial, conflict avoidance, and what the authors called "substantial cognitive deflection about actual local practices" (p. 68), resulting in inaccurate claims of being in compliance with the Court's rulings. The lawsuits discussed later in this book, filed as recently as the late twentieth and early twenty-first centuries against continuing school-sponsored prayers, tend to bear out Dolbeare and Hammond's conclusion that decisions such as *Engel* and *Abington* were merely "the opening of a long struggle in which lower level power holders often have the last word" (p. 153). As they further observed, compliance with the Court's rulings is likely to be enforced only when, and if, at least one resident or public official is willing to go to court. Understandably, people who see nothing wrong with school-sponsored prayer are frustrated to find that even if an overwhelming majority of residents want it to continue, their wishes can be overridden by anyone who chooses to sue. Accordingly, opponents of *Engel* and *Abington* initiated what became a decades-long effort to reverse the Court's rulings and reinstate traditional public-school devotionals.

7

Picnic with a Tiger

[T]he greatest safeguard against the eventual loss or frittering away
of these precious guarantees of individual liberty is to keep them as
they are. If we start to tinker with them, and to amend them here,
and amend them there, we will soon find good reasons for restrict-
ing this liberty, or narrowing that safeguard, and will eventually wake
up to find that we have lost the essential safeguards which these
amendments can and should protect.

—*Erwin N. Griswold*

In a free society such as the United States, people who disagree with the
actions of any government agency are entitled to say so as emphatically as they
wish. Nevertheless, as a matter of practical reality, disputing with the Supreme
Court about interpreting the Constitution is like the proverbial picnic with a
tiger: it may be fun for a while, but the tiger always eats last. Opponents may
protest to their hearts' content that the Court is wrong, but its interpretation of
the Constitution is binding unless the Court itself reverses an earlier ruling—
or unless the document is changed. If the Constitution were amended to say
that state-sponsored school prayer is permissible, then earlier rulings banning
it would be superseded, and all subsequent lawsuits would have to be decided
in accord with the new provision. In order to be enacted, however, a constitutional amendment requires a two-thirds vote in both Houses of Congress and
ratification by three-quarters of the states.[1] These requirements, designed to
ensure that any change to the Constitution will have broad-based support, are
intentionally difficult to meet.

POGO RULES
Calls for a constitutional amendment to restore state-sponsored school prayer
began immediately after *Engel* and escalated dramatically after *Abington*.

Although it is difficult to alter the Constitution, it is certainly not impossible, and the overwhelming popularity of school prayer appeared to make an amendment feasible. Nevertheless, in the four decades that have elapsed since then, only four such proposals have come up for a vote in either House of Congress, and none has passed. The reason for this is not that the foes of a school-prayer amendment are necessarily unbeatable, although they have undoubtedly exerted some influence. The problem, from the viewpoint of amendment supporters, is best expressed in a line from a classic *Pogo* comic strip: "We have met the enemy, and he is us." Over the years, national polls have shown widespread agreement on school prayer in the abstract, but the devil, as the saying goes, is in the details. People who wholeheartedly answer "Yes" when asked whether they support school prayer are far less united when the time comes to put pen to paper (or fingers to keyboard) to draft the actual language of a constitutional amendment. It is the continuing inability of school-prayer supporters to unite behind a single proposal, more than any action by their opponents, that has doomed every effort to pass a constitutional amendment.

Disagreements over the wording of an amendment often begin with a discussion of its ideal scope. Some supporters prefer to focus narrowly on religion in the public schools, whereas others see the legislation as an opportunity to have a broader impact on the relationship between religion and government. Accordingly, some proposed school-prayer amendments have also dealt with such matters as tax-funded chaplains, the inclusion of "under God" in the Pledge of Allegiance, and tax support for religious institutions. Inevitably, the introduction of each new topic makes consensus harder to reach, since people who favor school prayer might not share the other goals.

With respect to school prayer itself, the same two fundamental and inescapable issues that have dominated the controversies discussed in earlier chapters also emerged as impediments to reaching consensus on a constitutional amendment.

1. *Should the amendment stipulate that dissenting students must be allowed to opt out?*
    YES: School prayer is not primarily a community activity or a statement of group identity but an act of worship. If a student does not wish to pray, or to pray in a particular manner, the state has no right to compel him or her to do so. Without an opt-out clause, the amendment would invite abuses of the sort that occurred in the nineteenth and early twentieth centuries, when the children of religious minorities were compelled to

engage in majoritarian religious exercises in the public schools. Under no circumstances should state officials ever again have the authority to coerce students in matters of faith.

NO: The primary reason for amending the Constitution is to undo the Supreme Court's ruling that the First Amendment applies to the states as well as to Congress. In accord with the original meaning of the First Amendment, each state should have complete control of its own policies with regard to religion, and any federal restriction—such as a constitutionally mandated opt-out provision—would violate this principle. Moreover, since prayer promotes good morals, common values, and a communal identity, it would not be unreasonable to require all students to participate, and no student's personal beliefs would justify an exemption from the common school program. Indeed, students who seek to be excused may be the very ones most in need of exposure to school prayer, as it is unlikely that they are taught the value of American-style prayer in their homes.

2. *Should the amendment specify that school prayer has to be nonsectarian?*
   YES: Religious observances would be counterproductive if they caused strife or failed to include as many willing participants as possible. Since even the broadest of sectarian practices, such as reading the Bible, might promote discord, a generic invocation similar to the Regents' Prayer would be preferable. In addition, as a matter of principle, government agencies should not have the power to endorse any particular religious view or practice.

   NO: Like a federally mandated opt-out policy, constitutionally required nonsectarianism would violate the right of each state to set its own policies regarding religion. Moreover, the courts might interpret the term "nonsectarian" so broadly that every attempt at school prayer, no matter how bland or inclusive, would be found to favor some religious view over others. Alternatively, the inclusion of that word might advance a watered-down civic religion over more creedal faiths by barring such practices as Bible-reading and the Lord's Prayer from every school regardless of the wishes of the local community.

As these examples suggest, whenever momentum begins to build up behind any school-prayer proposal, it is gradually dissipated by differences over specific provisions. The stakes are especially high because constitutional amendments tend to be one-time events. With an ordinary bill, people who compromise on a particular issue can try to get what they want through further legislation. But once a constitutional amendment is ratified, a second one on the same issue is unlikely to be enacted until years have elapsed—if ever. Accordingly, amendment supporters are reluctant to settle for language that either includes something they find unacceptable or omits a provision they deem essential, and the result has been a series of standoffs. Naturally, these disagreements are exploited to the full by opponents of state-sponsored school prayer, who subject each new proposal to a storm of queries about opt-out policies, nonsectarian prayer, and other divisive issues. The resulting disunity among the proposal's supporters brings about its defeat, thus strengthening the widespread perception that a constitutional amendment on school prayer is impracticable. Over the years, this pattern has became so familiar that when the House of Representatives voted on a school-prayer amendment in 1998, the process was so predictable as to appear choreographed (see Chapter Fifteen). Such was not the case, however, in the immediate aftermath of *Abington,* when Congress undertook its first serious consideration of constitutional amendments aimed at restoring state-sponsored school prayer. At that early stage, people on all sides of the issue were just beginning to articulate their own positions as well as developing strategies for outflanking one another.

The first of the post-*Abington* proposals to emerge as a serious contender for passage was sponsored by Representative Frank Becker (R–New York). Of all the members of Congress who introduced school-prayer amendments at that time, only he was willing to expend the time and energy necessary to move the proposal forward. One of his colleagues, former Representative Peter Rodino (D–New Jersey), later described him as "a likeable fellow, but strongly opinionated." With regard to school prayer, Rodino recalled, "He went beyond dedicated to more like obsessed" (July 23, 1996; all Rodino quotations are from this interview).

Given the popularity of school prayer, it may seem odd that members of Congress were not vying for the privilege of leading the fight, but that role was less appealing than it appeared. For one thing, it was already evident that school-prayer supporters were far from unanimous about what the amendment should say. Moreover, most of the Democratic leaders of the House came from heterogeneous urban communities where religion in the public schools was a divisive issue, and in some instances they themselves were members of minority faiths who had had unpleasant experiences with majoritarian school prayer. Since it is all but impossible to bring a bill to the floor of the House over the objections of the leadership of the majority party—in this instance, the Democrats—even those members of Congress who gave impassioned pro-prayer speeches were unwilling to invest further effort in what appeared to be a lost cause.

When Becker decided to challenge these odds, the first obstacle he faced was the House Judiciary Committee, to which all proposed constitutional amendments are referred. That committee was notorious for blocking any measure with which key members disagreed, and its chairperson, Representative Emanuel Celler (D–New York), was a powerful and determined foe of government-sponsored school prayer. Rodino, a personal friend of Celler and his successor as committee chairperson, said that Celler enjoyed parliamentary maneuvering and "did not hesitate to demonstrate legerdemain." At the time the Becker Amendment appeared, he had enjoyed such a productive forty-year career in the House that "the walls of his office were plastered with the bills he had introduced," Rodino recalled. "*All* the walls," he clarified.

At first, it did not appear that Celler's special talents would be needed to deflect the Becker Amendment. Like all chairpersons, he could ordinarily bury any bill referred to his committee simply by ignoring it. As long as he did not put it on the agenda, the committee could not vote on whether to send it on for consideration by the full House. Naturally, Becker and his allies criticized what they saw as Celler's autocratic veto of a proposal that had more than enough support to pass, but their accusation that he was single-handedly thwarting the will of the House was not quite accurate. Some members of both political parties were reluctant to amend the Constitution as a means of reintroducing school prayer, but because of its popularity few of them were willing to say so. There was thus less pressure on Celler than might have been expected, since as long as he blocked the amendment, his ambivalent colleagues could speak in support of school prayer without having to vote on any specific measure.

HONORABLE DISCHARGE

Becker had one chance, though a slim one, to prevent Celler from keeping the amendment bottled up in committee. If 218 of the 435 House members sign a document known as a discharge petition, the full House can decide whether to vote on a bill that has not been sent forward by the relevant committee. The committee is thereby discharged from further consideration of the proposal—hence the term "discharge petition." Understandably, the speaker, committee chairpersons, and other House leaders frown on this procedure because it undermines their control over the agenda. Nevertheless, Becker filed a discharge petition and set about getting the necessary signatures, which was no easy task because his colleagues were well aware of all the ways in which the leadership could retaliate. "I agree that Members will not sign petitions having to do with things that are Caesar's," he urged in a typical speech, "but I feel that when it comes to the area of Almighty God, no man can use the excuse that he does not sign discharge petitions" (*Congressional Record*, July 16, 1963, p. 12763).

Once the drive for signatures was in motion, Becker set about replacing his original proposal, a simple call for the restoration of school prayer, with whatever language was most likely to attract the necessary two-thirds vote. To this end, he convened a meeting of all the House members who had introduced school-prayer amendments and asked them to elect three Republicans and three Democrats to draft a bipartisan measure. After critiquing several drafts, the group agreed on a new Becker Amendment:

> Nothing in this Constitution shall be deemed to prohibit the offering, reading from, or listening to prayers or biblical scriptures, if participation therein is on a voluntary basis, in any governmental or public school, institution, or place. Nothing in this Constitution shall be deemed to prohibit making reference to belief in, reliance upon, or invoking the aid of God or a Supreme Being in any governmental or public document, proceeding, activity, ceremony, school, institution, or place, or upon any coinage, currency, or obligation of the United States. Nothing in this article shall constitute an establishment of religion. ("School Prayers," p. 22; hereafter "Becker hearings")

The suspicion that the Becker Amendment was crafted by a committee would probably cross the mind of anyone who read it, since the imperative factor in its composition was not elegance or even coherence but the necessity of attracting enough votes to pass. In its level of detail, it looks more like a statute than a constitutional amendment, which would ordinarily be framed as a broad statement of principle rather than as a lengthy enumeration of applications. Concern about Justice William O. Douglas's remarks in *Engel* and *Abington* is evident in its sweeping protection of any and all religion-related government practices, and although the words "on a voluntary basis" could be interpreted as some form of opt-out policy, its exact nature and scope are unspecified. The amendment is silent on the subject of sectarian/nonsectarian prayer, but the reference to "biblical scriptures" suggests the traditional public-school devotionals banned by *Abington*. One of the most significant parts of the amendment is its final sentence, whose assertion that "Nothing in this article shall constitute an establishment of religion" was ridiculed by people who felt that that was precisely what the measure was designed to achieve. Their jibes recalled an anecdote attributed to Abraham Lincoln, in which he allegedly asked how many legs a sheep would have if you called a tail a leg. "Five," someone said, whereupon Lincoln pointed out that calling a tail a leg doesn't make it one. By the same logic, Becker's opponents maintained that no amount of calling his proposal a nonestablishment of religion would make it so. Nevertheless, the drafters' decision to include this disclaimer was significant, for it reflected a long-standing and fundamental disagreement about the meaning of the Establishment Clause: "Congress shall make no law respecting an establishment of religion."

Becker and his supporters argued that the Establishment Clause was intended to prevent the federal government from setting up a national church, and from that perspective it was perfectly reasonable to claim that the Becker Amendment did not establish religion. Among the authorities cited in defense of this position was Justice Joseph Story, whose support for the Christian Nation theory was mentioned in Chapter Six. His *Commentaries on the Constitution* included a passage that might have been explicitly designed to support the contention that the Becker Amendment did not violate the Establishment Clause. "Indeed," Story wrote, "the right of a society or government to interfere in matters of religion will hardly be contested by any persons, who believe that piety, religion, and morality are intimately connected with the well being of the state, and indispensable to the administration of civil justice.... And at all events, it is impossible for those, who believe in the truth of Christianity, as a divine revelation, to doubt, that it is the especial duty of government to foster, and encourage it among all the citizens and subjects. This is a point wholly distinct from that of the right of private judgment in matters of religion, and of the freedom of public worship according to the dictates of one's own conscience" (pp. 698–99).

Story's assertion that government support for Christianity is "wholly distinct" from personal religious freedom reflects a standard known as religious toleration. It is based on the premise that although members of minority faiths have the right to worship as they see fit, that does not diminish the government's ability and indeed its duty to endorse and promote the majority religion. Underlying this standard is the conviction that the religion in which the majority believes, however it is defined, is inherently worthy of greater deference than any other belief system. If dissenters fail to see the light of religious truth, the argument runs, they are free to follow the dictates of their own consciences, but they have no legal or moral right to purge the majority faith from government documents, events, or programs. Their personal religious beliefs are not persecuted by the government, and that is the extent of the religious liberty to which they are entitled. Indeed, some Becker Amendment supporters went so far as to suggest that even that may be negotiable. Representative Richard Roudebush (R-Indiana), for instance, issued a warning to minorities about the folly of impeding the highly popular school-prayer proposal. "[T]he time is here," he declared, "when the minority... should display a little more tolerance toward the majority since the concept of religious freedom, under which so many sects flourish, is clearly a constitutional requirement only so long as the majority wills it so" (Becker hearings, p. 312).

Rejecting this majority-oriented notion of religious toleration, foes of the Becker Amendment embraced a model known as religious equality. As the name implies, religious equality requires the government to treat all views about religion—including nonbelief—exactly the same. To adherents of the religious equality principle, any endorsement of a particular religious view would denigrate and marginalize other belief systems. Reverend Edward O. Miller, rector of St. George's Episcopal Church in New York City, explained the concept in these terms: "For members of the minority, who are no less citizens because their faith is different, the result [of state-sponsored prayer] is not merely a moment or two of inconvenience but an impairment of equal citizenship. For to the extent that the 'free exercise' of religion by the majority is repeated, ostentatious, and collective in a public institution, to that extent the minority are less participants in, proprietors of, that public institution" (pp. 1572–73). Unlike proponents of religious toleration, who argued that excluding religion from government-run activities would establish atheism, advocates of religious equality maintained that the government would endorse atheism only if it explicitly affirmed that there is no God. To them, the absence of any statement about the existence of God, one way or the other, would not represent hostility toward religion but would demonstrate the governmental neutrality required by the Establishment Clause. The government, they argued, must refrain not only from preferring one religion over another but also from advancing religion in general over nonbelief. They further refuted the charge that the absence of school-run devotionals would turn the public schools into atheistic institutions by pointing out that the Supreme Court's decisions dealt with government-sponsored prayer, not with the students' personal right to pray. In their view, the students' ability to pray on their own was all that was either needed or permitted in the way of proof that the schools were neutral rather than hostile toward religion.

The lobbying campaign for the Becker Amendment benefited enormously from the extraordinary dedication of Representative Becker himself, who did everything possible to get the necessary signatures on the discharge petition. He was aided by a grassroots effort run largely by evangelical groups, such as the National Association of Evangelicals, the International Council of Christian Churches, the Children's Bible Mission, and the National Sunday School Association. Among the printed materials circulated by these groups was a memo prepared by Citizens for Public Prayer, described by Representative Philip Philbin (D-Massachusetts) as "a vigorous group of loyal, God-fearing Americans of Rutland, Massachusetts, in my district." "'Wake up, America!'" it declaimed. "'Do not sit by while Communists, atheists, agnostics, materialists, bleeding hearts, and their unwitting dupes tamper with and imperil the very foundation stones, sacred beliefs, and shrines of our great majestic Nation'" (*Congressional Record,* October 10, 1963, p. 19278). Such material was mailed in bulk to potential supporters, often accompanied by pre-printed postcards to send to their congressional representatives. Members of Congress and their staffs realized, of course, that many of the letters and postcards they received were identical and that some people were calling or writing over and over. Nevertheless, all this activity showed that a large number of voters cared about school prayer, and the discharge petition continued to gain signatures.

Opponents of the Becker Amendment were relatively inactive for the same reason that motivated its supporters to be particularly energetic: the assumption that Celler would keep the proposal bottled up in his committee. His ability to do so was threatened, however, by the slow but sure increase in the number of signatures on the discharge petition. Obviously, Celler did not want the bill to pass, but he was working on several other matters and was also running for reelection. (Becker had decided not to seek another term.) As a result, he was neither willing nor able to match Becker's dedication to this particular cause. Lacking single-minded leadership comparable to Becker's, the anti-amendment lobbying campaign was slow to get off the ground, and the delay was costly. By the beginning of 1964, the discharge petition had more than half of the necessary 218 signatures, and some undecided representatives were warning Celler that constituent pressure would soon force them to sign. He, in turn, was exasperated with anti-amendment advocacy groups that were, in his view, leaving too much of the burden on his shoulders. The time had come, he felt, for them to do more to spread the anti-amendment message. In order to give them breathing space to develop a strategy, he announced that the Judiciary Committee would hold hearings on the amendment, thus stalling Becker's drive for signatures by creating the appearance that the measure was moving forward. Then Celler ordered his staff to prepare a report on school prayer and postponed the hearings until it was ready.

Prominent among the advocacy groups that joined together in an anti-Becker coalition were Protestants and Other Americans United for Separation of Church and State,[2] the American Civil Liberties Union, the Anti-Defamation League of B'nai B'rith,[3] the American Jewish Congress, the National Council of Churches of Christ in the U.S.A., and the Baptist Joint Committee on Public Affairs. To their chagrin, they quickly determined that Becker's proposal would almost certainly pass in the Judiciary Committee if the members were given a chance to act on it; and even if Celler kept it off the committee agenda, it could pass in the House if it came up for a vote as a result of the discharge petition. Feeling that Becker had been getting his message out to legislators and the public with little effective rebuttal, the anti-amendment groups set about presenting persuasive counterarguments that would cause all but the most committed advocates of the amendment to take a closer look at its implications and possible results. Above all, they were determined to neutralize the perception that a vote against the amendment would be a vote against God, since they could not win a debate that was framed as an epic struggle between religion and traditional values on one side and atheism and amorality on the other. Moreover, although Jewish organizations were among the most dedicated foes of government-sponsored prayer and employed some of the nation's most distinguished First Amendment experts, they agreed that Christian clerics should take the lead in public appearances in order to prevent the coalition's efforts from being characterized as an attack on Christianity by non-Christians. Some pro-Becker advocacy groups were already emphasizing the role played by Jewish organizations, lawyers, and plaintiffs in *Engel* and *Abington*, as well as the fact that Celler and other prominent opponents of the amendment were Jews. Becker himself singled out the American Jewish Congress as the primary obstacle to the amendment's passage, leading Celler to accuse him of implying that only non-Christians opposed it.

With these various problems in mind, the coalition selected as its leader and spokesperson the Reverend Dean M. Kelley, a United Methodist minister who served as executive director of the National Council of Churches. His credentials included an outstanding reputation, political connections, and experience, but above all he was a living refutation of the notion that opposing the amendment was tantamount to denying God. He also persuaded other clerics to come forward in opposition to the amendment, with the result that coalition members who lobbied members of Congress were often accompanied by clergy from the member's home district. In addition, the coalition started its own grassroots campaign as well as mobilizing law school deans and professors to write to Congress and to the newspapers. Gradually, the public began to hear more about the negative effects of state-sponsored school prayer, and principled opposition by people of faith became more visible. In addition to demonstrating that religious believers held more varied views on school prayer than Becker was suggesting, this activism encouraged anti-amendment members of Congress to speak out, since they could refute the charge of ungodliness by pointing to all the religious leaders and legal experts who shared their view.

Anti-amendment advocacy groups also worked with Celler and his staff to line up impressive witnesses for the upcoming hearings, but they did not follow the example set two years earlier by the Senate Judiciary Committee, which had heard testimony only from advocates of school prayer. In addition to wanting the hearings to be perceived as fair, the Celler team felt that amendment supporters had benefited from presenting their case on their own terms without encountering meaningful questions or challenges. Consequently, foes of the amendment were eager to create a forum in which they could point out inconsistencies, raise objections, and force their opponents to address divisive topics. Moreover, with large numbers of witnesses testifying on both sides, the hearings would run close to the summer adjournment, thus leaving little opportunity for further action. Time was not on Becker's side; his momentum was peaking, whereas his opponents were just beginning to organize, and his decision not to seek another term meant that this was his only chance to bring his proposal to a vote.

When the hearings finally got under way, it seemed as if they were never going to stop. They took place on April 22, 23, 24, 28, 29, and 30; May 1, 6, 7, 8, 13, 14, 15, 20, 21, 27, and 28; and June 3. It took fifty-nine single-spaced pages of small type just to print the school-prayer resolutions being considered, which by then had grown to 154 proposals introduced by 115 members of Congress. (Many of them repeated or resembled the Becker Amendment, although they were listed under other sponsors' names.) Among the witnesses were 99 members of Congress, including future president Gerald

Ford (R-Michigan), who endorsed the amendment. In addition, the committee heard testimony from lawyers, teachers, actors, clergymen, war veterans, community activists, homemakers, students, school administrators, and farmers. The witness list ran to eight pages of small print and was followed by a twenty-one-page list of prepared statements and additional materials submitted to the committee. The transcript of the proceedings, along with supplementary items such as newspaper editorials and committee correspondence, fills three thick volumes. Whatever Celler's reasons for amassing so much material, the hearings he chaired remain an impressive compendium of American thought on prayer in public schools.

Obviously, it would not be feasible to summarize eighteen days of testimony and hundreds of pages of supporting documents, but it might be possible to convey the gist and tone of the proceedings by discussing half a dozen of the major topics they covered:

- Was state-sponsored school prayer beneficial in the past?
- How does school prayer relate to states' rights and racial desegregation?
- Does the majority have a right to decide what school prayers, if any, should be said?
- Does the state have a legitimate interest in overriding dissenting parents in order to expose children to majoritarian religious beliefs and practices?
- Does school prayer promote morality and guard against Communism?
- Is a vote against state-sponsored school prayer a vote against God?

(For further summary and analysis of the Becker hearings, see John H. Laubach's *School Prayers: Congress, the Courts, and the Public*, 1969. This book also deals with the Dirksen Amendment, which is discussed in Chapter Eight.)

AH, FOR THE GOOD OLD DAYS:
PERCEPTIONS OF THE HISTORY OF SCHOOL PRAYER

In his multiple appearances before the House Judiciary Committee, Becker repeatedly emphasized what he saw as the need to turn back the clock on the Supreme Court's school-prayer decisions. Among the many amendment supporters who endorsed that view was Representative John Dowdy (D-Texas), who gave the following response to a query about what would happen if state-sponsored prayer were reintroduced into the schools: "The same thing that has been happening for 175 years in the United States, and I don't know that anybody has gone to hell because they said a few prayers in school or read the

Bible in school. It has not hurt our country. We have come a long, long way in 175 years" (Becker hearings p. 1581). Representative Joseph Waggonner (D-Louisiana) gave voice to similar sentiment in more colorful terms when he protested that the Supreme Court had "killed the goose that lays the golden egg and we are left with a dead goose and a mess of scrambled eggs" (p. 503). Such assertions were, of course, based on a benign view of the way school prayer had operated in the past; and with a few exceptions, notably Becker himself, the witnesses who expressed it came from the South and from rural areas of the Midwest, where a strong Christian majority prevailed. Witnesses from more diverse urban areas, such as New York, Chicago, and southern California, tended to emphasize past problems and future risks. Among these was Reverend Edward Miller of New York, who mentioned such early controversies as Bishop Hughes's struggles with the New York authorities (Chapter Two) and the tarring and feathering of Father John Bapst (Chapter Three). In his view, state-sponsored school prayer would be no more peaceful or unifying today than it was in the past. "In the lower East Side," he said, "you have gang wars now which are in part religious wars. You have Orthodox Jewish boys and you have Puerto Ricans fighting with them. To have one of those Orthodox Jews get up in a school and walk out because the name of Jesus was said would mean murder, and any policeman would tell you that in New York" (pp. 1587–88).

THE GEORGE WALLACE FACTOR:
CIVIL RIGHTS, STATES' RIGHTS, AND SCHOOL PRAYER

Expressions of concern about the stormy past of state-sponsored school prayer and its ongoing potential for divisiveness were particularly frustrating to Becker and his allies because their foes showed no such compunction about the upheaval caused by the civil rights movement. On the contrary, the Becker forces protested, activists who were turning this country into a battleground over racial issues had recently been rewarded by the passage of the Civil Rights Act of 1964, which banned racial discrimination in employment, education, and other areas of society. Firmly backed by President Lyndon B. Johnson and other leading Democrats, the bill was anathema to many supporters of the Becker Amendment, including Democrats from the South. With Celler's help, it had zipped through the House Judiciary Committee with very little opportunity for discussion, leading school-prayer advocates to draw cynical comparisons between that process and the treatment being accorded to their proposal. Surely, they expostulated, racial issues have a more troubled past and raise more difficult questions than does school prayer, but that had not stopped Celler and his allies from muscling a civil rights bill through the Judiciary Committee and then through the House. That being so, they found it absurd to suppose that such astute and creative politicians were suddenly overwhelmed by the past or potential contentiousness of school prayer. In their eyes, the real issue was a battle between two sets of values and two ways of life: traditional Americanism, based on majority rule, states' rights, and an association of patriotism with religion; and an atheistic, amoral, socialistic state controlled by a liberal federal bureaucracy that favored Jews, blacks, and other minorities. As later chapters illustrate, this comparison of school prayer with civil rights soon evolved into the assertion that prayer under government auspices *is* a civil right that should be upheld under the same standards that protect Americans from racial discrimination.

Far from denying that a link existed between racial issues and school prayer, Celler and his allies used it to charge their opponents with hypocrisy. What was the point of making a great public display of religion, they demanded, while at the same time seeking to deny basic human rights to non-whites? To them, both racial segregation and state-sponsored prayer relied on the misuse of government power to secure special privileges for the majority while condemning minorities to second-class status. "We don't expect too much," sniffed Representative Roland Libonati (D-Illinois), "from persons who love God and hate their fellow man" (p. 861).

The discussion of racial issues reached a climax with the testimony of Governor George Wallace of Alabama. A year earlier, he had stood in the doorway of a University of Alabama building, blocking the passage of the first African Americans who came to register under a federal desegregation order. He had yielded only when threatened with federal force authorized by President John F. Kennedy, and in his testimony before the Judiciary Committee, he passionately maintained that all of America's social problems stemmed from federal interference with states' rights. He was particularly contemptuous of the Supreme Court, which he described as "nine unelected people in this country who say who rides in schoolbuses" (p. 865). Like many proponents of segregation (and, earlier, of slavery), he associated racial separatism with the American religious tradition, which in turn differentiated this nation from its Communist enemies.

LOCUS OF CONTROL I:
IS SCHOOL PRAYER SUBJECT TO MAJORITY RULE?

While Wallace and other amendment supporters tried to direct the committee's attention to such broad issues as states' rights, the alleged perils of liberalism, and the purported political activism of the Supreme Court, Celler and his allies doggedly hammered away at the practical details of the proposed return to school prayer. Among the most persistent of what Representative William Cramer (R-Florida) reviled as "all these nit-picking suggestions" (p. 357) was the contention that if group prayers were once again recited in the public schools, *someone* would have to write, select, or prescribe them. Supporters of the amendment were infuriated by questions about how this process would work for the same reason that its opponents kept asking them: they shone a spotlight on contentious issues that Becker would have preferred to finesse, notably the decades-long conflict between majority and minority rights with regard to school prayer.

All the plans suggested by Becker's supporters involved some form of majority rule, since they would have placed decisions about school prayer in the hands of elected bodies, such as state legislatures or school boards, or in those of administrators who served at the pleasure of such bodies. Advocates of the amendment also saw no reason to exclude sectarian prayers as long as they met with the approval of the local majority. As the more politically sophisticated of Becker's supporters had feared, the prospect of imposing majoritarian prayers on schoolchildren and using the machinery of the state to promote sectarian beliefs was singularly unappealing to members of Congress who were as yet uncommitted. The suggested procedures for handling school prayer also gave credibility to the prediction that this amendment would lead to competition, divisiveness, and bad feeling among religious groups.

In hindsight, the most novel and interesting of the proposed plans for implementing school-prayer programs was presented by Reverend Carl McIntire, president of the International Council of Christian Churches. Although it attracted little attention at the time, his suggestion that the students themselves should decide what prayers they wanted to say foreshadowed the current policies discussed in Chapters Eleven and Twelve. At the time of the Becker hearings, however, most people were still thinking in terms of adult-directed arrangements. Moreover, the prospect of having students vote on the content of school prayer raised—and continues to raise—the fear that religion might become a source of competition and divisiveness among the students and might generate undue peer pressure to participate in the majority's prayers.

LOCUS OF CONTROL II: WHOSE KIDS ARE THEY, ANYWAY?

Inextricably linked with the question of who would select school prayers was the right of parents to direct their children's religious upbringing. Celler and his associates, believing in religious equality, saw no justification for a double standard whereby parents of the majority faith could depend on public-school devotionals to bolster the beliefs they taught at home, whereas the religious teachings of other parents would be undermined by competition from the school authorities. Becker and his supporters, who preferred religious tolera- tion, retorted that the parents' freedom to practice the religion of their choice at home did not affect the majority's right to have its prayers said in the public schools. Like the nineteenth-century nativists, they maintained that public schools have an obligation to expose all students to distinctively American reli- gious observances, such as the King James Bible and its version of the Lord's Prayer. To them, the fact that such observances would conflict with the reli- gious practices taught in some families was not a disadvantage but a benefit, since one of their goals was to "Americanize" children from backgrounds they considered alien.

Becker and his associates were even more harsh toward nonbelievers, maintaining that the decision to avoid inculcating *any* religion was not a legit- imate parental choice but an error that the government had an obligation to remedy. Indeed, in Becker's view, any tension that school prayer might cause for the children of nonbelievers was attributable to the nonbelievers them- selves. "The parent who is an atheist or unbeliever or nonbeliever," he testi- fied, "seems to be the one who wants his children to be disassociated from prayer and Bible reading. It is not the children's decision. Actually, I think that we tend to overemphasize the dilemma faced by the children, stimulated by *the inter- ference of the parent*" (p. 238; emphasis added).

HOMELAND SECURITY:
SCHOOL PRAYER, MORALITY, AND COMMUNISM

To many amendment supporters, concern about such matters as who would select school prayers or how some parents might feel about them paled to insignificance before the conviction that fidelity to God is the only sure way to preserve the American way of life, including its moral values and its system of government, from a Communist takeover. Indeed, they portrayed Commu- nism not merely as the enemy of American culture but as its antithesis: col- lective rather than individual, amoral, undemocratic, and above all atheistic. In their certainty that religious faith is not only symbolically but materially essential to national security, they echoed the past even as they foreshadowed the future. Like the nineteenth-century nativists, Becker and his supporters believed that majoritarian religion—Protestantism in the nineteenth century, a broader form of monotheism in the twentieth—was the only dependable bulwark against dangerous foreign foes who sought to overturn America's social and political system by corrupting from within while attacking from without. Half a century later, in the aftermath of the 1999 Columbine school shootings and the terrorist attacks of September 11, 2001, some current members of Congress continue to use the same reasoning to justify a return to state-sponsored school prayer. Only by fostering belief in God, they assert, can the nation hope to preserve and enhance the divine protection it has historically enjoyed because of its religious traditions and identity (see Chapters Fifteen and Sixteen).

While acknowledging that ethical precepts are taught in the Bible and that majoritarian religion has long been linked with democracy, individual rights, and American institutions, foes of the Becker Amendment balked at the corollary that similar values are not to be found in any other belief system. In particular, they challenged the claim that majoritarian school prayer is a necessary element of morality and patriotism by pointing out that prior to *Abington* school prayer had been required in only twelve states, while nine states had forbidden it and the rest had left the decision to local authorities (see Chapter Four). They defied amendment supporters to show that the residents of Wyoming, for instance, were less moral, less patriotic, or less fully and distinctively American than those of New Jersey, although school prayer had been banned in one state and required in the other. (The public schools' duty to promote morality and love of country, together with the philosophical and legal issues surrounding various methods of achieving this goal, is discussed in depth in *Making Good Citizens: Education and Civil Society*, a collection of essays edited by Diane Ravitch and Joseph P. Viteritti [2001].)

IS A VOTE FOR THE BECKER AMENDMENT A VOTE FOR GOD?

As their references to a so-called American way of life suggest, Becker and his supporters saw themselves as defenders of an integral cluster of mutually dependent values resting on a foundation of majoritarian faith, and to their way of thinking, anyone who disagreed with any element of that cluster—including state-sponsored school prayer—must be an enemy of the whole thing. Becker himself introduced this theme on the first day of testimony, when he characterized opponents of his amendment as a "fraternity of secularists" who wanted to "create in the minds of our children and young people the feeling that a tribute to God in relation to the affairs of our Nation is a misdemeanor, if not a crime" (p. 212). He and his allies had been making such remarks for months without encountering much opposition, but at the hearings they were peppered with hostile questions that broke the momentum of their "be on God's side" rhetoric. Foes of the amendment also vented their frustration at what they saw as the substitution of hyperbole, name-calling, and emotionalism for intelligent discussion.

By far the most serious challenge to the notion that opposing the Becker Amendment was tantamount to rejecting God came from clergy associated with the National Council of Churches, who asserted that using the power of the state to promote majoritarian religious beliefs would be unjust, immoral, and dangerous. Their viewpoint was effectively summarized by Edwin Tuller, general secretary of the American Baptist Convention, who testified on behalf of the NCC. According to Tuller, "Another very real danger is the possibility that in time this amendment could bring about a kind of 'state religion' in which forms of religious observance and patriotism could become confused.... The act of worship might become part of being an American or being patriotic and in time the ideas of God and the Nation can fuse into one. There would be a real danger, then, that religion could become the tool of the state and eventually be used for the state's purposes as has already happened in the history of many countries" (p. 660).

In an effort to minimize the effectiveness of such witnesses, Becker and his allies characterized them as effete intellectuals who did not speak for the true religious community. Pointing to polls that showed strong support for school prayer among grassroots Americans, they accused anti-amendment clerics of substituting their own intellectual pride for majority rule and divine will. Among other things, this populist approach allowed Becker's supporters to counter their opponents' impressive credentials by turning prestige and accomplishments into liabilities. Paradoxically, the more distinguished and imposing a religious leader was, the more pretentious and detached from the common people he could be made to appear. Some of the pro-amendment clerical witnesses were, of course, just as well-educated and distinguished as their opponents, but they were spared the charge of elitism because they endorsed a populist view of school prayer.

To further this strategy, Becker's allies emphasized the academic credentials of opposing clerics rather than their religious calling. Representative William Widnall (R–New Jersey), for instance, declared, "I have had several college men get in touch with me against the amendment, and at the same time I have had the vast majority of their congregation get in touch with me and they are wholeheartedly for the amendment. They certainly are not speaking for the people in their own church when they write to me about it" (p. 474). Widnall's use of the term "college men" rather than "ministers" obfuscated the witnesses' religious identity while implying that they were remote and ivory-towerish. Representative George Goodling (R-Pennsylvania) expressed similar views in a letter he sent to the NCC when it assumed leadership of the anti-amendment coalition. "'Frankly, I am somewhat annoyed and greatly concerned about the present-day philosophy of some of our so-called religious leaders,'" he wrote. "'Let me suggest you come from your exalted position and mingle with the 40 million rank and file as I do constantly. You will discover beyond any shadow of doubt the chiefs and indians are in violent disagreement'" (p. 520).

Attempts to marginalize anti-amendment clerics suffered a serious setback when several Protestant denominations passed anti-amendment resolutions at their conventions. Although each denomination follows its own procedures for selecting delegates to these meetings, in general they are local pastors and lay people who cannot credibly be dismissed as out-of-touch elitists. Among the organizations whose conventions passed such resolutions were the United Presbyterian Church in the U.S.A., the Alabama Baptist State Convention, the Southern Baptist Convention, the American Baptist Convention, the North American Division of the Seventh-Day Adventists, the United Church of Christ, and the Unitarian-Universalist Association. Similarly, a poll conducted by the United Presbyterian Church showed that fewer than one-third of its 3.3 million members supported state-sponsored school prayer. Representatives of other mainstream Protestant faiths, including the Lutheran, Methodist, and Episcopal Churches, testified that although their denominations had not conducted a formal vote, many of their members opposed the Becker Amendment.

Becker's supporters tried to turn the tables by pointing to pro-amendment endorsements from such groups as the Convocation of the Bible Way Church, the Carolina Christian Union, the North Pacific Ministerial Association of the Evangelical Mission Covenant Church of America, the Independent Fundamental Churches of America, and the Massachusetts Congregational Christian Conference. Although these organizations were small and not well-known, Becker tried to turn that to his advantage by claiming that their grassroots quality made them more representative of "real" Americans than were what he saw as the snobbish, spiritless mainstream churches. He and his allies also introduced statements from people who indignantly disagreed with the anti-amendment resolutions passed by the conventions of their denominations. Nevertheless, his early prediction that most if not all people of faith would support his amendment had clearly failed to stand up under scrutiny. Since his opponents had made the more modest claim that religious people were divided in their views, the cacophony of conflicting opinions did more harm to Becker's position than to theirs.

BUT THE WHOLE COUNTRY ISN'T PROTESTANT

Although the most dramatic conflicts between supporters and opponents of the Becker Amendment involved a clash of Protestant perspectives, Catholic and Jewish spokespersons also lent their voices to the debate. (Members of other faiths did not become a factor in school-prayer hearings until the late twentieth century; see Chapter Fifteen.) The only Catholic bishop to speak at the hearings was Fulton J. Sheen, Auxiliary Bishop of New York, best known for a weekly television program largely devoted to anti-Communist speeches. He advocated nondenominational prayer in the public schools but was reluctant to amend the Constitution for this purpose. A similar ambivalence was evident in letters written to the House Judiciary Committee by Catholic bishops who wanted prayer in the public schools but would support the Becker Amendment only if it required that the prayer be nondenominational and that dissenters be excused. Some of them also reintroduced the long-standing argument that if religious observances were permitted in the public schools, there would be no justification for denying public funding to religious schools. Becker himself conducted a survey of the American Catholic bishops, and of the fifty-five who responded, thirty-six supported the amendment, nine opposed it, and the rest were undecided. Despite the almost two-to-one margin in his favor, the poll did not bear out his prediction that the bishops would be unanimous or close to it in supporting the amendment, and Catholics who testified as individuals expressed a wide range of views.

The reaction of Jewish organizations to the Becker Amendment can be summarized very easily: they wanted no part of it. Among their primary concerns were religious divisiveness, the potential ostracism of their children, and the implication that there is no meaningful distinction among different religions. As Leo Pfeffer testified on behalf of the American Jewish Congress, the Spanish Inquisition had murdered Jews who would not convert to Christianity, which hardly supports the notion of a universally shared faith. While acknowledging that majoritarian prayers are considerably less troublesome than the rack or the stake, he asserted that pressure to bow to government-approved religious practices is objectionable in any form. Although a few Jewish individuals expressed pro-amendment sentiments, the overwhelming opposition of the Jewish community could not be denied.

After eighteen days of testimony, support for the Becker Amendment was hopelessly eroded, and only fifteen of the thirty-five Judiciary Committee members remained committed to voting for it. Since its supporters had no interest in forcing a vote, even if they could have done so, it died in committee. Its demise did not, however, signal the end of the battle over *Engel* and *Abington*. Across the Capitol in the Senate, powerful supporters of state-sponsored school prayer were about to undertake their own effort to amend the Constitution.

8

Beware of the Leopard

I do not deny that there may be other well-founded causes for the
hatred which various classes feel toward politicians, but the main
one seems to me that politicians are symbols of the fact that every
class must take every other class into account.

—José Ortega y Gasset

Like the Becker Amendment, which had been sparked by outrage over *Abington v. Schempp,* the next attempt to restore state-sponsored school prayer was
at least partially motivated by an action of the Supreme Court. In this instance,
the catalyst was not that the Court had issued an unpopular decision but that it
had declined to review a controversial lower-court ruling. The cause of the
uproar was a case called *Stein v. Oshinsky,* in which a federal appeals court had
said that school officials cannot be compelled to allow prayer in the classroom
even if it is allegedly initiated by students. When the Supreme Court declined
to intervene, forty-eight of the one hundred U.S. senators co-sponsored a new
proposal to amend the Constitution.

BACK TO NEW YORK AGAIN

The events leading up to *Stein* began in fall 1962 as a reaction to the Supreme
Court's ruling in *Engel v. Vitale.* Outraged by the termination of the Regents'
Prayer, fifteen parents in Whitestone, New York—in Queens, not far from Man-
hattan—set about finding a way to keep prayer in the schools. All of them had
children who were about to enter kindergarten, and they told the teachers that
their children were to recite prayers before their morning and afternoon snacks.
The morning prayer was "'God is great, God is good, and we thank Him for our
food, Amen.'" The afternoon prayer was "'Thank You for the world so sweet /
Thank You for the food we eat / Thank You for the birds that sing / Thank You
God for everything'" (*Stein v. Oshinsky,* 224 F. Supp. 757 [1963], p. 757).

The principal, Elihu Oshinsky, forbade the classroom recitation of the prayers, saying that since the children were only five years old, the teachers would have to prompt them and help them with the words. He also worried about the reactions of other parents, since in his view the anti-*Engel* parents were trying to use their children as a means of making prayer a part of the school day for all kindergarteners. As evidence, he pointed to their demand that the prayers be said in the classroom, not in a separate place to which their children might be taken. As they later stated in their lawsuit, they believed that their children's religious rights included praying aloud in their classmates' presence. They also maintained that this arrangement would not necessarily imply that the teachers approved of the prayers, but Oshinsky questioned whether five-year-olds would understand that.

When the principal's decision was confirmed by the New York City School Board and the New York State Board of Regents, the parents sued Oshinsky and the two boards in federal district court. A child named Kimberly Stein was listed first among the plaintiffs—hence the title *Stein v. Oshinsky*. The parents, who identified themselves as Protestant, Catholic, Jewish, Episcopalian, and Armenian Apostolic, asked the court to require the school authorities "to afford the [children] an opportunity to express their love and affection to Almighty God each day through a prayer, voluntarily offered in their respective class-rooms...and to declare such prayers constitutional" (p. 757). The court obliged, ruling that the prayers were permissible because they did "not involve a State statute requiring the children or personnel to actively engage in or refrain from acknowledging their complete dependence upon God. It is merely a voluntary desire of the children without any coercion or pressure being brought to offer a prayer to the Almighty." With regard to the involvement of school personnel, the court declared that there has to be some cooperation between government and religion or "Municipalities would not be permitted to render police or fire protection to religious groups. Policemen who helped parishioners into their places of worship would violate the Constitution" (p. 759). This being so, the court ruled, the teachers' cooperation in overseeing the prayers was permissible.

The case then went to the Court of Appeals for the Second Circuit,[1] which agreed with the district court that nothing would prevent school officials from allowing such prayers if they wished to do so. Nevertheless, it found, saying that school officials are free to do something does not mean that they are com-pelled to do it. Although the prayers at issue in *Stein* were allegedly student-initiated rather than state-sponsored, the appeals court echoed the reasoning of *Cincinnati v. Minor* (see Chapter Four) and other early decisions indicating that the same authority that empowers school officials to permit prayer also empowers them to decline to do so. Accordingly, the appeals court found that the controlling issue in *Stein* was not the students' religious rights but the locus of control in the public schools. Ironically, this was the same reasoning once used to justify such actions as the expulsion of Bridget Donohoe and the caning of Thomas Wall (see Chapter Three) on the ground that school officials, not parents, have the final word on classroom prayer. What had changed was not the underlying logic of the legal decisions but the attitude of school officials— and courts—toward public-school devotionals. As the *Stein* court observed, "Determination of what is to go on in public schools is primarily for the school authorities. Against the desire of these parents . . . the authorities were entitled to weigh the likely desire of other parents not to have their children present at such prayers, either because the prayers were too religious or not religious enough; and the wisdom of having public educational institutions stick to education and keep out of religion, with all the bickering that intrusion into the latter is likely to produce. The authorities acted well within their powers in concluding that plaintiffs must content themselves with having their children say these prayers before nine or after three" (*Stein v. Oshinsky*, 348 F. 2d 999 [1965], p. 1002).

As a further irony, the decision in *Stein*, though reviled by school-prayer advocates, was entirely consistent with the Becker Amendment. Both of them said that nothing in the Constitution prohibits school prayer, but neither required officials to include it. The difference was that Becker and his supporters assumed that state and local authorities wanted prayer but were being hindered by the federal courts, as was indeed true in many of their home districts. Forced to confront the unwelcome revelation that some school authorities preferred to exclude religious observances, they were faced with an apparent conflict between their support for local control and their desire to have prayer in all schools. Their solution was to assert that states and local districts should be free to make the *right* choices. The logic behind this contention might be expressed thus:

- State and local authorities are sworn to uphold the Constitution.
- The Constitution (as school-prayer advocates interpret it) protects the right of religious people to have organized vocal prayer in the public schools.
- Therefore, it does not violate legitimate state or local authority to say that officials are free to include school prayer but not to exclude it, just as they are free to enforce racial justice but not to deny it.

As Chapters Eleven and Twelve explain, proponents of this view later won some, though not all, of what they wanted. States and local school districts continue to be prohibited from sponsoring or encouraging prayer, but they are also forbidden from interfering with student-initiated vocal prayer during noninstructional periods of the school day. Whether children as young as five are in fact capable of initiating prayer on their own remains in dispute.

BE CAREFUL WHAT YOU PRAY FOR

Since the Supreme Court hears fewer than five percent of the cases it is asked to review, its refusal to consider *Stein* did not necessarily signal agreement with the appeals court's decision; indeed, it is not unusual for the Court to reject two or more cases in which the same issue has been decided in contradictory ways by different courts. Nevertheless, some school-prayer advocates treated the Court's refusal to hear *Stein* as if it were an explicit denial of the students' right to pray voluntarily. The combined result of *Engel, Abington,* and *Stein,* they alleged, loaded the dice against prayer because school officials were forbidden to encourage it but were free to inhibit it even when it was constitutionally permissible.

People who cringed at the thought of little children being forbidden to say what became known as "milk and cookie prayers" found an influential spokesman in Senator Everett Dirksen (R-Illinois), who was then minority leader of the Senate. "Prayer," he declared, "is the roadmap to God. It should become the greatest adventure for young minds.... This can come only from practice and rehearsal day after day when young minds are alert. How strange that we spend hundreds of millions of public funds every year to develop physical fitness and harden the muscles of American youth, but when it comes to hardening the spiritual muscles through the practice and rehearsal of prayer, it becomes enshrouded in quaint legalism and the jargon of church and state" (*Congressional Record,* March 22, 1966, p. 6478). In order to supersede what he viewed as the Supreme Court's misconstruction of the Constitution, Dirksen introduced a constitutional amendment stating, "Nothing contained in this Constitution shall prohibit the authority administering any school, school system, educational institution or other public building supported in whole or in part through the expenditure of public funds from providing for or permitting the voluntary participation by students or others in prayer. Nothing contained in this article shall authorize any such authority to prescribe the form or content of any prayer" ("School Prayer," p. 1; hereafter "Dirksen hearings").

Determined to avoid the pitfalls that had doomed the Becker Amendment two years earlier, Dirksen kept his proposal relatively simple, omitting the long list of applications that had encumbered the earlier measure. Nevertheless, it drew fire because the very simplicity that was supposed to make it less controversial than the Becker Amendment also created a great deal of uncertainty about exactly what it would accomplish. As an example, "the authority administering any school, school system, educational institution or other public building" could mean the principal, the state or local school board, or the state legislature, and the locus of control would be even less clear in public buildings other than schools. Similarly, there was confusion about how much government activism might be encompassed by "providing for" prayer, and about whether the phrase "students or others" implied that teachers or invited clergy could lead prayers. Perhaps, a spokesperson for the Methodist Church suggested, "any passing religious crackpot could be allowed onto the school premises ... if only some school authority could be prevailed upon to give the necessary permission" (Dirksen hearings, p. 553). The amendment's lack of specificity also alienated some staunch supporters of school prayer, who considered it too weak to accomplish its stated goal. Ostensibly a reaction to *Stein*, it merely provided that nothing in the Constitution prohibited state and local officials from permitting voluntary prayer; it did not require them to do so. As a result, even if it had been in effect when *Stein* was decided, there is no reason to suppose that the outcome would have been different. Dirksen, echoing Representative William Cramer's (R-Florida) objection to "all these nit-picking suggestions" (Becker hearings, p. 357), dismissed these concerns as "just tortured interpretation" and "going around Robin Hood's barn" (Dirksen hearings, p. 13).

In an effort to garner public support for the amendment, Dirksen gave numerous speeches about the need to turn back the tide of secularization that prevented schoolchildren from engaging in voluntary worship. "[I]f their parents want them to utter a little prayer," he pleaded during a television talk show, "let there be a little corner, a little space, a little vestibule, a little room, I don't care what it is. Take them on top of the roof of the school building if they like or down in the deepest basement of the school, but wherever it is, let them, of course, keep that connection and never cut that pipeline [to God]" (Laubach, 1969, p. 142). Like the phrase "milk and cookie prayers," this suggested something so minimal and innocent that only the most rabidly antireligious curmudgeon would have the heart to refuse. Nevertheless, it is interesting to speculate about the probable reaction of Dirksen and other school-prayer supporters if children who asked to pray were in fact sent down to the basement or put out on the roof with the pigeons. Indeed, the plaintiffs in *Stein* had rejected the suggestion of a separate room for prayer; the whole point of the lawsuit was their demand to have their children pray aloud in the classroom in the presence of the other students.

LET THE GAMES BEGIN

Dirksen's proposal was referred to the Senate Judiciary Committee and from there to the Subcommittee on Constitutional Amendments, whose chairperson, Senator Birch Bayh (D-Indiana), was a determined opponent of state-sponsored school prayer. Nevertheless, Dirksen was not only the minority leader but also the ranking Republican on both the Judiciary Committee and Bayh's subcommittee, and he had persuaded forty-seven of his Senate colleagues to sign on as co-sponsors. Since Bayh could not simply bury an amendment that had so much support, he lost no time in announcing that he would hold hearings, thus frustrating an attempt by Dirksen to bypass the subcommittee and get his proposal on a fast track to a Senate vote. Bayh then set about reprising the role Celler had played in the House two years earlier, orchestrating hearings designed to bring out the ambiguities and weaknesses of the proposal.

Compared with Celler's tour de force, the Dirksen Amendment hearings, which took only a week, were over in a flash. Forty-two witnesses were heard, of whom a noticeable but not indecent majority favored Bayh's point of view. Since the Becker hearings had taken place so recently, many of the same witnesses were called to testify again, and the two sets of hearings were largely repetitious. Nevertheless, one new issue that emerged during the Dirksen hearings deserves mention because of its relevance to later controversies discussed in this book. In addition to making the often-repeated arguments about the inadequacy of opt-out policies, some foes of the amendment went on to suggest that if the government provides an opportunity for people to join voluntarily in majoritarian prayers, then dissenters deserve not only a chance to opt out but also an equal opportunity to say their own prayers or to express nonreligious thoughts. This topic arose when Edward J. Bazarian, the attorney who had represented the plaintiffs in *Stein*, made the tactical error of alleging that the federal courts had burdened the right to voluntary prayer that American students had enjoyed for 150 years. Senator Joseph Tydings (D-Maryland) tartly observed that reading the King James Bible under threat of being beaten or expelled was not what most people meant by "voluntary." Bazarian conceded the point, and Tydings pressed his advantage by asking how the right to voluntary prayer would be upheld for students who did not want to say whatever prayer was selected for use in the school. Even if they were excused from participating in the majoritarian prayer, he inquired, what about their right to say their own prayers? At the time, his purpose was to challenge what he saw as an attempt to use the students' personal religious rights as a pretext to mask what would really be governmental favoritism toward majoritarian religion. Since then, however, the assertion that the religious liberty of dissenters requires not only an opt-out provision but an equal opportunity to engage in their own prayers has become a major factor in the national debate over religious expression in the public schools, and controversies involving this issue are discussed from Chapter Eleven onward. The same is true of a similar claim regarding the students' right to express secular beliefs, which was introduced into the Dirksen hearings by Robert Alley, whose school-prayer scholarship is mentioned elsewhere in this book. Testifying on behalf of the Virginia Baptist Convention, he maintained that if the government created special forums open exclusively to prayer, as the Dirksen Amendment would have done, it would thereby favor religion over nonreligion and religious speech over secular speech. "[T]he first amendment, which has stood as a protection of all minorities," he protested, "would be limited to the protections of those only who have some religious sentiment. Only the human rights of 'religious' persons would have absolute protection" (p. 566).

VOX POPULI, VOX DEI

At the conclusion of the hearings, the members of Bayh's subcommittee were so divided over the amendment that they sent it to the Judiciary Committee with no recommendation one way or the other. Following a heated debate, the Judiciary Committee voted it down, which would ordinarily have concluded the matter. Dirksen, however, was determined to bring his proposal before the full Senate even without the committee's support. Since the rules of the Senate differ from those of the House,[2] he could not resort to a discharge petition as Becker had done. Instead, he took advantage of a Senate procedure that allows the sponsor of a piece of legislation to ask the Senate to substitute a different bill in its place. Dirksen had introduced a proposal commemorating the anniversary of the United Nations International Children's Emergency Fund, and when it was about to come up for a vote, he persuaded his fellow senators to consider the school-prayer amendment instead.

Addressing the Senate, Dirksen spoke wrathfully of the National Council of Churches, which had led the religious opposition to his amendment as it had to the Becker Amendment two years earlier. In his view, the mainstream clergy who had testified against his amendment were "the social engineers, the panacea hunters, the world savers, and the brittle professors," "a few ivory-towered leaders here who have lost contact with the people of this country" (*Congressional Record,* September 21, 1966, p. 23532). Indeed, he averred, the disregard they displayed for the wishes of the majority—which he habitually referred to as "the common man"—smacked of anti-democracy and thus of Communism. Dirksen, who had supported the anti-Communist crusade of Senator Joseph R. McCarthy (R-Wisconsin) a decade earlier, went on to castigate the NCC for supporting the admission of Communist China into the United Nations. "I want to establish the fact that these social engineers have been giving too much time to things like the recognition of China instead of to a little soul saving," he said. "We might not have some of the [civil rights] riots in this country if we had prayer in schools and a little more religious tradition." He went on to make an emotional appeal suggesting that eliminating school prayer would replace wholesome American traditions with sterile Soviet atheism. "[B]rutal cynicism is on the march in this country today," he declaimed, "rivaled only by the efforts made in the Soviet Union where they eliminated Santa Claus and called him 'Grandfather Frost.' Will that satisfy the children of America? Will it? Will that enrich them? Will that inspire them? Will that bring animation and happiness to their little faces, and warmth to the hearts of their parents in the wintertime? This I have got to see" (*Congressional Record,* September 19, 1966, pp. 23069, 23078).

BY BAYH

Obviously, anything equated with the common man and Santa Claus is hard to oppose, and with the election of 1966 approaching, senators were under a great deal of pressure to defend school prayer. To give wavering senators an alternate way to show their support for religious values, Bayh introduced a "sense of Congress" resolution—a type of legislation that indicates Congress's sentiments on a particular subject but has no binding legal force. It stated, "[I]t is the sense of the Congress that nothing in the Constitution or the Supreme Court decisions relating to religious practices in our public schools prohibits local school officials from permitting individual students to engage in *silent,* voluntary prayer or meditation" (*Congressional Record,* September 20, 1966, p. 23161; emphasis added). The question of silent prayer had arisen in both the Becker and Dirksen hearings, where school-prayer supporters had emphatically rejected it. In response to Bayh's proposed resolution, Dirksen protested that "the purpose of prayer is to articulate it and fashion a bond of communion with the Almighty, who has had such a high place in American history. Well, this does not do it." He also objected to Bayh's deference to local education authorities. "You have gone right back to the school officials. You have set-tled exactly nothing," he told Bayh. "So school officials become the arbiters. That is precisely what we are quarreling about, because Mr. Oshinsky, the principal of the school in New York, notwithstanding there was voluntary prayer, called in all teachers and said: 'No prayer of any kind'" (*Congressional Record,* September 21, 1966, p. 23533). These statements were perplexing because his own amendment said merely that nothing in the Constitution prohibited school officials from permitting prayer, which appeared to leave the matter up to them—which is exactly what the decision in *Stein v. Oshinsky* had said. Nat-urally, Dirksen's opponents suggested that his remarks to Bayh raised suspi-cions about the true intent of his amendment, since he seemed to assume that it would—perhaps in conjunction with political activism by school-prayer advo-cates—effectively force all schools to have religious observances. In the end, Bayh's resolution failed, and the Dirksen Amendment received a simple major-ity of votes but not the two-thirds needed for a constitutional amendment.

Determined to try again, Dirksen reserved the number "Senate Joint Resolu-tion No. 1" so that school prayer would be the first item on record for the congres-sional session beginning in 1967. His new amendment stated, "Nothing in this Constitution shall abridge the right of persons lawfully assembled in any public building which is supported in whole or in part through the expenditure of public funds, to participate in non-denominational prayer." Unlike Dirksen 1, Dirksen 2 did not even mention school officials but focused on the rights of people who wanted to pray, so that under this version the outcome of *Stein* would unquestion-ably have been different. Dirksen 2 also specified nondenominational prayer, which pleased some people and antagonized others. In the ensuing furor, Dirk-sen replaced "nondenominational prayer" with "private, voluntary prayer," but that was generally rejected as being too close to what was already permitted. Absent strong support for Dirksen 2, the Senate took no action on it.

For a few years after the demise of Dirksen 2, members of both Houses of Congress introduced one school-prayer proposal after another, but to no avail. Among the sponsors of such measures was future president George Bush (R-Texas), then serving in the House. "I believe," he said, "that there can be no morals without religion, hence some religious content is necessary for the schools to fulfill our expectations" (*Congressional Record,* February 7, 1968, p. 2407). Nevertheless, although there was certainly no shortage of proposals to choose from, neither the House nor the Senate showed much interest in debating a school-prayer amendment.

The catalyst that shook Congress out of its lethargy with regard to school prayer was an Ohio homemaker, Mrs. Ben Ruhlin. Fearing for the morals of her teenage sons and their friends, Ruhlin consulted her congressional representative, William Ayres (R-Ohio), about counteracting what she saw as the offensive secularism of the public schools. Acting on Ayres's advice, she spent six thousand dollars on newspaper advertisements asking people all over the country to write to the House Judiciary Committee in support of a constitutional amendment. She also met with the chairpersons of the House and Senate Judiciary Committees and formed a lobbying group, the Prayer Campaign Committee. Among the issues she emphasized was yet another federal court decision, *DeSpain v. DeKalb County Community School District*, which in some ways was *Stein* in reverse. In *Stein*, the plaintiff parents wanted school officials to allow kindergarten children to pray even if the teachers had to help them; in *DeSpain*, school officials permitted teacher-led kindergarten prayers, and the plaintiff parents sued to stop them.

STEIN AGAIN, BACKWARDS

When the son of Lyle and Mary DeSpain started kindergarten in DeKalb County, Illinois, his parents were irritated to learn that his kindergarten teacher was requiring the children to recite a daily prayer: "'We thank you for the flowers so sweet; / We thank you for the food we eat; / We thank you for the birds that sing; / We thank you [God] for everything'" (*DeSpain v. DeKalb County Community School District*, 255 F. Supp. 655 [1966], p. 655). The DeSpains threatened legal action, whereupon the teacher dropped the word "God" but left the rest of the language intact. According to the DeSpains' complaint, she continued to require the children to recite the statement every day and "to fold their hands in their laps, close their eyes and assume a traditional devotional and prayerful attitude immediately prior to its recitation" (pp. 655–56). School officials refused to intervene, and the DeSpains filed a federal lawsuit alleging that this part of the daily routine was a state-sponsored supplication to a divinity even if none were named. The school authorities replied that the recitation had a secular purpose because the verses were meant "to instill in the child his place in society and the community and to inculcate good manners, graciousness, and gratefulness into his character. The many exhibits indicate that through verse, the child is taught to realize his dependence upon tradespeople who serve him: the milkman, the mailman, the plumber, and similar occupations.... He is taught politeness: to say thanks, pardon me, etc." (p. 656). As to the posture the children were required to adopt, the school officials explained that "The child is instructed in 'finger exercises'" and "The gesture is made for the practical purpose of preventing one child partaking of his food before another does so and from spilling the milk or dropping the crackers" (p. 656).

The federal district court agreed with the teacher and the school officials, going so far as to express regret that they had been troubled with a lawsuit over a minor matter that could easily have been settled by mutual agreement had the plaintiffs been more reasonable. The Court of Appeals for the Seventh Circuit overturned this decision, finding "that the verse is a prayer and that its compulsory recitation by kindergarten students in a public school comes within the proscription of the first amendment, as interpreted by the Supreme Court in the 'school prayer' cases" (*DeSpain v. DeKalb County*, 384 F. 2d 836 [1967], p. 837). With regard to alleged secular purposes, the decision stated, "The fact, however, that children through the use of required schoolroom prayer are likely to become more grateful for the things they receive or that they may become better citizens does not justify the use of compulsory prayer in our public school systems" (p. 839). The appeals court acknowledged that the verses were "as innocuous as could be insofar as constituting an imposition of religious tenets upon nonbelievers. The plaintiffs have forced the constitutional issue to its outer limits" (p. 840). Nevertheless, the court found, governmental neutrality toward religion did not permit the compulsory recitation of any prayer in a public school, no matter how generic or appealing it might be. As it had done in *Stein*, the Supreme Court declined to hear an appeal.

DIRKSEN REDIVIVUS

The outcome of *DeSpain* provided ammunition for Ruhlin's newly formed Prayer Campaign Committee (PCC), which set out to convince Congress that the time was ripe for another attempt at a school-prayer amendment. These efforts suffered a brief setback when Representative Ayres lost his seat in the election of 1970, but his role was soon filled by Representative Chalmers Wylie (R-Ohio), who introduced a school-prayer amendment identical to Dirksen 2. It went to the House Judiciary Committee, where Chairman Emanuel Celler (D–New York) added it to the pile of school-prayer proposals about which he intended to do nothing. Years later, Wylie reminisced about his efforts to persuade Celler to take his proposal seriously, including threatening to file a discharge petition as Becker had done. "Well," Wylie recalled, "Chairman Celler in his inimitable way put his arm around my shoulder and he said, 'My boy, that is provided for within the rules of the House.' Well, he had thrown down the gauntlet, in fact, and I did file my discharge petition" (*Congressional Record*, March 5, 1984, p. 4421).

If that scene did take place as Wylie recalled it, Celler soon had cause to regret his insouciance. A survey conducted by the PCC showed that more than half of the members of the House would support a discharge petition, which would allow the House to bypass Celler's committee and proceed to a vote on the amendment. As soon as Wiley filed the petition, the PCC began contacting the representatives who had promised to sign it. Those who delayed too long received visits from irate constituents, and throughout the summer of 1971, the National Association of Evangelicals and several smaller organizations worked with the PCC to demand that representatives who had responded affirmatively to the survey must keep their word. This effort received valuable publicity courtesy of Project Prayer, a celebrity organization headed by singer Pat Boone. Its members included Ginger Rogers, Gloria Swanson, Danny Thomas, and John Wayne, but by far its most prominent participant was future president Ronald Reagan, a former head of the Screen Actors Guild.

As they had done in response to the Becker Amendment, anti-amendment advocacy groups delayed organizing because they did not think that Wylie's proposal would ever emerge from the House Judiciary Committee. By September, however, the discharge petition had so many signatures that the Baptist Joint Committee on Public Affairs, which had been active in the anti-Becker clergy coalition, drafted a statement opposing the Wylie Amendment. Among the religious groups that endorsed the statement were eight Baptist conventions, the Lutheran Church in America, the Presbyterian Church in the U.S.A., the United Presbyterian Church, the Church of the Brethren, the Friends Committee on National Legislation, the Episcopal Church, the United Church of Christ, the Synagogue Council of America, the National Jewish Community Relations Advisory Council, the Unitarian-Universalist Association, and the United Methodist Church. The statement was hand-delivered to all the House members, but it was too little, too late. Within a week of its distribution, Wylie announced that 111 Republicans and 107 Democrats had signed his petition, giving him the 218 names he needed.

Wylie followed up on this success by urging his colleagues to show that they were on God's side by voting for his amendment. This long-standing equation of state-sponsored school prayer with love of God had lost none of its power; as a House staffer told the *Congressional Quarterly,* "'It's just very difficult to explain a vote against prayer. If you are voting strictly on political considerations, you vote for it'" ("School Prayer: Pressures Mount As House Vote Nears," November 6, 1971, p. 2295). In an effort to reassure representatives that they "would not be committing political suicide by voting against a prayer amendment" (p. 2294), Celler joined several religious leaders, including the president of the Southern Baptist Convention, in a press conference spotlighting religious opposition to the Wylie Amendment. He also announced the formation of an ad hoc group, the Congressional Committee to Preserve Religious Freedom (CCPRF), made up of sixty-seven anti-amendment representatives: fifty-nine Democrats and eight Republicans. Interestingly, the CCPRF included some representatives who had signed the discharge petition. Their explanation for this apparent inconsistency was that they wanted the matter to come up for a vote (hence the petition) but did not want it to pass (hence the CCPRF). This development worried Wylie, Ruhlin, and their associates because although the discharge petition required only a simple majority, the amendment itself needed a two-thirds vote to pass. As they struggled to attract additional votes over and above those representatives who had signed the petition, the prospect of losing some of the signers was cause for concern.

DOWN IN THE CELLER

Although Wylie's discharge petition had received its crucial 218th signature in September, it was not acted upon until November. The reason for the delay was that several generations of House leaders, who detested having their control of the agenda superseded by discharge petitions, had developed rules making this procedure cumbersome in the extreme. An analogy may be found in *The Hitchhiker's Guide to the Galaxy*, a science fiction novel by Douglas Adams. (Anyone who would contend that there can be no comparison between science fiction and politics has not been paying attention.) In the novel, a recalcitrant local council, forced to make its plans for a highway bypass available to the public, selects as a display area an unlighted basement with no stairs leading to it. The documents are then placed in the bottom drawer of a locked filing cabinet in an unused bathroom with a sign on the door saying "Beware of the Leopard." The House rules governing discharge petitions appear to have been conceived in the same spirit.

To begin with, no discharge petition can be filed until the relevant committee has had the legislation for thirty legislative days. Even if this meant thirty working days when Congress is in session, it would represent a minimum delay of more than a month. A legislative day, however, begins when the House comes back into session after an adjournment and continues until the House adjourns again. This period may be a single day, but it may also be several days or, on rare occasions, weeks. Then, after a discharge petition has received the required signatures, its sponsor must wait for seven more legislative days before asking to have it considered by the full House, which can be done only on the second or fourth Monday of the month. Since Congress is often out of session on Mondays and Fridays to allow members to spend long weekends in their home districts, months may pass between a discharge petition's endorsement by 218 members and its consideration by the House.

When Wylie's opportunity to call for a vote on his discharge petition finally arrived, he offered as evidence of popular support a poll that had recently been conducted by the *National Enquirer*. The *Enquirer* editors had invited readers to express their views about the proposal and had published pro-amendment pleas from Wylie and Senator Strom Thurmond (R–South Carolina). More than fifty thousand responses had been received within a two-week period, Wylie announced, 92.6 percent of which favored his amendment. "This, Mr. Speaker," Wylie crowed, "is no piddling poll" (*Congressional Record,* November 2, 1971, p. 38719). A similar deference to majority sentiment was expressed by several of his colleagues, notably Representative Gillespie (Sonny) Montgomery (D-Mississippi), who declared with remarkable candor,

> Most Americans are not interested in the arguments about whether or not the prayer amendment will change the Bill of Rights or weaken the Constitution. What the American people are interested in is that the Supreme Court has restricted prayer in public schools and they do not like it one bit. If the people want voluntary prayer in the public schools and we represent the people, then I think we should approve this resolution. Let us lay our cards on the table. A vote for the proposed constitutional amendment is going to be a lot easier to explain back home than a vote against it. I know that if I vote against the resolution today, my opponent next year will make me do a lot of explaining. (*Congressional Record,* November 8, 1971, p. 39890)

WHAT'S IN A WORD

Despite these attempts to focus attention on the popularity of school prayer, Wylie—like Becker and Dirksen before him—was called upon to defend not only the rationale of his proposal but also its specific provisions. One bone of contention was the phrase "lawfully assembled," originally inserted by Dirksen to avoid aiding the pray-ins, kneel-ins, and other religion-related demonstrations then taking place as part of the civil rights movement. Representative Frederick Schwengel (R-Iowa) was one of several representatives who protested that if that phrase were not carefully defined, government officials could use it to void the religious rights of unpopular sects merely by declaring that they were unlawfully assembled. He also questioned how unlawful assembly could affect anyone's constitutional right to freedom of religion, since it would be out of all proportion for such mild misbehavior to result in the loss of a fundamental liberty. In response to the claim that the Wylie Amendment would not change the First Amendment, he scoffed, "This reminds me of the man who was caught in bed with another man's wife. He sat right up in bed and denied it" (*Congressional Record,* November 4, 1971, p. 39384).

Of all the words in the Wylie Amendment, perhaps the most contentious was "non-denominational," which alienated school-prayer advocates who wanted children to read the Bible and pray in the name of Jesus. It was unlikely that the courts would regard such practices as nondenominational, as they had done in the nineteenth century, and some people feared that school prayer might be limited to bland, one-size-fits-all formulations. In an effort to allay these concerns, Wylie sent a long letter to Representative Sam Gibbons (D-Florida), who read it into the *Congressional Record.* "'What is a nondenominational prayer,'" Wylie wrote, "'is not the kind of question which requires a uniform national solution.'" Each community, he suggested, would be free to design prayers reflecting its own religious makeup. Diverse urban areas would no doubt use broadly nondenominational prayers, if any, but that would not prevent more homogeneous districts from taking into account only those faiths represented in their own schools. According to Wylie's letter, local officials would be able to decide whether praying in the name of Jesus was to be deemed denominational or nondenominational. Even sectarian prayers would be permissible if members of different faiths took turns, since each prayer "could be nondenominational in the context of the overall school program even if it would be regarded as sectarian if considered in isolation" (*Congressional Record,* November 2, 1971, p. 38694).

Opponents of the amendment pointed out that nothing Wylie said would be binding on the courts, which are free to use their own discretion about how much weight to place on the statements of legislators. In light of what the courts had done in the past, they predicted that "nondenominational" would be interpreted so broadly that any meaningful prayer would be disqualified. As it was intended to do, this rebuttal to Wylie's claims scared off some potential supporters of the amendment, who worried about the possible legal consequences of including the word "nondenominational." It also provided an unusual opportunity for adamant foes of state-sponsored school prayer to talk about how deeply religious they were. "Prayer is a private thing between a man and his God," declared Representative Abner Mikva (D-Illinois), "and my God is not nondenominational, and neither is yours. I do not want my children's prayers to start out 'To Whom It May Concern'" (*Congressional Record*, November 4, 1971, p. 39425). Representative Edward Boland (D-Massachusetts) took a slightly different approach by asking his colleagues to imagine that Shintoism were the dominant religion of America and that the Shinto majority voted to "compose a prayer and stipulate that your children must dutifully and docilely recite it each schoolday.... Would you consider it religious freedom even if the prayer is nondenominational—that is, vague enough to avoid quarrelsome disputes among Shinto sects but still alien to you?" (*Congressional Record*, November 8, 1971, p. 39927).

Perhaps the most serious blow to the provision for nondenominational prayer was struck by the U.S. Catholic Conference (USCC), which represents the American Catholic bishops. Those bishops who had commented on earlier school-prayer bills had not opposed nondenominational worship—indeed, some had made it a condition of their support—but the Wylie Amendment was different because it was not limited to public schools. Its provisions extended to all tax-supported buildings, including places like hospitals and memorials where denominational prayer was already allowed. In its attempt to cover as much ground as possible, the amendment seemed likely to trigger the law of unintended consequences; as the USCC explained in a letter to the House Judiciary Committee, it could inadvertently "'represent a threat to the existing legality of denominational prayer'" in some public buildings (*Congressional Record*, November 8, 1971, p. 39895). A related consideration for the USCC was that Catholic schools received tax support for such things as textbooks, transportation, and lunches for low-income students, and the bishops hoped that in the future the government might provide more direct funding for religious schools. If the amendment passed, and the Catholic Church accepted tax money for its schools, then prayer in those schools would arguably have to be nondenominational. A report prepared for Congress by the Legislative Research Service supported the bishops' arguments, cautioning that the wording of the amendment could indeed cause it to apply to parochial schools receiving public funds, thus inadvertently excluding Catholic prayers from Catholic schools.

After days of contentious debate, the House voted on whether to discharge the Judiciary Committee from further consideration of the Wylie Amendment. That motion, which required only a simple majority, passed. When the House went on to vote on the Wylie Amendment itself, the tally was 240 yea,

163 nay, and 27 not voting—twenty-eight votes short of the two-thirds required for passage. Sixteen representatives who had signed the discharge petition voted against the amendment, and twelve others were absent, which added up to the twenty-eight votes by which it had failed. Not surprisingly, Ruhlin and the PCC were particularly infuriated with those representatives, feeling that they had tried to reap the political benefit of appearing to support the amendment without actually doing so. She and her supporters repeatedly tried to get another vote, but for more than a decade there was no effective movement toward a school-prayer amendment.

GORDIAN KNOT

Although each of the amendments discussed in this chapter and the previous one presented some distinctive features, all of them fell victim to the same underlying problem. As long as the discussion remained at the level of "Who wants to be on God's side," support for state-sponsored school prayer appeared to be unbeatably strong. It invariably fragmented, however, in relation to any proposal that included *this* word instead of *that* word, one provision but not another. While some of the blame may have rested with the drafters, this divisiveness also reflected the reality that not enough Americans agreed on any particular form of school prayer to meet the high standards of a constitutional amendment. By the time the language had been softened enough to reassure people who feared government intrusion into religious matters, there was too little substance left to satisfy those who wanted to restore Christian prayers to the public schools.

As the Dirksen and Wylie Amendments demonstrated, it was possible to garner a simple majority of votes for a school-prayer proposal, but the two-thirds supermajority proved frustratingly elusive. Facing the near certainty that their hope of amending the Constitution was not going to be fulfilled, advocates of state-sponsored school prayer began to experiment with a variety of legislative strategies aimed at restoring total control over that issue to the states. Their goal was to find a way to exclude federal agencies, particularly the courts, from participating in disputes over religion in the public schools.

9
Full Court Press

If there are such things as political axioms, the propriety of the judicial power of a government being coextensive with its legislative may
be ranked among the number. The mere necessity of uniformity in
the interpretation of the national laws decides the question. Thirteen
independent courts of final jurisdiction over the same causes, arising
upon the same laws, is a hydra in government from which nothing
but contradiction and confusion can proceed.

—*Alexander Hamilton*

The successive defeats of the Becker, Dirksen, and Wylie Amendments left
advocates of state-sponsored school prayer 0 for 3, and the death of Senator
Everett Dirksen (R-Illinois) in 1969 deprived them of a powerful champion.
That void was filled when Senator Jesse Helms (R–North Carolina), first elected
in 1972, emerged as the leader of an effort to insert school-prayer provisions
into all sorts of legislation, from a bill on the permissible size of the national
debt to a constitutional amendment on equal rights for women. Although these
attempts usually failed, they forced opponents to keep "voting against God," and
they prevented the ban on school-organized prayer from being shrugged off as a
fait accompli.

Among the bills most likely to become vehicles for school-prayer amendments are those involving the so-called power of the purse—Congress's control over the distribution of federal funds. Every year, Congress appropriates
money to keep federal departments and agencies running, and this legislation
routinely sets limits on the ways in which the funds may be spent; for
instance, the federal funds allotted to welfare programs cannot be used to pay
for abortions. Such provisions require only a simple majority vote, and in
most instances they are defensible in court because they do not require or prohibit any action but merely specify what use may be made of the funds in a

particular appropriations bill. Throughout his thirty years in the Senate, Helms made a practice of introducing legislation to prohibit various federal agencies from using their funds to enforce bans on school prayer, and since his retirement in 2002, other senators have continued to follow that example. Many of these proposals are purely symbolic because the money would not have been used for that purpose in any event; for instance, since fiscal year 1981, appropriations bills funding the U.S. Department of Education have stated that the money cannot be used "to prevent the implementation of programs of voluntary prayer and meditation in the public schools" (Public Law 106–554, Title III, Section 303). This tactic is by no means peculiar to school prayer; as an example, the Department of Education is also forbidden to pay "for the transportation of students or teachers . . . in order to carry out a plan of racial desegregation" (Section 301). Such provisions tend to pass easily because they have no practical effect, as it is not the Department of Education but states and school districts that establish policies for school prayer and local school transportation. Since the appropriations process is inherently contentious and delicate, senators who oppose these measures in principle are rarely willing to expend political capital on a prolonged fight over something that makes no real difference.

More troubling to opponents of state-sponsored school prayer are efforts to amend appropriations bills affecting the federal courts. An early example arose in 1981, when Senator Lowell Weicker (R-Connecticut) led the fight against a bill that included the words, "No funds appropriated under this act may be used to prevent the implementation of programs of voluntary prayer and meditation in the public schools" (*Congressional Record,* November 16, 1981, p. 27491). Since the "funds appropriated under this act" included the operating budgets of the federal courts, that provision could have been interpreted to mean that the courts would not be authorized to incur the expense of hearing school-prayer cases. To be sure, any such regulation might have been found unconstitutional, but it would at the very least have caused confusion. Weicker, admonishing his colleagues not to "come out here and try to slap this stuff on appropriations bills," protested that "the appropriations process has been brought to a dead halt by this type of social legislation" (*Congressional Record,* November 18, 1981, p. 27896). When prolonged debate failed to resolve the matter to his satisfaction, he refused to let the bill out of the subcommittee he chaired, and the funds were supplied through a different mechanism. Attempts to include school-prayer language in Justice Department appropriations bills in subsequent years were similarly unsuccessful.

THE BATTLE OF ARTICLE III

Although it is open to debate whether an appropriations bill could be used to prevent the federal courts from hearing school-prayer cases, there can be no doubt that that goal is dear to the hearts of those who advocate a return to state-sponsored school prayer. As a matter of principle, they believe that each state should be able to enact its own policies on religion without intervention by the federal courts. From a practical perspective, the whole point of their efforts is to restore traditional public-school devotionals that are inherently incompatible with the Supreme Court's rulings. Since any school-prayer policy that went far enough to satisfy them would be doomed the moment it reached a federal court, their best chance of achieving their aim would be to deprive those courts of jurisdiction over cases involving religion in the public schools.

As matters now stand, anyone who has a complaint about school prayer can file a lawsuit in either state or federal court, and no matter which route is chosen, any dissatisfied party can ask the U.S. Supreme Court to hear an appeal. Advocates of state-sponsored religious observances want to pass a law requiring all school-prayer lawsuits to be filed in state courts and prohibiting the Supreme Court from hearing any appeals in such cases. Only thus would it be possible to restore the pre-1930s status quo described in Chapter Four, under which state courts had sole responsibility for deciding school-prayer lawsuits.

These highly controversial attempts to deprive the federal courts of authority to decide school-prayer cases—colloquially known as "court-stripping"[1]—are based on Article III of the Constitution. The relevant portions state:

> The judicial power of the United States, shall be vested in one Supreme Court, and in such inferior courts as the Congress may from time to time ordain and establish.... The judicial power shall extend to all cases, in law and equity, arising under this Constitution, the laws of the United States and treaties made, or which shall be made, under their authority.... In all cases affecting ambassadors, other public ministers and consuls, and those in which a state shall be party, the Supreme Court shall have original jurisdiction. In all the other cases before mentioned, the Supreme Court shall have appellate jurisdiction, both as to law and fact, with such exceptions, and under such regulations as the Congress shall make.

In accord with Article III, only the Supreme Court was established by the Constitution. All other federal courts were set up by Congress, which retains some degree of control over them—exactly how much is the subject of considerable dispute. Advocates of court-stripping maintain that Congress's power over the lower federal courts includes the authority to prohibit them from hearing lawsuits on certain topics, such as school prayer. Their opponents disagree, of course, but even if court-stripping supporters won that argument, it would be a hollow victory. If the lower federal courts could not hear school-prayer cases and all such lawsuits were forced into state courts, the federal judiciary would still have the final word as long as the U.S. Supreme Court retains its power to reverse state-court decisions. The only way to give the states total control over school prayer would be to move all such cases into the state courts *and* prevent the Supreme Court from deciding them on appeal. Advocates of court-stripping claim that it would indeed be possible to do this because Article III's statement that the Supreme Court has the authority to hear appeals "with such exceptions, and under such regulations as the Congress shall make" means that Congress could tell the Court not to review any decisions involving a particular topic, such as school prayer.

When, in 1974, Helms and his allies undertook a concerted effort to neutralize the power of the federal judiciary and thus place school prayer once again under the sole authority of the states, they were by no means breaking new ground. Proposals to curtail the authority of the federal courts had been made many times in U.S. history, notably during the post–Civil War period and the New Deal. Among more recent examples, Dirksen had attempted in 1969 to revoke the federal courts' power to reverse jury verdicts involving the definition of obscenity, and three years later a proposal to prevent the federal courts from ruling on mandatory desegregation busing had failed in the Senate by one vote. Following in the tradition of these earlier attempts, Helms's court-stripping proposal stated, "[T]he Supreme Court shall not have jurisdiction to review, by appeal, writ of certiorari, or otherwise, any case arising out of... any Act interpreting, applying, or enforcing a State statute, ordinance, rule, or regulation, which relates to voluntary prayers in public schools and public buildings." To remove the option of filing school-prayer cases in the lower federal courts, it also stipulated that "[T]he district courts shall not have jurisdiction of any case or question which the Supreme Court does not have jurisdiction to review" (*Congressional Record,* September 11, 1974, p. 30721).

Helms's proposal, which would prevent any federal court from deciding cases involving either the wording of a state school-prayer law or the manner in which it is carried out, was referred to the Senate Judiciary Committee. Chairman Strom Thurmond (R–South Carolina) was a co-sponsor, but even so the committee did not act on it that year—or the next, or the next. For almost five years, Helms and other court-stripping advocates introduced the same proposal over and over without generating so much as a serious debate about it. Then in 1979, when the Senate was considering President Jimmy Carter's proposal to create the U.S. Department of Education, Helms suddenly rose and asked the Senate to attach his court-stripping language as an amendment to the Department of Education bill. To the shock and dismay of Carter's supporters, the Senate did so.

MINUET IN D MAJOR

No doubt Helms's success owed more to the unpopularity of the Carter plan, even among some Democrats, than to any sudden upsurge in support for court-stripping. Nonetheless, this unexpected victory placed him and his associates in an enviable situation. At the very least, school prayer would be a major focus of debate when the legislation went to the House of Representatives and perhaps in any subsequent conference held to reconcile the House and Senate versions of the bill. In the unlikely event that the legislation passed both Houses with the court-stripping provision still attached, Carter would face an uncomfortable choice. If he signed it, the whole bill—including the removal of the federal courts' jurisdiction over school-prayer cases—would become law. If he vetoed it because of that provision, his highly publicized plan to form a Department of Education would fail, and he would be marked as a foe of school prayer.

Senate Majority Leader Robert Byrd (D–West Virginia) led the effort to remove the Helms language from the Department of Education bill before it went to the House of Representatives. After several days of arm-twisting and parliamentary maneuvering that rivaled Emanuel Celler (D–New York) at his best, Byrd and his allies managed to reopen the topic for further consideration. During the subsequent debate, several supporters of the Carter plan complained about the unexpectedness with which Helms had interjected the court-stripping measure into the Department of Education debate, although they must have known that it would come up. It had, after all, been proposed on every conceivable occasion for the past five years, so they could hardly claim to be flabbergasted by its appearance during a debate about public education. What they were objecting to was that they had not known exactly *when* it would arise and had thus been unprepared to respond effectively.

Over the years, Helms developed such skill at using this tactic, which his foes described as "legislation by ambush," that it became his hallmark. On the other side of the aisle, Senator Edward Kennedy (D-Massachusetts) often took the lead in countering Helms's efforts. In an interview for this book, a former Helms staffer recalled how he used to bring his "briefing book"—a thick blue looseleaf binder containing information that might be needed during a debate—into the Senate chamber whenever Helms was about to introduce a proposal. After a while, he noticed that Kennedy seemed to be acquiring an uncanny knack for arriving just in time to foil Helms's surprise moves. Suspecting that Kennedy's aides had figured out what the appearance of the big blue book signified, he formed the habit of carrying it with him everywhere, including the men's room. This account was confirmed in an interview with a longtime Kennedy staffer. When asked how Kennedy's aides knew when Helms was about to propose legislation, he began his reply with the words, "Do you know what a briefing book is?"

Kennedy had not been present when Helms first introduced his amendment to the Department of Education bill, but when the debate resumed, he carried the bulk of the responsibility for promoting a plan hatched by Carter's supporters. They proposed to remove Helms's court-stripping language from the Department of Education bill and attach it instead to a piece of legislation sponsored by Senator Dennis DeConcini (D-Arizona), who sought to give the Supreme Court greater discretion in selecting the cases it wished to review. Of course, Helms opposed this plan. He had no interest in making it easier for Carter and his allies to create a Department of Education, and he knew that the DeConcini bill was destined for oblivion. Although it seemed likely to pass the Senate, it would then go to the House, where it would be consigned to the dreaded Judiciary Committee. Representative Peter Rodino (D–New Jersey), who had succeeded Celler as committee chairperson, had already stated his opposition to the DeConcini bill. There was, Helms dryly noted, "some question about whether Chairman Rodino ... will bury the DeConcini bill so deep that it will require fourteen bulldozers just to scratch the surface" (*Congressional Record*, April 9, 1979, p. 7630). Nevertheless, he was unable to dissuade the Senate from attaching his amendment to the DeConcini bill and removing it from the Department of Education bill, which subsequently passed both Houses and was signed by President Carter.

OUTRUNNING THE BULLDOZERS

When the DeConcini bill reached the House with Helms's proposal attached, House members who agreed with Helms seized upon the opportunity to request committee hearings on federal court jurisdiction over school prayer. Since the bill had been sent from the House Judiciary Committee to its Subcommittee on Courts, Civil Liberties, and the Administration of Justice, it was not Rodino but the subcommittee chairperson, Representative Robert Kastenmeier (D-Wisconsin), to whom the request for hearings was addressed. Kastenmeier, who was even more adamantly opposed to court-stripping than Rodino was, refused. Court-stripping advocates then followed the time-honored procedure of filing a discharge petition and obtaining enough signatures to show that the issue could not be buried, whereupon Kastenmeier capitulated and held five days of hearings. Feeling that the atmosphere surrounding them had been excessively heated, he conducted additional hearings the following year. At about the same time, Senator Orrin Hatch (R-Utah) also conducted subcommittee hearings on court-stripping. The 1980 and 1981 hearings were not limited to the topic of school prayer; among other things, witnesses proposed curtailing the power of the federal courts to decide cases involving school desegregation, the treatment of women in the military, abortion, legislative redistricting, and certain aspects of criminal law. Faced with such a multiplicity of proposals, witnesses had little choice but to move beyond discussions of school prayer to a more comprehensive consideration of the relationship between Congress and the federal courts. Although some of the testimony was rather technical, it is well worth considering because of the potential impact of court-stripping on the American system of government. As several witnesses explained, the purpose of court-stripping is to increase the majority's power by giving the final say on controversial social issues to elected officials who can be voted out of office. Taken to its extreme, it would give near total control over constitutional law to Congress and the states. This chapter provides a brief summary of the main arguments on both sides of this debate, followed by a consideration of two of the most important questions it raises: If the federal courts were deprived of jurisdiction over certain issues, would the result be a wide variation in the way different states interpret some of the rights guaranteed under the U.S. Constitution? And if so, would that result be good or bad?

ONCE MORE, WITH DETAIL

The View from the Pro-Court-Stripping Side

As noted earlier, court-stripping advocates rely heavily on their interpretation of Article III of the U.S. Constitution, which states, "In all the other cases before mentioned, the Supreme Court shall have appellate jurisdiction, both as to law and fact, *with such exceptions, and under such regulations as the Congress shall make*" (emphasis added). In their view, the italicized words—known as the "Exceptions Clause"—give Congress the power to limit the Supreme Court's authority to hear appeals in any or all cases. Accordingly, they maintain that if Congress were to declare that a particular topic is an exception to the Supreme Court's appellate jurisdiction, then the Court could hear no appeals in cases involving that topic. They further assert that Congress should use this means of curtailing the power of the Supreme Court in order to remedy what they see as its usurpation of power that rightfully belongs to Congress and the states. As this suggests, supporters of court-stripping believe that the federal judicial branch has inappropriately assumed a legislative function by creating new laws under the guise of interpreting the U.S. Constitution, state constitutions, and federal and state statutes. They also maintain that the Constitution is being used as a pretext for protecting alleged rights that it does not in fact cover, such as access to abortion and freedom from racial segregation and from state-sponsored prayer. Indeed, the very fact that the Supreme Court decides cases involving those issues, regardless of what the decisions say, implies that such matters are not wholly under state control but are subject to federal review. To those who believe that the primary purpose of the Constitution is to protect states' rights from federal interference, these actions on the part of the Court have seriously upset the balance of power between the federal government and the states. Since supporters of court-stripping view state legislatures and courts (particularly in states whose judges are elected) as being far more likely than the federal judiciary to carry out the will of the majority, they argue that it is undemocratic and tyrannical to subjugate the majority's representatives to what they consider elitist federal courts.

The View from the Anti-Court-Stripping Side

Opponents of court-stripping deny that the Exceptions Clause gives Congress the power to single out any particular constitutional right and declare that lawsuits involving it are ineligible for review by the Supreme Court. By definition, they assert, an exception is an aberration from a norm, not the destruction of the norm itself. It is thus ridiculous to claim that Congress could remove all the Supreme Court's power to hear cases involving school prayer, for instance, and call that an "exception" to its appellate jurisdiction over school prayer. That result, they assert, would not be an exception to the Court's jurisdiction but its total destruction with respect to school prayer. The Exceptions Clause, as they see it, merely allows Congress to make adjustments to the appeals process, such as DeConcini's proposal to give the Court greater discretion in deciding whether to hear certain appeals. That bill failed, but Congress has on occasion changed the ways in which various kinds of appeals reach the Court. Such changes can have a significant effect on the processing of appeals, but they are a far cry from the near annihilation of the Court's power that the court-strippers' view of Article III would permit.

To foes of court-stripping, it is inconceivable that Article III could have been intended to leave the federal courts almost entirely at the mercy of Congress, as that would be inconsistent with any reasonable balance of power among the three branches of the federal government. If it were true that Congress has the authority to remove all the Supreme Court's appellate jurisdiction at will, they add, then the Court could well be left with little if anything more than its original jurisdiction over a handful of specialized lawsuits. Combined with the other element of the Helms plan—the removal of cases involving certain topics from the lower federal courts—the federal judiciary as a whole would have no power to interpret the Constitution and federal laws in many critical areas. To Helms's foes, it is this prospect rather than the current situation that would represent an imbalance of power among the three branches of the federal government, since it would dramatically weaken the judicial branch. If the Framers had intended to make the federal judiciary so wholly subservient to Congress, they argue, then the Constitution would not provide for unelected federal judges who retain their positions for life except under unusual circumstances. In their view, the whole point of this arrangement is to establish one branch of government that is able to protect minority and majority rights equally, and to interpret and uphold the Constitution, independent of the political passions of the day. They also protest that the accusation that the federal courts have usurped the authority of Congress and the states rests on the assumption that certain cases have been wrongly decided, whereas that is merely the view of people who disagree with those rulings; there is no objective proof that the courts have in fact erred. *Someone* has to have the final word on what the Constitution and the laws mean, and in their view that responsibility should rest with the federal judiciary. Court-stripping plans, they aver, seek to substitute Congress's constitutional and legal interpretations for those of the federal courts, which would make Congress an intruder into the rightful domain of another branch of government.

Wrapup

To some degree, the court-stripping debate is yet another way of addressing the same issues that arose in the early nineteenth-century disputes discussed in Chapters Two and Three, the post–Civil War lawsuits discussed in Chapter Four, the Supreme Court cases discussed in Chapters Five and Six, and the hearings on proposed constitutional amendments discussed in Chapters Seven and Eight. On one side, proponents of court-stripping argue in favor of majority rule, states' rights, populism, and a system of law that fosters traditional beliefs and practices that they view as quintessentially American. To them, the most important imperatives are to vindicate the sovereignty of the states over the power of the federal government, and to subordinate unelected judges with lifetime terms to the authority of legislators and other elected officials who represent the will of the people. On the other side, opponents of court-stripping seek a consistent interpretation of the Constitution guaranteeing certain basic rights to all Americans throughout the country. To them, the point is not to protect the states from the federal government or to save democracy from an elitist oligarchy, but to vindicate the rights of individuals against infringement by any level of government or by the tyranny of the majority.

THE CASE OF THE STATE: WOULD COURT-STRIPPING MAKE A REAL DIFFERENCE TO SCHOOL PRAYER?

In one sense, Helms's proposal might appear pointless because even if the Supreme Court were prevented from hearing any further appeals in school-prayer cases, the state courts would nonetheless be legally obliged to adhere to any decisions the Court had already issued before that prohibition went into effect. Since only the Court itself can overturn or modify its earlier rulings, the law would require all new school-prayer cases to be decided in conformity with *Engel v. Vitale, Abington v. Schempp,* and other existing Supreme Court precedents. This would be true even if a case were heard in state court and even if the Supreme Court could not review it. From this perspective, preventing the Supreme Court from continuing to decide school-prayer cases might be worse than useless because it would eliminate any chance that the Court might overturn a controversial precedent. In the words of Professor Laurence Tribe of Harvard Law School, court-stripping would, at least in theory, "create an ice age in constitutional law, paralyzing the law as of the moment the [court-stripping] laws were enacted, with the State courts not free to develop or change, but free only to parrot what the Supreme Court had done, and indeed to parrot decisions that were the very occasion for these measures" ("Statutory Limits on Federal Jurisdiction," hereafter "1981 House hearings," p. 49). In reality, neither Tribe nor anyone else believed that all state courts would conscientiously adhere to unpopular Supreme Court precedents if the possibility of review by the federal courts were removed. As witnesses on both sides acknowledged, the whole point of the proposed court-stripping legislation was to restore state-sponsored school prayer and other practices that could not take place if the Court's interpretation of the Constitution were followed. The titles, rationales, and plain language of the court-stripping bills, as well as the speeches of their supporters, made it unmistakably clear that the outcome of school-prayer lawsuits in some states was expected to change dramatically once the federal courts were out of the way. The question was not whether state courts would disregard their legal obligation to follow Supreme Court precedents—it was generally assumed that some would—but whether that would be a godsend or a catastrophe.

Opponents of court-stripping, appalled by the prospect of having as many as fifty different interpretations of the U.S. Constitution, argued that the Constitution assigns to the federal courts certain core functions, sometimes called essential functions, that must not be hampered by any use of Article III. Although there are variations in the definition of these functions, they are generally held to include at least three duties: resolving conflicts between federal and state courts about the meaning of the Constitution and federal laws, ensuring that federally guaranteed rights are interpreted uniformly throughout the country, and upholding the sovereignty of federal law over state and local policies. Consistent with this "essential functions" argument, witnesses who opposed court-stripping asserted that the federal judiciary bears the ultimate responsibility for ensuring that all the rights guaranteed by the Constitution are enforced throughout the country. Congress cannot place any specific constitutional right outside the reach of the federal courts, they maintained, because such judicial gerrymandering would create a blacklist of disfavored rights that would be denied the benefit of judicial review that protects those rights of which Congress approves. Professor Tribe, among others, testified that the very notion of picking and choosing which constitutional rights are to be excluded from the federal courts violates the overall sense of the Constitution. "It is," he said, "rather like declaring open season on particular rights, a free fire zone in which people exercising those rights are told, 'You have to stand on your own against hostile and injurious action by State and local officials'" (p. 43). To opponents of court-stripping, it would be meaningless to say that everyone has certain rights under the Constitution if the federal courts were forced to stand idly by while state and local officials violated those rights at will.

By contrast, witnesses who favored court-stripping vehemently denied the need for a single interpretation of the Constitution that would be the same in all states. While acknowledging that people are entitled to their day in court if they believe their rights under the Constitution have been violated, they argued that the state courts are fully capable of serving that function. In fact, they asserted, state courts would do a better job than federal courts because they are more responsive to the wishes of the people. Echoing the populist rhetoric of some witnesses at the Becker and Dirksen hearings, they alleged that the federal courts favor elitists and liberals, who benefit from anti-majoritarian policies. This being so, they suggested, the Supreme Court's misguided interpretations of the Constitution have created such havoc and injustice that disregarding them would be justifiable as an act of self-defense.

PLAY IT AGAIN, JESSE

As expected, the DeConcini bill never emerged from the House Judiciary Committee, nor was any action taken on the court-stripping proposals discussed during the 1980 and 1981 House and Senate hearings. Nevertheless, far from signaling the end of the debate, this lack of closure merely left unresolved the underlying tensions between states' rights and federal authority, and between majoritarianism and individual liberty. These issues resurfaced in another concerted attack on the federal courts, this one launched in 1997, shortly after President William Clinton embarked on his second term of office. Some of his opponents, disturbed by his judicial appointments and critical of the decisions of some federal courts, undertook a massive publicity campaign that coincided with another round of hearings: three in the House and three in the Senate. Although court-stripping was mentioned during these hearings, most of the testimony focused on other methods of curbing the power of the federal judiciary, such as establishing term limits for federal judges, requiring the popular election of federal judges, and blocking the appointment of new judges deemed likely to hand down unpopular decisions. One of the most widely discussed proposals was made by House Majority Whip Tom DeLay (R-Texas), who suggested that the desired results might be achieved by impeaching judges whose decisions conflicted with Congress's view of the Constitution. "'Congress has thrown out judges for being drunk,'" declared DeLay spokesperson Tony Rudy. "'We can't see any reason for not throwing them out for being drunk with power'" (Gil Klein, "Impeachment Move a Stunner: GOP Law-maker Announces Drive Against Federal Judges," *Denver Rocky Mountain News,* March 30, 1997, p. 4A). Defenders of the courts, of course, ridiculed the sug-gestion that unpopular judicial rulings are impeachable offenses. As Professor Herman Schwartz of American University Law School wrote, "Should anyone think that for a judge to displease the GOP majority is not usually considered an impeachable offense, DeLay has asserted 'an impeachable offense is what-ever a majority of the House of Representatives considers it to be at a given moment in history.' DeLay has obviously studied Communist legal practice closely" ("Judge Bashing: Political Partisans Hold Court Appointments Hostage," [Wilmington, Delaware] *News Journal,* July 20, 1997, p. H1). Among those who disagreed with DeLay were many of his fellow conservatives, notably Chief Jus-tice William Rehnquist and Justice Antonin Scalia, who argued against any attempt to weaken judicial independence through ideologically based impeach-ments or by any other means.

As these examples suggest, recent proposals for lessening the power of the federal courts, like those discussed in the 1980s hearings, are based on the belief that federal judges are usurping power that rightfully belongs to Con-gress and the states—an accusation that is now called "judicial activism." This viewpoint was summarized very effectively in a statement by Senator John Ashcroft (R-Missouri), who chaired the 1997 hearings before the Senate Sub-committee on the Constitution, Federalism, and Property Rights. (In 2001, Ashcroft became U.S. attorney general under President George W. Bush.) According to Ashcroft,

> [J]udicial activism strikes at the heart of our system of separation of powers and it represents a real and, I believe, a tangible threat to the people's freedom to govern themselves. When we in the Congress do something that the people don't like ... the people have an opportunity to vote us out of office. The same thing applies to the President, to the State legislatures, Governors, and even to the vast majority of State judges. Not so with the unelected Federal judiciary. Of course, when Federal judges stay within their proper role and interpret the text of the laws that come from Congress or interpret the text of the Constitution, the Federal judiciary safeguards the people's constitutional rights and poses no threat to the freedom of the people. The people can

still address their concerns to the political branches of government.... But when the courts go beyond the text of the laws and
start making law, then there is a real threat to the people's freedom. When individuals who are not elected and can only be
removed with great difficulty are making policy judgments
unguided by a congressional or constitutional text, then the people lose their constitutional rights and the freedom to make their
own decisions and govern their own institutions. ("Judicial
Activism: Defining the Problem and Its Impact," pp. 1–2)

Ashcroft's reiteration of "the people" eight times in as many sentences leaves
no doubt about the populist character of his argument. Like Dirksen's
repeated use of the term "the common man," Ashcroft's phrasing appears to
imply that most Americans—or at least those who deserve consideration—
share his views. His statement sets up a Manichaean contrast between elected
officials who can be removed if they violate the will of "the people," and
appointed federal judges with lifetime tenure who allegedly carry out an elitist
agenda by imposing tyrannical edicts on an unwilling public. Underlying this
argument is the equation of liberty and self-government with the unfettered
rule of "the people."

These themes were repeated in advocacy group mailings that peaked at the
time of the House and Senate hearings in 1997 and 1998. According to
Thomas Jipping, director of the Free Congress Foundation's Judicial Selection
Monitoring Project, "Judicial activism, then, means the American people are
not able to govern themselves. The people should be able to decide issues
such as abortion, school prayer, homosexual rights, education policy, or
pornography. Unless judges stay within their proper role, our liberty remains
at risk" ("America: Governed by Courts—Not 'We the People,'" *TVC Report*,
Summer 1997, p. 7). Similarly, a newsletter written by Phyllis Schlafly declared
that the Supreme Court had overstepped its bounds "in the areas of racial
preferences and quotas, criminal procedures, pornography, forced busing,
prayer and the Ten Commandments in public schools, internal security, and
term limits. The courts have invented new 'rights' such as the right to abortion and to receive welfare payments" ("Congress Must Curb the Imperial
Judiciary," *The Phyllis Schlafly Report*, February 1997, p. 1). As these remarks
indicate, foes of the federal judiciary believe that the majority is entitled to
exercise direct control over certain social issues, including school prayer. This
view is intimately linked to states'-rights activism by the assumption that

states would uphold the majority's wishes if they were not impeded by the federal courts.

THE OTHER TEAM AT BAT

Defenders of the federal judiciary responded to this attack by questioning whether most Americans do indeed favor all the policies their foes described as the will of "the people." They also challenged the rationale that lies at the heart of the anti-court movement: the belief that the correct interpretation of the Constitution must coincide with the will of the majority at any given time. While agreeing that the federal judiciary must function within a democratic process, they asserted that the courts' proper role therein is to make decisions based not on polling data but on a Constitution that contains numerous protections for unpopular minority rights. Roger Pilon, representing the libertarian Cato Institute, explained this viewpoint in his testimony before a House subcommittee: "[T]he problem of 'judicial activism' is seriously misstated when it is cast, as it often is, as involving judges overruling the will of the people. In our legal system, judicial review often requires a judge to do just that. In such a case, were the judge to defer to the political will, exercising 'judicial restraint' when the law requires active judicial intercession, that restraint would itself be a kind of activism, for it would amount to an 'active' failure to apply the law in deference to democratic or majoritarian values. The judge in such circumstances would be shirking his judicial responsibilities every bit as much as if he overrode a legitimate exercise of political will in the name of other values" ("Judicial Misconduct and Discipline," p. 71). Moreover, foes of the anti-court movement pointed out, Congress sometimes passes legislation in which contentious issues are couched in vague or confusing language. When such laws are challenged in federal courts, judges are forced to decide what the ambiguous provisions mean, and anyone who is displeased with the outcome may raise the cry of judicial activism.

Some defenders of the federal courts also went on the offensive, alleging that critics of so-called judicial activism were willfully blind to the transgressions of judges who erred in the conservative interest. Referring to DeLay, attorney Bruce Fein testified, "One Honorable Member of the House of Representatives has avowed that 'I do not advocate impeachment for judges whose opinions [sic] I disagree. I advocate impeachment of those judges who consistently ignore their constitutional role, violate their oath of office and breach the separation of powers.' But his bill of indictment against federal judges cites only rulings with which he disagrees (e.g., decisions that favor abortion rights, pro-choice,

racial preferences, and a judicial power to impose taxes to remedy a constitutional violation)" (p. 35). As examples of conservative judicial activists, Fein
mentioned John Sprizzo, a federal district court judge in New York, and Roy
Moore, then a county court judge in Alabama. (In 2000, Moore was elected
chief justice of the Alabama State Supreme Court; see Chapter Fifteen for a
further discussion of his activities.) According to Fein, Sprizzo

> acquitted two churchmen of their concededly illegal obstructions
> of an abortion clinic because the violations were religiously moti-
> vated, a defense utterly without legal basis. Judge Sprizzo further
> pontificated that judges could decline enforcement of the Consti-
> tution and laws of the United States if obedience would be
> morally unattractive.... [DeLay] has been similarly close-mouthed
> about Judge Roy Moore, an Alabama state judge, who defied
> church–state precedents of the U.S. Supreme Court in posting a
> copy of the Ten Commandments in his courtroom and in invit-
> ing clergy to lead juries in prayer prior to hearing cases.... In
> sum, [DeLay] seems [to be] aiming to undermine judicial inde-
> pendence by hanging a Sword of Damocles above the heads of
> judges whose opinions he finds politically unappealing while
> granting amnesty for those who abuse their authority to further a
> popular cause. (p. 36)

THE SCORE AT PRESENT

Neither DeLay's impeachment suggestion nor any of the other proposals discussed during the 1997 and 1998 hearings came anywhere near being
enacted. Unpopular as some court rulings may be, it appears that tampering
with judicial independence, like amending the Constitution, is too wide-rang-
ing and drastic an approach to win the necessary support. The initiatives that
tend to succeed involve working within the present system, such as electing a
president and senators who are likely to nominate and confirm one type of
judge rather than another. Professor Barry Friedman of Vanderbilt University
Law School, testifying at a 1997 Senate hearing, offered an explanation for this
phenomenon: "History teaches that challenges to judicial independence have
come from both sides of the political spectrum. It is easy to forget this,
because in recent years complaints about judges generally have come from
conservatives, concerned about what they perceive as liberal decisions. In the
first half of this century, however, it was exactly the opposite. Perhaps it is for

this very reason that the people have developed a deep-seated caution about those attacks, concerned about creating a precedent that might come back to haunt them. Today it might be a liberal judicial ox that is gored, but tomorrow it may be a conservative one. Meanwhile, the very idea of independence itself is threatened" ("Judicial Activism: Defining the Problem and Its Impact," p. 105). "[T]he public," he added, "has chosen regularly to support the system that we have, warts and all. Often it takes time for the public to focus its attention fully on what is happening in Washington, D.C., and attempts to limit judicial independence have gotten quite far before being derailed. But for the most part derailed is what they have been" (p. 107).

Since all the school-prayer initiatives discussed so far have failed, it might seem as if any effort to accommodate religion in the public schools must be hopeless. As the following chapters show, however, some school-prayer proposals have gained enough acceptance to be enacted into law, and the federal courts have upheld them. Predictably, these successful measures are relatively modest in scope and do not affect such values as judicial independence and the freedoms guaranteed by the First Amendment. Instead, they represent compromises by which the students' personal religious practices are accommodated to some extent, but not at a price that too many Americans are unwilling to pay.

10

The Rest Is Silence

Where shall the word be found, where will the word
Resound? Not here, there is not enough silence.

T. S. Eliot

Throughout the school-prayer conflicts that have taken place since the nine-teenth century, seekers after compromise have repeatedly suggested that replacing vocal prayer with moments of silence might reduce the tension sur-rounding religion in the public schools. Any student who wishes to pray would be able to do so in his or her own way, and since the students would not hear one another's prayers, there would be no need for the generic formula-tions that offend some religious people. Moreover, they suggest, silence is not inherently religious, so no one would have to leave the room to avoid partici-pating in a religious observance or appearing to do so. They also maintain that neutral moments of silence—as opposed to explicit invitations to silent prayer—would not implicate the state in promoting religion; each student could use the time at his or her discretion, free from the influence or criticism of school officials and classmates.

Attractive as this reasoning may appear, it draws the same two-pronged criticism that greeted Horace Mann when he substituted pan-Protestant observances for doctrinal religion, and the New York State Board of Regents when it recommended the Regents' Prayer as a replacement for pan-Protes-tantism. To advocates of vocal prayer, silence represents a surrender to the forces of atheism that seek to mute America's hitherto proud religious her-itage. School prayer must be vocal, they assert, if it is to serve as a common statement of belief in God and as a model for students who do not pray at home. A different set of objections is raised by opponents of school-sponsored prayer, who point out that students can already pray silently without any statute or regulation to authorize it, and that nothing stops school personnel from requiring silence whenever it would serve any secular purpose. This being so, they argue, formal moments of silence have no purpose or effect other than to signal governmental encouragement of prayer.

WHERE IS SOLOMON WHEN YOU NEED HIM?

Despite such criticisms, moments of silence enjoy widespread support, and approximately half the states either permit or require their use in the public schools. When opponents challenge such laws, it becomes the courts' business to determine whether they violate Supreme Court precedents. Since silence, unlike vocal prayer, is commonly used for a variety of secular purposes, the courts must take into account the specific facts underlying the enactment and enforcement of the particular statute under challenge. Three examples of such decisions may serve to illustrate the disparate outcomes produced by this process before the issue reached the Supreme Court in the mid-1980s.

The first of these cases, in chronological order, began when the Massachusetts legislature amended a 1966 law stating, "'At the commencement of the first class of each day ... a period of silence not to exceed one minute in duration shall be observed for meditation, and during any such period silence shall be maintained and no activities engaged in'" (*Gaines v. Anderson*, 421 F. Supp. 337 [1976], p. 339). The revision, enacted in 1973, inserted "or prayer" after "meditation." Twelve families sued on the grounds that the law established a religious exercise, mandated a particular form of worship, and interfered with the parents' right to control their children's religious upbringing. A federal district court disagreed, finding the new law constitutional because "[T]he act of meditating is not necessarily a religious exercise. Used in its ordinary sense 'meditation' connotes serious reflection or contemplation on a subject which may be religious, irreligious or nonreligious" (p. 342). As to the addition of "or prayer," the court ruled that "the statute as amended permits meditation or prayer without mandating the one or the other. Thus, the effect of the amended statute is to accommodate students who desire to use the minute of silence for prayer or religious meditation, and also other students who prefer to reflect upon secular matters" (p. 343). The decision was not appealed.[1]

Gaines was unusual in that it upheld a moment-of-silence law even after the legislature had made a point of enhancing the religious connotation of "meditation" by adding the word "prayer." In other cases, courts have found religious purposes in moments of silence for far less reason than that. An example may be found in a Tennessee case filed by three families who challenged a statute that provided, "At the commencement of the first class of each day... a period of silence not to exceed one minute of duration shall be observed for meditation or prayer or personal beliefs and during any such period, silence shall be maintained" (*Beck v. McElrath*, 548 F. Supp. 1161 [1982], p. 1161). Before this legislation was enacted by the state legislature, some of its supporters had made remarks similar to this one by a state senator: "'If there is one thing the people of this state want, they want prayer in the public schools. The fact of the matter is this is a vote on prayer in public schools'" (p. 1164). The legislature later asserted that the law was constitutional because it included secular alternatives to prayer, but the federal district court, while acknowledging that "a moment of silence in and of itself [may be] nondiscriminatory and may serve a secular purpose in aid of the educative function," struck down this particular statute because "it is difficult to escape the conclusion that the legislative purpose was advancement of religious exercises in the classroom" (p. 1163). Before an appeal could be heard, the Tennessee legislature repealed the challenged statute and substituted a different moment-of-silence law. Following two more revisions, current Tennessee law provides for a minute of silence "for all students and teachers to prepare themselves for the activities of the day," with the stipulation that teachers "shall not indicate or suggest to the students any action to be taken by them during this time" (Tenn. Code Ann. § 49-6-1004).

While *Beck* was in progress in Tennessee, a similar dispute was brewing in New Mexico, where a pro-prayer activist named Jean Walsh persuaded her state representative to introduce a moment-of-silence bill. The legislator directed the State Department of Education's attorney to draft a bill "which would authorize some form of prayer in New Mexico public schools" (*Duffy v. Las Cruces*, 557 F. Supp. 1013 [1983], p. 1015). Prompted by a suggestion from Walsh, the attorney modeled the bill on the Massachusetts statute upheld in *Gaines*. The resulting law permitted but did not require local boards to institute moments of silence, and Walsh, a resident of Las Cruces, then urged her town's school board to enact one. Community support was strong, and the board complied, fearing that if voters were antagonized, they might reject a proposed bond measure to provide additional money for the schools. As the court later observed, "While it perhaps cannot be said that the Board members favored prayer in public schools as an abstract proposition, it is clear that they intended to implement a program of prayer in the schools in order to avoid the political wrath of their constituents" (p. 1016). In addition to striking down the Las Cruces policy, the court declared the state law unconstitutional, finding that its "pre-eminent purpose... was to establish a devotional exercise in the classrooms of New Mexico public schools" (p. 1015). To the court, "The ill lies in the public's *perception* of the moment of silence as a devotional exercise. If the public perceives the State to have approved a daily devotional exercise in public school classrooms, the effect of the State's action is the advancement of religion." The court also denied that the inclusion of alternatives to prayer made the law neutral with regard to religion. "It cannot be seriously argued," the decision stated, "and certainly cannot be assumed that children can discern the nice distinctions concerning the meanings of 'meditation,' 'contemplation' and 'prayer'" (p. 1016). The decision was not appealed.[2]

THE BIG TIME

When the moment-of-silence issue finally made its way to the Supreme Court, it did so in a case that originated as a protest against vocal prayer but evolved into a challenge to a state-established moment of silence. It began in spring 1982, when a five-year-old boy in Mobile, Alabama, told his agnostic father and Bahai mother that he was learning Christian prayers in his public-school kindergarten class. The father, Ishmael Jaffree, questioned his other two school-aged children, who told him that the Lord's Prayer and grace before meals were said in their classes as well. Jaffree, a lawyer, protested to school officials that such practices were unconstitutional. When nothing changed, he sued the school officials in federal district court.

Shortly after Jaffree's complaint was filed, Governor Fob James, Jr., called a special session of the Alabama state legislature in which he proposed a new law empowering public-school officials to lead children in a prayer composed by his son, Fob James III. The statute, which passed within a week, provided that

> [A]ny teacher or professor in any public educational institution
> within the State of Alabama, recognizing that the Lord God is
> one, at the beginning of any homeroom or any class, may pray,
> *may lead willing students in prayer,* or may lead the willing stu-
> dents in the following prayer to God: "Almighty God, You alone
> are our God. We acknowledge You as the Creator and Supreme
> Judge of the world. May Your justice, Your truth, and Your peace
> abound this day in the hearts of our countrymen, in the counsels
> of our government, in the sanctity of our homes and in the class-
> rooms of our schools *in the name of our Lord.* Amen." (*Jaffree v.
> James,* 544 F. Supp. 727 [1982], p. 731)

Jaffree amended his complaint to include the new statute and to add the governor and other state officials to the list of defendants. In addition, he challenged a moment-of-silence statute that he found while searching the Alabama state code for additional references to prayer in the public schools. The state legislature, he discovered, had passed a 1978 law stating, "At the commencement of the first class of each day in all grades in all public schools, the teacher in charge of the room in which each such class is held may announce that a period of silence not to exceed one minute in duration shall be observed for meditation, and during any such period no other activities shall be engaged in" (p. 731). In 1981, the Alabama legislature had amended this law to insert "or voluntary prayer" after "meditation." As the plaintiffs in *Gaines* had done, Jaffree challenged the addition of the word "prayer" to a law that already permitted meditation, presumably including meditation on religious topics.

ENTER THE INTERVENORS

As the trial approached, some pro-prayer Alabamians lost faith in the school board's attorney, who had expressed doubts about the constitutionality of religious observances in the public schools. Fearing that his defense of the prayers would be halfhearted, 624 citizens, led by Pastor Fred Wolfe of Cottage Hill Baptist Church, asked to join the case on the school board's side. Although both Jaffree and the school board objected to the inclusion of the defendant-intervenors, whose lawyers would be able to argue before the court, call witnesses, and cross-examine other witnesses, Judge Brevard Hand admitted them. Their legal fees and expenses were covered by Pat Robertson's National Legal Foundation, a conservative Christian advocacy group that has since been succeeded by the Christian Coalition and the American Center for Law and Justice.

Shortly after being admitted, the defendant-intervenors began presenting testimony and exhibits to show that the history, social studies, and home economics textbooks used in the Alabama schools were promoting the religion of secular humanism. As they defined it, secular humanism is the modernist opposite of fundamentalist Christianity—a belief system that advances such concepts as evolution, feminism, personal decision-making, critical thinking, vegetarianism, pacifism, disrespect for authority, skepticism about anything that is not empirically verifiable, and other notions that conflict with a literal interpretation of the Bible. All this was relevant to Jaffree's lawsuit, they alleged, because if Christian prayers were eliminated under the Establishment Clause, then the same standard should be applied to the textbooks, which in their view presented a competing religious ideology. This new assault placed the school officials in the unenviable position of fighting on two fronts at the same time: against Jaffree's accusation that they were establishing Christianity through classroom prayer, and against the intervenors' allegation that they were advancing secular humanism through their selection of textbooks.

Treating the whole discussion of textbooks as a diversion, Jaffree's attorney sought to focus the court's attention on school prayer. Among other things, he questioned the sponsor of the revised moment-of-silence statute, State Senator Donald Holmes (R), about his reasons for adding "or voluntary prayer" to the 1978 law. At the lawyer's request, Holmes read aloud a political speech in which he had declared, "'The United States as well as the State of Alabama was founded by people who believe in God. I believe this effort to return voluntary prayer to our public schools for its return to us to the original position of the writers of the Constitution, this local philosophies and beliefs hundreds of Alabamians have urged my continuous support for permitting school prayer. Since coming to the Alabama Senate I have worked hard on this legislation to accomplish the return of voluntary prayer in our public schools and return to the basic moral fiber.... [E]ven though this is a far cry from where this country and state stood years ago, it is a beginning and a step in the right direction'" (*Jaffree v. James*, transcript of hearing, August 2, 1982, p. 50; syntax as in the original). Asked whether he had proposed the legislation for any reason other than the advancement of prayer, he replied, "No, I did not have no other purpose in mind" (p. 52).

Far from denying that the challenged state laws were religious, some defense witnesses praised the state legislature for upholding religious liberty. They urged Judge Hand to follow the legislature's example in ignoring what they considered the Supreme Court's erroneous interpretation of the Constitution, thus striking a blow for states' rights with regard to religion. Among the most eloquent of these witnesses was James McClellan, a former political science professor who had served as an aide to Senator Jesse Helms (R–North Carolina) at the height of the court-stripping battles, during which similar arguments had been made. McClellan expounded a theory of history leading to the conclusion that the Establishment Clause applies only to Congress and not to the states. Drawing on Justice Joseph Story's account of the Framers' intentions (see Chapters Six and Seven), he contended that even Congress is free to support Christianity as long as it shows no favoritism toward any particular Christian sect.

McClellan's testimony found a receptive audience in Judge Hand, who quoted it extensively in his decision. In defiance of Supreme Court decisions to the contrary, Hand declared that the Establishment Clause does not apply to the states, which he deemed free to establish any religious policies they like. Accordingly, he found that the teachers' classroom prayers, the James prayer law, and the revised moment-of-silence law were all constitutional. As he explained, "the relevant legislative history surrounding the adoption of both the first amendment and of the fourteenth amendment, together with the plain language of those amendments, leaves no doubt that those amendments were not intended to forbid religious prayers in the schools which the states and their political subdivisions mandate" (*Jaffree v. Board of School Commissioners of Mobile County*, 554 F. Supp. 1104 [1983], p. 1128).

Like all federal judges, Hand had sworn to uphold the Constitution, and in his view that oath created a conflict between his legal obligation to follow Supreme Court precedents and his duty to enforce what he considered the true meaning of the Constitution. "What is a court to do," he mused, "when faced with a direct challenge to settled precedent?" His answer: "[I]n cases involving the federal constitution, where correction through legislative action is practically impossible, a court should be willing to examine earlier precedent and to overrule it if the court is persuaded that the earlier precedent was wrongly decided." He further maintained "that the United States Supreme Court has erred in its reading of history. Perhaps this opinion will be no more than a voice crying in the wilderness and this attempt to right that which this Court is persuaded is a misreading of history will come to nothing more than blowing in the hurricane, but be that as it may" (pp. 1126, 1127, 1128).

Although Hand's entire decision was controversial, its most startling statements appeared at the end. The final sentence threatened, "If the appellate courts disagree with this Court in its examination of history and conclusion of constitutional interpretation thereof, then this Court will look again at the record in this case and reach conclusions which it is not now forced to reach." In a footnote, he explained that he was referring to the defendant-intervenors' claims about the allegedly secular humanist textbooks. Case law, he observed, "deals generally with removing the teachings of the Christian ethic from the scholastic effort but totally ignores the teaching of the secular humanist ethic. It was pointed out in the testimony that the curriculum in the public schools of Mobile County is rife with efforts at teaching or encouraging secular humanism—all without opposition from any other ethic—to such an extent that it becomes a brainwashing effort. If this Court is compelled to purge 'God is great, God is good, we thank Him for our daily food' from the classroom, then this Court must also purge from the classroom those things that serve to teach that salvation is through one's self rather than through a deity" (p. 1129, note 41).

In reversing Hand's decision, the Court of Appeals for the Eleventh Circuit noted that it "was contrary to the entire body of United States Supreme Court and Eleventh Circuit precedent," being based on the judge's personal view that "'the United States Supreme Court has erred in its reading of history'" (*Jaffree v. Wallace*, 705 F. 2d 1526 [1983], p. 1530). But, the appeals court averred, "Under our form of government and long established law and custom, the Supreme Court is the ultimate authority on the interpretation of our Constitution and laws; its interpretations may not be disregarded.... If the Supreme Court errs, no other court may correct it" (pp. 1532–33).

Citing the Supreme Court's rulings on school prayer, the appeals court did not hesitate to strike down the teacher-led prayers and the James prayer law, but the moment-of-silence statute presented a far less settled question. Although the court ultimately decided that the history of Alabama's attempts to return state-sponsored prayer to the public schools, combined with the legislators' religious speeches, rendered the revised moment-of-silence law unconstitutional, it qualified its ruling with this observation: "We do not imply that simple meditation or silence is barred from the public schools; we hold that the state cannot participate in the advancement of religious activities through any guise, including teacher-led meditation. It is not the activity itself that concerns us; it is the purpose of the activity that we shall scrutinize" (pp. 1535–36). As is customary, this decision was made by a panel of three judges, and Jaffree's opponents asked for a rehearing *en banc*—that is, a reconsideration of the case by all the judges on the Court of Appeals for the Eleventh Circuit. This request was denied over the vigorous protests of four judges who felt that the moment-of-silence question was novel enough to warrant further examination. Jaffree had argued that amending an existing statute solely to add the word "prayer" automatically advanced religion, but the dissenting judges, like the court in *Gaines*, were not sure about that. Since the revised statute included both religious and secular alternatives, they mused, perhaps it should be allowed to stand despite the legislators' statements of religious intent. These unsettled questions were referred to the Supreme Court, which summarily affirmed the appeals court's ruling that the vocal prayers were unconstitutional and agreed to hear an appeal on the more difficult question of the revised moment-of-silence law.

THE SUPREME COURT SPEAKS

As the appeals court had done, the Supreme Court rejected Hand's use of what he mistakenly "perceived to be newly discovered historical evidence" leading to the "remarkable conclusion that the Federal Constitution imposes no obstacle to Alabama's establishment of a state religion" (*Wallace v. Jaffree*, 472 U.S. 38; 105 S. Ct. 2479 [1985], pp. 45, 48). On the contrary, the decision stated, the Court has rejected that interpretation of history many times and has ruled definitively that the First Amendment does indeed apply to the states. The Court also disagreed with Hand's finding that although the government may not favor any particular faith, it is entitled to promote religion over nonreligion. With respect to the revised moment-of-silence statute, the Court explored the Alabama legislature's purpose in adding the words "or voluntary prayer." The state's attorneys had argued that the revised law should be judged on its own merits without regard to any remarks made by its sponsor or other legislators, since all that mattered was that it treated religion and nonreligion even-handedly. The Court, however, found that

> The legislative intent to return prayer to the public schools is, of course, quite different from merely protecting every student's right to engage in voluntary prayer during an appropriate moment of silence during the schoolday. The 1978 statute already protected that right, containing nothing that prevented any student from engaging in voluntary prayer during a silent minute of meditation. Appellants have not identified any secular purpose that was not fully served by [the earlier version] before the enactment of [the revised version]. Thus, only two conclusions are consistent with the text of [the revised version]: (1) the statute was enacted to convey a message of state endorsement and promotion of prayer; or (2) the statute was enacted for no purpose. No one suggests that the statute was nothing but a meaningless or irrational act. (p. 59)

Despite its negative ruling on the Alabama moment-of-silence law, the Court's reference to "every student's right to engage in voluntary prayer during an appropriate moment of silence during the schoolday" suggested support for moments of silence that were demonstrably neutral with regard to religion. This possibility was explored more explicitly in a concurring opinion by Justice Sandra Day O'Connor. "[A] moment of silence," she wrote, "is not inherently religious" and "need not be associated with a religious exercise," so that "a pupil who participates in a moment of silence need not compromise his or her beliefs. During a moment of silence, a student who objects to prayer is left to his or her own thoughts, and is not compelled to listen to the prayers or thoughts of others.... The crucial question is whether the State has conveyed or attempted to convey the message that children should use the moment of silence for prayer. This question cannot be answered in the abstract, but instead requires courts to examine the history, language, and administration of a particular statute to determine whether it operates as an endorsement of religion" (pp. 72, 73–74). Her reasoning was endorsed by Justice Lewis Powell, who wrote, "I agree fully with Justice O'Connor's assertion that some moment-of-silence statutes may be constitutional, a suggestion set forth in the Court's opinion as well" (p. 62).

Two of the three justices who dissented from the Court's opinion, Chief Justice Warren Burger and Justice Byron White, disregarded the Alabama statute's history and treated the case as if it hinged solely on the inclusion of prayer among the permissible uses of a moment of silence. As White explained, "[I]f a student asked whether he could pray during that moment, it is difficult to believe that the teacher could not answer in the affirmative. If that is the case, I would not invalidate a statute that at the outset provided the legislative answer to the question 'May I pray?'" (p. 91). The third dissenter, Justice (later Chief Justice) William Rehnquist, was the only member of the Court to adopt an interpretation of history similar to that of McClellan and Hand. Among other things, he advocated a return to the original meaning of the First Amendment as explained by Justice Story (see Chapters Six and Seven), under which the government was able to promote religion over nonreligion and Christianity over other traditions. "As its history abundantly shows," he wrote, "nothing in the Establishment Clause requires government to be strictly neutral between religion and irreligion, nor does that Clause prohibit Congress or the States from pursuing legitimate secular ends through nondiscriminatory sectarian means" (p. 113).[3]

When the Supreme Court's decision reached Judge Hand, he fulfilled his promise to examine the question of secular humanism in the textbooks used in the Alabama schools. Dismissing Jaffree from the case, he reconfigured it so that the former defendant-intervenors became the new plaintiffs, suing the school officials for allegedly promoting the anti-Christian religion of secular humanism. Hand emphatically asserted that this was not a new case but a continuation of *Jaffree;* to him, it was important that the same lawsuit that had challenged Christianity in the public schools should also explore charges of anti-Christianity. Attorneys for the school officials pointed out that *Jaffree* had been decided by the Supreme Court and was now over, but their protest fell on deaf ears. The revived lawsuit proceeded, with the National Legal Foundation continuing to provide representation to the anti-textbook group. The school board was aided by People for the American Way, a liberal group founded by television producer Norman Lear to create a counterweight to the influence of religious conservatives. After a five-day trial, Hand ordered the Mobile County schools to stop using all the challenged social studies and home economics textbooks and all but one of the history books. His ruling was reversed by the Eleventh Circuit, and the Supreme Court refused to hear an appeal.[4]

SOMETIMES SILENCE *IS* GOLDEN

Naturally, the Supreme Court's decision in *Wallace v. Jaffree* affected other moment-of-silence cases making their way through the courts. Among these was a challenge to a 1982 New Jersey statute whose history was not unlike that of the Alabama law. The New Jersey state legislature had passed moment-of-silence bills in 1969, 1971, and 1978, but these had been vetoed by three successive governors on the ground that they impermissibly established religion. For this reason, Assemblyman James Zangari, who sponsored the 1982 proposal, was careful to word it in a neutral manner: "Principals and teachers in each public elementary and secondary school of each school district in this State shall permit students to observe a 1 minute period of silence to be used solely at the discretion of the individual student, before the opening exercises of each school day for quiet and private contemplation or introspection" (*May v. Cooperman*, 572 F. Supp. 1561 [1983], p. 1562). Nevertheless, supporters of the bill left little doubt that their intention was to restore state-sponsored religion to the public schools, and the measure was widely perceived as a school-prayer proposal. A staffer at the New Jersey School Board Association later testified that Zangari had stated at a legislative hearing that it was "important that society get back to deeply embedded religious values" and that although students were free to pray silently on their own, "'They [students] publicly won't do it [pray] unless they are directed'" (p. 1564). Other witnesses confirmed that no secular purpose was ever mentioned at the hearings.

The state legislature passed the bill and later overrode Governor Brendan Byrne's veto, whereupon school officials tried to implement the new law. They were perplexed, however, because it ordered them to permit rather than require students to observe a minute of silence, and there would be no quiet setting for students who chose to participate in a moment of silence unless the other students were silent as well. Some school officials attempted to finesse this difficulty by ordering all students to be quiet, either because they were opting to observe a moment of silence "for quiet and private contemplation or intro-spection" or because they were being considerate of those classmates who were doing so. Among these was the principal of a high school in Edison Township, who distributed a memo stating, "You will note that the Bill says students shall be permitted to observe a minute of silence. That will be interpreted to mean that there will be a minute of silence in the classroom so that each student may use that time as the individual interprets his or her desire to do so" (*May v. Cooperman*, 780 F. 2d 240 [1985], p. 248). A teacher named Jeffrey May, declar-ing that the moment of silence was a religious practice, refused to observe it. He and the parents of six students then filed suit in federal district court; as described in the subsequent decision, the plaintiffs "either are not religious and view the minute of silence as an enforced religious observance or else are religious and oppose required participation in this particular observance" (*May v. Cooperman*, 572 F. Supp. 1561 [1983], p. 1562). The defendants were the state commissioner of education, Dr. Saul Cooperman, and other state and local school officials.

At first, it looked as if the plaintiffs would prevail without a fight because Cooperman and the other state officials agreed with them that the law was unconstitutional, and the local school officials were willing to stop enforcing it if instructed to do so. In order to give the state legislature and its two presiding officers, Speaker of the General Assembly Alan Karcher and President of the Senate Carmen Orechio, an opportunity to defend their action, the court admit-ted them to the case as defendant-intervenors. The lawsuit then proceeded with the legislature's attorneys carrying the burden of demonstrating that the moment of silence was constitutional because it had the secular purpose of quieting the students so that they could begin the school day. Several educa-tion experts attacked this rationale, but by far the most damaging testimony was offered by Professor Adam Scrupski of the Rutgers Graduate School of Education. Several months after the law was enacted, he said, a friend who worked on a legislative committee had asked whether Scrupski could think of a secular use for the moment of silence, and he had suggested using it "as an opening exercise forming the boundary between school and not-school." As the decision noted, "Dr. Scrupski found a secular consequence and was retained to testify concerning it" (pp. 1569, 1570), but "only the utterly naïve would con-clude that the Bill's advocates were fighting passionately for establishment of such a boundary. It is abundantly clear that once the Governor's veto had been overridden and litigation commenced, [the new law] became a statute in search of a secular purpose" (p. 1573). Accordingly, the court struck it down.

The case then went to the Court of Appeals for the Third Circuit, which was more favorably disposed toward the moment-of-silence statute than the district court had been. Among other things, it found that requiring all students to refrain from making any noise was not the same as forcing them to participate in a state-mandated moment of silence defined as a time for "quiet and private contemplation or introspection." Nevertheless, the appeals court upheld the district court's decision because the purpose of the law "was religious, at least to the extent of requiring school districts to accommodate those students desiring the opportunity to engage in prayer at some point during the school day" (p. 252). Alan Karcher and Carmen Orechio tried to take the case to the Supreme Court, but both of them had lost their leadership posts. Since they had been admitted to the case only in official capacities they no longer held, the Court ruled that they had no standing to pursue the appeal.

LET'S HEAR IT FOR SILENCE

All the courts that struck down moment-of-silence laws took pains to clarify that the outcome was based on the specific history and intent of the challenged policy and not on a blanket condemnation of moments of silence as such. In accord with this distinction, some courts have ruled in favor of carefully crafted policies whose treatment of moments of silence was found to be neutral toward religion. Among these was a 1994 Georgia law upheld by the Court of Appeals for the Eleventh Circuit—the same court that had struck down the Alabama law in *Jaffree*. Its legislative sponsor, while serving on a committee seeking to reduce school violence, noticed that when students were killed or injured, other students spontaneously initiated moments of silence that seemed to have a calming effect. Hoping that a moment of silence at the beginning of each school day might encourage students to improve their self-control and reflectiveness, he included such a plan in a package of three anti-violence measures. As passed by the Georgia legislature, the moment-of-silence provision stated,

> (a) In each public school classroom, the teacher in charge shall, at the opening of school upon every school day, conduct a brief period of quiet reflection for not more than 60 seconds with the participation of all the pupils therein assembled.

(b) The moment of quiet reflection authorized by subsection (a) of this Code section is not intended to be and shall not be conducted as a religious service or exercise but shall be considered as an opportunity for a moment of silent reflection on the anticipated activities of the day.

(c) The provisions of subsections (a) and (b) of this Code section shall not prevent student initiated voluntary school prayers at schools or school related events which are nonsectarian and nonproselytizing in nature. (*Bown v. Gwinnett County School District*, 895 F. Supp. 1564 [1995], p. 1566)

(Subsection (c) was added by the Georgia House of Representatives over the sponsor's objections.)

Shortly before the 1994–95 school year started, a social studies teacher named Brian Bown protested without avail that the moment of silence was unconstitutional. During homeroom period on the first day of school, his principal said over the loudspeaker: "'As we begin another school day, let us take a few moments to reflect quietly on our day, our activities and what we hope to accomplish.'" As Bown later testified, he told his students, "'You may do as you wish. That's your option. But I am going to continue with my lesson'" (p. 1565). Although homeroom period does not ordinarily include academic instruction, he proceeded to lecture on the political power the Catholic Church had once exerted over European governments. When he persisted in refusing to comply with the law, he was suspended and subsequently fired.

Bown fared no better in court than he did with the school officials. While acknowledging that some legislators had expressed religious motivations, the federal district court found those statements insufficient to overshadow what it saw as the clearly secular intent of the statute itself. This ruling was upheld by the Court of Appeals for the Eleventh Circuit, which declared, "Although some Georgia legislators expressed religious motives for voting for the Act, the fact remains that the language of the statute as enacted reveals a clearly secular legislative purpose: to provide students with a moment of quiet reflection to think about the upcoming day" (*Bown v. Gwinnett*, 112 F. 3d 1464 [1997], p. 1472).

YES, VIRGINIA, THERE IS A SILENCE CLAUSE

A similar result was reached in a challenge to a Virginia moment-of-silence statute enacted in 2000. It provides that "the school board of each school division shall establish the daily observance of one minute of silence in each class-room of the division." The stated purpose is "that each pupil may, in the exercise of his or her individual choice, meditate, pray, or engage in any other silent activity which does not interfere with, distract, or impede other pupils in the like exercise of individual choice. The Office of the Attorney General shall intervene and shall provide legal defense of this law" (Va. Code Ann. § 22.1-203). An earlier version of this statute, enacted in 1950 and amended in 1976, was almost identical to the current language except that school districts are now required rather than permitted to institute moments of silence, and the attorney general is obliged to defend the statute.

The 2000 revision of Virginia's moment-of-silence law was inspired by conservative Christian activist Rita Warren, whose book, *Mom, They Won't Let Us Pray* (1975), explains her convictions. When her local school board declined to institute a moment of silence under the old law, she persuaded State Senator Warren Barry (R) to introduce a revised version making the practice mandatory. He also attempted to insert a clause requiring teachers to announce that students had the option of praying, lest "students who wanted to pray might not realize that it was an acceptable activity during the silence" (Justin Blum, "Va. Senate Approves a Minute of School Silence," *Washington Post*, February 2, 2000, p. A1). This provision did not pass, and the Virginia Department of Education warned teachers neither to suggest prayer nor to discourage it. Among the lawmakers who disagreed with this position was Delegate Robert G. Marshall (R), who said, "'This is a very tepid response to a moral crisis in this country.... If they're so timid about mentioning the word "prayer," I'm doubtful about what [the law] will do.'" Similarly, Delegate Lionell Spruill (D) said, "'I'm definitely going to bring it back to put some teeth into it'" (Liz Seymour, "Don't Raise Prayer Issue, Schools Told," *Washington Post*, June 14, 2000, pp. A1, A26). Citing such statements as evidence that the intent of the new law was religious, the Virginia affiliate of the American Civil Liberties Union filed suit in federal district court on behalf of eight students and their parents. According to its executive director, "'From its beginnings, this law has had state-sanctioned prayer written all over it.... Every student who has ever attended public schools knows that they can pray to themselves. That's not a secret.'" Attorney General Mark Earley responded that the ACLU's opposition to a moment of silence ran contrary to Virginia's efforts to curb school violence. Senator Barry added that the word "prayer" was included "'because we didn't want to discriminate against prayer'" (Patricia Davis and Liz Seymour, "ACLU Challenges Virginia's Minute of Silence," *Washington Post*, June 23, 2000, p. B8).

Like the *Bown* court, the federal district court that heard the Virginia case balanced the religious statements of some lawmakers and other officials against the neutral language of the law itself. It concluded that the statute was sufficiently secular to withstand constitutional scrutiny, and the Court of Appeals for the Fourth Circuit agreed. "In sum," the appeals court stated, "in establishing a minute of silence, during which students may choose to pray or to meditate in a silent and nonthreatening manner, Virginia has introduced at most a minor and nonintrusive accommodation of religion that does not establish religion" (*Brown v. Gilmore,* 258 F. 3d 265 [2001], p. 278). The Supreme Court refused to hear an appeal.

ONCE MORE, IN REVERSE

In the Virginia case, as in *Jaffree* and the other lawsuits discussed so far in this chapter, the plaintiffs asserted or implied that school officials were compensating for the absence of state-sponsored vocal prayer by establishing moments of silence. The reverse was true in a Louisiana case, *Doe v. Ouachita Parish School Board,* in which the state legislature started with a moment-of-silence law and gradually altered it to a provision for vocal prayer. The process began with a 1976 statute providing that "a brief time in silent meditation" should open each school day. It was revised in 1992 to permit "silent prayer or meditation," and in 1999 the word "silent" was removed. When students and parents challenged the new law in court, Governor Murphy J. Foster III retorted that they had no standing to sue because, among other things, no one was forced to pray or meditate. He also denied that any student could conceivably be injured by the revised statute. Nevertheless, both the federal district court and the Court of Appeals for the Fifth Circuit found that the plaintiffs not only had standing but were also correct in considering the law unconstitutional. As the appeals court stated, "[T]here is no doubt that the 1999 amendment was motivated by a wholly religious purpose. It accomplished only one thing—the deletion of the word 'silent' from a statute that authorized 'silent prayer or meditation.' The purpose of the amendment is clear on its face—it is to authorize *verbal* prayer in schools" (*Doe v. Ouachita Parish School Board,* 274 F. 3d 289 [2001], p. 294).

SO WHERE DOES ALL THIS LEAVE US?

A search of state codes reveals that approximately half of them include provisions for moments of silence in the public schools. A few merely acknowledge the students' right to pray silently, but most establish formal moments of silence as part of the official school program. They are more or less evenly divided between those that use the word "prayer," usually as an alternative to meditation or reflection, and those that do not. In some states, moments of silence are incorporated into laws that also include such matters as graduation prayer (Delaware), Bible study (Florida), and Scripture-reading (Maryland), whereas other states explicitly disclaim any association between moments of silence and religion. Although legal thought on moment-of-silence statutes is still evolving, it seems likely that they can, in some circumstances, be constitutionally sound. "The crucial question," as Justice O'Connor observed, "is whether the State has conveyed or attempted to convey the message that children should use the moment of silence for prayer" (*Wallace v. Jaffree,* pp. 73–74). Even the explicit use of the word "prayer" does not appear to be an automatic disqualifier if presented as an option, not a preferred activity. To be upheld in court, moment-of-silence laws must manifest a secular purpose, but beyond that lie the murkiest of legal waters. A comparable lack of clarity about their political usefulness is created by ongoing protests to the effect that they are either too religious or not religious enough, but since they exist in approximately half the states but have generated only a handful of lawsuits, they would appear to enjoy broader public support—or at least tolerance—than do proposals to amend the Constitution, reduce the power of the federal courts, or institute state-run vocal prayer.

The comparative success of religiously neutral moments of silence is attributable to three characteristics: the ability of each student to pray as he or she likes or not pray at all, the absence of governmental encouragement or discouragement of religion, and the lack of opportunities for government officials to compose or select prayers. Among them, these factors eliminate most of the major sources of controversy that brought the legislative proposals of the 1960s, 1970s, and early 1980s down to defeat. Consequently, as the rest of this book demonstrates, the current phase of thought about prayer in the public schools centers around three questions:

- Could the features that make moments of silence comparatively attractive be incorporated into a plan for student-controlled vocal prayer?
- Could such a program be structured so that students could decline to participate without having to leave an ongoing school activity, such as homeroom period?
- Would this approach comply with the Supreme Court's rulings on school prayer?

11

Caution! Paradigms May Shift

JUSTICE POTTER STEWART: "But isn't it a gross interference with the free exercise of the religion of those in my imaginary case, those 98 percent of the student body who say our religious beliefs tell us that [Bible-reading] is what we want to do?"

ATTORNEY HENRY SAWYER: "Well, they have a right to do it, Your Honor, but they haven't got a right to get the state to help them."

Oral argument in Abington v. Schempp

When the Supreme Court struck down state-sponsored school prayer in *Engel* and *Abington,* those decisions were often taken to mean that no organized vocal prayer could occur during the school day or on school property. As some school-prayer advocates were quick to point out, however, such a total cleansing of worship from the public schools would prevent students from praying aloud on their own initiative during their free time, when they could talk among themselves about any other topic of their choice. In effect, such policies assumed that the Establishment Clause, which constrains the government's own speech about religion, also requires it to limit the speech of private citizens when they are on government property or participating in a government-sponsored program. By that standard, not only school officials but students were deemed to be involved in a government activity and thus unable to engage in religious exercises. Alternatively, students were thought to be so thoroughly under the control of school authorities that anything they were allowed to do, even outside of class, was presumed to carry the endorsement of the state.

People who wanted students to be able to pray challenged these assumptions, asserting that a clear distinction should be made between school personnel and students. In their view, it is appropriate to ask whether speech is religious only if it is sponsored by the school. If it is represented as being the students' private speech, then the first matter to be considered is not whether it is religious but whether it is indeed attributable to the students as individuals rather than to the school. Should that prove to be the case, they argued, then there is no reason that the speech should not be religious. In support of this assertion, they pointed out that the Establishment Clause applies only to the government, not to private citizens, and it gives the government no more right to hinder religion than to promote it. Noting that the students also have rights under the Free Exercise and Free Speech Clauses of the First Amendment,[1] they concluded that if prayer arises from voluntary student interactions outside of class, then school officials have neither the obligation nor the authority to act as "prayer police" to ensure that the students' private speech is exclusively secular.

THE LONG SHADOW OF THE '60S

The assumption that students have the right to engage in free speech within the public schools, which now plays a major role in discussions of school prayer, is based in part on 1960s decisions dealing with protests over civil rights and the Vietnam War. Although their subject matter was not religious, they limited the authority of school officials to suppress or regulate student speech, thus setting precedents that have since been applied to religious expression. Among the earliest of these cases was *Burnside v. Byars*, which arose in a small Mississippi town where, despite Supreme Court rulings to the contrary, the schools were racially segregated and African Americans were strongly discouraged from voting. In fall 1964, African American students at Booker T. Washington High School began wearing buttons saying, "One Man, One Vote." As they later testified, the buttons conveyed their desire to "'[g]o uptown and sit in the drugstores and wherever we buy things uptown we can sit down and won't have to walk right out at the time we get it.... And to register and vote without being beat up and killed'" (*Burnside v. Byars*, 363 F. 2d 744 [1966], p. 747, n. 5). The principal banned the buttons on the grounds that they "'didn't have any bearing on their education,' 'would cause commotion,' and 'would be disturbing [to] the school program by taking up time trying to get order, passing them around and discussing them in the classroom and explaining to the next child why they are wearing them'" (pp. 746–47). He suspended thirty to forty students, all but three of whom soon returned to school buttonless. The parents of the three holdouts sued, claiming that the exclusion of the buttons infringed the students' right to free speech.

A federal district court ruled against the parents, but the Court of Appeals for the Fifth Circuit reversed that decision. According to that court, "The record indicates only a showing of mild curiosity on the part of the other school children over the presence of some 30 or 40 children wearing such insignia.... Thus it appears that the presence of 'freedom buttons' did not hamper the school in carrying on its regular schedule of activities; nor would it seem likely that the simple wearing of buttons unaccompanied by improper conduct would ever do so." While emphasizing that "the regulation forbidding the presence of buttons on school grounds would have been reasonable" if the display had interrupted the school's educational effort, the court ruled that in the absence of any disturbance, the rule was "arbitrary and unreasonable, and an unnecessary infringement on the students' protected right of free expression in the circumstances revealed by the record" (pp. 748–49).

On the same day that it decided *Burnside,* the Fifth Circuit also ruled on another case concerning the right of African American students in a segregated Mississippi high school to wear "freedom buttons." Unlike the students at Booker T. Washington, however, the students at Henry Weathers High School also engaged in demonstrations that "created a state of confusion, disrupted class instruction, and resulted in a general breakdown of orderly discipline, causing the principal to assemble the students in the cafeteria and inform them that they were forbidden to wear the buttons at school" (*Blackwell v. Issaquena County,* 363 F. 2d 749 [1966], p. 751). The appeals court concluded that the students' disruptive behavior justified the ban. "In this case," the decision stated, "the reprehensible conduct described above was so inexorably tied to the wearing of the buttons that the two are not separable. In these circumstances we consider the rule of the school authorities reasonable" (p. 754).

Neither *Burnside* nor *Blackwell* reached the Supreme Court, but a year later the Court dealt with similar issues in a dispute that arose when protesters against the Vietnam War resolved to wear black arm bands for two weeks. School officials in Des Moines, Iowa, forbade students from wearing the arm bands, and three students who defied the ban were suspended. They remained out of school until the protest period had expired, whereupon their families sued the school district for violating their right to free speech. The federal district court ruled against them, finding that "While the arm bands themselves may not be disruptive, the reactions and comments from other students as a result of the arm bands would be likely to disturb the disciplined atmosphere required for any classroom. It was not unreasonable in this instance for school officials to anticipate that the wearing of arm bands would create some type of classroom disturbance" (*Tinker v. Des Moines,* 258 F. Supp. 971 [1966],

p. 973). The case went to the Court of Appeals for the Eighth Circuit, where it was heard by a panel of three judges and subsequently reargued before the entire court. The resulting tie vote, reported without explanation, left the district court's ruling in place. This outcome was reversed by the Supreme Court, which said, "It can hardly be argued that either students or teachers shed their constitutional rights to freedom of speech or expression at the schoolhouse gate" (*Tinker v. Des Moines*, 393 U.S. 503; 89 S. Ct. 733 [1969], p. 506). According to the Court, "a silent, passive expression of opinion, unaccompanied by any disorder or disturbance *on the part of petitioners*" (emphasis added) is protected under the First Amendment. As long as the war protesters behaved well, the threat that their foes might become disruptive did not, in the Court's view, justify constraining their right to express a controversial view. "Any departure from absolute regimentation may cause trouble," the Court observed. "Any variation from the majority's opinion may inspire fear. Any word spoken, in class, in the lunchroom, or on the campus, that deviates from the views of another person may start an argument or cause a disturbance. But our Constitution says we must take this risk" (p. 508). The Court also noted that other kinds of symbolic expression were permitted in the Des Moines schools; only arm bands were singled out for exclusion, and then only when school officials learned of the plan to use them in an anti-war protest. "Clearly," the decision stated, "the prohibition of expression of one particular opinion, at least without evidence that it is necessary to avoid material and substantial interference with schoolwork or discipline, is not constitutionally permissible" (p. 511).

Tinker did not immediately affect religious expression in the public schools because most school-prayer advocates were still thinking in terms of state-sponsored, teacher-led prayer rather than private student devotionals. As efforts to reinstate traditional religious observances repeatedly failed, however, the student-centered *Tinker* model began to attract more attention. By the late 1970s, the assertion that students have a right to engage in religious speech whenever they are free to discuss secular topics of their choice—known as "equal access"—had become a regular feature of debates over school prayer.[2]

THE CORNERSTONE CASE

Equal-access proponents won their first major victory when a Christian club called Cornerstone sued the University of Missouri—Kansas City for prohibiting student religious groups from meeting on campus. As Cornerstone's leader, Florian Chess, explained, "Having to explain that we have to meet off campus tends to make students think that there is something 'wrong' with us and that there is something wrong with religion since it is banished from the campus. This leads to the kind of thinking which holds that religion is obsolete and has nothing to do with the realities of life. This type of thinking is a large barrier to the effectiveness of our message and the purposes of our group" (*Chess v. Widmar*, 480 F. Supp. 907 [1979], p. 912). Lawyers for UMKC retorted that far from suggesting hostility toward religion, the policy merely prevented the campus from being used as a place of worship in violation of the Establishment Clause. Since Cornerstone meetings were held at a house only a block away, they added, any burden on the students' rights to freedom of speech and religion was minimal. The federal district court ruled in favor of the university, but the students fared better in the Court of Appeals for the Eighth Circuit, whose decision pointed out that UMKC provided meeting space for more than ninety student groups representing a wide range of goals and viewpoints. The court found that permitting university students to establish such clubs unquestionably served valid social and educational purposes, and that the inclusion of religious groups "would no more commit the University, its administration or its faculty to religious goals than they are now committed to the goals of the Students for a Democratic Society, the Young Socialist Alliance, the Young Democrats or the Women's Union," which were already meeting on campus. In the court's view, "the University would not sponsor religious worship or teaching; sponsorship would lie with the recognized student groups" (*Chess v. Widmar*, 635 F.2d 1310 [1980], p. 1317).

In upholding this decision, the Supreme Court agreed with the Eighth Circuit that establishing opportunities for students to engage in the speech of their choice, some of which may be religious, is significantly different from creating a state-sponsored forum specifically for religious expression. Thus, the Court found, the central issue in *Widmar* "is not whether the creation of a religious forum would violate the Establishment Clause. The University has opened its facilities for use by student groups, and the question is whether it can now exclude groups because of the content of their speech" (*Widmar v. Vincent*, 454 U.S. 263; 102 S. Ct. 269 [1981], p. 273). (The title of the case changed because, when Chess graduated, Clark Vincent replaced him as the first-named plaintiff.) As the Court noted, previous decisions, such as *McCollum v. Board of Education* (see Chapter Four), had forbidden religious instruction in public schools even when carried out by nonschool personnel for the benefit of voluntary participants. In those cases, however, school officials had established a special opportunity for religious speech alone. By contrast, UMKC's forum was generally open to student groups of all kinds, so the question was not whether religious organizations could be given privileged access, as they had been in *McCollum*, but whether they could be singled out for exclusion. Cornerstone emerged victorious because the Court upheld both the students' right to free speech and the principle that UMKC could neither encourage *nor hinder* their religious beliefs and practices.

Although the reasoning of *Widmar* was all that proponents of equal access could have desired, the decision contained a footnote that raised questions about its applicability to elementary and secondary schools: "University students are, of course, young adults. They are less impressionable than younger students and should be able to appreciate that the University's policy is one of neutrality toward religion" (p. 274, note 14). To be sure, this statement did not explicitly prohibit student religious groups from meeting in elementary or secondary schools, but it prevented equal-access advocates from claiming that *Widmar* necessarily extended to all levels of public education. The inevitable result was a series of lawsuits exploring the distinction between government action and private speech as it applies to students of various ages. Among the earliest of these cases was *Brandon v. Board of Education of Guilderland,* which was going through the courts at the same time as *Widmar.*

Brandon was filed by the Catholic League for Religious and Civil Rights on behalf of high school students who wanted to establish a prayer group that would meet each day before school. School officials refused to allow the meetings because, like the UMKC administrators, they believed that no organized prayer was permitted in public schools. This view was upheld by the federal district court, which ruled that the central issue was not the students' right to free speech and free exercise of religion but the school's duty to avoid violating the Establishment Clause. Allowing the prayer meetings, it found, "would logically lead to the outward appearance of the placement of official state sanction on religious activity" (*Brandon v. Board of Education,* 487 F. Supp. 1219 [1980], p. 1229). The Court of Appeals for the Second Circuit agreed, stating, "Our nation's elementary and secondary schools play a unique role in transmitting basic and fundamental values to our youth. To an impressionable student, even the mere appearance of secular involvement in religious activities might indicate that the state has placed its imprimatur on a particular religious creed. This symbolic inference is too dangerous to permit" (*Brandon v. Board of Education,* 635 F. 2d 971 [1980], p. 978). The Supreme Court refused to hear an appeal, much to the dismay of equal-access proponents who had hoped that it would act quickly to extend *Widmar* to all public schools. If unfavorable lower-court decisions regarding elementary and secondary schools were allowed to stand, they feared, the notion that equal access applies only to higher education would become difficult to dislodge.

USING JUDICIAL LEMONS TO MAKE POLITICAL LEMONADE

Naturally, equal-access advocates disagreed with the entire decision in *Brandon*, but they were particularly incensed by the appeals court's use of the expression "too dangerous to permit." In context, those words referred not to prayer itself but to the perception that the state is favoring a particular religious belief. Nevertheless, according to an unpublished report by the Christian Legal Society (CLS), "Those words, 'too dangerous to permit,' galvanized the Christian legal community, both evangelical and nonevangelical, who suddenly saw much to fear in the state labeling private individuals' prayer and Bible reading as 'too dangerous to permit.' Four simple words became, in effect, a gauntlet that energized Christians across many theological divisions" ("Equal Access: The 14-Year Battle," 1993, p. 8).

Although many organizations advocated equal access, CLS's legal director, Samuel Ericsson, is generally regarded as the movement's most effective early leader. Ericsson, who has since left CLS, explained in an interview that in equal access he saw a way to restore prayer to the public schools without resorting to state control of religious exercises. State-prescribed devotionals, he feels, are objectionable both in principle and because they tend to promote what he calls "to-whom-it-may-concern prayer." As an example, he suggested that the Regents' Prayer was nonsectarian to the point of offending no one "except possibly God, and after all you can't please everybody." Similarly, he asserted, "if God had wanted [rote] prayer, He would have created a tape recorder on the sixth day." In his view, genuine prayer is by definition sectarian and thus inappropriate for a state-controlled program. "What's the point?" he asked, referring to battles over whose prayers should be said in the public schools. "To show that our faith trumps yours?" (interview, August 23, 1996). Nevertheless, he was deeply troubled by the exclusion of organized vocal prayer from the schools, and he felt that the solution was to allow students to pray among themselves without the involvement of school officials.

Fired by these convictions, Ericsson and other CLS attorneys spearheaded a two-pronged effort to open the public schools to student prayer groups. Together with lawyers from other advocacy groups, notably the National Association of Evangelicals, the National Council of Churches, and the Baptist Joint Committee on Public Affairs, they participated in lawsuits that they hoped would lead to judicial decisions upholding equal-access policies. They also pursued a legislative strategy, lobbying federal and state lawmakers to pass equal-access statutes. These two approaches converged in spring 1982, when Senator Mark Hatfield (R-Oregon), incensed by the outcome of *Brandon,* invited CLS to draft an equal-access bill. It stated: "No public secondary school receiving federal financial assistance, which generally allows groups of students to meet during non-instructional periods, shall discriminate against any meeting of students on the basis of the content of the speech at the meeting, provided that the meeting shall be voluntary and orderly and that no activity which is in and of itself unlawful need be permitted" ("Proposed Constitutional Amendment to Permit Voluntary Prayer," pp. 15–16; hereafter "1982 hearings"). A footnote suggested that "An alternative proposal might add the word 'religious' before the word 'content' in this statute" (p. 16). As Chapter Twelve explains, this uncertainty over whether the bill should protect all student speech or only religious expression later became one of the most contentious aspects of the debate over equal access.

DEEP IN THE HEART OF TEXAS

Hatfield explicitly described his proposal as an attempt to rebut *Brandon* by extending *Widmar* to secondary schools, and as it wended its way through the legislative process, it became connected with other lawsuits as well. Perhaps the most striking example of this association between legislation and litigation was the intervention of Hatfield and other senators in a Texas case that, like the equal-access bill, had the potential to bring about *Widmar*-like arrangements in secondary schools. Had the Supreme Court accepted the senators' arguments, there would probably have been no need for Hatfield's legislation because the same goal would have been achieved through the judicial process.

The dispute arose in Lubbock, Texas, whose public schools had a long tradition of school-sponsored religious exercises, such as teacher-led prayer, Bible-reading, Bible distribution, evangelical assemblies, advertisements of off-campus religious services, and moments of silent prayer. These practices, which had continued unabated after *Engel* and *Abington,* came under fire in the early 1970s from the local ACLU affiliate, the Lubbock Civil Liberties Union (LCLU). In response, the school board forbade school employees from encouraging prayer or arranging religious assemblies, although they "are not to be mislead [sic] by this letter into believing that the School District is prohibiting open prayer" (*Lubbock Civil Liberties Union v. Lubbock Independent School District,* 669 F. 2d 1038 [1982], p. 1039, note 2). These ambiguous instructions had no effect on the schools' religious practices, which continued despite repeated confrontations with the LCLU. In 1979, the school board tried to head off a lawsuit by stating that no school employee was to "compose, prescribe, or place his/her approval upon any particular prayer or form of religious activity; however, student initiated and directed religious activities will be permitted" (p. 1040, note 6). The LCLU sued nonetheless, describing the purported transfer of control to the students as a pretext designed to facilitate the continuation of traditional religious practices. The board then adopted another new policy, including among other things an equal-access provision allowing students "to gather at the school with supervision either before or after regular school hours on the same basis as other groups as determined by the school administration to meet for any educational, moral, religious or ethical purposes so long as attendance at such meetings is voluntary" (p. 1041, n. 7). Disparaging this new regulation as yet another sham, the LCLU alleged that the board's history of announcing one new policy after another without changing its practices clearly demonstrated that school-run religious activities would not cease without a court order.

The federal district court declined to issue such an order on the grounds that the new policy had been adopted in good faith and was constitutional on its face, thus ensuring against a recurrence of the impermissible practices of the past. In reversing this decision, the Court of Appeals for the Fifth Circuit found that although the equal-access provision might have been upheld in other circumstances, it was unconstitutional because, among other things, "it appears in the middle of a policy concerned with religious activities in the schools" (p. 1044). According to the court, the school officials had not created a true *Widmar*-style open forum in which diverse student groups met to express a variety of views; rather, the policy's overriding purpose was to allow school-sponsored prayer to continue with only cosmetic changes.

When the school officials petitioned the Supreme Court to hear an appeal, Hatfield and twenty-three other senators—fifteen Republicans and eight Democrats—interjected themselves into the case. Rejecting the appeals court's focus on the specific history of the Lubbock policy, they urged the Court to uphold the equal-access provision, whose wording they deemed unobjectionable. Otherwise, they feared, school officials throughout the country would feel obliged "to discriminate against students who wish to use school facilities outside school hours for discussion the school board considers to have religious content" or "to become the adversary of public school students who wish to engage in religious activities" (Brief Amici Curiae in Support of the Petition for a Writ of Certiorari, December 14, 1982, pp. 2, 11). Hatfield and the other senators also warned the Court that if it failed to prevent such evils, Congress would find a way to do so. As they pointed out in their brief, the Senate was once again discussing a proposal to strip the federal courts of jurisdiction over school prayer as well as a constitutional amendment that would supersede the Court's earlier decisions in that area. In their view, such radical steps had to be considered because of "the widespread perception that the courts are interpreting the Constitution in a way that is hostile to religion" (p. 3). If, however, the Court were to strike a blow for voluntary student prayer, the need for congressional action would be reduced or perhaps eliminated. Nevertheless, the Court refused to hear *Lubbock*, and the order terminating the religious activities was allowed to stand.

CLOSE BUT NO CIGAR, TWICE

Troubling as *Lubbock* was to equal-access advocates, they were perhaps even more disappointed by the outcome of *Bender v. Williamsport School District*, another lawsuit that was often mentioned during the debates over Hatfield's bill. Unlike *Lubbock*, which was cluttered with a variety of school-sponsored religious practices, *Bender* was a clear-cut equal-access case whose facts bore a close resemblance to the situation in *Widmar*. To all appearances, if any case involving secondary-school students could succeed, it was *Bender*.

Lisa Bender attended a high school in Williamsport, Pennsylvania, where students were given two half-hour periods each week to meet in clubs or informal groups. Students who did not wish to participate were free to engage in any other nondisruptive activity they chose. In fall 1981, Bender led a group of students who asked permission to form a club called Petros, which they described as "'a nondenominational prayer fellowship'" in which they would "'read some scriptures and pray to God that he might edify [their] minds'" (*Bender v. Williamsport Area School District*, 563 F. Supp. 697 [1983], p. 701). The school officials responded with a counterproposal: if the students could find a place to meet off campus, they would be given released time for that purpose. Instead, Ericsson and another CLS attorney, Kimberlee Colby, filed suit on their behalf, arguing that the principles on which *Widmar* had been decided should be extended to secondary schools.

The federal district court agreed. By establishing biweekly activity periods, its decision stated, the school had created a limited public forum in which student groups could gather for a variety of purposes. More than twenty-five groups were already meeting, and no student-initiated organization other than Petros had ever been excluded. The court found that "the high school's decision to create an activity hour to promote and stimulate student group participation is factually similar to the situation in *Widmar*" (p. 706), and that Petros could not be excluded from the forum solely because it was religious. To be sure, the court acknowledged, "there may be some instances in which a high school forum does not give rise to the same right of expression as does a university forum" (pp. 706–7), but in its view high school students are mature enough to understand that including Petros in the activity program would not constitute an endorsement of religion by school officials. "In essence," the court declared, "these students want the government passively to acknowledge that they have religious interests, just as others are 'benefiting' from the government's recognition that they are interested in sports, journalism or the theatre. By recognizing that students have these religious interests, the school would not be 'advancing' religion in the Establishment Clause sense.... Any advancement of religion would come from the students themselves, and this the Establishment Clause does not bar, it being a limitation on government conduct rather than on individual activity" (p. 711).

The Williamsport school board voted not to appeal, but one board member, John Youngman, appealed on his own. The Court of Appeals for the Third Circuit subsequently reversed the district court's decision, finding that school officials would indeed violate the Establishment Clause by permitting Petros to meet during the activity periods. While acknowledging that the Petros members had a legitimate free-speech claim, it ruled that the school's obligation to avoid endorsing religion took precedence over the students' desire to engage in religious speech during the activity periods. The appeals court also asserted that there is a greater difference between high schools and universities than the district court had recognized, which limited the applicability of *Widmar*. Among other things, the appeals court did not share the district court's certainty that high school students would distinguish between permitting a particular activity and endorsing it.

The Supreme Court agreed to consider the case but later concluded that Youngman should not have been allowed to take it to the Court of Appeals for the Third Circuit when the school board as a whole had voted against doing so. The appeals court's decision in favor of the school was thus declared null and void, which had the effect of reinstating the district court's ruling in favor of Petros. This result was a victory for Ericsson and Colby to the extent that Williamsport school officials had to allow the group to meet, but because the Supreme Court had not addressed the substantive issues of the case, its ruling in *Bender* did not set a meaningful precedent regarding student religious clubs in secondary schools. Nevertheless, while this outcome lessened the legal significance of *Bender,* it had the opposite effect on its political impact. Together with *Brandon* and *Lubbock, Bender* added credibility to the argument that equal-access legislation was necessary because the courts could not be relied upon to protect student-initiated religious speech. This interweaving of judicial decisions with the legislative process illustrates the ongoing interplay between Congress and the courts, often orchestrated by advocacy groups that carry out a coherent strategy of lobbying and litigating. It was neither coincidental nor unusual that the same CLS attorneys who filed *Bender* also drafted the equal-access bill and led the lobbying campaign in its favor.

THE MILLS OF CONGRESS GRIND EXCEEDING SLOW

Despite the increasing momentum in favor of equal access, Hatfield's bill was in its third legislative year before it finally came up for a vote—a delay largely attributable to school-prayer advocates who were unwilling to surrender their dream of restoring state-sponsored devotionals. Owing to their influence, Hatfield's proposal was held up until three other bills had been considered. Among them, they represented all the approaches that had been explored before equal access: court-stripping, a constitutional amendment, and silent prayer.

The first of these measures to be acted on was Senator Jesse Helms's (R–North Carolina) perennial proposal to deprive the federal courts of the authority to hear school-prayer cases (see Chapter Nine). He reintroduced it as an amendment to legislation that would raise the ceiling on the national debt, thus sparking a filibuster that was in progress when Hatfield introduced the equal-access bill. At the urging of Majority Leader Howard Baker (R-Tennessee), the Senate sent the debt-ceiling bill back to the Finance Committee to be stripped of all amendments and proposed amendments, including Helms's court-stripping language. The committee complied, and Baker warned against any further attempts to amend it. The bill passed amid bitter complaints that the fuss over court-stripping had prevented senators from amending or even discussing the Reagan administration's request to raise the ceiling on the national debt. (In the heat of this debate, a court-stripping opponent, Senator Dale Bumpers [D-Arkansas], inadvertently referred to Helms as "the senator from South Carolina." When the mistake was brought to his attention, Bumpers apologized immediately—to the State of South Carolina.)

Following the failure of Helms's court-stripping measure, the Senate took up a proposed constitutional amendment to restore state-sponsored school prayer. Ordinarily, the seeming impossibility of passing such legislation would have doomed it from the start, but it received special attention because it had been sent to Congress by President Ronald Reagan. He had made a campaign promise to try to reinstate school prayer, and at the urging of conservative Christian groups such as the Moral Majority, Concerned Women for America, and the Christian Broadcasting Network, he assigned attorneys from the White House and the Justice Department to join law professors and advocacy-group lawyers in drafting a constitutional amendment.

AND NOW A BRIEF WORD ABOUT THE SPONSORS

In view of the important role played in the 1980s by conservative Christian organizations that generally favored court-stripping and the Reagan Amendment over equal access, and by evangelical groups that took the opposite view, this would be a good place to explain the difference between the two. Although those Protestant groups tending toward theological, political, and social conservatism are often lumped together indiscriminately under the labels "evangelical" and "fundamentalist," those terms are not in fact synonymous. Rather, fundamentalists are a subset of evangelicals just as evangelicals are a subset of Protestants. According to the Merriam-Webster Online Dictionary (*www.m-w.com*), "evangelical" means "emphasizing salvation by faith in the atoning death of Jesus Christ through personal conversion, the authority of Scripture, and the importance of preaching as contrasted with ritual." As this definition implies, evangelicals are distinguished from mainstream Protestants by the degree to which they emphasize the Bible as the inerrant and sole source of divine teaching, and by their subordination of ecclesiastical structures to the immediate contact of the individual soul with God. Evangelical pastors are less likely than mainstream ministers to be employed as full-time clergy or to receive extensive formal training, which contributed to the distinctions drawn during the Becker and Dirksen hearings between so-called academic elites and more down-to-earth evangelical preachers.

All evangelicals place great importance on spreading their faith as they believe Jesus commanded them to do, but they differ widely in the extent to which they seek to use either the power of the majority or the machinery of the state to further this cause. Those described as fundamentalists are more likely to favor majoritarian, state-run religious practices, whereas nonfundamentalist evangelicals lean more toward enhancing opportunities for private individuals and groups to bear witness to their religious beliefs. Fundamentalists are also, as Merriam-Webster Online defines it, "marked by militant or crusading zeal" and inclined to emphasize "strict and literal adherence to a set of basic principles." In practical usage, the term "fundamentalist" may carry pejorative connotations to the extent that it has come to connote rigidity, intolerance, anti-intellectualism, and religious bullying, none of which is necessarily associated with the broader term "evangelical." For that reason, some fundamentalists prefer to be called something else, such as "conservative Christian." In general, the organizations associated with what author Matthew Moen calls "the Christian Right," also known as the Religious Right, are conservative Christian in orientation; among many others, these include the Moral Majority, the Christian Coalition, the Eagle Forum, and Concerned Women for America. (Although Moen's book, *The Christian Right and Congress* [1989], says little about the Reagan Amendment as such, it offers an in-depth assessment of the influence of Christian Right organizations during the Reagan administration.)

Neither conservative Christians nor evangelicals are as rigid and monolithic as they are sometimes portrayed, but evangelicals in particular are sometimes to be found allied with mainstream Protestant groups and even with such liberal organizations as the ACLU and People for the American Way. As Ericsson's efforts on behalf of equal access suggest, school prayer has been one of the issues on which evangelical groups such as the Christian Legal Society and the National Association of Evangelicals have parted company with their Christian Right counterparts. In an attempt to foster individual student prayer rather than school-sponsored majoritarian devotionals, they opted to support equal access in preference to the Reagan Amendment or court-stripping, which were backed by the Christian Right.

BACK TO THE REAGAN AMENDMENT

The amendment drafted by Christian Right groups and Reagan administration lawyers stated: "Nothing in this Constitution shall be construed to prohibit individual or group prayer in public schools or other public institutions. No person shall be required by the United States or by any State to participate in prayer" ("Proposed Constitutional Amendment to Permit Voluntary Prayer," p. 3; hereafter "1982 hearings"). It was sent to Congress accompanied by a letter from the president, the Justice Department's analysis of the proposal, and a further clarification in question-and-answer format. In his letter, Reagan declared that the restoration of traditional school prayer would foster democracy because "our liberty springs from and depends upon an abiding faith in God" ("Voluntary School Prayer Constitutional Amendment," p. 6; hereafter "1983 hearings"). He also said that the majority should rule in matters of religion and that states and local communities should be able to conduct any kind of school prayer they wish.

The Justice Department's analysis and the Q&A sheet expanded upon the notion that the amendment would allow states and local districts to make their own rules regarding public-school devotionals. Indeed, these documents asserted, state or local officials could go so far as to compose school prayers, which would not have to be nondenominational. As Chapters Seven and Eight indicate, earlier proposals to amend the Constitution had been buried under a mass of questions about exactly how school-prayer programs would be administered. By coming out squarely in favor of states' rights and local control, the Reagan administration offered a single reply to all such queries: let each state either determine its own policies or delegate that authority to local school districts. The only exception to this deference to states' rights was the stipulation that no state could require anyone to participate in prayer. Predictably, some states'-rights purists repeated the arguments they had made during the debates over the Becker, Dirksen, and Wylie Amendments, protesting that there should be no federal limitation on a state's authority with regard to religion. Reagan administration officials replied that without the opt-out provision, the amendment could be seen as a threat to the religious liberty of dissenters. Moreover, its passage would require the support of a broad coalition of school-prayer advocates, many of whom would not back any measure that would allow government officials to compel participation in divine worship.

The Reagan Amendment was sponsored in the Senate by Strom Thurmond (R–South Carolina), who as chairperson of the Judiciary Committee was ideally placed to advance it. This option was not available in the House, whose Judiciary Committee was chaired by Representative Peter Rodino (D–New Jersey), a long-standing foe of state-sponsored school prayer. Rodino later declared that his great respect for the presidency would have led him to respond deferentially if he had been approached about the Reagan Amendment, but when asked whether he might have been sufficiently impressed to let it out of his committee, he replied with a grin, "No way in hell" (interview, July 23, 1996). Reagan's staff did not even try to work with Rodino, choosing instead to have the amendment introduced in the House by Representative Thomas Kindness (R-Ohio). But no matter who sponsored it, it still had to be referred to the Judiciary Committee, from which it was unlikely ever to emerge. School-prayer stalwarts in the House filed a discharge petition in an effort to circumvent the committee, but with little chance of success. Even in the Senate, the Reagan Amendment did not come up for a vote during the 1982 congressional session, although Thurmond held three days of hearings on it. When Congress reconvened in 1983, he reintroduced it and then passed it along to one of its co-sponsors, Senator Orrin Hatch (R-Utah), who chaired the Judiciary Committee's Subcommittee on the Constitution. Hatch conducted further hearings at which many of the same organizations and individuals who had appeared at the Becker and Dirksen hearings testified yet again. Not surprisingly, the 1982 and 1983 hearings covered the same issues as did the earlier ones: majority rights versus individual liberty, states' rights versus federal control, the relationship between morality and school prayer, the adequacy of opt-out policies as a protection for minority rights, the threat of religious divisiveness and competition, and the accuracy of the Supreme Court's interpretation of the Constitution. Since these matters have already been discussed at length in previous chapters, they will not be repeated here.

In addition to recycling arguments from earlier debates, witnesses at the Reagan Amendment hearings raised a few new issues that were, on the whole, unfavorable to the proposal. Among the most damaging of these was the emergence of the competing equal-access model, which Hatfield outlined when he appeared as the first witness at the 1982 hearings. Hatfield, an evangelical Baptist and an influential member of Reagan's own Republican Party, explained why he favored a student-oriented, flexible approach over the traditional state-sponsored exercises envisioned by amendment supporters. "By chilling sincere efforts to pray for God's grace and forgiveness in voluntary meetings that do not disrupt the academic functions of a public school," he testified, "we do far more damage to the Nation's moral fiber than through any Supreme Court decision that invalidates a routine, formalistic, and spiritually bankrupt prayer" (p. 7). He made this point even more forcefully in a speech on the Senate floor in which he denied that state-sponsored prayer "is going to get anybody into Heaven or any place else in the hereafter. And merely because they get goosebumps when they hear Kate Smith sing 'God Bless America' or when they pledge allegiance to one nation under God or somehow they go through a ritualistic prayer in schools, they confuse that as being the spiritual sinew of America. I think that is pretty superficial and not at all in concert with what I feel is Biblical faith that is a foundation of my own religion" (*Congressional Record,* March 8, 1984, p. 4895).

The combination of Hatfield's sponsorship and the Christian Legal Society's authorship earned the equal-access bill a respectful hearing from other evangelical organizations, notably the National Association of Evangelicals. From a practical perspective, the NAE realized that the Reagan Amendment, designed primarily by and for the president's Christian Right supporters, was what NAE legal counsel Forest Montgomery later described as "a purely political act" rather than a viable piece of legislation (interview, August 4, 1995; all quotations from Montgomery are from this interview). While giving Reagan credit for opening a discussion on school prayer, the NAE felt that Hatfield's bill was more likely to bring about an actual change in the law. The group also agreed with Ericsson and Hatfield in preferring student-initiated prayer to state-controlled religious exercises as a matter of principle. "Evangelicals," Montgomery repeatedly asserted, "do not want Caesar in the prayer business." Despite these reservations, the NAE perfunctorily endorsed the amendment out of respect for the president, but its leaders did little to further it; instead, they urged their powerful network of religious broadcasters to throw their support behind equal access.

With evangelical organizations joining mainstream Protestant groups in preferring equal access to the Reagan Amendment, the last thing amendment supporters needed was opposition from the Catholic Church. To their dismay, the U.S. Catholic Conference wrote to the Senate Judiciary Committee to express the American bishops' collective disapproval of the amendment because it failed to provide for in-school religion classes. The bishops' protest harked back to nineteenth-century controversies in which their predecessors had objected to Bible-reading "without note or comment" in the public schools because they believed that Catholic children should be taught the Church's view of Scripture. Applying the same logic to the Reagan Amendment, the USCC maintained that if government-prescribed worship services were held in the public schools, they should be accompanied by an opportunity for children to be instructed in the beliefs of their own religions. "For many children," the letter explained, "prayer alone will not necessarily lead to a deeper understanding of faith, or even to the significance and importance of prayer itself. To this end religious instruction becomes an integral aspect of the prayer in schools issue. Prayer, without a framework of voluntary instruction in the child's religious tradition, is not sufficient fully to insure the individual's religious freedom" (1983 hearings, p. 618). Echoing a point Bishop Hughes had made almost a century and a half earlier, the USCC also noted that religion classes would weaken the distinction between public and parochial education, thus aiding the Church's long quest for tax-supported religious schools.

AN ALTERNATIVE IS HATCHED

From the viewpoint of the amendment's supporters, even worse than the opposition of evangelical groups and the Catholic Church was a marked lack of enthusiasm on the part of its most influential sponsors, Thurmond and

Hatch. According to their aides, the senators wanted to accommodate the president but were irked by what they deemed the Reagan administration's failure to include them in the drafting process. As they saw it, they had been called in at the last minute and asked, as a sign of loyalty to the president, to champion legislation they considered defective. In a 1998 interview, a senior staffer who had worked for Hatch in the 1980s used such terms as "caught off guard," "saddened," "hurt," and "taken aback" to describe the senator's responses. By endorsing the agenda of the Christian Right groups, Hatch felt, the White House was squandering an opportunity to promote more moderate school-prayer legislation that would have had a chance of passing. Hatch and Thurmond also resented the tactics of organizations that, as Moen observed, "ran simplistic pressure campaigns, bullied friends and allies, failed to unite behind legislative proposals, squandered valuable time and resources on quixotic tasks, applied pressure with imprecision, failed to exhibit a thorough understanding of issues and of legislative strategy, and neglected to appreciate the difference between the systematic [e.g., how many contributions they received, how many editorials endorsed their cause] and congressional agendas" (p. 155). Refusing to compromise in any way, they failed to comprehend that not even the president's influence could ensure the success of a proposal that lacked widespread appeal.

Hatch brought his dissatisfaction into the open during a subcommittee hearing in which he accused conservative Christian groups of pressuring what he saw as a naïve White House into supporting extreme measures, such as permitting government-composed prayer. He also complained bitterly about the way those groups treated senators who tried to educate them about political realities. As he told the *Congressional Quarterly,* "[S]ome of our right-wing friends continue to badger and fight and cause difficulties and disruptions and animosities and bad feelings because they can't get their most extreme approach on a lot of these issues. I think that the White House has to get its act in order" (Nadine Cohodas, "Senate Panel Bows to Pressure; Postpones School Prayer Vote," May 28, 1983, p. 1051). Convinced that the Reagan Amendment would not pass, Hatch presented his own proposed constitutional amendment: "Nothing in this Constitution shall be construed to prohibit individual or group silent prayer or meditation in public schools. Neither the United States nor any State shall require any person to participate in such prayer or meditation, nor shall they encourage any particular form of prayer or meditation. Nothing in this Constitution shall be construed to prohibit equal access to the use of public school facilities by all voluntary student groups" ("School Prayer Constitutional

Amendment," pp. 1–2). He emphasized that this amendment would permit government-endorsed silent prayer, not just neutral moments of silence, thus promoting religion without favoring any particular faith.

The main arguments for and against government-sponsored silent prayer are discussed in Chapter Ten and will not be repeated here, but this particular proposal generated additional strife because of the context in which it was offered. Obviously, it would do the Reagan Amendment no good for senators to know that if they voted against it, they would have another opportunity to cast a pro-prayer vote before the upcoming election. In addition, Hatch's use of equal-access language infuriated Hatfield, who had been honoring a request from his party's leadership to cease his direct competition with the Reagan Amendment. "Then," he declared indignantly, "I awaken to the fact that [equal access] has been offered and combined, fused, linked to the [Hatch] constitutional amendment" (*Congressional Record*, March 7, 1984, p. 4894). In a letter to his Senate colleagues, he protested that the inclusion of equal access in a constitutional amendment "undercuts the very heart of my legislation" (March 13, 1984), which was based on the contention that equal-access rights are already protected by the Constitution.

TAKE TWO

Chairman Thurmond was among those who preferred vocal to silent prayer, but instead of rejecting the Hatch Amendment outright, he used it as leverage to extract a concession from the White House. In exchange for Thurmond's promise that Hatch's proposal would not come up for a vote on the Senate floor, the following sentence was added to the Reagan Amendment: "Neither the United States nor any State shall compose the words of any prayer to be said in public schools" ("Voluntary School Prayer Amendment," p. 3). The Judiciary Committee then voted 14–3 to send both the revised Reagan Amendment and the Hatch Amendment to the full Senate with no recommendation on either of them. Although it was understood that only the Reagan Amendment would come up for a vote, its supporters were furious that even after the provision for government-composed prayer had been sacrificed, the Judiciary Committee had not given the proposal the resounding recommendation they felt it deserved.

The Senate took no action on the Reagan Amendment for almost a year, which left plenty of time for a lobbying war that heightened the tension between the Christian Right groups and professional politicians—even the president. Advocates of the Reagan Amendment expected him to act as the chief proponent for their cause, and although he gave a speech to the NAE and spoke with undecided senators, the activists wanted more. "'They should,'" said Gary Jarmin of Christian Voice,[3] "'have had the hinges on the doors at the White House swinging back and forth with senators coming in and out'" (Nadine Cohodas, "Senate Vote Set on Vocal Prayer Amendment," *Congressional Quarterly*, March 17, 1984, p. 633). One of the senators whom Reagan did lobby was Arlen Specter (R-Pennsylvania), who later voted against the amendment. As he described the meeting, the president "in a very low keyed and unpressured presentation, suggested that he was interested in having the amendment passed" (*Congressional Record*, March 19, 1984, p. 5834). Some of its most ardent supporters would have preferred a more aggressive approach.

GOD IS NOT CHEWING GUM

When the Reagan Amendment finally came up for debate on the Senate floor, Hatch put aside his irritation to lead the fight in its favor. Avoiding any discussion of its specific provisions, he focused on the value of prayer, and the debate he initiated sounded more theological than political as senators wrangled over the relative merits of different kinds of religious observances. According to Hatch, daily school-sponsored prayer would teach students "that there is something outside of self, that God is the ordering power and intelligence behind the universe, that he and the things he creates are good, and that therefore efforts to learn about the created order are worthwhile. Thus, through the very act of praying, a solid basis for learning is established" (*Congressional Record*, March 6, 1984, p. 4333). He also rejected the argument that state-sponsored majoritarian prayer would harm religious minorities. "I can remember as a young Mormon boy in Pittsburgh, Pa.," he recalled, "saying the Lord's Prayer every day in school, alongside of Jewish children, Jehovah's Witness children, and some who came from families who claimed to be agnostic or atheist. And I can tell you it did not hurt any of us and it did not hurt any of them" (*Congressional Record*, March 13, 1984, p. 5272).

Among the most vocal opponents of Hatch's viewpoint was Senator John Danforth (R-Missouri), an Episcopal priest, who protested that the heartfelt worship of God is not compatible with a formalistic prayer rattled off daily at the behest of the government. Prayer, he declared, "should not be cheapened. It should not be trivialized. It should not be prostituted." His most impassioned rhetoric was directed against the claim that God has been expelled from the schools: "To many religious people, God is not dependent on the Supreme Court or the Congress. Objects may be kept out of the classroom, chewing gum for example. God is not chewing gum. He is the Creator of heaven and Earth" (*Congressional Record*, March 6, p. 4581). Senator Charles Mathias (R-Maryland) enlarged on this point, asking, "Are the children in public schools, in fact, forbidden to pray? If so, who is stopping them? Has God really been banished from our classrooms? If so, what is the omnipotent force that has achieved such a feat?" (*Congressional Record*, March 8, 1984, p. 4887). Hatch decried this view as "the equivalent of saying that prisoners in Siberia cannot be prevented from praying for their salvation whenever they choose.... [It is] equivalent to saying that the State cannot mind read. So what? The issue ... is voluntary prayer, voluntary group prayer, voluntary group prayer accommodated by school authorities" (p. 4890). Without state recognition, Hatch maintained, prayer would be an underground activity rather than a recognized, respected part of the official school day.

Vice President George Bush presided over the vote on the Reagan Amendment, which received a simple majority of 56–44 but not the required two-thirds. As Minority Leader Robert Byrd (D–West Virginia) was quick to point out, this outcome was not attributable to either political party. Nineteen Democrats, including Byrd, voted for the amendment, and eighteen Republicans voted against it. The *Congressional Quarterly* suggested that the determining factor might have been election-year politics, since the strongest vote for the amendment came from the third of the Senate that would be up for reelection in 1984, followed by the third whose terms would end in 1986. The smallest number of favorable votes came from senators whose terms would not expire until 1988.

As soon as the Reagan Amendment had been dealt with, attention immediately turned to equal access. Reagan himself endorsed the concept, as did a wide variety of advocacy groups. Nevertheless, as Chapter Twelve explains, competing proposals and disagreements about specific provisions ensured that the fight was far from over.

12

Perkins's Last Stand

> The central question in this debate as I see it is simply: How can we adequately protect the right of our people to be free from having an alien religious practice forced upon their children by government action, but at the same time allow them to freely exercise their own religion without government hostility?
>
> —*Senator Mark Hatfield*

In spring 1983, while the Reagan Amendment was still making its way through the Senate Judiciary Committee, hearings began on two equal-access bills that were in hot competition with the president's plan and with each other. The first to be introduced was the Religious Speech Protection Act, sponsored in the Senate by Mark Hatfield (R-Oregon) and in the House of Representatives by Don Bonker (D-Washington). It provided: "It shall be unlawful for a public secondary school receiving Federal financial assistance, which generally allows groups of students to meet during noninstructional periods, to discriminate against any meeting of students on the basis of the religious content of the speech at such meeting, if (1) the meeting is voluntary and orderly, and (2) no activity which is in and of itself unlawful is permitted. Nothing in this Act shall be construed to permit the United States or any State or political subdivision thereof to (1) influence the form or content of any prayer or other religious activity, or (2) require any person to participate in prayer or other religious activity" ("Equal Access: A First Amendment Question," pp. 290–91; hereafter "Senate hearings").

Vying with the Hatfield/Bonker bill was the Equal Access Act, sponsored in the Senate by Jeremiah Denton (R-Alabama) and in the House by Trent Lott (R-Mississippi).[1] Although both proposals sparked debate, Denton/Lott was the more controversial of the two. Whereas Hatfield/Bonker applied only to secondary schools that accepted federal funds, Denton/Lott extended unconditionally to all public elementary, secondary, and post-secondary schools. It also provided that if any extracurricular activities were permitted, then not only students but also faculty would be entitled to engage in "prayer, religious discussion, or silent meditation" (p. 294). Finally, it did not prohibit government influence or coercion in religious matters.

PRACTICAL POLITICS

Despite their differences, either bill would have allowed students and parents to sue in federal court if they felt that their equal-access rights had been violated. Because this so-called judicial remedy would create a new basis for filing federal lawsuits, both proposals fell under Judiciary Committee jurisdiction. This posed no problem for the Senate versions of the two bills because the Senate Judiciary Committee, of which Denton was a member, supported equal access in principle despite some disagreement about specific provisions. The situation was different in the House, whose Judiciary Committee had been the burial place of countless earlier plans for bringing prayer back into the public schools.

Predictably, pro-equal-access lobbyists swarmed around House Judiciary Committee Chairman Peter Rodino (D–New Jersey) in the hope of persuading him that this new approach was a far cry from the school-prayer legislation he had so vigorously opposed in the past. Unimpressed, Rodino made it plain that any equal-access bill sent to his committee would sink without a trace. According to Mary Cooper, a lobbyist for the National Council of Churches, this forthright refusal was, in its own way, a favor. "He could have gotten us to let him have it and then bottled it up," she later recalled. "But he was an old friend, and he told us candidly that he would oppose it" (interview, August 2, 1993). Rodino himself described his attitude as having been ambivalent and pragmatic rather than hostile. He would have rejected any proposal that would "revive the whole school-prayer thing, be back-door school prayer," he explained, but if it were "just a way of letting the kids know they had a right to participate in something if they wanted to, I wasn't opposed to the concept as such." Nevertheless, he said, he was happy to direct the legislation away from his committee, where opposition by influential members "would have bogged down other things I wanted to expedite" (interview, July 23, 1996).

Since both equal-access bills were chiefly concerned with public education, the only reason for sending them to the House Judiciary Committee was the inclusion of a judicial remedy. Absent that provision, both bills would clearly belong in the House Education and Labor Committee, whose chair, Representative Carl Perkins (D-Kentucky), was favorably disposed toward equal access.

Accordingly, Bonker and Lott amended their respective proposals to say that noncompliant schools or school districts would lose all their federal funding. Few people genuinely favored such a draconian penalty, and it would have been all but impossible for the Department of Education, which oversees the disbursement of federal education money, to monitor compliance. As equal-access supporters openly acknowledged, the funding cutoff was a temporary measure designed to rescue the legislation from the House Judiciary Committee. Once an equal-access bill had passed both Houses, they promised, that provision would be eliminated in the House/Senate conference that would produce the final version of the legislation.

IS EQUAL-ACCESS LEGISLATION NECESSARY?

Shortly after the various equal-access measures were introduced, the Senate Judiciary Committee and the House Education and Labor Committee began holding hearings. Ignoring for a moment the differences among the various proposals, the testimony for and against the basic concept of equal access may be summarized as follows:

Top Five Reasons for Supporting Equal Access

- School officials who permit noncurricular activities thereby create an open forum in which students should be free to engage in religious as well as secular speech. Since the government may neither advance nor hinder religion, the practice of allowing secular activities but not student-initiated religious clubs violates the Establishment Clause by favoring secular speech over religious expression.
- Even if all school administrators allowed students to pray informally among themselves, there would still be a need for an equal-access bill because religious liberty requires not only ad hoc prayer but also the establishment of formal, school-recognized religious clubs if comparable secular groups are permitted.
- The federal courts are overly concerned with church/state separation and act slowly, if at all, to protect religious liberty. Moreover, their fact-specific, case-by-case approach yields piecemeal and contradictory results. Congress should therefore issue a broad-brush declaration that student religious groups have the unqualified right to function on equal terms with other noncurricular activities.
- Equal-access legislation would counteract the ACLU's long-standing practice of using lawsuits to intimidate school officials into excluding religion.

Under an equal-access policy, school-prayer advocates would be more likely
to prevail in court, and they would have a basis for threatening and filing
their own lawsuits.

- Religion has been excluded from the public schools, where children are
  punished for reading the Bible, reciting a blessing before meals, or even
  mentioning God. This has led to low test scores, drug use, violence, and a
  host of other evils. Although some school-prayer advocates favor student-
  controlled worship while others prefer state-sponsored prayer, an equal-
  access law would be at least a step toward returning God and morality to
  public education.

Top Five Reasons for Opposing Equal Access

- Nothing in current law prevents students from praying on their own, so
  there is no need for a new law to protect that right. The real effect of equal-
  access legislation would not be to uphold the students' personal religious
  liberty, which is already adequately covered, but to confer official school
  recognition on religious groups.
- It is true that some school administrators improperly interfere with student-initiated religious speech, but the solution to such errors is education,
  not legislation. Moreover, much of this confusion is caused by pro-prayer
  activists who trumpet the inaccurate statement that God has been kicked
  out of the schools. Equal-access supporters are thus trying to use the mistakes of some school officials, which arise in part from the pro-prayer side's
  own misrepresentations, as a reason for injecting formal, school-recognized religious activities into public education.
- An open-forum argument might be appropriate if a school admitted some
  ideological clubs, such as the Young Democrats or the Young Republicans,
  while excluding opposing viewpoints. But the existence of activity-oriented
  clubs, such as stamp-collecting and chess, does not justify the addition of
  organized religious activities to the official school program.
- School-prayer activists, including some school officials, are eager to use the
  claim of student initiative as a pretext for reinstituting majoritarian religious observances that would be widely understood to carry the endorsement of the school.
- The ACLU and other organizations have indeed sued to prevent state-
  sponsored prayer, but evangelical and fundamentalist groups have also
  filed numerous lawsuits, many of which have been successful. Far from
  leveling the playing field, equal-access legislation would encourage uncon-

stitutional religious activity by allowing activists to bully school officials into according it a privileged place.

WHAT SHOULD THE IDEAL EQUAL-ACCESS BILL LOOK LIKE?

Despite spirited opposition by some lobbyists and members of Congress, equal access had wide enough appeal to give the legislation a real chance of passing—*if* its proponents could agree on a single proposal. Accordingly, the sponsors of the various bills worked with their allies and potential allies to craft a composite version that would attract broad-based support. Denton and Lott agreed to omit faculty prayer at institutions of higher education and to prohibit government influence over religious activities, which left only two major areas of disagreement:

- Should the legislation apply to elementary as well as secondary school students?
- Should the legislation protect only religious speech or all lawful student expression?

Should Equal-Access Legislation Apply to Elementary as Well as Secondary School Students?

Denton agreed to drop college students from the bill because *Widmar* already protected their right to hold religious meetings on campus, but he was reluctant to exclude elementary school children. Regardless of age, he maintained, all students have a constitutional right to engage in private religious speech wherever secular conversation is permitted. This assertion was contradicted by people who considered elementary school children too young to run their own religious meetings or to understand that permission is not the same as approval. As John W. Baker, general counsel for the Baptist Joint Committee on Public Affairs, explained, "The lack of maturity in elementary school pupils requires that their school day be rigidly structured and supervised. The introduction of religion at this level would be neither voluntary nor student initiated. It would be the product of parents who want their own religious beliefs given voice to all the students in a class, or it would be a reflection of the religious beliefs of the teacher" (Senate hearings, p. 271). This view prevailed, and the equal-access bill that Hatfield and Denton later co-sponsored applied only to secondary schools.

Should the Bill Protect Only Religious Speech or All Lawful Student Expression?
The sponsors of the various equal-access bills limited them to religious groups because they felt that only religious speech was in need of statutory protection. According to Lott, for instance, "[T]he only student organizations which have been denied the right to use school facilities are voluntary religious organizations....While a few courts, including the Supreme Court, have protected religious rights in some places and under some circumstances, many more courts have denied voluntary religious groups the same rights enjoyed by others" ("Hearings on the Equal Access Act," p. 3; hereafter "1983 House hearings"). Similarly, Perkins and Bonker asserted in a letter to their House colleagues that "The purpose of the bill is to remove the double standard used against student religious groups when all other types of student groups are permitted to meet and exercise their right to free speech" (May 4, 1984). They also feared that if the equal-access legislation applied to all speech, it might be used by undesirable groups, such as hate groups or cults, as a means of demanding entry into the schools.

Those who opposed a religion-only bill denied that secular speech is already adequately protected. To be sure, they conceded, if an extracurricular program exists at all, some secular activity is presumably permitted. That does not mean, however, that any and all secular speech could find a place in that program. A school could, for instance, have a Young Homemakers Club but reject any group with a feminist orientation. For that reason, they maintained that a law that applied only to religious clubs would catapult religious expression into a privileged—not an equal—position. They also predicted that a religion-only bill would be declared unconstitutional on the ground that its intent and/or effect was to advance religion. More fundamentally, as Representative Gary Ackerman (D–New York) pointed out, it was far from clear "who makes the determination as to ... what is a religion and what isn't a religion?" ("Religious Speech Protection Act," p. 26). In his view, claims of religious belief could be used to force administrators to admit objectionable groups, including hate groups and cults, into the school. Conversely, little-known or unpopular sects might be discriminated against by school officials whose understanding of religion was limited to more familiar denominations, as had happened when the Jehovah's Witnesses were excluded from a program of religious instruction in Champaign, Illinois (see Chapter Four). In the words of Ruti Teitel of the Anti-Defamation League, "Should this legislation be enacted, the prayers that will echo in the halls of our public schools will not be the prayers of a single Buddhist or Jew in a small town somewhere, but rather the prayers of the prevailing majority students and faculty" (Senate hearings, p. 231).

Denton took the lead in ridiculing objections of this kind, but in so doing he displayed such a breezy disregard for unfamiliar belief systems that he appeared to confirm his opponents' predictions about the legislation's likely effect on minority faiths. According to Denton, "Senator [Dennis] DeConcini [D-Arizona], I believe it was, [said] that witchcraft or the Ku Klux Klan or the black revolutionary army of Libya or something could have meetings. So the school board will have the local and commonsense prerogative of making such obvious exclusions. However, there is no way they would be making exclusions on an [sic] anything like normal religious denominational basis" (1983 House hearings, p. 134). Among the witnesses who responded with horror to these remarks was Charles Bergstrom of the Lutheran Council in the U.S.A., who asked, "What in the world is a normal religion? To some it would include the fellow who, without clothing, danced on the bed of the metro and claimed his right to do that" (p. 185). Professor Arnold Loewy of the University of North Carolina School of Law added, "I do not think we can limit it to normal anything. The whole philosophy of an open forum is that the State doesn't care what is said so long as it is not unlawful speech, such as inciting the violent overthrow of the Government or something" (p. 201). Despite these arguments, most equal-access leaders preferred a religion-only bill and held out for that language as long as possible.

ACT ONE: THE HOUSE

Following the hearings, two revised versions of equal-access legislation were introduced, one in the House and one in the Senate. Both were entitled the Equal Access Act (EAA), and both applied only to public secondary schools that accept federal funds and generally allow noncurricular clubs to meet. Both of them further stated that schools could not discriminate against student-initiated religious clubs as long as their activities were voluntary, lawful, and free from involvement by school personnel except for nonparticipatory monitoring. The only substantive difference between the House and Senate bills lay in the penalty to be suffered by noncompliant schools. For the reasons explained earlier, the House version provided that they would lose their federal funding, whereas the Senate bill would allow them to be sued in federal court by interested parties who believed that the law was being violated. This revised equal-access legislation was developed in consultation with numerous members of Congress, legal scholars, and lobbyists—indeed, Hatfield later claimed that more than a thousand people had contributed input. The result was a delicately balanced, painstakingly crafted bill backed by an unusual coalition of Catholic, mainstream Protestant, and evangelical groups. The introduction of any controversial amendment could easily shatter this assortment of unlikely bedfellows, so of course foes of the EAA armed themselves with potentially disruptive proposals drafted by such groups as the American Jewish Congress, the American Civil Liberties Union, and Americans United for Separation of Church and State.

The first vote on the EAA was taken in the House, where Perkins's power as chairperson of the Education and Labor Committee facilitated prompt action. Given the importance of preserving the precise wording of the bill, his first step would ordinarily have been to ask the House Rules Committee to declare a so-called closed rule on the EAA, thus preventing House members from proposing any amendments to it. That route was blocked, however, because the Rules Committee was chaired by Representative Claude Pepper (D-Florida), a staunch opponent of equal access. As Perkins wryly observed, it would have taken not just an Act of Congress but an Act of God to induce Pepper to send the EAA to the floor with any kind of rule. Since he could not take the EAA through the Rules Committee, Perkins asked Speaker Tip O'Neill (D-Massachusetts) to place it on what is known as the suspension calendar. On the plus side, from Perkins's point of view, this parliamentary maneuver would not only allow the legislation to come directly to the floor without going through the Rules Committee but would also prohibit any amendments to it. The negative side was that bills brought to the floor in this way require a two-thirds majority to pass. O'Neill opposed the EAA, but he was inclined to oblige Perkins, who was a good friend and an influential colleague, because he did not believe that the bill would attract the necessary votes. After a delay brought about by Democrats who did not share O'Neill's confidence that the measure would fail, the EAA was put on the calendar for May 15.

On the day of the vote, foes of the EAA found themselves blessed with unexpected—and no doubt unintentional—assistance from Representative Newt Gingrich (R-Georgia), who later became speaker of the House. Because of events that had nothing to do with equal access, Gingrich happened to choose May 15 to make an hour-long speech blistering the Democrats for action they had taken with regard to the Sandinista government of Nicaragua. Majority Leader James Wright (D-Texas) demanded equal time for reply, and the ensuing discussion was acrimonious even by the elastic standards of the House. Despite the sponsorship of two prominent Democrats, Perkins and Bonker, the EAA was generally perceived as a Republican school-prayer measure originating with Hatfield; and by the time it came up for debate, few Democrats felt inclined to support anything that smelled Republican.

The opposition to the EAA was led by Representative Don Edwards (D-California), who placed great significance on the fact that Perkins's committee had voted against adopting provisions under which clergy would have been prevented from leading religious services in the schools, and religious meetings would have been limited to the periods before and after the school day. To him, this showed that the EAA was meant to permit clergy-led worship in the school building during school hours, just as the Reagan Amendment would have done. Ackerman added, "[T]his bill is not school prayer in sheep's clothing. It is the blatant establishment of religion, naked, and undisguised.... This bill opens the door so wide that not only prayer, but the entire church could be moved inside" (*Congressional Record,* May 15, 1984, p. 12219).

At the urging of education organizations, notably the National Education Association and the National School Boards Association, some House members also raised concerns about the possibility that disputes over religion would divert attention and resources away from the schools' primary educational mission and from the multitudinous problems they already faced. Moreover, they suggested, nothing in the EAA would prevent teachers from being forced to monitor religious activities against their will; alternatively, they might have to disclose their own religious beliefs in order to justify refusing to oversee certain clubs. At a minimum, the education organizations and their congressional allies called for a rewording of the EAA that would allow schools to continue offering activity-oriented, nonideological extracurricular clubs without having to allow religious clubs. In response, EAA supporters accused the education groups of seeking to deprive students of their constitutional rights merely to avoid inconveniencing school personnel. They were particularly emphatic in opposing any distinction between ideological and nonideological clubs, since the most effective way of ensuring the inclusion of religious clubs was to say that otherwise there would be no extracurricular program at all.

At the conclusion of the debate, most Republicans voted for the EAA, but more than half of the Democrats voted against it. The result was a simple majority of 270–151, which fell short of the required two-thirds vote. Afterward, Perkins walked back to his office with Samuel Ericsson, the Christian Legal Society attorney who had spearheaded the drafting of the original EAA. When Ericsson expressed great disappointment that the discussion of equal access was over in the House until the next session of Congress, Perkins, sounding uncharacteristically irritable, replied that if the Senate voted strongly in favor of the bill, it would get another chance in the House. "But, Mr. Chairman," Ericsson deferentially reminded him, "didn't the Speaker say that there would be only one vote on equal access this year?" "You handle the Senate," Perkins snapped, "and leave the House to me" (interview with Samuel Ericsson, August 23, 1996; all quotations from Ericsson are from this interview). To that, Ericsson observed with amusement, the only possible response was "Yessir," so he said it and then went looking for the ACLU lobbyist, Barry Lynn. (Lynn is now executive director of Americans United for Separation of Church and State.)

The reason Ericsson wanted to see Lynn was that the ACLU's determined opposition to equal access was a major obstacle to its success in the Senate, and Ericsson was anxious to explore the possibility of a compromise. According to interviews with both men, Ericsson confronted Lynn with the argument that the EAA protected free speech, which the ACLU claimed to support. Lynn retorted that the EAA covered only religious expression. When Ericsson replied that other forms of speech were not under attack, Lynn ridiculed the notion that students were generally free to form clubs supporting feminism, homosexuality, reproductive choice, and other controversial views. Finally, Ericsson asked what the ACLU would do if Hatfield agreed to return to the wording of the Christian Legal Society's original equal-access proposal, which would prevent discrimination on the basis of either secular or religious speech. Lynn, who had already discussed this possibility with the ACLU board, predicted that the organization would "go neutral"—that is, it would withdraw its opposition without providing positive support. As he later recalled, the ACLU board was experiencing "deep division about the wisdom of this compromise at this time." Some members viewed equal access with suspicion, seeing it as yet another attempt to return majoritarian religious proselytizing to the public schools. To them, there was no point in helping to improve the bill, since "the worse it was written the better the chance it would either fail or be struck down in court." Other board members felt obliged to support the EAA if it covered all voluntary student meetings, since protection of free speech is the ACLU's raison d'être. Following what Lynn later described as "an unusually lively debate, even for the ACLU" (interview, November 3, 1997), the board agreed to go neutral if the bill included secular as well as religious speech.

ACT TWO: THE SENATE

Having reached agreement, the two lobbyists embarked on the task of selling a content-neutral EAA to key advocacy groups whose help they would need when the bill came up for a vote in the Senate. On the conservative side, Ericsson and other CLS attorneys won over their counterparts in the National Association of Evangelicals, who joined them in approaching the Christian Right organizations that had supported the Reagan Amendment. Although those groups would have preferred a religion-only EAA, they were persuaded not to put a great deal of energy into fighting the change to a content-neutral version. The CLS and the ACLU also contacted mainstream Protestant groups, notably the National Council of Churches, which readily agreed to endorse the broader wording. Those organizations then worked with the ACLU in seeking support or at least neutrality from education groups, such as the National Education Association and the National School Boards Association; Jewish organizations, such as the American Jewish Congress and the Anti-Defamation League; and secular or nondenominational separationist groups, such as Americans United for Separation of Church and State and People for the American Way. (Separationists believe that the need for separation of church and state should be the paramount consideration in disputes over government involvement with religion. They deny that the removal of religious matters from the sphere of government promotes either atheism or hostility toward religion; to them, such neutrality is required by the Constitution and by the need to accommodate America's ever-increasing religious diversity.) The education organizations agreed to go neutral, at least temporarily, although they later objected to some of the specific provisions of the content-neutral EAA. But the Jewish organizations and their separationist allies fought the EAA to the bitter end. No matter what other interests it might serve, it would open the public schools to organized religious exercises, and they would have none of it. Although they were in the minority, their determined opposition to any version of the EAA garnered enough congressional support to raise significant doubt about whether changing to the content-neutral language would in fact ensure passage of the bill. For this reason among others, Hatfield and Denton decided against doing so at that time, and the revised EAA that they co-sponsored in summer 1984 remained religion-only. (For further information on the role played by religious organizations in supporting or opposing the EAA, see Allen D. Hertzke's 1988 book, *Representing God in Washington*.)

Denton introduced the new EAA as an amendment to the Education for Economic Security Act, whose purpose was to improve education in mathematics and science. The proposed amendment, which continued to be known as the Equal Access Act, stated:

It shall be unlawful for any state or local educational agency that receives Federal financial assistance and that by policy or practice generally allows groups of secondary school students to meet during non-instructional time to deny equal access and opportunity to, or discriminate against, any student meeting on the basis of the religious content of the speech at such meeting if—

(1) the activity is voluntary and student initiated;

(2) there is no sponsorship of the activity by the school, the government or its agents or employees;

(3) the activity is not in and of itself unlawful; and

(4) the activity does not materially and substantially interfere with the orderly conduct of educational activities within the school.

Nothing in this Act shall be construed to permit the United States or any State or political subdivision thereof to (1) influence the form or content of any prayer or other religious activity; (2) require any person to participate in prayer or other religious activity; or (3) expend public funds beyond the incidental cost of allowing student-initiated activities on institution or school premises. (*Congressional Record*, June 6, 1984, pp. 15003–4)

While Denton was leading a discussion of the EAA on the Senate floor, Lynn was meeting with staff members in the office of Senator Lowell Weicker (R-Connecticut), who had threatened a filibuster against the Reagan Amendment and was contemplating similar action against the EAA. Weicker, walking through the office on his way to a meeting with Hatfield, saw Lynn and invited him to come along. As Lynn later recalled, Weicker told Hatfield that he would oppose the EAA even if it were revised to cover all speech; the question was whether he would merely speak out against it or take stronger action. He finally decided that he would probably filibuster if the EAA remained religion-only, but not if it were broadened. According to a former Hatfield aide, this threat of a filibuster with so little time left in the congressional session was the final straw that persuaded Hatfield to switch to a content-neutral version of the EAA. With Denton's reluctant acquiescence, the change was made.

The content-neutral EAA was approximately twice as long as the religion-only version because it attempted to address at least some of the points that had been raised in discussions with the various advocacy groups. Among other things, it specified that an open forum would be created if even one non-curricular club were allowed to meet during noninstructional time, defined as "time set aside by the school before actual classroom instruction begins or after actual classroom instruction ends." No federally funded public secondary school that created such a forum would be permitted to discriminate against any student meeting "on the basis of the religious, political, philosophical, or other content of the speech at such meetings." The bill further stated that all noncurricular student groups must be voluntary, student-initiated, free from school sponsorship, nondisruptive, and lawful. Clubs could not be excluded for having too few members, and outsiders could not "direct, conduct, control, or regularly attend activities of student groups." School personnel could attend religious meetings "only in a nonparticipatory capacity" and need not attend any meeting whose content was "contrary to the beliefs of the agent or employee" (*Congressional Record*, June 27, 1984, p. 19219). School personnel could not influence the content of any religious meeting or coerce anyone to participate in it.

Hatfield defended the change to a content-neutral EAA by emphasizing the need for compromise. To be sure, he acknowledged, the bill was not as he would have written it had he been able to do so alone. "But," he said, "I have to recognize the reality that this is a body that reaches its final decisions by consensus and consensus is not always easily obtained, and it has certainly not been easily obtained in this case" (p. 19218). If this speech was intended to forestall demands for further changes, it failed. The debate continued hot and heavy, particularly with regard to the following questions:

- What is "noninstructional time"?
- Should the same restrictions apply to all noncurricular clubs?
- Would the EAA allow adult outsiders to demand access to the schools?
- Under the EAA, to what extent could school officials exclude controversial activities?
- Would the EAA facilitate aggressive student-to-student proselytizing?

What Is "Noninstructional Time"?
Ever since his meeting with Weicker and Hatfield, Lynn has steadfastly maintained that Hatfield promised to sponsor legislation that would apply only to meetings that took place before the school day began or after it ended. The bill itself, however, referred to periods before or after "actual classroom instruction," which could be interpreted to include intervals between classes, lunchtime,

or any other period when students are not in class. During the Senate debate, Hatfield intimated that religious meetings could take place during any free period, and Denton explicitly stated that the EAA would permit them whenever the participants were not in class. In opposition, education organizations averred that parents might be able to monitor what their children did before or after school hours, but they would have no control over participation in religious activities during the school day. The strongest opposition came from Jewish groups, which protested that students would be less able to avoid unwanted exposure to majoritarian religious practices or pressure to participate in them if they took place all day long.

Should the Same Restrictions Apply to All Noncurricular Clubs?
The restrictions that the EAA placed on noncurricular activities, such as forbidding school endorsement and faculty participation, had originally been developed with religious clubs in mind. Under the new version of the bill, most of those limitations would extend to all noncurricular groups, including secular clubs. Senator Slade Gorton (R-Washington) took the lead in objecting that teachers should not be prohibited from leading secular activities, such as debate teams or community service clubs, or from encouraging students to join them. Hatfield replied, "When you throw the net out, you are going to garner in a few other things, but I do not think to the detriment or the efficiency of what you were seeking. It will not create a difficult problem" (p. 19223). Gorton later observed that Hatfield "has cast a huge net to catch an important, but modestly sized, fish and has pulled in an entire boatload of unintended consequences" (p. 19248).

Would the EAA Allow Adult Outsiders to Demand Access to the Schools?
For many senators, the prospect of allowing nonschool personnel to participate in student activities was particularly troubling because it might lead to clergy-run religious observances. They also associated outsiders with cults, hate groups, and other undesirable organizations. Indeed, there seemed to be a widespread, if not entirely realistic, assumption that secondary school students would never initiate such groups, which could thus be excluded merely by preventing outside adults from leading them. EAA supporters claimed that the bill would not create any new right to bring outsiders into the schools, so local authorities could continue to set their own policies as they had done in the past. Opponents retorted that the EAA would indeed reduce the amount of flexibility school officials would enjoy, since it would force them to admit

virtually every student-initiated group and treat them all the same. In their view, if adult members of a local drama club were permitted to help with a student play, for instance, then clergy could not be barred from comparable participation in student religious groups.

Under the EAA, to What Extent Could School Officials Exclude Controversial Activities?

In response to the concern that undesirable clubs might come into the schools through the EAA, Hatfield suggested that its ban on disruptive activity would adequately safeguard against this. Once again, Gorton led the opposition. Drawing on his experience as attorney general of the State of Washington, he maintained that as long as a group conducted itself in an orderly manner and did not interfere with the running of the school, it could not be declared disruptive merely because the ideas it espoused were unpopular. If groups could be excluded on that basis, he maintained, then the EAA would be useless because school officials could ban any disfavored meeting merely by defining "disruptive" to mean anything that they, or the majority, did not like. Hatfield replied that the whole point of the EAA was to allow religious groups into the schools, and the broader language had been inserted only because the bill would probably not have passed without it. He would rather risk the problems Gorton was describing, he declared, than continue to allow religious groups to be banned from the schools.

Gorton's concerns were shared by Senator Howard Metzenbaum (D-Ohio), who scoffed at Hatfield's implication that a content-neutral EAA would not affect the school officials' authority to exclude controversial student clubs. "Now," he said to Hatfield, "let us assume that you or someone else is on the school board and a proposal is made to hold a meeting there of the John Birch Society, the Young Communist League, the Young Americans for Freedom, or the Social Democrats, and the principal or the administrator, whoever is making the determination, concludes that he or she thinks such a meeting would be disruptive. On that basis alone, without further evidence, would that principal or administrator have the right to deny the use of the school?" (p. 19231). After several attempts to evade the question, Hatfield replied that he could not anticipate every possible scenario and was primarily concerned with the plight of religious clubs "where there is discrimination, where there is a violation of the freedom of speech" (p. 19232). Despite Metzenbaum's increasingly caustic efforts, Hatfield either did not believe or would not acknowledge that a content-neutral EAA would protect controversial secular groups. The EAA's other lead sponsor, Denton, stated unequivocally that a content-neutral EAA would have no effect on secular speech, which was already receiving all possible protection. As he saw it, even the content-neutral EAA would truly affect only religious clubs.

Would the EAA Facilitate Aggressive Student-to-Student Proselytizing?
In addition to expressing concern about cults and hate groups, Metzenbaum worried about proselytizing and religious partisanship. "This bill," he declared, "would not only play into the hands of various cults of this country, but it would invite friction and divisiveness among different religious groups. Religious activities at school would encourage some students to tease and ridicule others who do not attend religious meetings before or after school. And allowing religious activity at the school gives this activity an aura of Government approval—if the meeting is being held in the school, it cannot be too bad; it must have the approval of the school authority" (p. 19227). Senator John Danforth (R-Missouri) agreed. In his view, "It is the nature of religion to conduct a missionary effort... to reach out for other people and to try to pull those other people into the religious community.... I think it is absolutely predictable that, if religious enterprise is to take place in public schools before school hours, after school hours, during school hours, whenever it is going to be, part of that enterprise is going to be to try to get other kids joining the group. In fact, if no effort is made to bring others into the group, then they are not really operating as a church at all" (p. 19228). Accordingly, Danforth proposed to amend the EAA by adding: "Nothing in this act shall be construed to limit the authority of the school, its agents, or employees to maintain order and discipline on school premises, to protect the well-being of students and faculty, and to assure the attendance of students at meetings as voluntary" (p. 19229). The amendment passed easily, and despite Danforth's assertion that its intent was to curb overly zealous student-to-student proselytizing, it was generally seen as a means of allowing school officials to exclude any group they considered unwholesome. To EAA supporters, it strengthened the bill's protection against the admission of hate groups and cults; to their foes, its vague and subjective language could be used by school officials in homogeneous communities to restrict minority faiths while permitting members of the majority religion to proselytize at will.

As this summary suggests, the Senate debate was dominated by a few vocal EAA opponents who forced Hatfield and Denton into a largely defensive posture. This was misleading, however, because most senators had already decided to vote for the EAA. Particularly in its content-neutral form, it represented an appealing compromise on school prayer, and it provided political cover for senators who had voted against the Reagan Amendment. It passed with a vote of 88–11, and the Education for Economic Security Act to which it was attached also passed.

ACT THREE: THE HOUSE AGAIN

After the EAA had failed in the House in May, Perkins had promised Ericsson that if it received strong support from the Senate, he would find a way to bring it up for another vote in the House. No one could deny that the Senate vote had been overwhelming, and the switch to content-neutral language eased Perkins's task because some House members who had voted against the religion-only version would willingly support the revised proposal. His main problem was that the version of the EAA the Senate sent to the House contained a judicial remedy, thus allowing Speaker O'Neill to refer it to the House Judiciary Committee. EAA supporters were outraged; Representative Connie Mack (R-Florida),[2] for instance, accused the speaker of consigning the EAA "to his favorite resting place, the Judiciary Committee; or, as Mr. Perkins calls it, the burial committee" (*Congressional Record,* June 29, 1984, p. 20181). O'Neill retorted that Chairman Perkins would have demanded the same deference with regard to any legislation that properly belonged in his own committee. Besides, he said, he had told the Judiciary Committee that they had to respond by August 6, so the EAA was not bottled up. What he did not say was that the committee's response would almost certainly be a negative vote, and in any event there would be too little time left in the session for further action. In an infuriated response, Perkins declared that he would resort to a seldom-used parliamentary procedure called "Calendar Wednesday," which allows a chairperson to bring to the floor any bill that has been reported out of his or her committee. Since the EAA had previously been reported out of Perkins's Education and Labor Committee, he was entitled to use that provision.

Naturally, the House leadership detests Calendar Wednesday as much as it does discharge petitions (see Chapter Seven), and any chairperson who uses it is thereby defying the heads of his or her own party. Recognizing the dedication Perkins was showing, pro-EAA lobbyists pulled out all the stops to support him. Forest Montgomery of the National Association of Evangelicals, for instance, turned to his organization's network of broadcast evangelists for help. Appearing on a popular radio show hosted by Focus on the Family leader James Dobson, he and Ericsson urged school-prayer supporters to call their congressional representatives. "Go bonkers for Bonker" was their slogan. "We really got 'em stirred up," Montgomery recalled. By his count, more than a hundred thousand calls flooded congressional offices that weekend in support of Perkins, whom he called "that grand old man" (interview, August 4, 1995).

The House debate began on Tuesday, July 24, with the expectation that Perkins would call for a vote the next day under the Calendar Wednesday procedure. O'Neill, who had apparently underestimated Perkins's determination to bring the EAA to a vote, did not want to force a showdown with a senior and highly respected member of his own party. He therefore allowed the EAA to come up for a vote under a suspension of the rules, as he had done two months earlier. Once again, no amendments were in order, and the bill required a two-thirds vote to pass. The debate, limited to an hour, covered essentially the same points that had arisen in the Senate, although there was less discussion of matters not directly related to religion. The EAA passed, 337–77, and the Education for Economic Security Act to which it was attached also passed.

The Equal Access Act was one of Perkins's most important legislative achievements, and it was also his last. Ten days after it passed the House, he suffered a fatal heart attack while flying home to Kentucky. EAA supporters, who had been planning a party in his honor, were stunned. In addition to mourning him, they felt that the EAA had had a close call. "If O'Neill hadn't pulled that stunt of putting equal access into the Judiciary Committee," Ericsson later reflected, "Perkins would never have gotten mad enough to threaten to use Calendar Wednesday." The bill would then have been postponed until the following fall, and since Perkins's chairmanship passed to Representative Augustus Hawkins (D-California), an EAA foe, the legislation would not have been able to clear either Education and Labor or Judiciary. As it was, President Ronald Reagan signed it into law on August 11, 1984.

CURTAIN CALL

The passage of the EAA by no means ended disagreements about exactly what it did or did not require public secondary schools to do. As the congressional hearings and floor debates had suggested, some of its language, such as its use of the terms "noninstructional" and "noncurricular," was susceptible to a variety of interpretations. A coalition of advocacy groups led by the Baptist Joint Committee on Public Affairs developed guidelines explaining some of the EAA's provisions, and these were read into the *Congressional Record*. Nevertheless, it was generally assumed that the federal courts would be called upon to interpret ambiguous wording and, of course, to decide whether the law itself was constitutional. Accordingly, advocacy groups hastened to provide legal representation for students, parents, and teachers in a variety of lawsuits testing the limits of the EAA. The result was a plethora of conflicting lower-court opinions, which all but guaranteed that the Supreme Court would agree to decide an EAA case.

The lawsuit that eventually reached the Court began when Bridget Mergens, a student at Westside High School in Omaha, Nebraska, sought to initiate a Bible club. The principal refused to declare it an official school club, although he had no objection to the students' engaging in religious activities on an informal basis. The superintendent agreed, asserting that the EAA did not apply because the school had no noncurricular clubs. Attorney Jay Sekulow of the American Center for Law and Justice filed suit on Mergens's behalf, whereupon the American Jewish Congress volunteered to assist the school district's attorneys. Challenging the school officials' assertion that the school had no noncurricular clubs, Sekulow accused them of using the terms "curriculum-related" and "school-sponsored" synonymously, as if any activity they chose to endorse thereby became curriculum-related for purposes of the EAA.

The federal district court found that the school did not have the kind of open forum that would trigger the EAA, but this decision was reversed by the Court of Appeals for the Eighth Circuit, which had upheld the right of university students to hold religious meetings on campus in *Widmar v. Vincent* (see Chapter Eleven). The appeals court found that although the school's written policy said that only curriculum-related activities were permitted, in practice some of its clubs were not curriculum-related. Among these was the chess club, whose purported relationship to the curriculum was that it promoted logic and critical thinking; and the scuba diving club, which school officials associated with the physical education program. Giving school officials such broad discretion to decide what is curriculum-related, the court ruled, "would make the EAA meaningless. A school's administration could simply declare that it maintains a closed forum and choose which student clubs it wanted to allow by tying the purposes of those student clubs to some broadly defined educational goal. At the same time the administration could arbitrarily deny access to school facilities to any unfavored student club on the basis of its speech content. This is exactly the result that Congress sought to prohibit by enacting the EAA" (*Mergens v. Board of Education of Westside Community Schools*, 867 F.2d 1076 [1989], p. 1078). The appeals court also rejected the school district's contention that the EAA is unconstitutional. Since the EAA's purpose is to apply *Widmar* to secondary schools, the decision stated, it could be struck down only

if university and secondary school students differ so much that what is constitutional for one group would be unconstitutional for the other. Congress had
determined that no such distinction exists, and the court accepted that
finding. Indeed, it declared, the facts in *Mergens* were so similar to those in
Widmar that "even if Congress had never passed the EAA, our decision would
be the same under *Widmar* alone" (p. 1080). The school authorities turned to
the Supreme Court, which granted a hearing.

Both sides agreed that the primary issue in *Mergens* was the definition of
"non-curriculum related," since the more latitude school officials were given to
decide what was related to the curriculum, the more flexibility they would have
to include some clubs and exclude others. Advocacy groups that had lobbied
against the EAA, such as the Anti-Defamation League, the ACLU, the National
School Boards Association, and People for the American Way, submitted amicus briefs urging the Court to allow schools to ban religious and political
meetings without sacrificing nonideological activities. Moreover, they argued,
local authorities should have the discretion to determine which clubs would
further the school's educational mission, broadly defined. Pro-EAA advocacy
groups retorted that the whole point of the law was to prevent school officials
from continuing to offer a wide range of secular clubs while discriminating
against religious groups. The Baptist Joint Committee on Public Affairs, the
Christian Legal Society, the National Association of Evangelicals, and the U.S.
Catholic Conference, among others, filed amicus briefs urging the Court to
say that no activity may be considered curricular unless it is closely linked to
courses taught in the school.

Like the amicus briefs, the oral arguments before the Supreme Court focused
on the vagueness and inconsistency of some of the EAA's provisions. For example, although the law focused on clubs that were student-initiated and student-
run, students could apparently demand to form such clubs if the school had *any*
noncurricular activities, including those that were established, sponsored, and
conducted by the school itself. Similarly, Solicitor General Kenneth Starr, appearing for the Bush administration in support of the EAA, acknowledged that Congress had apparently meant to grant special status to athletics, so that schools
could retain their sports teams without triggering the EAA. He attempted to justify this inconsistency by arguing that an athletic team is not "a student group
wishing to conduct a meeting," whereas a chess team or a stamp-collecting club
would be (oral argument, January 9, 1990, p. 50).

Citing "Congress' intent to provide a low threshold for triggering the Act's
requirements," the Supreme Court ruled that a student club qualifies as cur-

riculum-related "if the subject matter of the group is actually taught, or will soon be taught, in a regularly offered course; if the subject matter of the group concerns the body of courses as a whole; if participation in the group is required for a particular course; or if participation in the group results in academic credit" (*Westside Community Board of Education v. Mergens*, 496 U.S. 226; 110 S.Ct. 2356 [1990], pp. 239–40). Activities such as chess and stamp-collecting would trigger the EAA unless they clearly met one of these criteria, and no group could be deemed curricular on such broad grounds as developing logic or stimulating interest in other countries. By way of illustration, the Court said that a French club would be curricular in a school that offers or will soon offer French classes, but not elsewhere. Clearly, some of the clubs at Westside Community High School failed to meet the Court's test for curricular content.

Justice Anthony Kennedy, joined by Justice Antonin Scalia, filed a separate opinion agreeing with the outcome of the case but challenging the majority's assertion that the EAA is constitutional because, among other things, it does not involve school officials in the endorsement of any religious view. To them, the appropriate question was not "whether school officials, by complying with the Act, have endorsed religion," but whether "enforcement of the statute will result in the coercion of any student to participate in religious activity" (p. 261). In contrast, Justices Thurgood Marshall and William Brennan filed a concurring opinion saying that in their view, the school must "fully disassociate itself from the Club's religious speech and avoid appearing to sponsor or endorse the Club's goals" (p. 270). This conflict over whether public schools can endorse religious activities as long as no student is forced to participate was discussed more fully two years later in a Supreme Court decision dealing with graduation prayer, which is discussed in Chapter Fourteen.

The lone dissenter in *Mergens*, Justice John Paul Stevens, maintained that the Court's narrow definition of "noncurricular" would deprive school officials of their rightful authority to offer wholesome, nonideological activities without opening the door to almost anything any youngster might see fit to propose. Moreover, he declared, by preventing schools from making even the most common extracurricular activities available without triggering the EAA, the Court "comes perilously close to an outright command to allow organized prayer, and perhaps the kind of religious ceremonies involved in *Widmar*, on school premises" (p. 287).

ROAD MAPS

In the wake of *Mergens,* advocacy groups rushed to publish new guidelines for use in the schools. Notable among these was *The Equal Access Act and the Public Schools: Questions and Answers,* drafted by lawyers from the Baptist Joint Committee on Public Affairs, the American Jewish Congress, and the National Council of Churches and signed by eighteen other education and religious groups. Obviously, the concurrence of so many organizations enhanced the credibility of these guidelines, but some gray areas remained because the groups disagreed about parts of the EAA that were not addressed in *Mergens.* Accordingly, some groups composed additional guidelines based on their own views, such as the CLS's *A Guide to the Equal Access Act.*

Advocacy-group lawyers also used other outlets, such as press conferences, newsletters, and fund-raising appeals, to communicate conflicting views about the EAA. One such exchange began when Bridget Mergens's attorney, Jay Sekulow of the American Center for Law and Justice, sent warning letters to approximately eighty school districts that were allegedly in violation of the EAA. "We will not hesitate to send legal SWAT teams anywhere in this country," he declared, whenever "any public school that receives federal funding" failed to comply with the EAA. According to Sekulow, "If a school permits a French club or a science club to meet, they must permit the formation of a Bible club or a prayer club. It's that simple." He also wrote to Attorney General Janet Reno asking for a Justice Department investigation of purported violations of the EAA, and to Secretary of Education Richard Riley urging him "to make school districts who receive federal funds prove that they are complying with the Equal Access Act" (ACLJ press release, February 16, 1994). In response, Elliot Mincberg, legal director of People for the American Way, wrote to the same school districts to assert that the ACLJ statement was "a fundamental misinterpretation of several aspects of the Act." He also wrote to Sekulow pointing out that the EAA does not apply to all public schools that receive federal funds but only to secondary schools, and it is not triggered by such examples as French and science clubs if they are curriculum-related. Moreover, he asserted that it was misleading to write to Reno and Riley, neither of whom had any role to play in implementing the EAA. "[B]y publicly suggesting that districts may somehow be subject to federal enforcement," he scolded, "you have unnecessarily confused and frightened many educators" (February 25, 1994). (A 2001 law requires local education agencies seeking federal funds to certify annually that their policies do not burden anyone's religious rights—see Chapter Fifteen.) Similarly, August Steinhilber, general counsel for the

National School Boards Association, protested that "most schools abide by the law, and that ACLJ is targeting schools unfairly to promote its own agenda" ("NSBA Calls 'Bible Clubs' Initiative Misleading, Provocative," *School Law News*, March 11, 1994, p. 4).

TESTING THE LIMITS

In addition to publishing warring guidelines, press releases, and open letters, advocacy groups participated in lawsuits aimed at bolstering certain interpretations of the EAA. As an example, Kimberlee Colby of the CLS, Sekulow, and other advocacy-group attorneys wrote amicus briefs in a case entitled *Ceniceros v. Board of Trustees*, which addressed the question of "noninstructional time." The EAA defines it as "time set aside by the school before actual classroom instruction begins or after actual classroom instruction ends," which could refer either to the periods before the first class and after the last class of the day or, more broadly, to any interval between the end of one class and the start of the next. The student plaintiffs in *Ceniceros* wanted to hold religious gatherings at lunchtime, when other clubs were allowed to meet. Their claim was supported by an amicus brief from the U.S. Justice Department, written in part by attorney Lowell Sturgill, who as an assistant to Ericsson at the CLS had helped to write the original draft of the EAA. In a victory for the broader interpretation, the Court of Appeals for the Ninth Circuit found that the overriding sense of the EAA is that religious clubs should be treated the same as secular clubs. Almost a decade later, the Ninth Circuit further declared in *Prince v. Jacoby* that school officials may not create a two-tiered system under which clubs initiated by students pursuant to the EAA enjoy fewer privileges and receive less support than do noncurricular clubs with which the school has chosen to identify itself. Other post-EAA lawsuits reflected attempts to extend the EAA beyond secondary school students. In *May v. Evansville*, for instance, a federal district court found that the EAA does not cover religious meetings of school employees. The question of elementary school students' right to pray in school was addressed in several cases, notably *Herdahl v. Pontotoc County*, discussed in the next chapter. Perhaps the most far-fetched of these lawsuits was *Hunt v. Bullard*, in which a death-row prisoner complained that inmates could lead law classes and self-help groups but not worship services. The court found that the EAA does not apply because prisons and secondary schools are two different things—a point some teenagers might contest.

The scope of the EAA was tested in a somewhat different way in a case filed by CLS attorneys on behalf of high school students in Renton, Washington, who were denied permission to form a religious club. In addition to claiming that all the clubs in their schools were noncurricular, Renton officials maintained that the EAA did not apply because the Washington state constitution forbids religious meetings in public schools. They prevailed in the federal district court and in the Court of Appeals for the Ninth Circuit, but the Supreme Court vacated the judgment and sent it back for further consideration in light of *Mergens*. Although the district court then found that some of the school clubs were noncurricular under *Mergens*, it continued to uphold the exclusion of the religious club because of the state constitution's requirement for strict separation of church and state. Nevertheless, unlike Judge Brevard Hand in *Jaffree v. Wallace* (see Chapter Ten), the *Renton* court neither defied Supreme Court precedents nor denied the supremacy of the U.S. Constitution and federal statutes over state constitutions and laws. Rather, its decision was based on a provision of the EAA stating that school officials may not be compelled "'to sanction meetings that are otherwise unlawful'" (*Garnett v. Renton School District*, 772 F. Supp. 531 [1991], p. 537). Since prayer in public schools is unlawful under the Washington state constitution, the court held, the EAA does not require the public schools of that state to grant official recognition to religious clubs. In reversing that decision, the Court of Appeals for the Ninth Circuit stated, "If the EAA did not preempt state law, then states could freely opt out of its requirements. Congress did not intend to permit the states to thwart its objectives by outlawing speech based on its religious content, and thereby discriminate on that basis" (*Garnett v. Renton*, 987 F.2d 641 [1993], p. 646).

HOW EQUAL IS EQUAL?

Among the most aggressive of the post-*Mergens* lawsuits was *Hsu v. Roslyn Union Free School District*, which tested the proposition that the same rules must apply to both secular and religious noncurricular clubs. During the congressional debates over the EAA, some legislators had worried that the constraints required for religious clubs might unnecessarily restrict secular clubs. In *Hsu*, Jay Sekulow of the ACLJ, who had represented the students in *Mergens*, argued the matter the other way around. In his view, religious clubs should be subject to fewer, not more, restrictions than secular groups. If school rules that apply to secular groups conflict with the message a religious club wishes to promote, he asserted, then the students' right to free exercise of religion justifies an exemption from regulations that all other clubs must obey.

The dispute arose in a small town on Long Island, where students wanted to form the Roslyn High School Walking on Water Club. Their purpose was to share "'testimonies of their belief, faith, walk, experiences in or with Christ Jesus'" (*Hsu v. Roslyn*, 876 F. Supp. 445 [1995], p. 455). School officials were willing to allow informal meetings, but before granting official status to the club, they required a change in its proposed constitution. Everyone agreed that the club meetings would be open to all students, but the club founders wanted to say that "'Accepting Jesus Christ as savior is a requirement for all officers'" (Amended Verified Complaint, March 24, 1994, p. 16). When the school officials objected that this restriction conflicted with a policy forbidding discrimination on the basis of race, gender, or religion in any school-recognized activity, the students protested that the club's officers must "be sensitive to the direction of the Holy Spirit in all matters" and serve as spokespersons "in relating the Christian perspective on any particular issue" (p. 18). Indeed, they alleged, they should not even have to submit their club's rules for the principal's approval because that process impermissibly entangled the school with religion. They also claimed that without the religious test they were seeking, non-Christians might hijack the club by joining in large numbers and then electing nonbelievers to office. The school officials retorted that the EAA guarantees religious clubs equal access to school facilities, not the right to dictate their own terms. The Walking on Water Club could restrict its choice of officers if it met as a private group, they declared, but if it sought official school recognition, its members would have to abide by the same regulations as everyone else. In their view, what the club was seeking was not equal access but preferential treatment that would permit it to violate the rights of other students. They also felt that they could not exempt one club from the nondiscrimination rule but continue to enforce it against all other groups.

Sekulow disputed the school's contention that it had to treat all clubs equally. In his view, an exemption could be granted to the Walking on Water Club without affecting the school's ability to prevent the exclusion of African Americans, for instance, from a white supremacist club. "That's not a religious exclusion but a political club," he asserted, "and that wouldn't apply" (transcript, May 13, 1994, pp. 21–22). His case was founded on the free exercise of religion, he explained, and the same deference was not necessarily due to choices made on any other basis. When the judge asked, "Let's assume your religious organization believes that blacks should not be part of their group, can they do it?" Sekulow replied, "Oh, certainly" (p. 37). In his view, religious groups have a near-absolute right to set their own policies without hindrance from government officials or from rules that restrict secular groups.

Unpersuaded by these arguments, the federal district court found that the

Roslyn school officials would adequately comply with the EAA if they offered official recognition to the Walking on Water Club on the same basis as all other clubs. In the court's view, the nondiscrimination policy did not burden the students' right to express their religious beliefs; it merely prevented them from violating the rights of other students. Sekulow then turned to the Court of Appeals for the Second Circuit, where he was supported by an amicus brief written by Colby and other lawyers and submitted on behalf of the CLS, NCC, NAE, and Christian Life Commission of the Southern Baptist Convention. Religious groups, they argued, have a right to choose their leaders as they see fit, and the "requirement that officers of the group adhere to a 'statement of faith' is unquestionably part of the group's religious expression" (p. 13). On the other side, an amicus brief filed by the Anti-Defamation League denied that the rights enjoyed by private religious groups necessarily extend to a club that demands official recognition as a part of a public-school program. If the Walking on Water Club wanted to come under the same rules as churches, synagogues, and other private religious entities, the brief asserted, it should meet as a private group; as an official school club, it should be subject to the same rules as all other school groups. The brief also stated that granting special treatment to a religious club would have no secular purpose or effect but would show favoritism toward religion, thus violating the Establishment Clause.

The appeals court agreed with Sekulow and the Christian organizations, at least in part. "[T]he club's Christian officer requirement," the decision stated, "as applied to some of the club's officers, is essential to the expressive content of the meetings and to the group's preservation of its purpose and identity, and is therefore protected by the Equal Access Act" (*Hsu v. Roslyn,* 85 F.3d 839 [1996], p. 848). Accordingly, the court declared the religious test appropriate for the president, vice president, and music coordinator, whose responsibilities related directly to the club's speech; but not for the activities coordinator and secretary. The school district appealed to the Supreme Court, which refused to hear the case.

WHAT GOES AROUND COMES AROUND

As these examples suggest, almost all the disputes in which the EAA has been invoked have dealt with religious clubs. Indeed, for the first ten years after it was enacted it might as well have applied only to religious speech, since it appeared to have no other effect. By the mid-1990s, however, students in several states had begun to use its content-neutral language to protect unpopular secular clubs, such as Gay/Straight Alliances and Young Atheists Clubs. The most widely publicized of these disputes began when students at East High School in Salt Lake City, Utah, asked to form a Gay/Straight Alliance, whose goal would be to improve the social status and peer acceptance of homosexual students. Having ascertained through his own investigation that homosexuals were in fact mistreated by their peers, the principal granted the request. The school district's lawyer also noted that since East High had other noncurricular clubs, the Gay/Straight Alliance could not be excluded. Nevertheless, the school board banned the club amid a barrage of lobbying by the local chapter of the Eagle Forum, which called it a device for recruiting students to homosexuality. This set off a bitter dispute involving the Utah state legislature and U.S. Senator Orrin Hatch (R-Utah), as well as advocacy groups on both sides. The board finally decreed that only curriculum-related clubs would be allowed in the Salt Lake City schools, whereupon Bible clubs, Students Against Drunk Driving, clubs celebrating various ethnicities, and other popular activities either ceased to exist or met in the evening as private groups.

Represented by attorneys from the ACLU and the Lambda Legal Defense and Education Fund, students filed a lawsuit entitled *East High Gay/Straight Alliance v. Board of Education*. They argued that some of the clubs retained by the board, such as Future Business Leaders of America and Future Homemakers of America, did not meet the *Mergens* standard for determining that a club is curricular. Under these circumstances, they asserted, the Gay/Straight Alliance could not be excluded. The school officials, represented by the Utah attorney general with assistance from Rutherford Institute lawyers, replied that all the clubs retained under the new policy were curricular because they related either to a specific course or to the curriculum as a whole. The federal district court found that the Gay/Straight Alliance had been unjustly excluded during the 1997–98 school year, when other noncurricular clubs were still meeting, but that all the clubs in existence at the time of the lawsuit in 1999 were curriculum-related. Accordingly, the students' demand for recognition of the Gay/Straight Alliance as a school club was denied.

The school district fared less well in a lawsuit filed by a student club called PRISM (People Recognizing Important Social Movements), whose stated purpose was to "'serve as a prism through which historical and current events, institutions and culture can be viewed in terms of the impact, experience and contributions of gays and lesbians'" (*East High School PRISM Club v. Seidel*, 95 F. Supp. 2d 1239 [2000], p. 1243). The students argued that their club was curriculum-related because it dealt with the same subject matter as did the school's history and civics courses. Cynthia Seidel, the administrator charged with making such decisions, retorted that PRISM focused on the role of homosexuals in history and current events. "'This subject matter,'" she wrote to the students, "'is not taught in the courses you cite'" (p. 1243). *PRISM v. Seidel* was, of course, the converse of *Gay/Straight Alliance v. Board*. Whereas the Gay/Straight Alliance conceded that it was noncurricular and attempted to show that the same was also true of other clubs, PRISM claimed curricular status for itself. The question it raised was whether school officials have the authority to declare that a particular subject matter, such as American history or current events, becomes noncurricular when addressed from a disfavored perspective. Finding that PRISM had a reasonable chance of prevailing at trial, the federal district court granted an injunction ordering the school to admit the club. Five months later, in September 2000, the board rescinded its requirement that all school clubs must be curriculum-related, thus placing Salt Lake City once again within the scope of the EAA. Nevertheless, influential officials, notably Senator Hatch, continue to press for the exclusion of pro-homosexual clubs, citing the provisions of the EAA that protect schools from having to allow groups that are likely to be disruptive to the school and harmful to the students' welfare.

In most states that have faced controversies such as these, the most common pattern is that a school district seeks to exclude such groups as the Gay/Straight Alliance and the Young Atheists Club while finding ways to classify some traditional activities as curriculum-related, thereby retaining them. An interesting contrast may be found in a dispute involving the Boulder Valley School District in Colorado, which has refused approval for a Bible club while trying to retain the Gay/Straight Alliance and the Multicultural Club. According to a federal lawsuit filed in January 2003, the school claims that all its existing clubs are curriculum-related: the Gay/Straight Alliance is allegedly related to the health curriculum, while the Multicultural Club supports instruction in diversity. The would-be founders of the Bible club retort that the literature, history, art, and music taught in the school owe more to the Bible than the health curriculum owes to homosexuality. No court action has yet taken place in this case.

FOREVER AFTER, AT LEAST FOR NOW

As noted earlier, the Supreme Court's early decisions regarding school prayer were based almost exclusively on the Establishment Clause, under which the government must neither advance nor hinder religion. Since the school officials in those cases overtly sponsored devotionals, the resulting rulings said more about the need to prevent the government from promoting religion than about the concomitant ban on impeding it. A more balanced treatment of the Establishment Clause was one of the most important results of the shift to the equal-access paradigm, which also led to an increased focus on the Free Exercise and Free Speech Clauses. Since the cases discussed in the rest of this book revolve around conflicting views of the ways in which these clauses, particularly the two involving religion, relate to each other, it might be well to provide a brief explanation of this difference of opinion before moving on to the next chapter.

To some school-prayer advocates, equal access is primarily a vehicle for easing the return of majoritarian prayer to the public schools. While recognizing that equal access requires prayers to be controlled by students and not by school personnel, they resent what they see as pointless scrutiny of the extent to which school officials organize, facilitate, and encourage such prayers. Believing that the Free Exercise Clause gives students a near-absolute right to pray aloud in school, they assert that even the most permissive approach to the involvement of school personnel would create no conflict with the Establishment Clause. As they see it, the Establishment Clause pertains to such things as the official creation of a national church, so that merely accommodating or aiding students in the free exercise of their religion cannot conceivably rise to the level of an Establishment Clause violation.

Opponents of school-organized prayer agree that there is no conflict between the Establishment and Free Exercise Clauses, but for quite different reasons and with a very different practical outcome. To them, governmental aid to any view about religion, including belief in God over disbelief, is *both* an establishment of religion *and* a violation of the free-exercise rights of private individuals, in whose hands the government should leave total control of religion. The Establishment Clause and the Free Exercise Clause thus work together, in their view, to prevent the government from aiding the perpetuation or spread of anyone's beliefs or practices in preference to anyone else's. To them, the fact that a religious exercise is carried out, or even initiated, by student volunteers does not justify school officials in becoming excessively involved with it, as by creating special opportunities for prayer. As the rest of this book illustrates, people who want to make equal access workable in the real world of American public schools are presently seeking a balance that will exclude school sponsorship of religion without preventing school personnel from providing reasonable accommodation to genuinely student-initiated religious activity—whatever "reasonable" and "genuine" may be taken to mean.

One other effect of the shift from state-sponsored devotionals to equal access should be mentioned before proceeding to discuss specific examples of conflicts arising from this new paradigm. In the earliest school-prayer cases mentioned in this book, the central question was whether certain religious practices, particularly Bible-reading, were sectarian. By the time of *Murray* and *Abington,* the focus had broadened to include the advancement of religion in general over nonreligion. As a result, the threshold question that had to be answered in order to prove a constitutional violation went from "Does this practice promote a particular religion?" to "Does this practice advance religion in its broadest sense?" But under the equal-access model, the threshold question no longer focuses on some variant of "How religious is the challenged speech?" What today's courts need to know is, "*Whose* speech is it?"

13
Mississippi Learning

Scarcely any political question arises in the United States that is not resolved, sooner or later, into a judicial question.

—*Alexis de Tocqueville*

Despite the controversy surrounding its enactment, the Equal Access Act is quite limited in its application, since it pertains only to the formation of officially recognized student-initiated clubs in secondary schools that accept federal funds and allow at least one noncurricular club to meet. But the term "equal access" is also used in a broader sense, referring not to the specific provisions of the EAA but to its underlying premise: that an important difference exists between the actions of government agencies, such as state legislatures and public schools, and those of students who enjoy constitutional rights, as private individuals, to free speech and free exercise of religion. As the previous chapter indicated, this distinction is widely accepted in principle, but in practice there is far less agreement about defining exactly what qualifies as equal access. In particular, heated debates arise when equal access is invoked to justify student-led prayer at times when no comparable opportunity exists for other student speech—for instance, when student volunteers are allowed to pray aloud before school assemblies, but the microphone is not then handed to other students who may wish to say different prayers or make secular statements.

School officials who create special opportunities for student-led vocal prayer either ignore or deny the premise that students are entitled to pray aloud only when—and because—they would be equally free to engage in other forms of secular or religious speech. To defenders of such practices, the fact that secular speech occupies most of the school day means that not only equal access but the students' right to free exercise of religion demands the inclusion of majoritarian prayer in the school day. The lack of a parallel opportunity for secular speech or for other religious speech at that precise time is, in their view, irrelevant. Their opponents, of course, equate the creation of special opportunities for prayer with state sponsorship of religious worship, not with equal access, no matter who says the prayer. To them, equal access applies only when students are on their own time and free to move about and choose among a variety of activities, since only then is prayer truly voluntary, student-initiated, and free from school involvement. In essence, what is at issue is the claim that any prayer led by a willing student is automatically permissible under the distinction between student initiative and government action.

THE SCHOOL OF HARD KNOX

A highly publicized example of this kind of dispute arose in Jackson, Mississippi, where a high school principal suggested that the students might want to vote on whether to institute daily prayers over the loudspeaker. The deputy superintendent and the school district attorney told the principal, Dr. Bishop Earl Knox, that any such practice would be illegal. (Bishop is his first name, not a religious title.) The next day, Knox showed the student council a pamphlet published by the American Center for Law and Justice, which had successfully represented student Bible clubs in *Mergens* and *Hsu* (see Chapter Twelve). The pamphlet discussed another ACLJ case, *Jones v. Clear Creek*, in which the Court of Appeals for the Fifth Circuit had upheld a policy allowing high school students to vote on whether to have nonsectarian, nonproselytizing, student-led prayer at graduation. (*Jones* is discussed in the Chapter Fourteen.) Focusing on the pamphlet's distinction between state-mandated action and student-initiated prayer, Knox said that daily prayer over the school loudspeaker would be acceptable if the students voted to have it. The student council president, Kim Fails, was worried about violating Supreme Court rulings, but Knox assured her that he had consulted the school board's attorney. The council then agreed to put the matter to a vote of the student body. The result was 490 aye, 96 nay, 310 not voting.

Knox approved the prayer Fails proposed: "'Almighty God, we ask that You bless our parents, teachers and country throughout the day. In Your name we pray. Amen'" (Carol Innerst, "Legal Groups, Students Help Principal Fired Over Prayer," *Washington Times*, December 9, 1993, p. A1). She read it over the loudspeaker for the first time on November 9—the day after the school district attorney had warned Knox for the second time that the practice would be illegal. On November 10, the attorney again admonished him that the loudspeaker prayers would expose the school district to adverse judicial action and financial costs. When Knox continued to allow the prayers, he was placed on leave and later fired. The dismissal was put on hold pending a school board hearing, whereupon students walked out of class to show solidarity with Knox. His supporters also marched on the State Capitol, and state legislators proposed draconian measures against any school that did not allow prayer. Although Knox is African American and the outcry was biracial, some demonstrators waved Confederate flags and sang "Dixie" to protest what they saw as the Supreme Court's usurpation of sacred traditions and states' rights. Appearing on the Larry King Show, Mississippi Governor Kirk Fordice asserted that "'Any place that Americans want to pray ought to be the place for religion'" ("Mississippi Fights Ban on Prayers in Schools," *New York Times,* November 7, 1993, p. B8).

Inevitably, advocacy groups became involved. The Mississippi affiliate of the American Civil Liberties Union helped to organize Jackson residents who opposed the prayers, while Knox was aided by "a veritable Noah's ark of interest groups" (Vern Smith, "A Principal's Troubling Prayer," *Newsweek,* December 20, 1993, p. 107). Prominent among these were the American Family Association, whose lawyers represented him, and Concerned Women for America, which led a letter-writing campaign on his behalf. The ACLJ's chief litigator, Jay Sekulow, gained amnesty for students who had been suspended for leaving class in support of Knox.

At his hearing before the school board, Knox stated that although the deputy superintendent had told him the prayer was illegal, the only direct order to stop it had come from the school district attorney, whom he was not obliged to obey. He also asserted that he had proposed the prayers at the request of several students, who were not identified. By a unanimous vote, the board rescinded his dismissal but suspended him without pay until July 1. According to a news report, Knox "appeared stunned" and said, "'This is simply a decision I hadn't anticipated'" (Cathy Hayden, "Knox Gets His Wingfield Job Back in '94," *Clarion-Ledger,* December 16, 1993, p. 1A). His attorneys assured reporters that he had received several other job offers.

Knox appealed his suspension to the Hinds County Chancery Court, and the attorneys on both sides agreed that the case was about his alleged insubordination and not about school prayer. Judge W. O. Dillard saw it differently. "We have completely missed the main objective of the founding fathers of our country," his decision stated, "when we reach the point where we construe our constitution to allow students to have abortions yet forbid them to pray in our schools" (unpublished opinion, *Knox v. Board of Trustees* [April 22, 1994], p. 1). Having written a great deal more about abortion, HIV, school violence, and the relevance of the King James Bible to American democracy, Dillard concluded that Knox had not violated the Supreme Court's school-prayer rulings. Despite Knox's meeting with the student council and Fails's testimony that she had participated only because of his implication that the school district attorney had approved the loudspeaker prayer, the court treated it as a student initiative. The decision also described it as entirely voluntary on the part of the students in the high school, ignoring the ninety-six of them who had voted against it. Knox was vindicated, and the school board was told to "draw up guidelines for all their schools consistent with this opinion and then strictly enforce them" (p. 17).

Pending the school board's appeal, the Supreme Court of Mississippi stayed Dillard's order to develop a school-prayer policy. Knox's early reinstatement was allowed to stand, but the court postponed any decision about whether he should receive back pay for the time he was suspended. Three years later, the school board won its appeal, and Dillard's ruling was reversed. According to the state supreme court, the pertinent issue was not school prayer but the board's decision to suspend Knox when he "consciously disregarded his school district's position regarding a legal issue, as stated to him on four occasions by the district's attorney" (*Board of Trustees v. Knox*, 688 So. 2d 778 [1997], p. 780). The court found that "In this age of litigious students and parents and of shrinking school budgets, a school district must have the ability to control its employees in such a manner as to protect itself from having to defend against lawsuits which may arise from the conduct of a principal or teacher" (p. 781).

EVEN THE SINNERS ARE FOR IT

Although Judge Dillard's ruling was overturned, he was by no means alone in favoring the reinstatement of organized prayer in the public schools of Mississippi. The state legislature, quick to support this popular cause, passed a resolution praising Knox "for his forthright action [which] has been the catalyst for a renewed effort all over this state and nation to return prayer to our public schools." Ignoring its counsel's advice to the contrary, the legislature then passed a bill legalizing what Knox had done. Among other things, the new law provided that "on public school property, other public property or other property, invocations, benedictions or nonsectarian, nonproselytizing student-initiated voluntary prayer shall be permitted during compulsory or noncompulsory school-related student assemblies, student sporting events, graduation or commencement ceremonies and other school-related student events" (*Ingebretsen v. Jackson Public School District*, 864 F. Supp. 1473 [1994], p. 1479).[1] As one Mississippi legislator explained, "'This cuts across racial lines, social lines. Heck, even the sinners are for it.... People are saying we're tired of giving up our rights because the federal government says we have to.'" But one of his fellow legislators, a pastor, disagreed. "'There are enough issues to deal with out there that we don't need to bring the divine creator into a political gimmick.... This bill is pure partisan politics and has nothing to do with prayer whatsoever,'" he said (Emily Wagster, "School Prayer Bill May Still Be Sent to Fordice," *Clarion-Ledger,* March 30, 1994, p. A1). Other legislators expressed mixed feelings. "'We had to deal with the constitutional and emotional sides of the issue,' [a state representative] said. "'I voted for the law because I believe in school prayer, but it is not constitutional'" (Jerry Mitchell, "ACLU Asks Judge to Kill Prayer Law," *Clarion-Ledger,* July 16, 1994, p. A1).

That last assessment was shared by David Ingebretsen, executive director of the Mississippi ACLU and father of a child in the Jackson public schools. Together with other parents, and represented by a volunteer attorney from the Mississippi ACLU and by staff attorneys from People for the American Way, he filed a lawsuit asking the federal district court to declare the statute unconstitutional and prevent it from being implemented. The American Family Association, which was representing Knox in his lawsuit against the school district, also attempted to join the case. It asked the court to admit three pro-prayer parents as defendant-intervenors, which would have allowed AFA lawyers to call and question witnesses, argue before the court, and decide whether to pursue an appeal. The request to intervene stated, "The axiom that students do not shed their rights to freedom of speech or expression at the school house gate is often times lost amidst the shrill yelps of those whose creed has no tolerance for others who would have the temerity to actually express their faith in a public school" (Intervenors' Memorandum in Opposition to Plaintiffs' Motion for Preliminary Injunction, August 7, 1994, p. 2). To them, the Mississippi ACLU was "a wolf coming as a wolf seeking to devour Intervenors' constitutional rights" (p. 24). The court denied the AFA motion on the ground that Mississippians who supported school prayer were adequately represented by the state attorney general.

When the case went to court, one of the first questions the judge asked was whether the statute's reference to "compulsory events" meant that teachers would have to permit students to pray aloud in class. Assistant Attorney General T. Hunt Cole, Jr., refused to commit himself on that point. It was well known that the governor and other supporters of the bill wanted students to be able to pray in class, but that was the last place where vocal prayer was likely to be found constitutional. Cole temporized by saying that "a classroom instructional setting is not the central focus of this statute." The judge asked again, and Cole replied, "I've never thought of a classroom as being included, and that's our position" (transcript of hearing, August 4, 1994, p. 90). When the judge persisted, Cole said that there was no clear yes or no answer because different schools might do different things. The statute, he noted, did not mention classes, and the court should interpret it in whatever way would cause it to be upheld.

A FUNNY THING HAPPENED ON THE WAY TO THE FORUM

Among the other issues raised in the case was the question of what an open forum is and whether the students have a right to pray aloud only in the context of such a forum. During the lawsuits and congressional debates leading up to the EAA, the phrase "open forum" usually referred to periods when students were out of class and free to talk about any topic of their choice. Most commonly, it was associated with club activity periods, during which students met for a variety of purposes. To supporters of the Mississippi law, however, the fact that an assembly, a class, a graduation ceremony, or any other activity was taking place meant that a forum had been created, and the exclusion of prayer was thus an unjust limitation on religious speech. In their view, people who wished to pray aloud should be able to do so at any time, regardless of what anyone else was doing. Their opponents retorted that allowing students to lead a class or assembly in prayer when other students were not free to engage in the speech of their choice was not equal treatment of religious expression but governmental favoritism toward it.

The attorney general's case rested largely on the argument that the law did not compel anyone to do anything but merely allowed students to engage in voluntary prayer if they wished to do so. Thus, he asserted, the plaintiffs had no legitimate case against the state because whatever prayers might be said would not be a state action but the free choice of private individuals. "The ACLU Plaintiffs," he wrote, "may not use the guise of the Establishment Clause to censor or silence private speech or religious viewpoints with which they disagree. There is no hecklers' veto" (Memorandum of Law in Support of State's Motion to Dismiss or for Summary Judgment, August 3, 1994, pp. 30–31). The plaintiffs replied that the new law did indeed compel action: it required school personnel to allow students to begin, end, or interrupt any event with prayer. They also challenged the attorney general's claim that the law merely affirmed the students' rights to freedom of speech and religion under the Constitution, since in their view the issue was not the students' right to pray but the state's creation of countless opportunities for prayer that would not be open to any other manifestation of the students' right to free speech.

The court blocked implementation of the new law pending another hearing, and on the day before it was to take place, supporters of the statute converged on the State Capitol with signs saying, "Go God" and "God Rulz." At the hearing, school officials expressed practical concerns about the law, since it did not allow them to limit the number of students who could pray or how much time they could consume. "I'm trying to protect the instructional time in the classroom," said Interim Superintendent Daniel Merritt, whose understanding of adolescent behavior was perhaps less idealistic than that of the legislature (transcript of hearing, August 16, 1994, p. 28). Over Cole's repeated objections, he also raised the two oldest and most troublesome questions in the generations-long debate over school prayer: What was a teacher supposed to do if a child said a sectarian prayer, and were dissenters free to walk out? To counter Merritt's testimony, Cole argued that since the law did not compel anyone to pray, no one knew how many students would do so, what they would say, how long they would take, or whether anyone would leave the room. Thus, he alleged, the plaintiffs' lawsuit was premature because they were merely speculating about a law that had never been implemented. When he suggested that perhaps no one would pray, the judge interrupted. "So seemingly what you are telling me," he said, "is that even though there has been this outburst of energy, concern, speeches on the issue... they will simply fold up their tents, go home and say we now have a statute but we don't wish to pray under it?" Cole refused to speculate. The judge persisted, mentioning the extensive news coverage of the previous day's rally at the State Capitol. "Your Honor," Cole replied, "frankly I don't read the papers that closely." "Nor watch television?" the judge asked. "I watch television every once in a while," Cole conceded. "Nor look out your window over by the Capitol?" "My office looks out over the funeral home, Your Honor" (pp. 81–82).

The court ruled against the statute, describing it as "a legislative enactment which potentially empowers third parties, at their whim, to offer prayers, with or without student body agreement, at all school events and assemblies, whether compulsory or noncompulsory. If this empowerment in all other respects oversteps the bounds of the Establishment Clause, the state may not escape liability... by claiming that the school-prayer statute merely authorizes private parties to take these actions" (Memorandum Opinion and Order, September 2, 1994, pp. 18–19). The Mississippi attorney general asked the Court of Appeals for the Fifth Circuit to overturn this decision, arguing that the district court had had no basis for ruling that "a statute which passively acknowledges the existence of private religious speech rights creates some kind of improper 'platform for prayer' on public property" (Reply Brief of Appellant Attorney General, May 19, 1995, p. 3). The plaintiffs reiterated their claim that the new law "establishes a state preference for religious speech and the concomitant conveyance of a message of government endorsement of, and favoritism toward, such speech" (Brief of Appellees, March 12, 1995, pp. 16–17).

Several advocacy groups also submitted briefs, one of which shifted the focus from the student speakers to the listeners. Written by Marc Stern of the American Jewish Congress, a nationally recognized expert in the law governing captive audiences, it argued that the Mississippi statute was fundamentally flawed because it attempted to "treat free speech rights as if they confer an unlimited right to compel others to listen" (Brief Amici Curiae of the American Jewish Congress, Anti-Defamation League of B'nai B'rith, and Americans United for Separation of Church and State, March 27, 1995, p. 1). While acknowledging that "the general principle [is] that the listener has to close his or her ears, and not the speaker's mouth," Stern denied that people can be "enlisted as passive but unwilling participants in someone else's ideological campaign" (pp. 4, 5). In response to the claim that responsibility for the prayers rested with the students, he wrote, "Mississippi could not stand idly by if students determined that only Blacks or Christians could attend graduation, or that only Christians could offer graduation prayers. We assume that Mississippi would not dare come to this Court to absolve itself of liability for such decisions on the ground that they were student decisions" (p. 13). This concern about captive audiences was reflected in the decision of the appeals court, which upheld the district court's ruling on the grounds that the challenged statute "sets aside special time for prayer that it does not set aside for anything else. It also places the coercive power of the state in the position of forcing students to attend school and then forcing them to listen to prayers offered there." Moreover, the court found, the students' free speech and free exercise of religion were sufficiently protected by their ability to pray aloud "in groups before or after school or in any limited open forum created by the school" (*Ingebretsen v. Jackson Public School District*, 88 F. 3d 274 [1996], p. 280). The case was not appealed to the Supreme Court.

STRANGER AT THE GATES

Although school officials in the city of Jackson disagreed with Knox's actions and with the statute struck down in *Ingebretsen*, their counterparts in less urban areas saw no problem at all with state-sponsored prayer. Indeed, as anticipated by Kenneth Dolbeare and Phillip Hammond in their 1971 study of local responses to *Abington* (see Chapter Six), schools in homogeneous communities had quietly continued their traditional religious exercises for decades after the Supreme Court had declared them unconstitutional. Of course, those activities would not stand up in court, but that is irrelevant until someone shocks the local community by filing a lawsuit. By coincidence, an incident of that kind was taking place in rural Pontotoc County, Mississippi, at the same time as *Ingebretsen* was raging in Jackson. It arose because a newcomer viewed with alien eyes practices that seemed as unremarkable as air to the longtime residents of Pontotoc County.

Lisa Herdahl had lived in California and Wisconsin before moving to Mississippi with her husband and six children. She enrolled five of her children in the North Pontotoc Attendance Center (NPAC), which served approximately thirteen hundred students in grades K–12. One son was in high school, and the other four children were in the elementary grades. Having heard from Pontotoc residents that the school had prayers and Bible classes, she asked that her children be excused. They attended Sunday school at a Pentecostal church, and, as she later explained in court documents, she felt that "what a school is for is for them to go to learn how to add, subtract, and read, and that I do not believe that the—that them learning about God in the school is the right thing to do" (deposition, January 27, 1995, p. 143).

Herdahl was referred to Vice-Principal Rodney Flowers, who, she later testified, rudely insisted that NPAC's traditional procedures were the only right way to do things. For his part, Flowers found Herdahl abrasive and critical, objecting not only to religious observances but also to other school practices, such as corporal punishment. When they were unable to agree on excusing her children from the prayers and Bible classes, she wrote to the Mississippi ACLU, which was interested but short of resources because of its commitment to *Ingebretsen*. PFAW, also participating in *Ingebretsen*, provided two staff attorneys to work on Herdahl's case with two volunteer lawyers from the Mississippi ACLU, one of whom was the lead attorney in *Ingebretsen*. Similarly, the school district's attorneys were assisted by AFA lawyers who were also working on *Ingebretsen*. The AFA's connection with the Herdahl case was later severed because of disputes over strategy, and a lawyer from the Christian Life Commission of the Southern Baptist Convention stepped in.

CHARGE ONE: LOUDSPEAKER PRAYER

Beginning in 1978, secondary school students at NPAC who belonged to an extracurricular group called the Christ-in-Us Club opened each school day by reading Bible verses and prayers over the loudspeaker to the entire school. In 1993, the year Herdahl moved to Pontotoc County, the student group became an Aletheia Club—a student organization affiliated with the AFA. Student members and faculty advisors were required to sign a statement declaring belief in Christ as savior and in the literal truth of the Bible, although Herdahl's lawyers were unable to learn whether the NPAC advisor had done so.

When Herdahl challenged the daily Bible-reading and prayer, school officials defended it as a student-initiated club project protected by the Equal Access Act. If the drama club could present plays, they argued, the Aletheia Club could lead prayers. They also alleged that it was the students' choice and not the school's action that made the daily message religious. Herdahl retorted that other clubs were given access to the microphone to make announcements, not to conduct their business; the drama club did not put on plays over the loudspeaker. School officials then offered to excuse her children from the prayers, which was all she had originally requested. Like Madalyn Murray O'Hair and the Schempps, however, once she had filed a lawsuit, she sought the termination of the religious practices. Moreover, having found that the prayers were not said in each classroom but broadcast over the loudspeaker, she argued that there was no way to avoid them. Going into the hallway or another room, she alleged, subjected her children to ridicule but did not prevent them from hearing the prayers. She also testified that one teacher had put headphones on her eight-year-old son to muffle the prayers, causing classmates to call him "football head" and "baseball head" because the headphones looked like a helmet.

CHARGE TWO: DOCTRINAL BIBLE CLASSES

In addition to challenging the loudspeaker prayers, Herdahl objected to the Bible classes taught at NPAC.[2] In grades 1–6, Bible teachers came into each classroom once a week in a rotation system that also included art, music, and physical education; in the higher grades, students could take Bible as an elective. Thus, her oldest son could easily avoid it, but the younger children had to make special arrangements to go elsewhere. While the school claimed that the classes were secular, Herdahl alleged that the manner of hiring and paying the teachers, the content, and the teaching methods showed that they were not only religious but sectarian.

Although the Bible teachers worked full-time in the public schools, they were selected, paid, and evaluated by the Pontotoc Bible Instructional Committee, whose members represented approximately forty Protestant churches. When a job opened up, the committee either accepted the departing teacher's suggestion for a replacement or asked an instructor at a local Bible college to recommend someone. The jobs were never advertised, and school officials approved the committee's selections but played no further role. When PFAW attorney Elliot Mincberg asked Superintendent Jerry Horton how the Bible teachers were paid, his lawyer objected that the question called for speculation. "You're the superintendent," Mincberg asked incredulously, "and you have to speculate as to how one of your teachers is paid?" (deposition, January 31, 1995, p. 88).

In light of the nineteenth-century disputes discussed earlier in this book, the most obvious basis for Herdahl's claim that the content of the Bible classes was sectarian was the exclusive use of the King James Bible and the presentation of the Old Testament solely as a preparation for the coming of Christ. Beyond that, however, in these classes the Bible was by no means read "without note or comment," as advocated by early educational reformers who called for generic Protestantism in the public schools. The Bible Committee adhered to an understanding of nonsectarianism that its president described as not saying whether a teacher was Baptist or Methodist, and the classes it sponsored presented a nondenominational but distinctly fundamentalist perspective on the inerrancy of Scripture, the meaning of the various books of the Bible, and the significance of the Bible in the students' daily lives. In accord with these instructional goals, the Bible Committee quizzed prospective teachers about their religious beliefs, and the minutes of their job interviews are filled with accounts of their salvation experiences and their "Walk with Christ." The teaching method they used was to go through the KJB each year, having the students fill out worksheets, memorize verses, and learn to name the books of the Bible in order. Identical lessons were taught in grades 1 and 2, and similar plans were used for grades 3–6. To Herdahl's attorneys, this suggested "not a secular class but a class intended to drill the Bible into students through repetition of the same 'course' for [several] consecutive years" (Memorandum of Points and Authorities, December 12, 1995, p. 26). The secondary-school lessons resembled those in the elementary grades, adjusted for the age of the students.

As school officials who defended the classes were quick to point out, the Supreme Court has repeatedly declared that the Bible can be taught as history or literature. To the Bible teachers, this meant teaching that every word of

Scripture is historically accurate. When teacher Michael Thompson was asked how he dealt with the Virgin Birth, the miracles of Christ, and the Resurrection, he replied, "We just study it as the Bible explains it: This event happened, this event happened, this event. We're teaching the historical account, so I want my students to understand the details of those events" (deposition, July 18, 1995, p. 464). Asked whether he cared whether his students believed that Jesus is the Savior and the Son of God, Thompson replied, "'Yes, ma'am, just as any—a math teacher believes that one plus one is two and feels that is important and vital to them. I mean they need to believe that one plus one is two" (deposition, July 17, 1995, p. 130). This doctrinal orientation was also evident in annual reports presented to the Bible Committee by teachers and students, which appeared as exhibits in the lawsuit. The minutes of one meeting, for instance, include the Bible teachers' assurance "that their students seem responsive to God's word." The secretary's rough notes add that students "were telling [the teacher] about their salvation experiences." The testimony of Bible teacher Larry Dean Patterson was particularly passionate on this point, since he felt that he owed his salvation to his high school Bible teacher and hoped that his own instruction would have the same effect on his students.

RATHER FIGHT THAN SWITCH

Among the points school officials raised to legitimize the Bible classes was the fact that at the high school level they carried social studies credit toward graduation. This matter was in flux, however, when Herdahl filed her lawsuit in 1995. For years, the Mississippi State Department of Education (MSDE) had given graduation credit for any Bible course, but in 1992 it stated that although Bible classes could continue, they would not carry credit. Alarmed by the prospect of shrinking enrollments, the Bible teachers met with MSDE officials to plan a course called "Biblical History of the Middle East." It was approved in 1993 as a pilot course for secondary schools, which meant that it would carry graduation credit for three years pending a final decision based on annual MSDE evaluations. The plan called for a broad-based course on Middle Eastern history in which the Bible would be one of several texts; but according to Patterson, the Bible teachers and their AFA advisors saw it as a way to "'preserve the integrity and essence of what [they] had been teaching already'" (Plaintiff's Motion for Summary Judgment, December 12, 1995, p. 18).

When Joann Prewitt, an MSDE social studies specialist, visited the schools to evaluate the pilot program for the first time, she noted that although the course had been approved only for secondary school, it was being taught in all grades. She also found no evidence of the agreed-upon Middle Eastern history curriculum. As she later testified, "the climate was very emotional, defensive and any expansion of the course is seen as a threat" (deposition, October 2, 1995, p. 149). She experienced difficulty in obtaining copies of course materials, being told repeatedly that things had been misplaced; when she persisted, she was given copies of tests and worksheets with some items whited out. She also reported receiving folders of material that did not correspond with what she found on the students' desks. Moreover, she asserted, some principals were as resistant to changing the course as the Bible teachers were. One of them, she recalled, protested, "'You cannot teach without interjecting your own personal beliefs. There is only the Bible.' . . . He seemed to think to change the course of doctrine would be to change his beliefs" (p. 235). Teachers and principals quizzed her about her own faith, she said, and she tried to explain that no one's personal beliefs were at issue; the goal was to develop a course on Middle Eastern history in biblical times.

Based on Prewitt's findings, the MSDE wrote to the school superintendents in each of the three years of the pilot program cautioning them about teaching the course in elementary school and noting that it "needs more references to the historical background including the ancient Mesopotamians, Egyptians, Assyrians, Babylonians, Persians, Greeks, and Romans if it is truly to be a history course." The MSDE also admonished, "Care should be taken that a discussion of sin, punishment, repentance, and deliverance be treated as a recurring literary theme and not as doctrine" (letter of March 3, 1993). Of particular concern to the MSDE was the use of tests and worksheets requiring students to profess certain religious beliefs. Prewitt collected numerous examples that appeared as exhibits in the legal proceedings; for example:

- "Do I have room in my heart for Jesus?"
- "From your own experience, tell how God has used events or situations in your own life to strengthen your faith."
- "Explain who your God is to a person who is from a foreign country and doesn't know our God of the Bible."
- "Explain, out of your own experience and using Biblical references, how sin has crouched at your door and how you mastered it. Include the temptation experience and what kept you from falling into sin."

In the second and third years of the pilot program, some teachers listed nonscriptural texts in the folders they gave Prewitt, but she continued to see no evidence of anything but the Bible in lesson plans or tests. Thompson later testified that he had indeed added material on other cultures even if it did not appear in his course materials. Asked for an example, he said, "Well, we discussed many, I'm sure. I mean I can't say when or where or how, but I'm sure we discussed many of the larger religions of the world" (deposition, July 18, 1995, p. 453). In an attempt to explain why the Bible teachers resisted the proposed revisions, Patterson said, "[W]e just felt... that we soon wouldn't be teaching the bible history anymore, we'd be teaching world history or world religions or whatever" (deposition, August 16, 1995, p. 139). While acknowledging that he taught the same material six times in elementary school and then again in secondary school, he protested that there was no room in the course for anything but the Bible. "If I did [what the MSDE wanted]," he remarked, "I would never get to *Nehemiah*" (p. 174).

The Bible teachers' objections to expanding the course were set out in a letter from an AFA attorney to the MSDE, dated April 28, 1994: "It is the concern of the Bible Committee, which we share, that in the name of preventing the establishment of religion the State of Mississippi might inadvertently destroy all legitimate attempts to instruct students in a Biblical history course." It also warned "of the danger of offending First Amendment precedent by virtue of your numerous suggestions for revisions to the course as currently taught." Nevertheless, the MSDE decided that the course would no longer carry graduation credit, and Prewitt's data became a centerpiece of Herdahl's case because it provided evidence that "the Bible teachers dressed up the curriculum with references to numerous non-biblical resources, instructional materials, and student activities that plainly and admittedly are not being used" (Plaintiff's Post-Trial Brief, March 26, 1996, p. 34). Herdahl also cited the teachers' behavior as evidence that nothing short of a court order was likely to be effective.

FAMILY CONFLICT

Although the disagreement between the Bible teachers and the MSDE played a role in *Herdahl*, it is important to note that it had been in progress for three years before the lawsuit was filed. Unlike the Aletheia Club devotionals, which had been unchallenged until a stranger came to town, the Bible classes had already generated conflict within the Mississippi education establishment itself. This controversy recalls Dolbeare and Hammond's 1971 analysis of responses to *Abington* in the Midwest (see Chapter Six), which focuses on tension between "elites" and "nonelites" in state politics, the education profession, and the local community. Although their study preceded the Pontotoc dispute by more than twenty years, the dynamics it outlines are clearly applicable. In the Mississippi conflict, state education officials showed themselves to be more in tune with the Supreme Court's view of church/state separation than they were with the desire to preserve a traditional way of life that remained sacred to local school personnel and the community they served. As a result, the MSDE's behavior struck the Bible teachers as a perversion of rightful governmental authority and a usurpation of their religious and academic freedom. This rationale would justify civil disobedience to defend what the teachers viewed as their sacred rights and as God's will—hence the vanishing lesson plans and the whited-out test items. In this respect, the Mississippi conflict brings to mind the congressional hearings on court-stripping discussed in Chapter Nine, in which some witnesses argued that finding a way to disregard or defy the Supreme Court's school-prayer rulings was a necessary act of self-defense whose end would justify the means.

The conflict between the "elites" of the MSDE and the "nonelite" Bible teachers and local school officials in Pontotoc County also resembles the Becker, Dirksen, and Reagan Amendment hearings, where witnesses and members of Congress representing a conservative Christian viewpoint presented themselves as down-to-earth, grassroots, "real" Americans and Christians. By contrast, as they saw it, opponents of state-sponsored majoritarian prayer were effete adherents of elitist mainstream faiths who, corrupted by liberalism and secularism, shilled for church/state separation and political correctness at the expense of the populist values of majority rights and religious freedom. As a final comparison illustrating the persistence of certain themes and dynamics, the ultimatum delivered by the MSDE to the Pontotoc schools was in some respects a milder version of the post-*Abington* New Jersey litigation discussed in Chapter Six, in which state officials forced unwilling local communities to conform to national standards, values, and expectations. Such clashes between "elite" and "nonelite" imperatives are an integral part of the evolution of public policy on school prayer, and as the last chapter of this book demonstrates, they are anything but a thing of the past.

A ROSE IS A ROSE IS A ROSE

Shortly before the court was to hear arguments in Herdahl's case, signs decked with red, white, and blue ribbons went up all over Pontotoc County. The words "Religious Freedom" were printed inside a picture of a schoolhouse with a bell in its pointed spire and "A+" on its sides. Local stores sold similarly decorated T-shirts and baseball caps produced by the Parent Teacher

Organization to raise funds for the lawsuit. The irony—or at least ambiguity—of the phrase "Religious Freedom" was apparent in an anecdote Herdahl told a reporter. Her children, she said, "'thought all those signs meant those families agreed with us.... I had to tell them, "No, I don't think so"'" (Laurie Ann Lattimore, "The Herdahl Family's Hurdle," *Liberty*, May/June, 1996, p. 19). One of her attorneys, Elliot Mincberg, had a similar experience. When he went into a shop to buy some of the baseball caps, the shopkeeper asked him earnestly whether he thinks religious freedom is important. "Oh yes," he replied with equal earnestness. "I think it's very important" (interview, July 9, 1996). Simple as this two-sentence exchange is, the conflicting definitions of religious freedom underlying it embody decades, and indeed centuries, of debate over the scope and meaning of that expression. What was under discussion in the Pontotoc community as well as in the courts was whether the principle of religious liberty means that the majority has the right to decide what religious practices should take place in the public schools, or whether it entitles each individual to equal treatment from a government that offers to no one what it does not provide for everyone.

To state the obvious, the evolution of legal thought on school prayer traced in Chapters Four through Six has led to Supreme Court precedents that clearly coincide with Herdahl's view. In accord with those precedents, the federal district court granted her request for a preliminary injunction blocking the loudspeaker prayer pending final resolution of the lawsuit. The school officials had attempted to protect the prayers by arguing that they represented not state action but an exercise of the free-speech and religious rights of the Aletheia Club members, but to no avail. As the decision explained, "When a student is told to be silent and listen to the school's official morning announcements, at the conclusion of which the school principal hands control of the address system over to a student solely for the purpose of prayer and scripture reading, the students reasonably believe that the school, a government institution, is advocating religion and, in particular, the Christian faith" (*Herdahl v. Pontotoc County Board of Education*, 887 F. Supp. 902 [1995], pp. 908–9). This decision did not mean, however, that the Aletheia Club had to stop conducting daily prayer services. Even before the hearing took place, both sides had agreed that the club members were at liberty to pray aloud if they did so within an EAA-style neutral activity period open to other noncurricular meetings of secondary-school students. Nevertheless, although Herdahl's attorneys were fully supportive of such activities on the part of older students, they were dismayed when the court said that children in the elementary grades could, with their parents' permission, attend prayer meetings led by the high school students in the Aletheia Club. Moreover, as the lawyers indignantly pointed out in later proceedings, no announcement was made about the creation of a neutral activity period, and the students were not invited to form other clubs that could meet at the same time as the Aletheia Club. The only change was a ten-minute delay in the start of classes to allow any student who wished to do so to attend devotionals led by the Aletheia Club in the gym. The elementary teachers distributed and collected permission slips composed by the club, and secondary-school students were asked to submit their own forms to the club, indicating whether they would attend the prayers.

When the newly organized prayer services began, participating secondary-school students went from their school buses to the gym, while their nonparticipating classmates remained outside. Later, in response to objections, they were allowed into a small annex in inclement weather. Elementary-school students whose parents had given permission for them to attend prayers first reported to their classrooms, where they were lined up and escorted to the gym by a teacher, a teacher's aide, or a volunteer parent. School officials stated that this degree of school involvement was necessary because of the children's age. Their classmates who did not go to prayers made their own way from the buses to the cafeteria and thence to their classrooms, where they sat in silence. At first, preachers, politicians, and other community members attended the prayer meetings to show support, but this slackened off over time. By most estimates, more than two-thirds of the students participated at first, although this too later diminished.

THE BIG WIDE WORLD

Like *Lubbock, Brandon, Bender,* and other lawsuits used as ammunition in the fight over the EAA, Herdahl's ongoing case quickly became a factor in congressional debates over school prayer and related issues. Speaker of the House Newt Gingrich (R-Georgia), for instance, mentioned it to support his call for school vouchers. "'My attitude,'" he said, "'is that we'll give [Herdahl] a voucher for the value of your child's education.... Go find a school you like. But don't dictate to everybody else in your community based on your particular prejudices.'" When it was pointed out that there were no other schools in Pontotoc, he shot back, "'But there would be if you had vouchers.'" Herdahl said that Gingrich's remark was "'completely nuts,'" adding, "'The Constitution was not written for the minority or the majority but for everybody'" (Reuter News Service, "Gingrich Voucher Remark Is Called 'Nuts,'" *Washington Post*, June 19, 1995, p. A11).

Herdahl also became a rallying cry for supporters of Representative Ernest Istook's (R-Oklahoma) proposal for a new constitutional amendment on school prayer, discussed in Chapter Fifteen. The Traditional Values Coalition, a California-based group that drafted and promoted one version of the Istook Amendment, invited Pontotoc County students to a press conference at the National Press Club in Washington, D.C. There, TVC leader Reverend Louis Sheldon pointed to them as living exhibits of the extent to which American Christians are ridiculed, disenfranchised, and silenced. Similarly, William Murray, son of atheist activist Madalyn Murray O'Hair, led an anti-Herdahl rally at a conservative National Affairs Briefing attended by presidential candidates and other politicians. Murray, a staunch supporter of state-sponsored prayer, gave a colorful speech comparing Lisa Herdahl to his mother, whom he accused, among other things, of emasculating the males in the Murray family. Turning his attention to PFAW, he described the group as the tool of "powerful left wing Hollywood types" who, he alleged, "want the people of little Pontotoc County to stop praying in the schools and start promoting homosexuality and the worship of nature. The bottom line is that People for the un-American Way is just another group of pro-homosexual activists that want to destroy the last vestige of morality in America" ("Stand at Pontotoc," *The William J. Murray Report*, January/February 1996, p. 1). He urged his listeners to support the Istook Amendment, which would help to restore traditional values to the public square.

Herdahl articulated her own views about the Istook Amendment in her testimony before both the House Subcommittee on the Constitution and the Senate Judiciary Committee. "I am a Christian," she declared, "and I am raising my children to be Christians, and I believe that it is my job as a parent, not the job of a public school, to teach my children about religion and prayer" ("Religious Liberty," p. 16). The Pontotoc school district submitted a written rebuttal to Herdahl's remarks, alleging among other things that the ACLU and PFAW "have consistently sought to intimidate students and parents who have tried to express deeply held religious beliefs in the public arena.... What this really means is that it is alright [sic] to be a Christian, or a member of any other religious group, as long as you do not tell anyone about it" (p. 198).

MEANWHILE, BACK IN THE COURT

Amid all this national publicity, *Herdahl* went to trial in spring 1996. Among other things, Herdahl asked the court to make permanent its injunction against the loudspeaker prayers, require the establishment of a meaningful open forum for secondary-school clubs, halt the participation of the elementary grades in Aletheia Club meetings, and prohibit doctrinal Bible classes. The two sides soon reached agreement about creating a neutral activity period before school each morning, but the school officials defended the elementary students' participation in the Aletheia Club's prayer meetings and sought to retain the Bible classes. They also asked the court to reinstate the loudspeaker prayers, which they preferred to the meetings in the gym.

The court's decision gave something to each side. The loudspeaker prayers were prohibited, but the morning devotionals were upheld for both elementary- and secondary-school students. A similar dichotomy existed with respect to the Bible classes. On the one hand, the court ruled that by offering "a course based on the community's Protestant beliefs, the District has abandoned its institutional role and blurred the line between secular and parochial education" (*Herdahl v. Pontotoc County School Board,* 933 F. Supp. 582 [1996], p. 595, note 9). School officials were therefore ordered to terminate any class that used the Bible "as the only source of historical fact or as if the Bible were actual literal history" (p. 600). On the other hand, the court not only upheld NPAC's right to offer secular courses that used the Bible among other texts, but also allowed the Bible Committee to continue selecting and paying the teachers as long as no religious test was involved in their hiring.

Some community activists, including several preachers, urged the school board to keep fighting all the way to the Supreme Court if necessary, but lawyers from the Christian Life Commission of the Southern Baptist Convention warned that the right to appeal goes both ways. If the board tried to win back the loudspeaker prayers and traditional Bible classes, Herdahl would almost certainly renew her effort to exclude the elementary grades from the Aletheia Club meetings and to end the Bible Committee's role in the classes. Accordingly, the school board voted to let the case rest. Herdahl, too, decided against appealing, feeling that her family had had enough controversy. She had won with regard to the loudspeaker prayers, and she decided to wait and see how the Bible classes would be taught. Since they were now supposed to be secular, she saw no reason to have her children excused, and following the first Bible class of the 1996 fall term, she called Mincberg to say that the children had drawn a lake. "This is fine," he said. "They can draw all the lakes they want. But next week, if there's anybody walking on that lake, we might be going back to court" (interview, August 19, 1996). By 1999, the board had voluntarily suspended Bible classes in grades 1–3 because the teachers could not determine how to present the material to such young children in a nondoctrinal way.

Although this dispute over prayer and Bible classes took place in the 1990s, it fit a pattern that would have been equally familiar a hundred years earlier. Its starting point was the school's enforcement of a community orthodoxy so ingrained that it was seen not as promoting any sectarian view but simply as acknowledging an obvious and universally accepted reality. This perception made it difficult for school officials to conceive that anyone could have a valid basis for wishing to be excused, as illustrated by the anger and even shock with which Vice-Principal Rodney Flowers greeted Lisa Herdahl's initial challenge. Like the protests of nineteenth-century Catholics against the use of the KJB, her insistence that her family had the right to opt out of traditional observances conflicted with the majority's conviction that those practices represented something absolute, universal, and transcendent rather than merely manifesting one group's subjective preferences against another's. Far worse, from the standpoint of traditionalists, even when they made at least a gesture toward excusing her children, this upstart invader to their community demanded nothing less than the termination of the challenged practices. Clearly, the Pontotoc school officials and their supporters adhered to the model of religious toleration described in Chapter Seven, under which dissenters from the majority view were held to be sufficiently protected if they were not impeded in the private practice of their beliefs regarding religion. In contrast, Herdahl, her PFAW attorneys, and the MSDE called for the model of religious equality. As they (and the court) understood it, the concept of religious liberty prevents American public-school officials from suggesting that any religious system, no matter how generic, long-standing, or widely accepted, is more "American" or more of a governmental norm than any other.

THE HALL OF JUSTICE

Herdahl was by no means the first lawsuit to deal with Bible classes in the public schools; indeed, the Court of Appeals for the Fifth Circuit, where any appeal in *Herdahl* would have gone, had already decided a similar case involving loudspeaker prayers and a "Bible-as-literature" course in an Alabama school. That case, *Hall v. School Commissioners,* was dismissed by Judge Brevard Hand, mentioned in Chapter Ten in conjunction with his decisions in *Wallace v. Jaffree.* The appeals court reversed his decision in *Hall* and ordered him to issue an injunction against the loudspeaker prayers. It also declared the Bible classes unconstitutional because they were based solely on the KJB and a textbook entitled *The Bible for Youthful Patriots,* which "reveals a fundamentalist Christian approach to the study of the Bible devoid of any discussion of its literary qualities" (*Hall v. Board of School Commissioners of Conecuh County*, 656 F.2d 999 [1981], p. 1002).

Although *Hall* indicated in general terms that a secular Bible course would be permissible, other pre-*Herdahl* decisions included more specific instructions regarding the distinction between secular and doctrinal instruction. An example was *Wiley v. Franklin*, which arose in Chattanooga, Tennessee, and was decided in conjunction with a similar lawsuit, *Schwartz v. Dobson*, from nearby Hamilton County. At issue in both cases were elementary-school Bible classes whose teachers were selected and paid by a Bible Study Committee. The written policies of both school districts required the classes to be secular, but in practice the curriculum was determined by the committee, which equated "nonsectarian" with "nondenominational fundamentalist Protestant." In finding that the Bible classes in both school districts were unacceptably religious, the federal district court clarified that the problem was "not the Bible itself, but rather the selectivity, emphasis, objectivity, and interpretative manner, or lack thereof, with which the Bible is taught" (*Wiley v. Franklin*, 468 F. Supp. 133 [1979], p. 150). Accordingly, the Bible classes were suspended while school officials developed a plan that would fulfill several conditions set by the court. The school officials in both districts complied, but the case was back in court the following summer. The plaintiffs protested that although both school districts claimed to have eschewed religious tests, almost all the newly approved teachers had been trained at sectarian Bible colleges. The court ruled that excluding teachers because they had attended those schools would be a religious test in itself, just as requiring such attendance would be. The plaintiffs also objected to the way the courses were taught, and the decision on this matter was split: the Chattanooga classes were upheld, but those in Hamilton County were struck down because they treated accounts of divine intervention as fact. Hamilton County later developed a new Bible curriculum based on the Chattanooga model.

HOT WEATHER IN FLORIDA

A similarly solomonic approach was evident in a post-*Herdahl* decision dealing with Bible classes in Fort Myers, Florida. The dispute began when a school-board member saw a plan for a two-semester Bible course published by the National Council on Bible Curriculum in Public Schools. (The NCBCPS curricula may be found at *www.bibleinschools.org*, and a rebuttal appears at *www.pfaw.org/issues/liberty/fl-bible-ncbcpsfacts.shtml*.) He recommended it to the board, but because of concerns about the NCBCPS's fundamentalist orientation, the board formed a citizens' committee to develop two courses: Bible History I: Old Testament, and Bible History II: New Testament. Most of the Bible Curriculum Committee's fifteen members were Protestants, but Catholics and Jews were also represented.

From the time it was convened in June 1996, the committee was able to agree on almost nothing, which is one of the most striking differences between this dispute and *Herdahl*. Unlike Pontotoc County, Fort Myers was not a place where almost everyone supported doctrinal Bible classes. The Pontotoc case showed what happened when alien voices were raised against a long-standing and well-loved tradition; Fort Myers was a tale of conflict within a diversified community in which Bible classes were being proposed de novo. The Bible Curriculum Committee appears to have represented a good cross-section of the population, which explains why it deadlocked. Some members wanted nothing less than the NCBCPS curriculum, which treated the Bible as fact, while others were repelled by what they saw as blatant sectarianism.

When the committee was unable to agree on a curriculum for Bible History I, the school district staff drafted one. Despite revisions made at the committee's behest, some members still felt that it diluted the Bible with too much extraneous material, while others questioned teaching such things as the six days of creation as history. Nevertheless, prodded by school officials who wanted to have the course in place by January 1997, the committee presented the proposed Bible History I curriculum to the board, together with a dissenting minority report. The board's attorney warned that the course was probably actionable, and although he resigned when his concerns appeared in the press, they were echoed by his successor and by an outside law firm the board hired as advisors. Following a raucous public meeting on August 6, the board voted 3–2 to approve a version of Bible History I that included some of its own lawyer's suggestions but not those of the outside firm. When school principals pointed out that there was no time for teacher training before September, the course was put off until the spring semester.

Meanwhile, the Bible Curriculum Committee had been working on Bible History II, but to no avail. Foes of a doctrinal Bible course, including lawyers advising the board, objected to presenting miracles and the Resurrection as historical facts. Naturally, this infuriated advocates of the NCBCPS approach. According to a lawsuit later filed in federal district court, one committee member "literally shredded a copy of the lawyer-edited curriculum at the September 23, 1997, meeting and threw it over his head saying: 'This class is not history; this is censorship outright.... I move we cease discussions of this garbage on the floor, this atrocity, this blatant malignancy... Christians died over the last week of Jesus' life. Christians died over this'" (*Gibson v. Lee County School Board*, Complaint, p. 14). Hopelessly conflicted, the committee voted to disband itself and to recommend the adoption of the NCBCPS New Testament curriculum. Both votes were 6–5.

When the school board met on October 21, 1997, the proceedings opened with a prayer in the name of Jesus. The standing-room-only crowd was vociferous; some called for an explicitly Christian curriculum, while others wanted to know why the district had spent thirty-seven thousand dollars to develop Bible courses in which few students had indicated any interest. Neither the lawyers nor the school superintendent favored the NCBCPS course, which presented the Bible as fact and emphasized memorization. Nevertheless, when the board was assured that the American Center for Law and Justice would charge nothing for defending that curriculum in court, it was adopted by a vote of 3–2. A month later, the board accepted ACLJ representation by another vote of 3–2.

Bible History I was scheduled to be taught for the first time in January 1998, and Bible History II was to begin in March. When plaintiffs represented by the Florida ACLU and PFAW asked the federal district court to prevent either course from being taught, the court issued a *Wiley*-style compromise decision balancing the need to avoid indoctrination against a recognition of "the importance of the Bible independent of its religious significance, and the influence that this book has had on Western civilization" (*Gibson v. Lee County School Board*, 1 F. Supp. 2d 1426 [1998], p. 1431). On the basis of this standard, the court upheld Bible History I but not Bible History II. Ironically, the revisions made to Bible History I by its opponents proved to be its salvation because they demonstrated a reasonable effort to construct a secular course. "The Court expects that Plaintiffs will videotape the classes," the decision added, which "may prevent any veiled attempt to promote religion or Christianity in the guise of teaching history." If the plaintiffs were dissatisfied, they could return to court with evidence to support their claims. In declining to make a similar arrangement for Bible History II, which consisted of the NCBCPS curriculum, the decision referred to the objections expressed by the board's lawyers. "This Court too finds it difficult to conceive how the account of the resurrection or of miracles could be taught as secular history" (p. 1434), it stated.

Lost in the tumult over demands for Christian-centered Bible instruction was the plight of teachers who had no intention of teaching Scripture as dogma but wanted students to understand the Bible as a seminal text of western civi-

lization. "'In other situations,'" one such teacher said, "'people have acted irre-
sponsibly, so I'm afraid of being lumped into that category in somebody's
mind who isn't being that objective either'" (Shelby Oppel, "Public School
Class to Learn Bible History," *St. Petersburg Times,* December 7, 1997, p. 1B).
Obviously, adding the tension of the lawsuit and the glare of media spotlights
to the inherent difficulty of teaching a secular Bible course in a public school
created an almost impossible situation for any instructor. As the *New York
Times* described the first day of the course, "[The teacher] was being cautious
because . . . the textbook was the Bible, and every word he said was being video-
taped for review by lawyers and a Federal judge in a pioneering legal case."
Then a student asked where Cain and Abel came from. "'For whatever reason,
we're not supposed to talk about that' [the teacher] said. 'You just read it on
your own. I don't know why. Please don't ask me why'" (Mireya Navarro,
"Florida Case Highlights Conflicts on Use of the Bible as a Textbook," *New
York Times,* February 17, 1998, pp. A1, A13). Within a week, the school board
decided to scrap the Bible History I and II approach. Instead, it set about
developing a new course called "Introduction to the Bible," thus addressing
the plaintiffs' objection that the title "Bible History" implies that the Bible is
factually true. The board also agreed to develop companion courses in world
history and world religions. By April, the board and the plaintiffs had worked
out a settlement that included agreement on a textbook and a course outline.
Nevertheless, the final blow to doctrinal Bible courses—at least for the time
being—came not in court but at the polls. Following the 1998 school-board
election, the small majority in favor of the NCBCPS curriculum became a
large majority against it.

In 2000, PFAW issued a report entitled "The Good Book Taught Wrong:
'Bible History' Classes in Florida's Public Schools." Among other things, the
group objected to the use of such test questions as "Why is it hard for a non-
Christian to understand things about God?" and "Who, according to Jesus, is
the father of the Jews?" to which the answer is "The devil" (*www.pfaw.org/issues/
liberty/florida-bible.shtml*). The Florida Department of Education later removed
Bible History from its list of approved courses and replaced it with two humani-
ties courses which, in PFAW's view, "conform to the Constitution, if implemented properly by the local school districts" (press release, March 16, 2000).

A WILEY JUDGE

Another post-*Herdahl* lawsuit brought the question of public-school Bible
classes back to the same district court that had decided *Wiley v. Franklin* two

decades earlier. This case, *Doe v. Porter*, arose in Rhea County, Tennessee, site of the famous Scopes "monkey trial" in which creationist William Jennings Bryan had faced evolutionist Clarence Darrow. A college named for Bryan had been established nearby, and students from its Bible Education Ministry taught the elementary-school Bible classes challenged in the lawsuit. The BEM classes ran for half an hour a week in grades K–5, and although school officials claimed that participation was voluntary, they neither announced an opt-out policy nor sought parental permission. Unlike all other instruction in the Rhea County schools, the Bible classes were completely unsupervised by school officials, which led the court to conclude that "The School Board and Superintendent have essentially turned over the operation of the BEM program to Bryan College, making a place in the regular school curriculum and in the classrooms for the program" (*Doe v. Porter*, 188 F. Supp. 2d 904 [2002], p. 907). The court also found that the Bible was being taught as inerrant truth and that the children were being encouraged to apply it to their lives. As evidence, the decision cited lesson plans containing such objectives as "Believe that Jesus can perform miracles," "I hope to convey the truth of the gospel that everything Jesus did was b/c he loves us," "The kids should see that the Bible is full of instructions for us and is a source of light," and "That the Bible is true and it is the instrument that can give guidance and direction in your life" (p. 912, note 2). Like almost all post-*Abington* school-prayer decisions, *Doe* made short work of the claim that local majorities are entitled to decide whether they want such instruction. "Counsel for defendants," it stated, "contended at oral argument that since 'Rhea County is a place where they respect the Bible,' it ought therefore to be at liberty to teach the tenets of the Bible in its public schools as truth.... It is probably true that the citizens of Rhea County who are of the Christian faith are in the majority. This, however, does not give them license to teach their religion in the public schools" (p. 915).

A WIDER NET

This chapter set out to demonstrate how the equal-access model is affecting disputes over religious expression during the regular public-school day, but it cannot claim to have dealt with all the specific forms such controversies may take. If space permitted, additional examples might include such matters as distributing religious literature, singing religious songs, having holiday celebrations and displays, and incorporating religious material into school assignments. But covering all these bases in any degree of detail would obviously result in an unwieldy book, and although the specific facts of such disputes differ from those of the cases discussed in this chapter, in many ways the analysis of the underlying principles would be repetitive. To summarize: student initiative, consistent rules for a given student activity, and freedom of choice for students are encouraged; whereas school involvement, discriminating for or against student-generated religious content in a given activity, or creating captive student audiences would at the very least raise questions. (A more detailed listing of the regulations governing such activities is provided by the U.S. Department of Education, whose guidelines are discussed in Chapter Fifteen.)

Somewhat different issues arise, however, with regard to school-sponsored events that take place outside the regular school day, such as graduation ceremonies, theatrical or musical performances, and athletic contests. As Chapter Fourteen demonstrates, the question of whether prayer is permissible at these functions is affected by such factors as voluntary attendance; the presence of parents and other community members, who may in fact outnumber the students; and the school officials' comparative lack of direct control over the participants' behavior. Inevitably, such differences as these, combined in some instances with long-standing traditions of having prayer at particular events, have led to lawsuits in which Establishment Clause concerns are weighed against the strong desire of some parents, students, and community members to engage in prayer.

14
The School and the Rabbi

A government cannot be premised on the belief that all persons are created equal when it asserts that God prefers some.

—*Justice Harry Blackmun*

For generations, a blessing by a member of the clergy was as integral a part of many graduation ceremonies as "Pomp and Circumstance." Certainly that was true in Providence, Rhode Island, where most graduations began and ended with prayer. Such prayers were ordinarily so bland that Daniel and Vivian Weisman had never really noticed them, but when their older daughter, Merith, graduated from Nathan Bishop Middle School, an ebullient Baptist minister called upon the audience to join hands and pray to Jesus. That got their attention. According to Robert E. Lee, who became principal of Nathan Bishop the following year, the minister had been selected because "it was just sort of the Baptists' turn" (interview, April 27, 1995; all quotations from Lee are from this interview). School officials had provided guidelines specifying, among other things, that the prayer should be brief, nonsectarian, and nonproselytizing; but unlike most clergy who prayed at school events, he had ignored them.

Disconcerted by this experience, the Weismans wanted no prayer when their younger daughter, Deborah, graduated from Nathan Bishop two years later. The Weismans are Jewish, and the teachers who had selected the minister tried to address their concerns by inviting a rabbi to pray at Deborah's graduation. Nevertheless, the family continued to assert that prayer should not be part of a public-school event. In fact, the choice of a rabbi made legal action more appealing to them because they could initiate it without appearing hostile to other people's religious beliefs. In an interview for this book, they also noted with amusement that they had less of a personal relationship with the rabbi than they had with the Baptist minister, an African American civil-rights advocate with whom they had worked in the past.

When the school officials refused to remove the invocation and benediction from the graduation program, Vivian Weisman, then-president of the Rhode Island affiliate of the American Civil Liberties Union, went to Sandra Blanding (now Lanni), a local lawyer. Blanding had been among the attorneys representing the RI ACLU in an earlier lawsuit concerning the inclusion of a nativity scene in a city's Christmas display, and at Weisman's request, she sought a temporary restraining order to prevent prayers from taking place at Deborah's graduation. The court declined to issue one, and the ceremony opened with an invocation by Rabbi Leslie Gutterman:

> God of the Free, Hope of the Brave: For the legacy of America
> where diversity is celebrated and the rights of minorities are pro-
> tected, we thank You. May these young men and women grow up
> to enrich it. For the liberty of America, we thank You. May these
> new graduates grow up to guard it. For the political process of
> America in which all its citizens may participate, for its court sys-
> tem where all can seek justice we thank You. May those we honor
> this morning always turn to it in trust. For the destiny of America
> we thank You.... May our aspirations for our country and for
> these young people... be richly fulfilled. Amen. (*Weisman v. Lee*,
> 728 F. Supp. 68 [1990], p. 70, note 2)

His closing benediction consisted of thanks, a blessing, and a quotation from the Book of *Micah*.

Although the Weismans' daughters had both graduated from middle school, the family had standing to sue as long as at least one of them had not yet graduated from high school. Accordingly, Blanding filed suit on behalf of Daniel Weisman, challenging a school district policy that permitted clergy-led prayers at graduation. This practice, she averred, should come under the same ban as school-sponsored classroom prayer because graduation was an official school event overseen by school personnel who chose the participating clergy and provided guidelines for the prayers. While conceding that no one was required to attend graduation, she quoted Supreme Court decisions, including *Abington*, stating that an unconstitutional practice does not become constitutional merely because people can decline to join in it. Moreover, she argued, missing such a significant occasion as graduation cannot be dismissed as a trivial burden. In response, the Providence school officials denied that graduation prayer is comparable to classroom devotionals. Rather, they asserted, it resem-

bles nothing so much as the invocations that open legislative and court proceedings. A few years earlier, in a case entitled *Marsh v. Chambers,* the
Supreme Court had upheld the practice of having legislatures appoint and pay
chaplains to open legislative sessions with prayer. The school board's lawyer,
Joseph Rotella, maintained that *Marsh,* not *Abington,* was the appropriate
precedent to apply to the long-standing tradition of using clergy-led invocations and benedictions to solemnize graduation ceremonies.

TEST QUESTION

At the federal district court hearing, Judge Francis J. Boyle asked Blanding a
hypothetical question. Suppose, he suggested, the rabbi had said, "'My fellow
citizens, to each according to his needs, from each according to his abilities.'
Would you let him say that?" Yes, she said, she would. "Because it's communist doctrine and communism denies a deity, right?" the judge shot back. "So
you can preach communism at an invocation, but he can't refer to 'in God we
trust'" (transcript of hearing, October 10, 1989, p. 7). Boyle went on to express
similar disgust with the Supreme Court's school-prayer decisions, but he
nonetheless declined to follow the example of judges mentioned in earlier
chapters, whose rulings flew in the face of those precedents. "The fact is," he
wrote, "that an unacceptably high number of citizens who are undergoing
difficult times in this country are children and young people. School-sponsored
prayer might provide hope to sustain them, and principles to guide them in the
difficult choices they confront today. But the Constitution as the Supreme
Court views it does not permit it. . . . Those who are anti-prayer thus have been
deemed the victors. This is the difficult but obligatory choice this Court makes
today" (*Weisman v. Lee,* p. 75).

In reaching this decision, Boyle applied a standard known as the *Lemon*
test, whose validity became an issue when the Weismans' case reached the
Supreme Court. It was first enunciated in *Lemon v. Kurtzman,* a 1971 Supreme
Court decision striking down tax subsidies for parochial schools.[1] In *Lemon,*
the Supreme Court declared that a state action may be held unconstitutional if
it violates any prong of a tripartite test: (1) the challenged state action must
have a secular purpose, (2) its primary effect must neither advance nor hinder
religion, and (3) it must not excessively entangle the government with religion. The first two of these prongs had appeared in *Abington,* and after 1971
the entire test was generally used in school-prayer cases. Applying the *Lemon*
test to the Providence graduation policy, Judge Boyle concluded that one or
more of its prongs were violated when school officials selected clergy to pray at

graduation, provided guidelines for the prayers, and made prayer an official part of the ceremony. His order to terminate those practices stunned the principal of Nathan Bishop Middle School, Robert Lee; as he later recalled, he and his colleagues had considered the Weismans' complaint "just a passing nuisance" that the court could not possibly take seriously. The Providence school district appealed Boyle's ruling to the Court of Appeals for the First Circuit, whose decision was succinct: "We are in agreement with the sound and pellucid opinion of the district court and see no reason to elaborate further" (*Lee v. Weisman*, 908 F.2d 1090 [1990], p. 1090).

The Supreme Court agreed to hear the case, and despite their defeats in the lower courts, the school officials were optimistic. "The district court was reluctant," Lee explained, "and then the appeals court was so terse, that it gave us hope that a higher court would have the power to change this." They hired a new attorney, Charles Cooper, who had once clerked for Justice (later Chief Justice) William Rehnquist. He had also worked in the U.S. Justice Department under President Ronald Reagan before joining a prestigious Washington law firm. He added several of the firm's attorneys to his legal team, which also included the school district's original attorney, Joseph Rotella, and Jay Sekulow of the American Center for Law and Justice. Blanding remained the lead attorney for Weisman, although she had never before argued in the Supreme Court and is quick to acknowledge that her regular practice has little to do with the Constitution. "It feels funny," she said, looking at the pile of *Lee* documents she had resurrected for a visiting writer. "One day you're in Family Court, then you're in the Supreme Court, and the next day you're back in Family Court" (interview, April 25, 1995; unless otherwise indicated, quotations from Blanding are from this interview). She was not alone, however. Although she did not have the kind of team assembled by Cooper, she was aided by advocacy-group lawyers, including the national ACLU legal director, Steven Shapiro; and by University of Texas law professor Douglas Laycock, a nationally known expert on church/state issues whose seminal essay on equal access in the *Northwestern University Law Review* (1986) had done much to bring that topic into the realm of academic discussion.

In approaching the Supreme Court, Cooper made a critical decision to change the fundamental argument on which the school district's case was based. Rotella had asserted that clergy-led graduation prayer should come under the same rules as the legislative chaplaincies upheld in *Marsh*, and Cooper never abandoned that position. But if he won *Lee* solely on that basis, the resulting decision might well affect only graduation ceremonies and perhaps other special events. Hoping to reinstate school-sponsored prayer in a broader range of venues, he asked the Court to abandon the *Lemon* test, which prevents the state from advancing religion. He also asked it to reject the so-called endorsement test, which forbids governmental preference for any particular view about religion. In their place, he urged the Court to apply a coercion test under which state officials would be free to promote religious beliefs as long as they did not compel anyone to assent to those beliefs. If the Court upheld the school district's policy under that standard, the effects of that decision would be likely to extend well beyond graduations, thus opening the door to a wide variety of state-sponsored religious activities.

In his arguments to the Supreme Court, Cooper maintained that the only thing a state should not be able to do with regard to religion is to compel belief in particular tenets. Unlike many proponents of a coercion standard who believe that the state cannot require attendance at prayer, he would uphold compulsory attendance on the ground that people have no inherent right not to hear things they do not like. He was, of course, dismissive of such psychological factors as social coercion or peer pressure, and he felt that a state should be able to endorse not only religion in general but a specific sectarian faith as long as no one is forced to embrace it. Since the prayers at the Providence graduation ceremonies did not violate the Establishment Clause as he defined it, he urged the Court to uphold them.

Blanding could have objected to Cooper's changing the focus of the case, since coercion had been mentioned only briefly in the lower courts. Once the Supreme Court had agreed to hear an appeal, however, she said little about her opponents' failure to preserve that issue. Cooper felt that the Court would be more likely to accept the case if it raised the coercion question, and he thought that framing his argument in that way would, at a minimum, do it no harm. Blanding disagreed. In her view, attempting to turn a rather narrow lawsuit into a means of legalizing state-supported sectarian religion was overambitious, and she thought it would backfire.

A MATTER OF PROVIDENCE

Shortly before the oral argument in the Supreme Court, Justice Thurgood Marshall, an implacable foe of state-sponsored prayer, retired. In his place, President George Bush appointed conservative Clarence Thomas, who took his seat just in time to participate in *Lee*. Cooper tried to improve his chances still further by framing his briefs with an eye toward Justice Anthony Kennedy's opinion in *ACLU v. Allegheny*, a 1989 decision involving religious displays on public property. Kennedy, partially concurring in the Court's opinion and partially dissenting, had indicated that he would favor the use of a coercion standard. Six months before the oral argument in the Weisman case, he had made similar observations in his concurrence in *Westside Community Schools v. Mergens,* which upheld the Equal Access Act (see Chapter Twelve). Cooper hoped to persuade him and other members of the Court to abandon the *Lemon* test in favor of a formulation that would be friendlier to state-sponsored prayer.

Among other things, Cooper pointed out that when this nation was founded, elected officials—some of whom helped to draft the Constitution—said public prayers and issued proclamations that clearly endorsed religion. Since the only thing they barred was overt governmental force, he saw no reason to forbid anything more today. Blanding replied that if the Court engaged in "blind validation of all practices arguably acceptable to the framers' generation," it would then "be compelled to uphold such practices as public whipping and racial segregation of schools. Discrimination against non-Christians would also be acceptable" (Respondent's Brief, July 17, 1991, pp. 32, 33). More significantly, she disagreed with Cooper about what those early prayers and proclamations signified. To her, the point of the First Amendment is that "government should not support or endorse religion.... The framers adopted the principle, and they applied it to all issues that were controversial among Protestants. They did not see its application to practices that substantially all Protestants could accept. But they put the principle in the Constitution, ready to be applied to new examples of the same evil" (p. 38).

In addition to differing about whether a coercion test should be used, the two attorneys clashed about whether school-sponsored, clergy-led graduation prayer is in fact coercive. Blanding argued: "Imagine the embarrassment and humiliation of a nonadhering child who attempts to withdraw from the room as all of his or her classmates are standing to begin an opening prayer. To deny that a child who wished to take such action is not [sic] coerced into conformity is nonsensical." It would be "nothing short of cruel" to say that "'if your beliefs are offended by our choice of religion, you are free to miss your graduation. We will mail you a diploma'" (Respondent's Brief, pp. 46, 47). Cooper countered: "Students choose to be present; the ceremony is short, occurs only once in a student's career, and does not involve teaching; and virtually all of the students who choose to attend the ceremony are in the company of their parents. Thus, the potentially coercive aspects of the classroom setting are not present at graduation exercises." Weisman, he noted, "does not contend that he or his daughter were subjected to unwanted efforts at indoctrination in Judaism, that they were penalized for not subscribing to Rabbi Gutterman's expression of religious values, or even that they were subject to pressure, ostracism, or embarrassment as a result of their views of the rabbi's prayers" (Petitioners' Reply Brief, pp. 19, 20).

AND IN THIS CORNER . . .

Inevitably, *Lee* attracted the attention of a wide range of advocacy groups, many of which filed amicus briefs. Among those favoring the Weismans were Jewish organizations, such as the American Jewish Congress and the Anti-Defamation League; separationist groups, such as Americans United for Separation of Church and State and People for the American Way; and some Protestant groups, such as the Baptist Joint Committee on Public Affairs and the National Council of Churches. On the other side, the Bush administration and several state attorneys general urged the Court to uphold the school district, as did the U.S. Catholic Conference, evangelical groups such as the Christian Legal Society and the National Association of Evangelicals, and Christian Right organizations such as Concerned Women for America and the Christian Life Commission of the Southern Baptist Convention.

Of the pro-Weisman briefs, the one that Blanding, Cooper, and the Court mentioned most often was written by Laycock on behalf of ten organizations headed by the American Jewish Congress. Emphasizing the harm that may be done to religion by too close an association with government, it stated, "There are still millions of Americans who believe that all religions are not equal... and that their faith should not be conglomerated into something that will not offend the great majority" (Brief Amici Curiae of the American Jewish Congress, et al., p. 53). As a further indication of harmful connections between religion and government, the brief used Rabbi Gutterman's invocation to illustrate how fragile is the line separating religious from political orthodoxy. "When government sponsors religious observances, it appropriates religion to its own uses and unites religious and governmental authority," Laycock wrote. "The message of Rabbi Gutterman's invocation is an essentially political message—that American government is good, that freedom is secure, that courts protect minority rights, that America is the land of the free and the home of the brave, etc.... The school can deliver that political message if it chooses. The rabbi can deliver that message if he chooses. But the school and the rabbi cannot unite the authority and prestige of church and state in support of that message" (pp. 54–55). Not surprisingly, the AJC brief also rejected

Cooper's definition of coercion, which assumed that "there is no coercion unless children are compelled to *believe in* the religious premises of the prayers. But that is absurd. That standard would permit the state to compel church attendance, or any other religious behavior. It is impossible to compel belief; outward manifestations of belief are all the state can ever hope to compel. When the state compels children to give respectful attention to prayers, it has violated even the coercion test" (p. 62).

On the school officials' side, the most important amicus brief was submitted by Solicitor General Kenneth Starr on behalf of the Bush administration. It endorsed Cooper's argument that the Court should return to the original meaning of the Constitution, in which "the essence of an establishment of religion was some form of legal coercion that, by its nature, negated religious liberty" (Brief for United States as Amicus Curiae, May 1991, p. 18). Accordingly, Starr advocated replacing the *Lemon* test with a "liberty-focused inquiry" involving "liberty, on the one hand, and compulsion and constraint, on the other" (p. 22). In his view, the dissenters' ability to stay away from graduation meant that there was no governmental coercion to participate in prayer, whereas those who wished to pray should be at liberty to do so.

TIE VOTE

Cooper managed to complete only one sentence of his oral argument before the justices began pelting him with questions. Among the most significant of these was a query posed by Justice Sandra Day O'Connor, who asked whether Cooper would consider it constitutional "if a State legislature were to adopt a particular religion as the State religion, just like they might pass a resolution saying the bolo tie is the State necktie?" "If it is purely noncoercive," he replied, "then I have a difficult time distinguishing that from the proclamation that I've just cited—[when President Reagan declared 1983 to be] the Year of the Bible." In reply to a follow-up question, he said, "Your Honor, I think that... some finding of Government coercion of religious sentiment is necessary to make out a violation." "Well," Justice O'Connor observed, "that certainly hasn't been our case holdings over a substantial period of time" (oral argument, November 6, 1991, pp. 13, 14). Years later, Cooper remarked that he still sometimes thought about that exchange, which may well have contributed to the loss of O'Connor's vote. "But there was nothing else I could have said that would have been credible," he said. "That's what my case was" (interview, August 16, 1995; unless otherwise specified, quotations from Cooper are from this interview).

Cooper yielded part of his time to Solicitor General Starr, who joined him in asserting that the government should be free to advance religion as long as it is nonsectarian. Just as nineteenth-century officials had considered pan-Protestantism nonsectarian, Cooper and Starr maintained that anything common to the Judeo-Christian tradition is nonsectarian in the context of America's religious heritage. Accordingly, when Starr was asked whether saying "God" rather than "Allah" would be sectarian, he replied, "Absolutely not, not in our traditions. It could be, at one level of generality, yes, of course. Because you are asserting a theological belief that stands squarely in the Judeo-Christian tradition, yes. But not sectarian in the sense that this Court has been concerned about it" (pp. 22–23). He also denied that people who attended graduation were coerced into at least appearing to pray, since, he said, dissenters could remain seated. Kennedy asked whether that was a viable option for students who "walked down as a class together to the strains of Elgar, and they sit as a class, and they're all asked to rise." Starr conceded that students thus situated might feel constrained to stand for the prayer. "But," he added, and Kennedy interrupted. "Cross their fingers?" he asked (p. 26).

Blanding's half hour at the podium was largely a repetition of arguments she had already made, although she too was subjected to a barrage of questions from the Court. Among other things, she denied that prayer is necessary to solemnize graduation, since Providence schools that chose not to have it were nonetheless able to conduct their ceremonies successfully. For the most part, she reiterated as often as possible that the *Lemon* test is preferable to a coercion standard but that Providence's graduation prayers would fail either way.

According to Blanding, when the oral argument ended she was the only person on her side of the case who believed she had won. Cooper recalled thinking that the oral argument had been unusually contentious and that the decision would be close. They were both correct. On June 24, 1992, the Court announced its 5–4 decision in favor of the Weismans. The opinion, written by Kennedy, said in essence that the Providence graduation-prayer policy was coercive, which was enough in itself to render it unconstitutional. There was thus no need for the Court to decide whether the policy would also have been struck down under any other standard, such as the *Lemon* test, or whether those other standards are valid. In finding the schools' practices coercive, the Court adopted a broad definition of the term that included both peer pressure and the threat of losing a valued benefit, such as the opportunity to attend one's graduation. In the Court's view, it is inconsistent to declare that graduation is such a uniquely important rite of passage that people's rights are burdened if the ceremony does not include prayer, but then to claim that dissenters' rights are adequately protected if they are allowed to stay away. "The Constitution forbids the State to exact religious conformity from a student as the price of attending her own high school graduation," Kennedy wrote (*Lee v. Weisman*, 505 U.S. 577, 112 S. Ct. 2649 [1992], p. 2660). Moreover, the Court found, students attending graduation were subject to peer pressure to stand for the prayers, and "the government may no more use social pressure to enforce orthodoxy than it may use more direct means" (p. 2659). As it had done in *Abington* and other school-prayer cases, the Court also said that it made no difference whether the prayers were nonsectarian. "The suggestion that government may establish an official or civic religion as a means of avoiding the establishment of a religion with more specific creeds strikes us as a contradiction that cannot be accepted" (p. 2657).

Justice Harry Blackmun, joined by Justices John Paul Stevens and O'Connor, wrote a concurrence emphasizing their belief that although governmental coercion in religious matters is always unconstitutional, it does not have to be present for a violation to occur. On the contrary, they wrote, previous Supreme Court decisions "have prohibited government endorsement of religion, its sponsorship, and active involvement in religion, whether or not citizens were coerced to conform" (p. 2667). Stevens and O'Connor also signed a concurrence written by Justice David Souter, who said that the state cannot prefer religion over nonreligion even if no coercion is involved.

Justice Antonin Scalia wrote the dissent, in which Chief Justice Rehnquist and Justices Byron White and Thomas joined. Among other things, they disagreed with the Court's finding that one reason the graduation prayers were unconstitutional was that the peer pressure they engendered was directly attributable to a school policy. But, Scalia wrote, "The deeper flaw in the Court's opinion does not lie in its wrong answer to the question whether there was state-induced 'peer-pressure' coercion; it lies, rather, in the Court's making violation of the Establishment Clause hinge on such a precious question. The coercion that was a hallmark of historical establishments of religion was coercion of religious orthodoxy and of financial support *by force of law and threat of penalty*" (p. 2683). Similarly, the dissenters asserted that if people chose to miss graduation rather than attend prayer, that was their personal choice and not a state-imposed penalty. Finally, they felt that the Court was ignoring the plain intent of the Framers by interpreting the Constitution to ban such a generic prayer as Rabbi Gutterman's. To be sure, they acknowledged, the Court has struck down state endorsement of practices that are sectarian "in the sense of specifying details upon which men and women who believe in a benevolent, omnipotent Creator and Ruler of the world, are known to differ (for example, the divinity of Christ). But there is simply no support for the proposition that the officially sponsored nondenominational invocation and benediction read by Rabbi Gutterman—with no one legally coerced to recite them—violate the Constitution of the United States. To the contrary, they are so characteristically American they could have come from the pen of George Washington or Abraham Lincoln himself" (p. 2684).

To summarize the arithmetic of the Court: the five justices who formed the majority found that a state action is unconstitutional if it involves coercion, which they defined to include not only overt compulsion by the state but also peer pressure and the threat of losing a significant benefit, such as the ability to attend graduation. By this standard, all five of those justices found the Providence graduation-prayer policy to be coercive. But of the five, only Kennedy thought that coercion *must* be present. The other four signed concurring opinions stating that although coercion is always sufficient to prove an Establishment Clause violation, it is not necessary; such violations may arise from other factors, such as a religious purpose or effect, entanglement of the state with religion, or state endorsement of religion. Taking a different view were the four dissenting justices, who agreed with the majority that coercion in religious matters is unconstitutional but disagreed with the majority's definition of that term. To the dissenters, coercion meant nothing less than the direct imposition of a state-inflicted penalty on people who declined to participate in prayer. Consequently, the four dissenting justices denied that the graduation prayers were in fact coercive. The closeness of the Court's vote on these critical issues in *Lee* and in other cases does much to explain the recurring political furor over judicial appointments (see Chapter Nine).

THE DAY THE PHONE FINALLY RANG

The Weismans had been awaiting the outcome with deep concern, fearing that a decision bearing their name might undermine the *Lemon* test and institute a coercion standard that would permit widespread state sponsorship of religion. "You have to understand," Daniel Weisman said. "It would be a terrible decision. And it would have our name on it. Every time they used it, they would say our name" (interview, April 27, 1995; all quotations from the Weismans are from this interview). Their suspense intensified when a *Good Morning America* producer phoned early one morning with the news that the decision would probably be announced that day. Vivian Weisman was at her job at the Jewish Community Center when a reporter called to say that the school district's policy had been struck down and the *Lemon* test had not been touched. "I screamed with joy," she said. "No dreadful thing was going to have our name on it."

As fate would have it, the decision was announced just as the 1992 graduation began at Nathan Bishop Middle School, and Principal Lee found out about it when he walked out of the ceremony into a swarm of reporters. He was flabbergasted by the decision, which years later still had him shaking his head. Opposition to sectarian worship makes sense, he said, but he was horrified by the banning of what he saw as harmless nonsectarian prayers.

In what was probably an understatement, Cooper described himself as disappointed by Justice Kennedy's role in the decision. The good news, from his point of view, was that *Lee* was not decided on the basis of either the *Lemon* test or the endorsement test, which to him suggested that the future of those standards is in limbo. But, he added with irritation, that victory makes little difference because anything that would fail those tests might well be found coercive under the Court's broad definition of the term. "If that's coercion, when would it not be present?" he asked. "If that qualifies as coercion, then there's no substance to the idea that you need coercion" to prove a constitutional violation.

Blanding's post-game analysis was that Rotella's attempt to extend *Marsh* to graduation ceremonies might have succeeded, whereas the Cooper team had contributed to its own defeat by trying to accomplish too much with a single case. On a more personal level, she had been stung by news coverage that lionized Cooper while she was portrayed as "a local nothing whose chief virtue was that I worked hard." Victory was sweet.

KEEPING UP WITH THE JONESES

Since *Lee* dealt with clergy-led, school-sponsored devotionals, those who favored graduation prayer did not despair of finding a way to preserve the practice in some form. The most popular approach was to allow the graduating class to decide whether to have a prayer and, if so, who would give it. The theory was that prayer may be included in the official graduation program without violating the First Amendment if it is attributable to students rather than to school officials. Some school districts had already implemented such procedures in the wake of the Equal Access Act, and more did so after *Lee*. Nevertheless, students cannot control any part of the ceremony unless school officials allow them to do so, and when prayer was authorized in the absence of any opportunity for other student-initiated speech, lawsuits became inevitable.

One of the first of these cases, filed two years before *Lee* and concluding after *Lee* had been decided, arose in Clear Creek, Texas, where graduations had long included Christian prayers. Two families represented by the Greater Houston ACLU sued to stop this practice, and attorneys from the American Center for Law and Justice provided legal assistance to the school authorities. Three weeks before the trial was to begin, the school district adopted a new policy stating that henceforth the senior class would vote on whether to have prayer at graduation, and the prayers would be nonsectarian and nonprosely-tizing. Defenders of this policy considered it constitutional because any prayers that were said would represent the voluntary choice of the students. They also felt that the school could not reasonably be perceived as advancing any religion if the prayers were nonsectarian and nonproselytizing. Their opponents retorted that school officials are not permitted to make prayer an official part of graduation, and this restriction cannot be circumvented by arranging for the students to ask them to violate the law. Moreover, the plaintiffs argued, the requirement for nonsectarian prayer did nothing to make the policy constitutional. On the contrary, it showed that the content of the prayers was regulated by school officials, who would further entangle themselves with religion by reviewing proposed prayers and banning any religious expression they deemed sectarian or proselytizing.

Both the federal district court and the Court of Appeals for the Fifth Circuit ruled in favor of the Clear Creek school district. In addition to finding that the policy had the secular purpose of solemnizing graduation, they held that the prayers did not advance religion because they were short, nonsectarian, student-controlled, and infrequent. Similarly, both courts denied that screening student prayers for sectarianism would constitute entanglement between church and state. The plaintiffs appealed to the Supreme Court, which delayed acting until *Lee* had been decided. Then it vacated the decision in *Jones* and sent it back to the Fifth Circuit for reconsideration in accord with *Lee*. As it had done in its earlier decision, the appeals court once again found that the Clear Creek policy passed all three prongs of the *Lemon* test. In deference to *Lee*, the court also considered whether the policy involved either coercion or governmental endorsement of religion and concluded that it did not. The court summarized its findings in the highly controversial statement that "[A] majority of students can do what the State acting on its own cannot do to incorporate prayer in public high school graduation ceremonies" (*Jones v. Clear Creek*, 977 F.2d 963 [1992], p. 972). The Supreme Court declined to hear an appeal.

Although *Jones* was decided by the Court of Appeals for the Fifth Circuit, whose rulings are binding only in Texas, Mississippi, and Louisiana, the ACLJ wrote to educators throughout the country implying that the Supreme Court's refusal to review this decision suggested agreement with it. The letter went on to admonish school officials that students have a right to pray aloud at graduation. An ACLU spokesperson responded with exasperation, "'Jay Sekulow knows very well that the Supreme Court's decision not to hear a case means nothing'" (Nancy E. Roman, "War Over Graduation Prayers Waged by Mail," *Washington Times*, July 18, 1993, p. A6).

Certainly other appeals courts did not hesitate to disagree with their brethren of the Fifth Circuit. In a decision involving graduation prayer in Idaho, the Court of Appeals for the Ninth Circuit stated outright, "We are not persuaded by the reasoning in *Jones*." On the contrary, it asserted, "elected officials cannot absolve themselves of a constitutional duty by delegating their responsibilities to a non-governmental entity. Even private citizens when acting with government authority must exercise that authority constitutionally" (*Harris v. Joint School District 241*, 41 F.3d 447 [1994], pp. 454, 455). *Harris* was later dismissed because the student plaintiff had graduated, but its reasoning was endorsed in a decision by the Court of Appeals for the Third Circuit. "Delegation of one aspect of the ceremony to a plurality of students does not constitute the absence of school officials' control over the graduation," the decision stated. "Students decided the question of prayer at graduation only because school officials agreed to let them decide that one question." Such an arrangement, the court found, "does not insulate the School Board from the reach of the First Amendment" (*ACLU v. Black Horse Pike Regional Board of Education*, 84 F.3d 1471 [1996], p. 1479).

In the lawsuits discussed so far, students were allowed to vote on whether to have prayer at graduation. By contrast, an Idaho case entitled *Doe v. Madison* dealt with a policy that permitted school officials to appoint at least four students, chosen solely on the basis of their grades, to speak at graduation. These neutrally selected students could say whatever they wished as long as they used "'appropriate language for the audience and occasion'" (*Doe v. Madison*, 7 F. Supp. 2d 1110 [1997], p. 1112). In a printed program distributed at the ceremony, the school disclaimed responsibility for the speakers' remarks. The disclaimer indicated that prayer might occur, but there was no evidence that school officials either encouraged or discouraged it. Thus, the Madison policy gave less control to the graduating class as a whole than did those in the other post-*Lee* lawsuits, since it was up to school officials, not a majority student vote, to decide whether speeches would be given and by whom. On the other hand, the individual students who spoke at the Madison graduations had greater latitude than their counterparts in the other cases because they were not constrained by having been appointed specifically to pray, but were free to speak as they chose.

While conceding that the Madison policy did not favor religious over secular speech, some parents sued on the ground that it opened the door to graduation prayer. To their dismay, the Court of Appeals for the Ninth Circuit, which had struck down the student-vote arrangement in *Harris,* upheld the right of neutrally selected speakers to engage in either religious or secular speech. This decision, like others discussed in this chapter, was later vacated because the student plaintiffs graduated while the lawsuit was still in progress. Despite all the dismissals, however, the growing pile of conflicting lower-court decisions made it likely that the Supreme Court would hear an appeal dealing with student-led prayer at graduations and other school-sponsored events. It did so in 2000, agreeing to decide a case that had arisen in the small town of Santa Fe, Texas.

LET THE GAMES BEGIN

For as long as anyone could remember, high school graduations and football games in Santa Fe had included student-led Protestant prayers. At first there were no formal guidelines, but when the Court of Appeals for the Fifth Circuit upheld the Clear Creek policy in *Jones,* the Santa Fe school board adopted graduation-prayer rules based on that model. Shortly afterward, two families, one Catholic and one Mormon, sued anonymously in a case entitled *Doe v. Santa Fe.* They challenged not only the graduation-prayer policy but the prayers at football games, which were usually delivered by an elected student called the "student council chaplain." The suit also included other issues, such as an episode in which a teacher admittedly told a Mormon child that her religion is a cult, but those were quickly resolved.

ACLJ attorneys headed by Jay Sekulow acted for the school district, while an ACLU volunteer attorney, Anthony Griffin, represented the Does. Griffin was best known for having successfully defended the Grand Dragon of the Texas Knights of the Ku Klux Klan from being forced to turn over the Klan's membership list to the state, which raised eyebrows because Griffin was, at the time, general counsel for the Texas chapter of the National Association for the Advancement of Colored People. A 1958 Supreme Court decision had upheld the NAACP's right to withhold its membership list from the State of Alabama, and Griffin accepted his unlikely client because "The rules have to be the same for everyone." This action led to the loss of his unpaid NAACP job, but he remained convinced that "If they can't do it, some day we won't be able to either. You can't have separate rules for groups you like and don't like" (interview, March 29, 2000).

Griffin's first action on behalf of the Does was to ask the federal district court to exclude organized prayer from the 1995 Santa Fe graduation. The request was denied. Since Texas is in the Fifth Circuit, *Jones v. Clear Creek* unquestionably applied, and the court ruled that graduation prayers led by an elected student were likely to be upheld as long as they were nonsectarian. The decision also suggested that nonsectarianism need not exclude "'[r]eference to any particular deity, by name, such as Mohammed, Jesus, Buddha, or the like'" (unpublished opinion, quoted in *Doe v. Santa Fe,* 168 F.3d 806 [1999], p. 811).

Since Santa Fe's policy required graduation prayers to be nonsectarian and nonproselytizing, it conformed to the court's ruling. Ironically, that provision was soon dropped because the court's statement that it was necessary drew the community's attention to it. Many of the townspeople had been unaware that any such restriction existed, and once they noticed it, they successfully pressured the school district to delete it and to fight in court for the students' right to pray as they chose. Only if the district lost its legal battle would the stipulation that the prayers had to be nonsectarian and nonproselytizing be restored. The board also adopted a "Football Prayer Policy" under which the student body would decide whether to have invocations at home games; if so, a student would be elected to deliver them throughout the season. The policy's stated purposes were "'to solemnize the event, to promote good sportsmanship and student safety, and to establish the appropriate environment for the competition'" (p. 812). The prayers would have to be nonsectarian and nonproselytizing only if a court ordered it. Later, the board removed the word "Prayer" from the policy's title and provided that the student body would decide whether to elect a speaker to deliver "an invocation and/or message" that would achieve the policy's goals.

The plaintiffs protested that the new policies were unconstitutional, but the federal district court upheld them on the condition that the school board implement its fallback provisions for requiring the prayers to be nonsectarian and nonproselytizing. Both sides appealed. The school board wanted to permit sectarian and proselytizing student-led prayers, while the plaintiffs said that *Jones v. Clear Creek* applied to graduations, not to football games. They also disagreed with the court's assertion that prayers offered in the name of Jesus, Mohammed, and so forth can be considered nonsectarian. In response, Sekulow conceded that the Clear Creek policy upheld in *Jones* required nonsectarian, nonprosely-tizing prayer, but in his view that provision was not essential to the outcome of the case. The deciding factor, he asserted, was not the content of the prayers but the fact that they were controlled by the students rather than by the school. By that standard, the Santa Fe policy was constitutional because it merely cre-ated an open forum in which students were free to engage in their own volun-tary speech, and a court-ordered ban on sectarian or proselytizing content would conflict with the school's determination to ensure that the speech was wholly controlled by the students.

Finding Sekulow's interpretation of its decision in *Jones* "specious at best" (p. 815), the Court of Appeals for the Fifth Circuit noted that Santa Fe's alleged open forum in reality allowed only one or two students "to deliver very circum-scribed statements that under any definition are prayers" (p. 820). In these cir-cumstances, the court ruled, requiring that the prayers be nonsectarian and nonproselytizing was an indispensable safeguard against violations of the *Lemon*, endorsement, and coercion tests. The court also remarked that "A nonsectar-ian, nonproselytizing prayer that, for example, invokes the name of Buddha or Mohammed or Jesus or Jehovah is an obvious oxymoron" (p. 822). Finally, the court rejected the contention that *Jones*, which upheld student-led nonsectar-ian prayer at graduation ceremonies, could be extended to cover football games. In the court's view, football games are "hardly the sober type of annual event that can be appropriately solemnized with prayer" (p. 823).

By the time this decision in *Doe v. Santa Fe* was issued, a student had already been elected to solemnize that season's home football games with "an invocation and/or message." Because of the court's ruling, the school officials reluctantly decreed that her message could not take the form of prayer. She then filed a separate lawsuit asking the federal district court to issue a tempo-rary injunction allowing her to pray at football games while *Doe v. Santa Fe* was making its way to the Supreme Court. The court did so, stating that "'Just as a school policy requiring student prayer would run afoul of the Establish-ment Clause, a school policy prohibiting prayer also runs afoul of the Estab-lishment Clause because it amounts to state sponsorship of atheism, i.e., state establishment of disbelief in a God instead of belief in a God'" (unpublished opinion, September 2, 1999; quoted in Brief Amici Curiae for Marian Ward et al., December 30, 1999, p. 27). The court also noted that football is at least as important as graduation to many students.

The Supreme Court agreed to hear arguments only on the following ques-tion: "Whether [the school district's] policy permitting student-led, student-initiated prayer at football games violates the Establishment Clause" (*Santa Fe v. Doe,* 528 U.S. 1002; 120 S. Ct. 494 [1999]). An amicus brief signed by then-Governor George W. Bush urged the Court to uphold the policy, as did briefs filed by evangelical and Christian Right groups and by several members of Congress, notably Texas Republicans Richard Armey and Tom DeLay, who were, respectively, the majority leader and majority whip of the U.S. House of Representatives. The House also passed a sense-of-Congress resolution supporting prayer at public-school sporting events.

The Does' brief to the Supreme Court was written by Griffin and two of the lawyers who had worked with Blanding on *Lee v. Weisman:* Steven Shapiro and Douglas Laycock. Rejecting the claim that the student elections promoted the independent private speech of individuals, they asserted that the machinery of the school was being used to advance a single majoritarian orthodoxy. They also scoffed at the notion that the school could disclaim responsibility for prayers said over its public address system at a school-sponsored event by a student chosen in accord with a school policy. Moreover, they argued, the policy's history showed that its purpose was not to create an open forum for the students' free speech but to continue having school-endorsed prayer. Similar arguments appeared in amicus briefs submitted by Jewish, separationist, and mainstream Protestant groups.

SCRUM

On the morning of the oral argument, a lone demonstrator stood outside the Supreme Court building holding a ten-foot wooden cross that contrasted starkly with the high-tech TV broadcasting equipment surrounding it. Inside, three long tables had been pushed together in the cafeteria to accommodate Sekulow and the attorneys who breakfasted with him. Sekulow, who had argued before the Court several times, projected his usual air of energy and confidence. A few tables away, Griffin talked earnestly with a handful of supporters. He had never before faced the Court, and as he left he remarked that he would really like to get to and from the podium without falling on his face.

Sekulow, who spoke first, took every opportunity to assert that the students acted as a "circuit breaker" disconnecting the school from any prayer that might be said (oral argument, March 29, 1999). If prayer took place, he declared, it was entirely attributable to a series of decisions by students. He also pointed out that the policy permitted both invocations and messages, which might be either religious or secular. Singling out religious speech for exclusion where secular speech was permitted would, he averred, demonstrate governmental hostility to religion. In response to questions about coercing captive audiences, he repeated his central message that the prayers were the action of the students, not the government, and hence not subject to those concerns. Justice Ruth Bader Ginsburg interjected an inquiry regarding the range of messages that might be permissible under the school policy. Suppose, she asked, a student were to say, "Break their necks! Make them wrecks! Buckle down, boys!" Would that, she asked amid laughter in the Court, be among the statements a student speaker might make under the Santa Fe policy? No, Sekulow replied, it would not. Justice Souter, pursuing this line of questioning, asked for an example of a nonreligious message that *would* satisfy the policy's purpose of solemnizing the games. When Sekulow responded with a statement about playing safely, Souter questioned whether that would qualify as "solemnizing" the event.

Texas Attorney General John Cornyn followed Sekulow. His intent was to defend the policy, but he may have done the school district's case more harm than good because he repeatedly asserted that the school officials had the authority to stop any speech they deemed "off topic." His emphasis on the school's control contrasted noticeably with Sekulow's remarks, and his statement strongly suggested that by "on topic" he meant religious speech.

Griffin's turn came next, and in accord with the hope he had expressed on leaving the cafeteria, he did indeed remain upright throughout the experience. Nevertheless, the half hour he spent at the podium had its rocky moments. Since the school board had passed several successive policies, the most recent of which had never been implemented, Griffin had to persuade the Court that the lawsuit was not premature. He addressed this issue by asserting that the history underlying the policy showed that all versions of it, including the latest, were attempts to preserve a school-created forum widely understood to be for prayer and nothing else. Chief Justice Rehnquist engaged Griffin in debate on this point, challenging his claim that the policy should be struck down because of its history even if its facial language appeared to be constitutional. Whereas Griffin saw the board's promulgation of one policy after another as evidence of its determination to use the students' religious rights as a pretext for state-sponsored prayer, in Rehnquist's eyes those same actions suggested a good-faith effort to develop a lawful policy.

In rebuttal, Sekulow reiterated his assertion that it was mere speculation to suggest that students would choose to pray, rather than to deliver a secular message, under the new policy. Justice Ginsburg pointed out that the student speaker elected for that year had already declared that she would pray in the name of Jesus. "Isn't it somewhat imaginary," Ginsburg asked, "to say we have to wait when we're told [by the student] 'I'm going to be honest about it. I'm going to give a prayer.' That's some message!" Sekulow, who is known to be a hard man to stop, uncharacteristically volunteered the information that his time had expired. The oral argument ended amid background laughter.

GAME OVER

Justice Stevens wrote the Court's opinion, in which Justices O'Connor, Kennedy, Souter, Ginsburg, and Stephen Breyer joined. "Contrary to the District's repeated assertions that it has adopted a 'hands-off' approach to the pregame invocation," it declared, "the realities of the situation plainly reveal that its policy involves both perceived and actual endorsement of religion" (*Santa Fe v. Doe*, 530 U.S. 290; 120 S.Ct. 2266 [2000], p. 305). Nor was the policy rendered constitutional because the student body had the option of declining to elect a speaker, or of choosing one who would engage in secular speech. "Government efforts to endorse religion cannot evade constitutional reproach based solely on the remote possibility that those attempts may fail," the decision stated (p. 316). Moreover, the Court found, putting the question of prayer to a vote under school auspices would be unconstitutional no matter what the outcome, since it subjected to majority rule an issue that should have been left to the individual conscience. That reliance on a majority vote also undercut the school officials' assertion that any message given at the football games represented the private speech of the individual student speaker. As the Court remarked, if the student body had been invited to decide "whether a political speech should be made, and whether the speaker should be a Democrat or a Republican, it would be rather clear that the public address system was being used to deliver a partisan message reflecting the viewpoint of the majority rather than a random statement by a private individual" (p. 305, note 15). To the Court, this promotion of a religious view "over the school's public address system, by a speaker representing the student body, under the supervision of school faculty, and pursuant to a school policy that explicitly and implicitly encourages public prayer—is not properly characterized as 'private' speech" (p. 310). The Court also agreed with Griffin that the policy could be properly understood only in light of its history. The school district "asks us to pretend that we do not recognize what every Santa Fe High School student understands clearly—that this policy is about prayer. The District further asks us to accept what is obviously untrue: that these messages are necessary to 'solemnize' a football game and that this single-student, year-long position is essential to the protection of student speech. We refuse to turn a blind eye to the context in which this policy arose, and that context quells any doubt that this policy was implemented with the purpose of endorsing school prayer" (p. 315). Consequently, the Court found that the Santa Fe policy failed all the tests commonly used to assess the constitutionality of state actions with regard to religion: it had a primarily religious purpose, advanced majoritarian religious views, and entangled the state with religion, thus violating all three prongs of the *Lemon* test. In addition, it endorsed religion, coerced students and others into participating in a worship service, and caused nonadherents to feel like outsiders with respect to the government's viewpoint.

The chief justice, joined by Justices Scalia and Thomas, wrote a dissent asserting that the majority opinion "bristles with hostility to all things religious in public life" (p. 318). They were particularly disturbed by the Court's use of the *Lemon* test, which in their view produces results that conflict with the original intent of the Constitution. Denying that the stated secular purposes of the Santa Fe policy were pretextual, they argued that less weight should be given to the policy's history than to the school officials' assurances about its intended use. "The policy at issue here may be applied in an unconstitutional manner," they acknowledged, "but it will be time enough to invalidate it if that is found to be the case" (p. 326).

OVERTIME

Immediately following *Santa Fe*, the Supreme Court sent two other student-prayer cases back to the lower courts for reconsideration in light of the new decision. The first of these, *Chandler v. James*, arose when Michael Chandler, an assistant principal in the DeKalb County, Alabama, school district and father of a public-school student, accused school officials of sponsoring a plethora of religious activities, such as prayer at graduation ceremonies and athletic events, classroom prayer, Bible distribution, and religious assemblies.[2] Represented by attorneys from Americans United for Separation of Church and State and the Alabama ACLU, Chandler and his adolescent son, Jesse, also challenged an Alabama school-prayer law containing the same provisions as the Mississippi statute struck down in *Ingebretsen v. Jackson Public Schools* (see Chapter Thirteen). These charges were answered by government and private attorneys acting for the governor, the State of Alabama, and DeKalb County, with the assistance of the Rutherford Institute and the ACLJ; indeed, Jay Sekulow was appointed an acting deputy state attorney general for the occasion. In all, seventeen lawyers went to court on behalf of the various parties.

The first result of all this legal activity was a victory for the Chandlers, as the federal district court struck down the challenged Alabama statute which, like its Mississippi counterpart, required teachers and administrators to permit student-led prayer at all compulsory and noncompulsory school events. He emphasized that his decision did not affect the students' right to engage in individual or group prayer on their own during noninstructional time, or their freedom to hold religious meetings in conformity with the Equal Access Act, express religious beliefs in their schoolwork, distribute religious literature on the same basis as other material, and so forth. He also noted that it is permissible to teach about religion and to use religious texts in relation to secular subjects, such as history, art, music, and literature.

Although this decision striking down the Alabama school-prayer statute was a victory for the plaintiffs, it did not resolve the entire dispute because most of the religious practices of the DeKalb County schools pre-dated the statute and were allegedly justified by the students' First Amendment rights to free speech and free exercise of religion. Moreover, Governor Fob James, Jr., was openly defying the court's ruling, as he had defied decisions in *Jaffree v. James* regarding vocal prayer and moments of silence (see Chapter Ten). In response, the court issued an injunction forbidding enforcement of the state school-prayer law and prohibiting the DeKalb County officials from "aiding, abetting, commanding, counseling, inducing, ordering, procuring, or permitting *school organized or officially sanctioned* religious activity in the classrooms of DeKalb County schools *including, but not limited to:* vocal prayer; Bible and religious devotional or scriptural readings; distribution of religious materials, texts, or announcements; and discussions of a devotional/inspirational nature, regardless of whether the activity is initiated, led by, or engaged in by students" (*Chandler v. James*, 985 F. Supp. 1062 [1997], p. 1063) (emphasis is in the original unless otherwise indicated). The court also ordered a halt to such practices as limiting attendance at graduation to students who also participated in religious baccalaureate services; failing to prevent the Gideons from tossing Bibles into the open windows of school buses; and providing for graduation prayer under the guise of "remarks" by a "student historian."

CREAM DEMENT

Following his earlier decision striking down the state school-prayer law, Judge Ira DeMent had been vilified by critics who besmirched his personal character and alleged that his rulings would establish atheism in the schools. He was even accused of forbidding practices that he had explicitly upheld. Accordingly, in his injunction, each proscription of a particular school-sponsored religious activity was followed by one or more paragraphs stating that "This PERMANENT INJUNCTION DOES NOT" ban comparable religious expression by the students as individuals. As an example, his exclusion of school-sponsored classroom prayer and Bible-reading was followed by the statement that students may "quietly engage in religious activity during noninstructional times, *so long as it does not unduly call attention thereto and so long as it does not interfere with the rights of other students to freely pass thereby or to avoid its imposition upon themselves*" (p. 1063). The limitations thus placed on the students' private religious activity, such as the word "quietly," later became an issue when the case went to the appeals court. Similarly, the injunction said not only that school officials could not encourage prayer by students or by community members attending school events, but that they could not permit it. This, too, became controversial on appeal.

Over the next two months, DeMent issued four more decisions clarifying or modifying the injunction and responding to motions by the various parties. Among other things, these decisions drew attention to the unremitting defiance that had led to the issuance of a permanent injunction. "[A]bsent permanent injunctive relief," one decision stated, "the substantial likelihood is that the DeKalb County Board of Education and its employees and agents will ignore the court's orders just as it has disobeyed the rulings of higher courts for years" (*Chandler v. James*, 985 F. Supp. 1068 [1997], p. 1074). Moreover, faced with yet another round of vociferous accusations that he was promoting atheism, he resorted to rebuttal by typeface: "The court notes that its October 29, 1997 Permanent Injunction merely PROHIBITS THE STATE FROM COERCING RELIGIOUS PRACTICES OR PROMOTING ONE TYPE OF RELIGIOUS ACTIVITY OR VIEWPOINT OVER ANOTHER. Indeed, the court's Permanent Injunction and March 1997 Opinion and Order goes to great length to articulate the activities permitted in public schools under the First Amendment" (p. 1093, note 54).

Governor James and the DeKalb County school officials appealed separately to the Court of Appeals for the Eleventh Circuit. James, whose main concern was the state school-prayer law, argued that the federal courts had no authority to strike it down because the First Amendment applies only to Congress, not to the states. (Earlier disputes over this principle are discussed in Chapters Four, Nine, and Ten.) The appeals court rejected this argument, and the part of the case relating to the state statute was over.

By no means could the same be said of the dispute regarding religious practices in the DeKalb County schools. While conceding that school-organized religious activities are unconstitutional, the school officials argued that the injunction inappropriately constrained the religious speech of the students as individuals. As explained earlier, each proscription of government-run religious activity was followed by a statement of what the students themselves remained free to do. In some of them, such terms as "quietly" and "brief" were used to describe permissible student prayer, leading to the objection that students should be able to pray as they wished outside of instructional time. Moreover, the school officials alleged, the injunction prevented them not only from encouraging prayer but also from permitting students and others to exercise their right, as private individuals, to pray "aloud in the classroom, over the public address system, or as part of the program at school-related assemblies and sporting events, or at a graduation ceremony" (*Chandler v. James*, 180 F.3d 1254 [1999], p. 1257). The Chandlers retorted that the injunction was far more generous toward student prayer than the defendants acknowledged. In their view, it merely prohibited school officials from permitting anyone to lead public prayers at school events, which were not open forums at which audience members generally made public statements. Although they had no objection to students praying on their own anywhere they liked, the plaintiffs declared, they supported the district court's ban on practices that would turn school events into worship services.

The appeals court's decision, although mixed, generally favored the school officials. It found that Judge DeMent had gone too far in his zeal to stop the use of student initiative as a cover for public prayer that was widely understood to be sponsored by the school. According to the court, school officials could not create special opportunities for student prayer, but neither could they single out religious speech for exclusion. Despite their past violations, they could not be required to ban public religious speech that was "genuinely" initiated by students or other private citizens—an adverb that appeared in the decision nine times. The Chandlers appealed to the Supreme Court, protesting that the appeals court's decision would allow students to lead captive audiences of other students, some as young as five years old, in group prayer. At school-sponsored events attended by outside adults, anyone in the audience could do the same. The school officials retorted that public religious speech by private persons is constitutionally protected whether other people wish to hear it or not. Without comment, the Supreme Court vacated the decision and ordered it to be reconsidered in light of *Santa Fe v. Doe*.

Once again, the appeals court ruled in favor of the school officials, finding that the injunction "assumed that virtually any religious speech in schools is attributable to the State. While the district court recognized that a student must be allowed to pray *silently* while in school, or even discuss his religious beliefs *quietly* with others, it enjoined the school district from *permitting* any prayer in a *public* context at any school function" (*Chandler v. Siegelman*, 230 F.3d 1313 [2000], p. 1316; the title of the case changed when Don Siegelman succeeded James as governor). The Supreme Court declined to hear an appeal, and the injunction was returned to Judge DeMent to be rewritten in conformity with the appeals court's decision. Before he could comply, Jesse Chandler graduated, and the case was dismissed as moot.

CASE NUMBER TWO

The second school-prayer case to be sent back to an appeals court in the wake of *Santa Fe v. Doe* arose in Duval County, Florida. In response to *Lee v. Weisman*, school officials replaced clergy-led graduation prayer with a new policy permitting the senior class to decide whether to have a message at graduation and, if so, which student would deliver it. Some parents and students sued on the ground that the policy's intent was to perpetuate the practice of having prayer at graduation, but the federal district court found it constitutional. By the time the case reached the appeals court, the student plaintiffs had graduated, and the lawsuit was dismissed. A year later, the suit was renewed on behalf of a new set of student plaintiffs, some as young as nine years old. Once again, the district court upheld the new graduation policy, but the Court of Appeals for the Eleventh Circuit reversed that decision. Among other things, the appeals court found that although the policy neither specified nor guaranteed that the "message" would be a prayer, its primary purpose was to allow graduation prayers to continue after *Lee*. Moreover, the court ruled, the prayers represented state action because graduation was controlled by the school, as was the student vote on whether to have a message that might well turn out to be a prayer.

In keeping with normal practice, the appeals court's decision was rendered by a panel of three judges. A year later, the court took the unusual step of rehearing the case en banc—that is, with all the Eleventh Circuit judges participating. It then reversed the panel's decision and upheld the policy, citing "the total absence of state involvement in deciding whether there will be a graduation message, who will speak, or what the speaker may say combined with the student speaker's complete autonomy over the content of the message" as its reasons for declaring that the speech is not state-sponsored. "To conclude otherwise would come perilously close to announcing an absolute rule that would excise *all* private religious expression from a public graduation ceremony, no matter how neutral the process of selecting the speaker may be, nor how autonomous the speaker may be in crafting her message" (*Adler v. Duval*, 206 F.3d 1070 [2000], p. 1071). The Supreme Court vacated this decision and sent it back to the Eleventh Circuit for reconsideration in light of *Santa Fe v. Doe*, whereupon the appeals court once again upheld the policy. Among other things, the decision noted that Duval County, unlike Santa Fe, did not restrict the content of the students' speech in a way that encouraged prayer. Indeed, the court observed, when the policy was implemented for one year, the graduating classes in seven of Duval County's seventeen high schools either voted not to have a speaker or elected one who delivered a secular message. The Supreme Court declined to review this decision.

COLE FACTS

A somewhat different type of graduation-prayer policy was at issue in a California case that reached the Court of Appeals for the Ninth Circuit in 2000. Each year, the senior class at Oroville High School elected a student to give a nonsectarian invocation. The valedictorian and salutatorian also gave brief speeches, and school officials reviewed the statements of all three in advance. In 1998, the principal told the valedictorian and the invocation-giver to remove sectarian and proselytizing language from their remarks. They refused. The valedictorian tried to deliver his speech at graduation, beginning with a warning that anyone who was offended by references to Jesus should leave. The principal stopped him, and both students sued.

The federal district court ruled in favor of the school officials, and the appeals court upheld that decision. According to the appeals court, the very appointment of an invocation-giver "appears to reflect an impermissible state purpose to encourage a religious message" (*Cole v. Oroville*, 228 F.3d 1092 [2000], p. 1102). The violation would be even more egregious, the court declared, if the school approved a blatantly sectarian prayer. The valedictorian, by contrast, was chosen by a neutral process, and the school neither encouraged nor discouraged religious content in his message. Nevertheless, citing the school officials' tight control over the proceedings and their prior review of the students' speeches, the court ruled that whatever transpired as an official part of the ceremony would be perceived as, and would indeed be, a state-approved message. "Even assuming the Oroville graduation ceremony was a public or limited public forum," the decision stated, "the District's refusal to allow the students to deliver a sectarian speech or prayer as part of the graduation was necessary to avoid violating the Establishment Clause" (p. 1101). The Supreme Court refused to hear an appeal. Three years later, the Ninth Circuit used *Cole* as the controlling precedent in a case involving school officials who prevented a neutrally selected student speaker from proselytizing in his graduation speech. The student was permitted to distribute his original speech in writing to anyone who wished to accept a copy, but the school officials and the court felt that graduation attendees constituted a captive audience that should not be subjected unwillingly to proselytizing at a public-school event. The decision is *Lassonde v. Pleasanton* (320 F.3d 979 [2003]).

As the decisions discussed in this chapter demonstrate, many unsettled questions remain with regard to policies that permit or facilitate student-led prayer at school-sponsored events outside the school day. Even if a student speaker is free to deliver any message of his or her choice, with no specific expectation that the message will be a prayer, that is still not an open forum of the kind that exists in public parks or in extracurricular programs offering a choice of several different activities. It is difficult, if not impossible, for dissenters to avoid whatever the speaker may choose to say, and they have no opportunity for rebuttal. Similarly, there is no provision for the delivery of multiple messages or for participation by everyone who chooses to join in the discourse. These considerations become particularly contentious when school officials react to the termination of traditional religious practices, such as clergy-led graduation prayer, by creating new opportunities for student speakers to address audiences at graduations, assemblies, games, and other school-sponsored events. While the facial language of such policies may be entirely constitutional, it is predictable that the effect will be to promote prayer, and in many instances school officials leave little doubt that such is their goal. In addition, the use of student elections, while ostensibly democratic, may represent an attempt to promote a majoritarian orthodoxy as opposed to facilitating genuinely independent expression by speakers selected without reference to what they are likely to say.

The situation is complicated, however, by the fact that the prevalence of prayer, and the predictability with which it occurs, may in some instances flow not from the school officials' actions but from the cumulative individual decisions of large numbers of private speakers within a relatively homogeneous community. The question then becomes whether a speaker should be denied an opportunity to exercise his/her personal choice to pray simply because that would also be the probable choice of other speakers given the freedom to say whatever they liked. If such a standard were established, the anomalous result would be that individual private speakers at graduation or other school events would be more likely to have an opportunity to speak, and thus to pray, if they lived in communities where other speakers would be relatively unlikely to make religious choices rather than in communities where a higher percentage of the individual private speech uttered under a neutral policy would take the form of prayer. To be sure, a policy would be suspect if student speakers were not allowed to express any secular message incompatible with the school's own viewpoint, since limiting the graduation speeches to school-approved messages would suggest that if prayer takes place, a judgment has been made that it too fits that category. The same would not be true, however, under a truly viewpoint-neutral policy such as that in *Doe v. Madison*, which allowed any student message couched in "appropriate language for the audience and occasion."

Somewhat different issues are raised by policies that permit student "messages" to be delivered over the loudspeaker at such events as football games, which unlike graduations do not ordinarily or inherently involve speech-making. While it is true that people who attend a public-school graduation might not expect to find themselves present for prayer, they certainly would understand that they are going to hear speeches, not only from school officials but also from students and outside speakers who clearly do not represent the school. In these circumstances, there is some validity to the argument that even at a school event expected to be innocuous and generally enjoyable, some audience members may be uncomfortable with something said by a particular speaker. Moreover, there is an almost inexhaustible supply of relevant messages, secular and religious, that might be delivered at graduation. At such events as football games, however, audience members might reasonably expect to hear no speeches other than announcements pertaining to the activity. As the courts noted in *Santa Fe v. Doe*, it is difficult to see what other secular speech would be relevant to the occasion or why a speech is appropriate at all. Thus, if school officials invite students to vote on whether they wish to elect someone to give a message at a football game, even without the inclusion of a word like "solemnize," a stronger argument can be made that the event is being gerrymandered, pulled out of its proper shape, to promote prayer.

Clearly, disputes over student-led prayer require courts to consider a wide range of issues, including the rights of people who wish to pray, the rights of those who prefer not to be present for prayer, and the duty of the state to uphold free exercise of religion and free speech without advancing or endorsing religion or coercing anyone into attending worship. As Chapter Fifteen illustrates, not only judges but advocacy groups, legislators, and scholars continue to seek a solomonic balance among these competing interests. The intensity of this debate can only grow as school officials experiment with an ever-widening variety of arrangements based on the distinction between government and private speech.

15

Zen and the Art of Constitution Maintenance

Mankind will in time discover that unbridled majorities are as tyrannical and cruel as unlimited despots.

—*John Adams*

As previous chapters have shown, the Supreme Court has not yet ruled on many of the questions surrounding religious expression in the public schools. The decisions it *has* handed down tend to be narrowly tailored to the facts of specific cases, and the lower courts are far from consistent in interpreting and applying these Supreme Court precedents. This complex judicial situation would be confusing enough, but when the contradictory advice disseminated by warring advocacy groups is added to the mix, it is no wonder that education officials have become desperate for definitive information. To be sure, some of them cherish agendas that they seek to carry out whether the courts agree or not, but most want to obey the law and are frustrated by their uncertainty as to what it requires or permits.

The first significant attempt to respond to this problem was initiated by a broad-based coalition of advocacy groups whose staff attorneys began interacting in the late 1980s, when they joined in support of a bill called the Religious Freedom Restoration Act.[1] This so-called RFRA coalition was remarkable for bringing to the table highly diverse groups ranging from the Christian Right to separationists, and coalition members have continued to meet to address a variety of church/state issues. In 1994, Marc Stern of the American Jewish Congress took the lead in drafting a proposal that would allow at least some members of this coalition to agree, as lawyers, on what current law says about religious expression in public schools. Naturally, it was understood that the various groups would continue their efforts to win court decisions and legislative battles that would further their preferences about the way prayer should be treated in the schools. As Mark Pelavin of the AJC expressed it, "We agree on the facts but disagree on the conclusions" (interview, June 23, 1995). Nevertheless, the participating attorneys proposed to put aside their ideological differences long enough to provide authoritative guidance to school officials regarding those matters that have been settled by the courts, as well as summarizing the current status of issues that remain in flux.

Unaware of this initiative, U.S. Secretary of Education Richard Riley instructed his staff to explore ways of addressing the misconceptions, hostile rhetoric, and atmosphere of suspicion that pervaded discussions of religion in the public schools. When his staff advised him that no such effort could succeed without the cooperation of the relevant advocacy groups, he invited representatives of key organizations to a conference at the White House. According to several advocacy-group attorneys who attended the meeting, one of them mentioned their proposed statement of current law to Riley, who greeted it with enthusiasm and promised to use the resources of the U.S. Department of Education (DOE) to further it. His support was, from the lawyers' standpoint, a mixed blessing. On the one hand, if their statement were disseminated by the DOE rather than by their own organizations, school officials would be more likely to regard it as authoritative. On the other hand, the Clinton administration's involvement inevitably politicized what had been a relatively non-political effort. The president, seeking reelection, was eager to associate himself with popular family-values issues, and groups that opposed him feared that their school-prayer document might become a feather in his political cap. The decision about whether to sign the statement in these circumstances was particularly difficult for conservative groups, since they wanted it to be as effective as possible but resented what they saw as the Clinton administration's attempt to hijack it. In the end, most of them declined to sign, but two evangelical groups—the Christian Legal Society and the National Association of Evangelicals—did so.

To the NAE and CLS, the main point was to reach school administrators who inappropriately prevented students from doing such things as saying grace before meals, reading the Bible when they were free to read other books of their choice, and saying the rosary on the school bus. With Riley's authority behind the statement, they reasoned, school officials who were enforcing such restrictions out of genuine confusion about the law would mend their ways. Not surprisingly, their decision was harshly criticized by such organizations as the Rutherford Institute, Wallbuilders, and Concerned Women for America. As they saw it, the CLS and NAE had been hoodwinked into lending their credibility to a measure that would undercut proposed new school-prayer legislation by suggesting that religious expression is already sufficiently protected. As an example, a Wallbuilders mailing directed against the CLS suggested that anyone who signed the statement must favor the removal of "In God We Trust" from currency and "under God" from the Pledge of Allegiance, as those would be among the consequences of failing to enact stringent new laws protecting religion. According to Forest Montgomery of the NAE, his group, too, was "blamed for consorting with the enemy." He also recalled having once been asked to leave a meeting of conservative advocacy-group lawyers with whom he disagreed. "That's okay," he added wryly. "I told them, 'I've been thrown out of better places than this!'" (interview, August 15, 1996; unless otherwise indicated, quotations from Montgomery are from this interview).

THE WORK UNVEILED

After undergoing many revisions, "Religion in the Public Schools: A Joint Statement of Current Law" was released in April 1995. In addition to Stern, the drafting committee included attorneys from the American Civil Liberties Union, American Jewish Committee, American Muslim Council, Anti-Defamation League, Baptist Joint Committee on Public Affairs, CLS, General Council of Seventh-day Adventists, NAE, National Council of Churches, People for the American Way, and Union of American Hebrew Congregations. This document, also endorsed by a variety of other groups, addresses fourteen headings, such as "Graduation Prayer and Baccalaureates," "Distribution of Religious Literature," "Equal Access Act," and "Released Time." Some of its assertions are categorical and unambiguous, such as "School officials may not mandate or organize prayer at graduation" (p. 2), and "It is both permissible and desirable to teach objectively about the role of religion in the history of the United States and other countries" (p. 4). Other topics receive more qualified treatment; for example, "Students have the right to pray individually or in groups or discuss their religious views with their peers" only as long as they are not allowed "to have a captive audience listen or to compel other students to participate" (p. 2). Similarly, "Students may express their religious beliefs in the form of reports, homework, and artwork," but if a student gives an oral presentation in class that amounts to "conducting a religious service, the school has the right—as well as the duty—to prevent itself from being used as a church" (pp. 4, 5). The law is frankly acknowledged to be unclear on some matters, such as the circumstances under which student-led graduation prayer is permissible and the point at which a student's religious speech becomes harassment of other students.[2]

Shortly after the Joint Statement was published, President Clinton announced that he had ordered the DOE to distribute a directive based on it to every public school in America. His foes were unimpressed. Jay Sekulow of the American Center for Law and Justice told a reporter that "'The president's remarks are a convenient afterthought to a national debate that has been raging for years.'" He also complained that the DOE directive was "'ambiguous and intended to appease rather than clarify this important issue'" (Terence Hunt, "School Prayer Measure Not Needed, Clinton Says," [Wilmington, Delaware] *News Journal*, July 13, 1995, p. A4). The Rutherford Institute, which was representing Paula Jones in her sexual harassment lawsuit against Clinton, issued a 1996 policy statement alleging that the DOE directive implied "that religious people in this country face no problem that education and clarification won't solve" ("Religious People in Public Schools: Can We Substitute Policy for the Law?"). At the other end of the political spectrum, separationists praised the president for addressing misconceptions about the exclusion of religion from the schools, but they criticized what they saw as his one-sided promotion of student prayer with insufficient protection for the separation of church and state. As a *New York Times* editorial observed, "Mr. Clinton invites proselytizers to turn schools into religion-saturated environments. The danger is that in some places where one faith has a heavy dominance... a religious minority will be inundated by a torrent of allegedly voluntary observances" ("School Prayer Anxieties," *New York Times*, July 13, 1995, p. A22).

Separationists were even more displeased when, four years after disseminating the directive on school prayer, the DOE launched a new program to encourage formal partnerships between public schools and religious institutions. In a radio address on December 18, 1999, Clinton defended this initiative by asserting that "children involved in religious activities are less likely to use drugs.... Common sense says that faith and faith-based organizations from all religious backgrounds can play an important role in helping children to reach their fullest potential." "'It certainly was a one-note address,' responded Barry Lynn of Americans United for Separation of Church and State. 'I kept saying, "Gee, where are the limits? Where is a specific and clear statement that these partnering programs cannot be used to evangelize and recruit students for specific religions?"'" (Hanna Rosin, "Church-Public School Partnerships Encouraged," *Washington Post*, December 19, 1999, p. A2). (As an ACLU lobbyist, Lynn had worked on the content-neutral version of the Equal Access Act; see Chapter Twelve.)

To promote its new program, the DOE posted on its website a long list of religious groups that had agreed to participate in partnerships with public schools. These included the African Methodist Episcopal Church, Evangelical Lutheran Church in America, Presbyterian Church (USA), NAE, Council of Jewish Federations, Southern Baptist Convention, U.S. Catholic Conference, Mormon Church, and Muslim Public Affairs Council, among many others. Although numerous faith groups were named, most were Christian, and all were monotheistic. Despite carefully drafted rules, such as a requirement that the partnerships have a secular purpose and ban proselytizing, separationists were far from reassured that these church/school partnerships would not become a vehicle for religious indoctrination. The partnership program remains on the DOE website (www.ed.gov) under the administration of President George W. Bush, as does a set of guidelines defining permissible religious activities in public schools. Pursuant to a 2001 law, the No Child Left Behind Act, local education agencies are required, as a condition of receiving federal funds, to certify annually that their policies in no way impede constitutionally protected prayer. Additional material on religion in the public schools, together with links to other sources of information on this topic, also appear on the DOE website.

WHEELS WITHIN WHEELS

As often happens in politics, the Clinton administration's support of student prayer served more than one purpose. In addition to being tied to the president's bid for reelection, it was intended to undercut congressional initiatives with which Clinton and his supporters disagreed. A year before the Joint Statement was published, the Republican Party had won majorities in both Houses of Congress for the first time in decades, and its leaders had unveiled a "Contract with America" including, among other things, a pledge to introduce a constitutional amendment to restore state-sponsored school prayer. Like some of the authors of the Joint Statement, Clinton and Riley openly acknowledged that one of their goals was to undermine this part of the Contract with America by demonstrating how much religious expression is already permitted in the schools. In response, some school-prayer advocates heatedly denounced what they saw as a disingenuous attempt to suggest that a mere explanation of current law somehow represented a material improvement in the school-prayer situation. Among these critics were advocacy groups that had endorsed the Joint Statement as an educational tool but felt that a constitutional amendment was also needed. As they pointed out, neither the Joint Statement nor the DOE directive addressed some of the issues they sought to incorporate into an amendment, such as the eligibility of religious programs for public funding.

The responsibility for developing the promised constitutional amendment was delegated to Representative Ernest Istook (R-Oklahoma), who had ardently lobbied Speaker Newt Gingrich (R-Georgia) for the assignment. Istook had introduced a school-prayer amendment while the Democrats were still in control of the House, but knowing that it would not come up for a vote, he had merely recycled the Reagan Amendment language. After the 1994 Republican victory, he authorized a committee of advocacy-group lawyers and law professors to draft a new proposal for him to introduce into Congress. Not surprisingly, the drafters soon found themselves facing the same problem that had bedeviled such efforts since the 1960s: the inability to agree on specific language. Some drafters sought to open the doors of schools and other public places to state-sponsored religious speech, sectarian as well as nonsectarian, with or without any provision for excusing dissenters. Others wanted to minimize state control while enhancing opportunities for students and other citizens to engage in a wide range of religious activities, some of which might be funded but not directed by the government. The inevitable result was a multiplicity of drafts produced by shifting coalitions of advocacy-group lawyers, law professors, and congressional staff. After months of occasionally acrimonious debate, this process yielded two proposals, one introduced by Istook and the other by Representative Henry Hyde (R-Illinois).

Among the organizations that remained most closely associated with the Istook version of the proposed constitutional amendment were Concerned Women for America, Wallbuilders, the Rutherford Institute, and the Traditional Values Coalition. Its chief author was Craig Parshall, an attorney in private practice who does work for CWA and Rutherford. While the drafting was in progress, he gave a speech at a Christian Coalition convention in Washington, D.C., in which he characterized the Joint Statement and the DOE directive as a wrongheaded effort to find common ground on religious issues when in truth there can be no compromise between good and evil. He exhorted American Christians to be vigilant in protecting their full religious rights and heritage, including school-organized prayer and other governmental acknowledgments of religion. Otherwise, he predicted, America will succumb to the tyranny of those who seek to destroy its religious freedom and traditions.

By contrast, the drafters of the Hyde Amendment sought to preserve more of a distinction between direct government involvement with religion, which they opposed, and government support for the religious efforts of private individuals and groups, which they favored. The committee was led by Michael McConnell, a prominent law professor at the University of Chicago who later taught at the University of Utah until President George W. Bush appointed him to the Court of Appeals for the Tenth Circuit in 2002. Working with McConnell were lawyers from a variety of advocacy groups, including the CLS and NAE. Although both the Istook and the Hyde drafters tried to keep their discussions confidential, it was widely understood that the Istook Amendment would permit governmental acknowledgments of religion, whereas the Hyde version would focus on the eligibility of religious programs for government funding.

As work on the Istook and Hyde proposals progressed, organizations that had been opposing school-prayer amendments since the 1960s prepared to mount yet another lobbying campaign against either or both of them. To coordinate their efforts, they formed the Coalition to Preserve Religious Liberty, cochaired by Brent Walker of the Baptist Joint Committee on Public Affairs and Rabbi David Saperstein of the Religious Action Center of Reform Judaism. CPRL members included separationist groups, such as the ACLU, Americans United for Separation of Church and State, and the People for the American Way Action Fund; religious institutions, such as the Episcopal, United Methodist, Evangelical Lutheran, and Presbyterian (USA) Churches; and education organizations, such as the American Association of School Administrators, American Federation of Teachers, and National Education Association.

The newest of the groups that make up the CPRL is the Interfaith Alliance, established in 1994 as a membership organization for clergy of all faiths who wish to challenge the decades-old allegation that anyone who opposes government-sponsored prayer must be anti-God. In the words of its former director, Jill Hanauer, it was founded "because the Religious Right so easily marginalized secular voices that spoke against them" (interview, August 31, 1995). Unlike other umbrella religious groups that have long opposed state-sponsored school prayer, such as the American Jewish Congress and the National Council of [Christian] Churches, the Interfaith Alliance is associated with no particular religious tradition. Its member clergy include not only Christians and Jews but also Muslims, Hindus, Buddhists, Shintoists, Taoists, Sikhs, Wiccans, Zoroastrians, and members of other faiths whose voices are just beginning to be heard in the school-prayer debate.

TAKING THE SHOW ON THE ROAD

Although some members of Congress go to great lengths to proclaim their independence from advocacy groups, Istook believed that organizations such as CWA and the Rutherford Institute represented the voice of the people. To him, the most compelling argument in favor of the amendment was that the majority wanted it, and his role was not to dictate policy but to carry out the people's wishes. Accordingly, his press releases routinely spotlighted not the congressman but the advocacy groups, leading to such headlines as "Christian Groups Craft 'Religious Equality' Amendment" over news articles that barely mentioned Istook (Gebe Martinez and David Savage, *Los Angeles Times,* April 15, 1995, p. A13). Similarly, inquiries to his office about the progress of the drafting were referred to advocacy-group lawyers with the candid acknowledgment that no one on the staff was actively participating in the process.

In accord with this populist approach, Istook wanted to give people throughout the country an opportunity to demonstrate their support for school prayer and to express their opinions about what the amendment should say. He therefore asked the chairperson of the House Subcommittee on the Constitution, Representative Charles Canady (R-Florida), to schedule a series of field hearings—that is, committee hearings held outside Washington—during summer 1995. After an initial event in Washington, the first of the field hearings took place in Harrisonburg, Virginia. Supporters of the amendment dominated in the audience as well as among the witnesses, prompting Brant Levine of the AJC to describe it as "a rally in support of the religious equality amendment" (letter to Mark Pelavin, June 13, 1995). According to news reports, however, both the testimony and the audience reactions became increasingly mixed in the later hearings, which took place in Tampa, New York, and Oklahoma City. When a final hearing that had been scheduled for Los Angeles was canceled, opponents were quick to suggest that, far from being a nationwide celebration of the amendment, the field hearings had become a public-relations embarrassment for Istook because public opinion was less one-sided than his majoritarian rhetoric had suggested.

Closely following the House field hearings were Senate Judiciary Committee hearings whose overall sense may be inferred from the opening exchange between Chairman Orrin Hatch (R-Utah) and the committee's ranking Democrat, Senator Joseph R. Biden, Jr. (D-Delaware). "I think it is fair to say," Hatch remarked, "that as government, often through the judicial branch, has harassed religious liberty and reduced its presence in the public square over the last few generations, our social life in this country has become more coarsened"

("Religious Liberty," p. 3). The government should foster spirituality, he suggested, as an antidote to moral decay. Biden replied, "The coin of religious freedom, we must never forget, has two sides" (p. 7). America is one of the most religious nations on Earth, he maintained, precisely because the government has stayed out of religion. In his view, the issue before the Senate was not whether religion is good but whether all Americans, including religious minorities, would benefit from increased governmental involvement with it.

LANGUAGE AT LAST

On November 15, 1995, Hyde introduced his proposed constitutional amendment: "Neither the United States nor any State shall deny benefits to or otherwise discriminate against any private person or group on account of religious expression, belief, or identity; nor shall the prohibition on laws respecting an establishment of religion be construed to require such discrimination" (104th Congress, H. J. Res. 121). Under current law, programs run by religious organizations are eligible for government funds only if there is no pervasively religious element in the activities those funds support; for instance, an essentially secular drug rehabilitation program run by a church may receive public funds, but a program based on conquering addiction by accepting Christ as one's savior may not. The point of the Hyde Amendment was to make religious and secular versions of the same undertakings equally eligible for government support. In the opinion of Hyde and his allies, it is ineligibility for government benefits, rather than any restriction on public religious speech, that most impedes individuals and private groups from pursuing their religious faith. Just as private persons have a right to engage in religious speech on the same basis as secular speech, they asserted, access to public funds should not be denied to an otherwise eligible private program solely because of its religious character.

Two weeks after the introduction of the Hyde Amendment, Istook presented his version: "To secure the people's right to acknowledge God according to the dictates of conscience: Nothing in this Constitution shall prohibit acknowledgments of the religious heritage, beliefs, or traditions of the people, or prohibit student-sponsored prayer in public schools. Neither the United States nor any State shall compose any official prayer or compel joining in prayer, or discriminate against religious expression or belief" (104th Congress, H. J. Res. 127). Of the two proposals, Istook's was far more similar to the Becker, Dirksen, Wylie, and Reagan Amendments of earlier decades, and indeed to the aims of nineteenth-century nativists who had fought to keep the King James Bible in the public schools. Like those earlier school-prayer advocates, Istook supporters asserted that America must remain true to its religious heritage because making God an official part of the nation's daily life is the only secure foundation for freedom and morality. They further echoed the arguments of earlier periods by calling for majority rule and states' rights with regard to religion.

Although both proposals shared the common goal of enhancing government support for religious activities, the Istook Amendment was a populist document, and the Hyde Amendment was a lawyerly one. Whereas the Istook Amendment sought to assuage the frustration, anger, and fear of conservative Christians who felt that they and their faith were being pushed to the margins of a country their forebears had founded, the Hyde Amendment was carefully crafted to affect the outcome of particular types of lawsuits involving the use of public funds for religious programs. Accordingly, when Istook supporters suggested that government-sponsored majoritarian prayer in public schools and other public places would turn back the clock on a whole host of social changes they deplored, Hyde advocates retorted that such observances were mere symbolic gestures that would achieve little more than satisfying some people's emotions. In the words of a CLS spokesperson interviewed for this book, "Istook supporters want the amendment to make them feel better about being Christian in America, but we've got bigger fish to fry. The goal isn't to feel good about being Christian in America but to expand the kingdom. The Hyde Amendment would help us get rid of legal obstacles to doing that." Nevertheless, there was no denying that the Hyde Amendment was more cerebral and less emotionally gratifying than the Istook version, and its supporters found themselves under attack from school-prayer advocates who considered them insufficiently committed to religion.

Naturally, opponents of both amendments continued to maintain that religious liberty was already in fine shape and could only be harmed by any change to the First Amendment. Like many recent political debates, this one was notable for the extent to which, as Rochelle L. Stanfield phrased it, "each side seems to have borrowed its new theme song from the old battle cries of its opponents. The religious Right is casting its crusade as a battle for freedom of speech, for example, while the opponents of an amendment describe their view as bolstering family values and restraining government influence" ("The Amen Amendment," *National Journal*, January 7, 1995, p. 23). An illustration of this phenomenon may be found in dueling op-ed pieces by Istook and Representative Barney Frank (D-Massachusetts) in the Capitol Hill newspaper *Roll Call* on July 10, 1995. In a column headed "A 'Constitutional Correction'

Is the Only Way," conservative Republican Istook called for diversity, tolerance, and inclusion. In "On Religion, One More GOP Inconsistency," liberal Democrat Frank defended states' rights and small government against what he described as an attempt to impose government-approved prayer by federal fiat (pp. 17, 27).

WEIGHING OPTIONS: ISTOOK

The most significant arguments pertaining to the Istook Amendment concerned its implications for government involvement with religion. Its use of the phrase "the people," for instance, might refer to private persons, singly or in groups, but it might also suggest that the people collectively—that is, the majority—could use their voting power to tell everyone what to do with regard to religion. Similarly, there was disagreement about whether "the people" would encompass government employees, thereby enabling them to use their official positions to promote religious views.

The amendment's provision that the government could not "compel *joining in* prayer" (emphasis added) was also controversial because it failed to guarantee that dissenters would not be forced to *attend* prayer. During the research for this book, this question was addressed in interviews with prominent supporters of the amendment, including Istook himself, who asserted that it would merely permit voluntary prayer by people who chose to participate. Without exception, when asked what kinds of arrangements they envisioned to permit dissenters to opt out of the prayer, they responded with indignant statements to the effect that religion is not a disease that people have to be able to avoid. Since liberals value tolerance, they added, presumably they can tolerate a brief prayer; and it is insulting to suggest that local majorities cannot be trusted to respect the rights of religious minorities in the absence of an explicit, federally mandated opt-out policy. These remarks, which recall attorney Charles Cooper's arguments in *Lee v. Weisman* (Chapter Fourteen), raise long-standing questions about the meaning of voluntary prayer under government auspices. To some people, the word "voluntary" signifies only that no one can be compelled to engage in meaningful communication with God, whereas others view coerced attendance as a negation of voluntariness. Similarly, opponents of a constitutional amendment are often accused of meanspiritedness for trying to prevent other people from praying even though they themselves would not have to participate, but the word "participate"— like "voluntary"—means different things to different people. Underlying these linguistic discrepancies is a fundamental disagreement about whether dissenters have a legitimate, inherent right to absent themselves from majoritarian prayer. The belief that they have not, expressed in many of the nineteenth-century disputes discussed in Chapters Two through Four, appears to have entered the twenty-first century alive and well, albeit significantly less prevalent than it was in earlier periods.

WEIGHING OPTIONS: HYDE

In contrast with the Istook Amendment, the Hyde version eschewed government-sponsored religious observances in favor of placing religious programs on an equal footing with their secular counterparts with respect to eligibility for public funding. To Hyde and his supporters, it is clearly inequitable for the government to fund such undertakings as counseling programs, day care centers, schools, homeless shelters, and facilities for troubled youths only if they are conducted in a secular manner. "We're united with our liberal friends on the right of conscience to believe whatever," remarked Forest Montgomery of the NAE. "But when the Supreme Court says *no* aid to religion, that's wrong because the secular or irreligious is being preferred to religion." He and other Hyde supporters felt that individuals and groups should not be forced to muffle their religious message as the price of securing government funds for charitable or educational activities. Indeed, they asserted, religion is the one sure route to morality, and in times such as these, religious voices are the last that should be suppressed.

Opponents of the Hyde Amendment retorted that although it would forbid discrimination against religion, it would do nothing to prevent discrimination in favor of any or all religions over nonreligion. They also maintained that people should not be taxed for the support of religious messages, and that the inevitable result of doing so would be favoritism toward the majority faith tempered by the need, at least in diverse communities, to provide some funds for minority religions, cults, and unpopular movements. Nor, they added, would government subsidies be truly beneficial to religion. In the words of Brent Walker of the Baptist Joint Committee on Public Affairs, co-chairperson of the CPRL, "When religion bellies up to the public trough, it becomes lazy and dependent. How can religion raise a prophetic fist against government when it has its other hand opened for a handout? It can't" ("Religious Liberty," p. 169).

The question of whether the Hyde Amendment would advance the majority faith was particularly contentious because, although its provisions were stated in terms of equal access to government benefits rather than the stark majoritarianism of Istook, its opponents had no doubt that the majority would

dominate as a matter of political inevitability. To be sure, the amendment neither favors the majority faith nor provides that all religions must be funded
equally; indeed, it does not oblige the government to fund any religious activity whatsoever. All it says is that programs would no longer be considered ineligible for funding solely because of their religious character. Nevertheless,
although the courts would determine which programs were eligible for funding, the actual allocation of money to one eligible applicant rather than
another would be made through a political process. To Hyde's opponents, it
would be naïve to suppose that decisions made by elected officials and their
appointees would not favor popular faiths and vocal religious groups. They
also pointed out that in sparsely populated regions a single government-subsi-
dized facility, such as a drug treatment program or counseling center, might
serve a wide area. If a religious program were the only one to receive government funds, then everyone who needed that type of help but could not afford
private care would have to submit to proselytizing as a condition of using tax-
subsidized services. Worse, they predicted, it was foreseeable that courts would
order indigent defendants into such programs, and if there were no subsidized secular facilities in the area, the result would be indoctrination that was
not only government-funded but court-ordered.

AND NOW A WORD ABOUT WORDING

The struggle over the Hyde and Istook Amendments, like the debates over the
Becker, Dirksen, Wylie, and Reagan Amendments, illustrates the critically
important role played by each word of a proposed constitutional amendment.
The measure's chance of success, to say nothing of its real-life effect on American society should it be enacted, hinges on its precise language. Accordingly,
it might be worthwhile to consider a few specific examples from the Hyde
Amendment in order to demonstrate how such crucial decisions about wording are made.

Kathryn Hazeem (now Lehman), chief counsel to the House Subcommittee on the Constitution, worked closely with the drafting committee as it tried
to anticipate all the possible ramifications each word or phrase might have.
"You can look at language for a month," she remarked, "before you realize that
it has, or could have, a significance you hadn't realized or hadn't intended"
(interview, August 29, 1996). To complicate matters further, she observed, the
language must not only achieve its intended effect in the courts but also
appeal to Congress, the press, and grassroots supporters. In her view, one of
the greatest challenges with respect to the Hyde Amendment was the need to

develop wording that would prevent the government from promoting religion but would not suggest that religion is a wholly private activity that has no place in public discourse. In the original version of the amendment that Hyde introduced in 1995, this purpose was served by the phrase "private person or group," which was meant to exclude public-school teachers and other government personnel from leading prayers. Because of fears about privatizing religion, however, the committee shied away from the word "private" in later versions. In its place, they considered inserting a provision that would prohibit coercion in matters of religion, but this gave rise to the concern that the word "coerce" might be interpreted—politically, popularly, or judicially—to mean that prayer was forbidden whenever there was any possibility of peer pressure or other forms of social compulsion. Ultimately, the revised version of the Hyde Amendment introduced by Representative Richard Armey (R-Texas) in 1996 omitted the word "private" and explicitly identified the government as the entity that was not authorized to coerce or inhibit religion.

The question of religious proselytizing by government officials also arose in conjunction with a passage written by Montgomery: "To secure the unalienable right of the people to acknowledge, worship, and serve their Creator, according to the dictates of conscience." This language formed the basis for the opening phrase of the Istook Amendment, and when Montgomery joined the Hyde Amendment team, he lobbied for its inclusion. The Constitution presently includes no mention of God, and Montgomery sought to insert one without altering the Hyde Amendment's meaning or effect. His fellow drafters protested that, like the Istook Amendment, Montgomery's language focused on emotional satisfaction rather than substance, and they feared that it might indeed affect the interpretation of the amendment. If, for instance, the right of every person "to worship God according to the dictates of conscience" is indeed unalienable, then it might be presumed to allow government officials to proselytize if their religious beliefs impelled them to do so. That provision might also suggest, to the public if not to the courts, that the amendment would apply only to people who believe in God. Despite these concerns, Montgomery's language carried enough congressional, popular, and advocacy-group support to cause it to appear in the title of the first version of the Hyde Amendment and in the text of the revised version—minus the word "unalienable."

BACK TO THE FRAY

After the Hyde and Istook Amendments had been written and debated, the two sets of drafters tried to formulate a single version that both sides could support. The Istook committee was willing to accept Hyde's provision for equal access to government benefits, but it wanted to retain its own explicit school-prayer language. The Hyde group refused to compromise on this point, and the House Republican leadership sought to resolve the impasse by endorsing a revised version of the Hyde Amendment that Armey introduced: "In order to secure the right of the people to acknowledge and serve God according to the dictates of conscience, neither the United States nor any State shall deny any person equal access to a benefit, or otherwise discriminate against any person, on account of religious belief, expression, or exercise. This amendment does not authorize government to coerce or inhibit religious belief, expression, or exercise" (104th Congress, 2d Session, H. J. Res. 184, July 16, 1996). Following an acrimonious exchange of views during committee hearings in the House, the 1996 congressional session ended with no further action on any of the three proposals.

When Congress reconvened in 1997, Istook announced a revised amendment that retained the overall sense of his original proposal while adding Hyde's "equal access to a benefit" language. True to his policy of deferring to the advocacy groups that supported him, his press release was headed, "Groups Announce Religious Freedom Amendment" (March 24, 1997). Among the groups it listed were the American Family Association, Concerned Women for America, the Family Research Council, Focus on the Family, and Wallbuilders. This new version of the amendment was referred to the Judiciary Committee, which made some additional changes and then sent it to the House for a vote. Following a floor debate that covered essentially the same points that had been raised with respect to earlier proposals for constitutional amendments on school prayer, the amendment received a simple majority of 224–203–7 but not the necessary two-thirds. Istook has repeatedly reintroduced it without success, and neither the Hyde Amendment nor the Armey Amendment has ever come up for a vote.

16
Deliver Us from Evil

So hope for a great sea-change
On the far side of revenge.
Believe that a further shore
Is reachable from here.

—*Sophocles*

Inevitably, the centuries-long battle over religious expression in American public schools took on renewed urgency following the 1999 shooting spree at Columbine High School and the terrorist attacks of September 11, 2001. To some people, these events and the long series of school shootings and acts of terrorism out of which they arose provide tragic proof of the need to reinstate public-school devotionals that clearly convey governmental and societal approval of prayer. Others assert that the lessons of Columbine and September 11 include the need for gun control, the danger of normalizing and glorifying violence, and above all the destructive fanaticism that can arise from the union of religious and national identities.

COLUMBINE
Typical of the flood of mailings sent out by advocacy groups in the wake of the Columbine shootings was a petition to the Supreme Court circulated by Dr. D. James Kennedy of Coral Ridge Ministries, a conservative Christian group headquartered in Florida. The petition attributed Columbine and other school tragedies to the Court's ban on school prayer, which has allegedly eroded moral values and respect for religion, thereby promoting inappropriate sexual activity, violence, low test scores, illiteracy, and gangs. Indeed, Kennedy suggested, "It is as if the blessing of God—so evident throughout so much of our history as a nation—was quietly and tragically withdrawn on that day [when *Engel v. Vitale* was decided]." The petition urged the Court, in the name of "We the

People of the United States," to reinstate the original meaning of the First Amendment, thus permitting states to reintroduce into their public schools Bible-reading, religious instruction, prayer, religious displays such as the posting of the Ten Commandments, and local control over the teaching of creationism rather than evolution.

Similar arguments also appeared in countless other advocacy-group appeals and grassroots campaigns, and several state legislatures debated proposals to bring references to God back into the public-school day. Most of these proposals were not new, but the Columbine tragedy energized their supporters and increased their opponents' vulnerability to the charge of obstructing the only effective means of stopping school violence. In its most common forms, this legislation involved either the posting of religious sayings or the recitation of religious excerpts from historical documents, such as the Declaration of Independence and state constitutions. Among the comparatively few proposals of this kind to be enacted was a 2001 Mississippi law requiring the "display on an appropriately framed background with minimum dimensions of eleven (11) inches by fourteen (14) inches, [of] the following motto of the United States of America in each classroom, school auditorium and school cafeteria... : 'IN GOD WE TRUST.'" (Miss. Code Ann. § 37-13-163). (The U.S. House of Representatives took similar action to convey its disagreement with the Supreme Court's decision in *Engel v. Vitale*—see Chapter Five.) Predictably, the Mississippi ACLU is monitoring the situation even as other states consider whether to follow Mississippi's lead.

The same post-Columbine dynamics were evident in Congress, where school violence was presented as an urgent justification for a variety of religious proposals. House Majority Whip Tom DeLay (R-Texas) became the chief spokesperson for this view, asserting that the responsibility for school violence rested with liberals who had taken God out of American schools. At Columbine, he said in a floor speech, "They sent counselors. They sent psychiatrists.... What did the kids do? They went to church. The kids went to church.... People have to be allowed freedom to exercise their religion. Barriers have to be removed to allow us to raise a culture that hopefully some day will eliminate kids killing kids" (*Congressional Record*, June 17, 1999, p. 4572). Later the same night, the House defeated gun-control legislation that had been passed by the Senate, and its disappointed supporters accused DeLay and his allies of using school prayer to divert attention from the relationship between adolescent violence and lax gun laws. Much of the time earmarked for the gun-control debate, they protested, had been squandered on a lengthy discussion of posting the

Ten Commandments and reinstating state-sponsored school prayer. "Perhaps," Senator Richard Durbin (D-Illinois) suggested ironically, "we could post the Ten Commandments at the gun shows... saying to people who want to buy and sell these guns without any background checks, accept your moral responsibility for what is about to occur" (*Congressional Record,* June 18, 1999, p. 7282).

DeLay's speech and others like it also impelled political commentators to ridicule the notion that an all-powerful God could be kicked out of the public schools. Among them was columnist Rick Horowitz, who satirically claimed to have seen a mob of liberals shouting into a megaphone, "'Come out with all Your commandments up!'" When God finally left the school, "all the liberals burst into cheers and went off to undermine family values." Some questioned whether God was really gone, Horowitz concluded, "But by midnight, there were scattered reports of children misbehaving all over town... and actions no longer had consequences. So when Tom DeLay talks, I listen" ("Liberals Must Have Sneaked Up Behind God," [Wilmington, Delaware] *News Journal,* June 26, 1999, p. A6).

TAKE TWO TABLETS

Displays of the Ten Commandments in public schools had been common in some parts of the country until 1980, when the Supreme Court struck down a Kentucky law requiring the Decalogue to be hung in every classroom. According to the Court, "The pre-eminent purpose of posting the Ten Commandments, which do not confine themselves to arguably secular matters, is plainly religious in nature, and the posting serves no constitutional educational function" (*Stone v. Graham,* 449 U.S. 39; 101 S. Ct. 192 [1980], p. 39). Not only are the Commandments part of certain religious traditions, the decision stated, but the first four (or the first three in the Catholic version—see Chapter Three) explicitly define "the religious duties of believers: worshipping the Lord God alone, avoiding idolatry, not using the Lord's name in vain, and observing the Sabbath Day" (p. 42). By the time the Columbine shootings took place in spring 1999, the question of circumventing this decision and finding ways to display the Commandments in schools and other public buildings was already in the national news because of a lawsuit filed by the Alabama chapter of the American Civil Liberties Union against a county court judge, Roy Moore, who displayed the Commandments in his courtroom and invited Protestant ministers to pray with juries. Coral Ridge Ministries funded his defense, and the case ended with a declaration by the Alabama Supreme Court that the plaintiffs had no standing to sue.

Members of the Alabama Supreme Court are elected by popular vote, and in 2000 Moore became chief justice, campaigning largely on the Ten Commandments issue. Shortly afterward, and without consulting the other justices, he brought workmen into the courthouse rotunda late one night to install a four-foot granite sculpture weighing more than two and a half tons. The sculpture consists of the Ten Commandments tablets atop a cube whose sides are inscribed with religious quotations from the Founders. As Moore explained at the unveiling, the monument was meant to serve not only as an assertion that American law is based on the Commandments but also as homage to the Judeo-Christian God. Coral Ridge Ministries was the only media outlet permitted to film either the installation of the sculpture or its unveiling the next morning. When the secular press questioned the legality of placing such a monument in the courthouse, Moore replied, "I'm the highest legal authority in the state, and I wanted it there.... Doesn't it look great?" (Jeffrey Gettleman, "Conviction Cast in Stone," *Los Angeles Times,* August 2, 2001, p. A9).

Not only individuals but also busloads of conservative Christian tourists began visiting the monument to kneel and pray, whereupon three lawyers who regularly use the courthouse sued, with representation by attorney Marc Stern of the American Jewish Congress. The federal district court, while painstakingly clarifying that not all displays of the Commandments are barred from government buildings, declared that Moore's stated intentions and the religious effect of the monument rendered this display unconstitutional. The Court of Appeals for the Eleventh Circuit agreed, and in September 2003 the monument was removed amid large but peaceful protests by its supporters. Judge Moore was suspended from his position for his earlier defiance of a federal court order to remove the monument.

AND CALL CONGRESS IN THE MORNING

Not surprisingly, Moore's actions became grist for several congressional debates over the role of religion in government. As explained in Chapter Nine, his name surfaced in this context during the 1997 House and Senate hearings on judicial activism, where he was depicted as a renegade jurist whose violations were ignored by congressional conservatives who sought to focus only on the alleged errors of liberal judges. Then, when the Alabama ACLU challenged his display of the Commandments in his county courtroom, Representative Robert Aderholt (R-Alabama) introduced a resolution expressing "the sense of Congress regarding the display of the Ten Commandments by Judge

Roy S. Moore." It described the Commandments as "a declaration of fundamental principles that are the cornerstones of a fair and just society" and
defended their display in courthouses and other government buildings (105th
Congress, H. Con. Res. 31). The Columbine shootings had not yet taken place
when this nonbinding resolution easily passed both Houses of Congress, and
after Columbine its advocates began lobbying for a similar measure that
would have the force of law.

In addition to forming the basis for post-Columbine legislative proposals,
calls for governmental promulgation of the Ten Commandments also appeared
in some of the invocations offered before Congress at that time. The Senate
chaplain, for instance, asked God to help the lawmakers "communicate to
[American children] Your love and Your righteousness so that they have...
charts to make it through these difficult waters. O Gracious God, help us to
communicate Your commandments and help them to know the joy of living
in faithfulness with You. In our quest to separate church and state, there are
times when we have divided God from our culture. Now when there is
nowhere else to turn, we return to You" (*Congressional Record*, April 27, 1999,
p. 4232). Another Senate session opened with a prayer by a guest chaplain
who stated that he was commemorating the 3,311th anniversary of the day on
which God gave the Commandments to Moses. Among other things, he
asked God to reward the Senate for beginning its sessions with public prayer
and to encourage other institutions, including public schools, to do the same.
(Invocations that convey the chaplain's attitudes are by no means confined to
the school-prayer debate or to the current era. In the Lincoln administration,
for instance, Senator Willard Saulsbury (D-Delaware) offered the following
motion: "Resolved, That the Chaplain of the Senate be respectfully requested
hereafter to pray to and supplicate Almighty God in our behalf, and not to lecture Him, inform Him what to do, or state to Him, under pretense of prayer,
his (the said Chaplain's) opinion in reference to His duty as the Almighty; and
that the said Chaplain be further requested, as aforesaid, not, under the form
of prayer, to lecture the Senate in relation to questions before the body"
[quoted in Sandburg, p. 369].)

To meet the demand for a measure that would carry more legislative force
than a chaplain's prayer or a sense-of-Congress resolution, Aderholt sponsored
the Ten Commandments Defense Act, which would allow each state to decide
whether to post the Commandments in schools and other public buildings. It
passed the House as an amendment to the Juvenile Justice Act, an omnibus bill
dealing with the prevention of juvenile crime. To the dismay of gun-control

advocates, the Ten Commandments measure and other religious amendments were inserted into the bill as replacements for the gun-control language it had originally contained. Representative Eddie Bernice Johnson (D-Texas), among others, fulminated that Congress was "in the grasp of the National Rifle Association and the religious right." "I would not be surprised," he added, "if this Congress would soon legislate the passing out of crucifixes in schools, under the guise of warding off vampires" (*Congressional Record*, June 17, 1999, p. 1399). The Senate restored the gun-control language and removed the religious provisions, but the session ended with the Juvenile Justice Act still unresolved.

Predictably, not only Congress but also several state legislatures considered post-Columbine proposals to display the Ten Commandments in public schools. Kentucky, whose earlier law had been struck down in *Stone v. Graham,* took the lead by passing laws that authorized school officials to post the Commandments and required the schools' insurance companies to pay the costs of any resulting lawsuits. This legislation, enacted in 2000, also provided that the Decalogue should be part of a larger exhibit of American flags, historical documents, portraits of the Founders, and so forth. The stated intent of this provision was to emphasize the historical rather than the religious significance of the Commandments, but opponents of such displays objected to what they saw as the implication that only one religious tradition has a place in America's national identity. Conversely, some of the strongest advocates of posting the Commandments opposed any attempt to make them look secular, since affirming the divine origin of those precepts was, in their view, the whole point of the display.

Despite these concerns, statutes similar to the Kentucky law have been enacted or are being considered in other states, and the inevitable lawsuits have followed. In June 2003, for instance, a judge ordered the removal of outdoor displays of the Commandments from the grounds of four Ohio schools, resulting in nonviolent clashes between protesters and police. An even more acrimonious discussion of this issue took place during a meeting of the South Carolina state school board, when a member named Henry Jordan responded to concerns about minority faiths with the words, "'Screw the Buddhists and kill the Muslims.... And put that in the minutes.'" Jordan later explained, "'What I want to do is promote Christianity as the only true religion.... This nation was founded to worship, honor and glorify Jesus Christ, not Mohammed, not Buddha'" ("Official Rejects Non-Christians," *Washington Post*, May 17, 1997, p. A2).

EVEN MORE SO

The reaction to Columbine and earlier school shootings was, of course, dwarfed by the outpouring of grief and anger that followed the terrorist attacks of September 11, when millions of Americans turned to God for solace, salvation, and an understanding of the deeper meaning of that event. Criticism of government-led prayers, including those in public schools, was equated with a lack of sympathy for the victims and survivors, hostility toward the spiritual yearnings felt by most Americans, and inadequate patriotic fervor. Not since the 1950s, when "under God" was added to the Pledge of Allegiance to assert that belief in God is the distinguishing factor between democracy and Communism, had religious faith been so strongly and so widely associated with national unity. Indeed, television preachers Jerry Falwell and Pat Robertson suggested that the sins of insufficiently religious persons had led an exasperated deity to withdraw his protection, thus exposing America to terrorist attack.

The association of religion with the American national identity was evident in numerous proposals introduced into Congress in the aftermath of 9/11, including a new version of the Istook Amendment that focused solely on school prayer. A press release from Representative Ernest Istook's (R-Oklahoma) office stated that at this "critical time for our country," it was crucial to "free the American people to honor and respect God in public places" ("Istook Introduces School Prayer Amendment," December 20, 2001). In opposition, the Coalition to Preserve Religious Liberty argued that the public outpouring of religious sentiment following the attacks left no doubt that prayer is alive and well in America, requiring neither aid nor intrusion from the government. "Governmental endorsement of religion," a CPRL fund-raising letter stated, "turns religion into a political tool and sends the message that those who don't hold a certain faith are second-class citizens" (November 28, 2001). In the end, the only school-prayer proposals to pass were nonbinding "sense of Congress" resolutions, such as a House bill stating that since the words "under God" appear in the Pledge, and since President George W. Bush had called for prayer following 9/11, "schools in the United States should set aside a sufficient period of time to allow children to pray for, or quietly reflect on behalf of, the Nation during this time of struggle against the forces of international terrorism" (107th Congress, 1st Session, H. Con. Res. 239 [2001]).

Like their federal counterparts, state and local officials suggested that the national crisis cried out for the reinstatement of school-organized prayer. Among them was Rick Perry, George W. Bush's successor as governor of Texas. After participating in a mandatory assembly at a public middle school where a preacher led the students in a prayer to Jesus, Perry was asked about promoting Christianity as part of the government's response to the terrorist attacks. He replied by minimizing the distinction between Christianity and other religions: "I happen to think we all pray to the same God.... I'll let the theologians split the hairs and do all those kind of things" (Associated Press, "Perry Wants School Prayer a Campaign Issue," *Houston Chronicle,* October 21, 2001, *www. chron.com/cs/CDA/story.hts/metropolitan/1098518*). As the arrangement at that Texas middle school suggested, the reaction to 9/11 tended to blur the distinction between the students' personal right to pray and the school's authority to run worship services, and opposition to the latter was harshly criticized as an attempt to impede the voluntary prayers of frightened children who naturally tended to seek God's protection.

Public schools also became the focal point of a controversy involving the post-9/11 use of "God Bless America" not only as a song but also as a motto. Those three words were displayed on billboards throughout the country in front of everything from churches and libraries to pizzerias and supermarkets. Inevitably, some people objected to the use of that expression in government displays, particularly in public schools, preferring such sayings as "America United" and "United We Stand." Regardless of their personal views about turning to God in times of crisis, they felt that 9/11 demonstrated the danger rather than the efficacy of uniting government with religion. The terrorists' actions were manifestations not of atheism, they pointed out, but of religious/nationalist extremism. To them, it was one thing for people to display "God Bless America" publicly on their homes, businesses, vehicles, and clothing, but quite another for the *government* to suggest that patriotism and religious belief go hand-in-hand, so that nonbelievers are at best second-class citizens out of step with the government as well as with the majority. Similarly, when supporters of governmental religious displays asserted, as Governor Perry did, that everyone prays to the same God, their opponents retorted that many Americans do not in fact pray to the Judeo-Christian God, whereas to others it would be unthinkable even to acknowledge that "God Bless America" might refer to anyone else.

Although disputes over "God Bless America" arose in several communities, national media attention focused on the Rocklin School District in California, where the Northern California ACLU affiliate wrote to the school board at the request of parents who objected to the posting of "God Bless America" on an outdoor school billboard. According to the Northern California ACLU, the display endorsed religion and was unconstitutional as well as divisive. No legal complaint was filed, but opposition to the display set off an explosion of protest led by conservative advocacy groups such as the American Center for Law and Justice, which offered to represent the school district in the event of a lawsuit. "America is at war," Jay Sekulow wrote in an undated fund-raising letter, and "*We could see a great renewal of faith in America as our citizens awaken to the vital importance of public faith in our lives.* Or, we could see a return to the ACLU's secular vision of our society—a vision that does not even allow our school children to see the Ten Commandments, sing 'God Bless America,' or recite the Pledge of Allegiance!" The U.S. House of Representatives joined the fray by passing a nonbinding resolution: "That it is the sense of the Congress that public schools may display the words 'God Bless America' as an expression of support for the Nation" (107th Congress, 1st Session, H. Con. Res. 248 [2001]). Some members of Congress defended this resolution on the ground that "God Bless America" is not a religious sentiment but an affirmation of patriotism, while others made no distinction between the students' right to say "God Bless America" and the schools' right to post it. No one spoke or voted against the resolution, although ten Democrats voted "Present" rather than Aye or Nay.

This patriotic/religious debate was renewed in summer 2002, when the Court of Appeals for the Ninth Circuit ruled in favor of an atheist who claimed that his daughter "is injured when she is compelled to 'watch and listen as her state-employed teacher in her state-run school leads her classmates in a ritual proclaiming that there is a God, and that our's [sic] is "one nation under God"'" (*Newdow v. U.S. Congress,* 292 F. 3d 597 [2002], p. 601). The plaintiff, Michael Newdow, also asserted that the 1954 federal statute adding "under God" to the Pledge of Allegiance violates the Establishment Clause. The district court dismissed his complaint, but in a highly controversial decision, the appeals court reversed that ruling and sent the case back to the district court for further consideration.

Crucial to the Ninth Circuit's decision was the fact that the words "under God" were not part of the original Pledge but were added later to proclaim the religious character of the United States in opposition to the atheism of the Soviet Union, and to make a profession of belief in God part of the official declaration of loyalty to this country. (Excerpts from the relevant congressional committee report appear in Chapter Five.) In the view of the appeals court, Newdow's challenge raised some of the same issues as did *Wallace v. Jaffree,* in which the Supreme Court struck down an Alabama law whose sole function was to add the words "or prayer" to an earlier moment-of-silence statute (see

Chapter Ten). Moreover, the *Newdow* decision stated, "The recitation that ours is a nation 'under God' is not a mere acknowledgment that many Americans believe in a deity. Nor is it merely descriptive of the undeniable historical significance of religion in the founding of the Republic. Rather, the phrase 'one nation under God' in the context of the Pledge is normative. To recite the Pledge ... is to swear allegiance to the values for which the flag stands: unity, indivisibility, liberty, justice, and—since 1954—monotheism. The text of the official Pledge ... impermissibly takes a position with respect to the purely religious question of the existence and identity of God" (p. 607). Accordingly, the court struck down the 1954 statute adding "under God" to the Pledge. It further ruled that making the Pledge an official part of the public-school day violates every test the Supreme Court uses to determine whether a government action is constitutional: its purpose and effect are to advance religion, it constitutes an endorsement of religion, and it coerces people into participating in, or at least being present for, professions of faith. Following the Ninth Circuit's rejection of repeated requests for a rehearing, both sides asked the Supreme Court to hear an appeal. As this book goes to press in fall 2003, the Court has not yet responded.

Not surprisingly, *Newdow* was highly unpopular, and members of Congress hastened to express their disagreement with it. Although the Senate had not been scheduled to meet on the day after the decision was issued, it rushed into session expressly for the purpose of reciting the Pledge, with discernible emphasis on the words "under God." By a vote of 99–0, it also authorized the Senate Legal Counsel to take action to defend the constitutionality of the 1954 law. In addition, both the Senate and the House passed resolutions reaffirming their commitment to retaining "under God" in the Pledge as well as the national motto, "In God We Trust." In March 2003, as a protest against the Ninth Circuit's refusal to reconsider its decision, the House passed a nonbinding resolution stating that belief in God formed the basis on which this nation was founded, and that reciting the Pledge is a patriotic rather than a religious act. The vote was 400–7, with fifteen members voting "present."

BACK TO THE FUTURE

The ongoing arguments over the Pledge, "God Bless America," and the Ten Commandments leave no doubt about the undiminished vigor of the debate over religion in the public schools. As this book goes to press, Congress is considering new versions of the Istook Amendment and the Ten Commandments Defense Act as well as other proposals dealing with religion in public education. School-prayer cases appear on court calendars throughout the country, and advocacy groups stand poised to file new lawsuits in addition to appealing earlier decisions. All this activity raises two inescapable questions: Has anything changed? Has any progress been made in resolving disagreements over religion in public schools? The answer to each question is, of course, yes and no, and the explanation calls for a brief recapitulation of the evolution of thought traced throughout this book.

As Chapters Two through Four demonstrated, there have been disputes about public-school religion for as long as public schools have existed. In the earliest instances, such as the expulsion of Bridget Donohoe and the beating of Thomas Wall, courts upheld the power of the majority not only to make religious practices part of the public-school program but also to enforce participation by all students. Over time, however, a marked trend toward individual choice has prevailed. The first wall to be breached was the notion that the government can compel attendance at prayer, and opt-out policies, relatively rare until the mid-twentieth century, were consistently required by state courts in some parts of the country. When the Supreme Court issued its decisions in *Engel v. Vitale* and *Abington v. Schempp* in the early 1960s, even opt-out policies, with their potential for social embarrassment and second-class status, were deemed insufficient. Since then, individual choice has prevailed to such an extent that the government is prevented not only from enforcing participation in prayer but from running public-school devotionals at all. As earlier chapters have shown, some school-prayer advocates protest that this limitation interferes with the individual choice of each member of the majority who would opt for school-organized prayer were it available, to which opponents retort that members of the majority have a right to pray on the same basis as everyone else, but not the right to band together to create for themselves an opportunity for government endorsement that is unavailable to religious minorities or nonbelievers.

Following *Engel* and *Abington,* differences of opinion among school-prayer advocates made efforts to restore traditional practices unexpectedly contentious, and out of the resulting stalemate grew ideas for innovative ways of conceptualizing religious expression in the public schools. When equal access emerged as the dominant model, the distinction it made between independent student action and state control carried the trend toward individual choice to a new level. By contrast with whole-school exercises that either favor the majority faith or are so generic as to approach meaninglessness, equal access gives public schools the potential to encompass any or all religious views as students take part in the worship of their choice—if any—during noninstructional periods.

Although equal access has made progress toward its original goal of aiding students who, for the reasons discussed in Chapter Eleven, were being prevented from praying on their own, it has come nowhere near restoring the level of religious activity that existed in the public schools of many states prior to the Supreme Court's intervention. As supporters of the Becker and Dirksen Amendments predicted when the ink was barely dry on *Abington,* the termination of school-run devotionals attended by the whole student body has dramatically reduced the prevalence and visibility of religion in American public schools. Although the Supreme Court has subsequently upheld religious activities whose locus of control lies with the students, the Becker and Dirksen advocates were correct in anticipating that many students will not engage in religious activities if left on their own. Under these circumstances, it is inevitable that the controversies surrounding equal access pit people who want more religion in the public schools against those who believe that the choice to pray should rest with the students and not with the state regardless of the outcome.

Such controversies notwithstanding, equal access appears to be firmly established as the dominant model for dealing with religion in today's public schools. Many highly creedal believers prefer it to traditional school prayer because it replaces rote recitation with an opportunity to engage in worship that is meaningful to each student's faith, and it has induced some separationists to become more accepting of the students' personal right to engage in religious speech on the same basis as secular speech. Naturally, it also appeals to people who want prayer in the schools but have no strong feelings about how it is carried out. Since these diverse thinkers find common ground in equal access, they see less need for creative new legislation than for clarification and enforcement of existing laws. Thus, equal access has filtered out of the school-prayer debate certain issues dealing with the students' personal right to pray in the absence of school control or endorsement, and it has generally satisfied people for whom that is the most important goal. To that extent, then, the answer to both of the questions posed earlier is yes. Yes, there has been real change not only in school-prayer practices but in the content of the debate itself; and yes, progress has been made in the sense of establishing new policies that many people accept and indeed prefer to earlier ones. Nevertheless, a great deal of tension remains between equal-access supporters and opponents who, though comparatively few in number, can only be described as intractable.

ETERNAL ENDGAME

Like Horace Mann's attempt to open public education to all students by permitting only those practices he considered nonsectarian, current efforts to
achieve the same goal by means of equal access arouse the ire of two sets of
foes: those for whom equal access permits too much religion in the schools,
and those for whom it permits too little. The first group is made up of strict separationists who believe that children should come home from school in the
afternoon with the same religious beliefs they held in the morning, untouched
by anything that happened during the school day. They do not trust school
officials to refrain from using equal access as a pretext for school-sponsored
prayer, and they feel that even student-initiated organized worship has no
place in the public schools. Although their passion remains undiminished,
their numbers have dwindled since the 1980s as more and more separationists
have embraced, or at least settled for, equal access. As a result, most of the continuing strife over religion in the public schools takes place between equal-
access supporters, joined in this instance by separationists, and diehard
advocates of traditional state-sponsored school prayer.

As earlier chapters explain, equal access does not permit school officials to
hinder students from praying on their own, but neither does it allow them to
accord any special recognition to religion in general or to the prayers of the
majority. Prayer takes place—or not—at the whim of the students and as their
private action, without official validation. Although many religious people prefer this hands-off approach, it enrages and energizes those who believe that
the nation itself must publicly and officially acknowledge the religious faith on
which it was founded and from which it continues to derive its liberties, its
governmental structure and principles, and its very identity. From this perspective, the students' own prayers, silent or vocal, are beside the point. What
is at issue is not the practice of religion by individuals but the furtherance of
America's commitment, as a nation, to its religious heritage.

The difficulty of defining exactly what is meant by the American religious
heritage is one of the major factors that helps to polarize the two sides of today's
disagreements over school prayer: those who want the students to join in a
common prayer, and those who favor either equal access or no religion in the
schools. In the past, disputes over whose prayers the students should recite were
resolved by means of the expansionist, common-denominator model favored by
Horace Mann as public-school religious exercises evolved from the practices of
specific Protestant denominations to pan-Protestant devotionals. Today, those
who seek a common public-school faith invoke a construct called "Judeo-

Christianity," which might best be described as a form of monotheism enlivened, in some parts of the country, by references to Jesus that are considered *Judeo*-Christian because Jesus was a Jew. Similarly, proponents of posting the Ten Commandments almost invariably mean the King James version, which they define as "Judeo-Christian" in a sense that is indistinguishable from the use of the term "nonsectarian" in the past. As was true in the nineteenth century, people who make this claim accept the KJB as their own religious text and dismiss as insignificant the differences between it and other versions of Scripture, as well as the concerns of Jews and Catholics over its historical uses and significance.

Even if the inclusion of so-called Judeo-Christianity in the public schools were trouble-free with respect to Catholics, Protestants, and Jews, it would nonetheless fail to encompass all believers because of the increasing number of students who practice Islam, Buddhism, Hinduism, Taoism, Shintoism, and various pantheistic or nontheistic faiths. As earlier chapters demonstrated, the expansionist model of broadening public-school prayers to accommodate incomers of different faiths has always been controversial, but in many parts of the country that option no longer exists at all. Despite their differences, Judaism and the various forms of Christianity all profess belief in the same God, but once the circle is expanded to include religions that worship different deities, the notion of common prayer approaches the farcical. Even Islam, whose adherents worship the same God as Christianity and Judaism, is unlikely to become part of a new "umbrella" tradition of Judeo-Christianity-Islam because just as Christianity views itself as the completion or perfection of Judaism, Islam defines itself as a further step in the same divine plan. If it were treated as part of the same religious thread as Judaism and Christianity, the culmination of that tradition would no longer be Christianity but a successor faith—a concept that would be anathema to the very people who are most determined to use the public schools to promote a common American religious tradition ostensibly based on the historical relationship of one faith to another.

To those who favor the equal-access approach, the increasing diversity of America's present-day blend of religious heritages cries out for individualized worship rather than for group prayer determined by the school. But just as nineteenth-century nativists asserted that the continuation of democracy, individual liberty, and Americanism required immigrant children of all backgrounds to respect Protestant principles, so contemporary advocates of state-sponsored prayer make the same argument about what they call Judeo-Christianity. In their view, the influx of students from outside that tradition merely increases the responsibility of the public schools to use majoritarian prayers to Americanize incomers, promote a common religious culture, and solemnize important events. To those who support common school prayer, giving up the link between the government and Judeo-Christianity would represent abject surrender to the notion that descendants of the first European Christian groups to settle in America have no special claim on it as "their" country. Like the nativists before them, they feel that immigrants of other faiths who are fortunate enough to be allowed to come here should acknowledge the primacy of the prevailing culture rather than diluting it or claiming equality with it. Otherwise, they fear, America will no longer be *their* country, which to them means that it will not be America at all.

Among the arguments used to defend the primacy of Judeo-Christianity in the public schools is the allegation that it was the faith on which the Founders built this nation—although in truth most of the founding generation would have been horrified by the thought of amalgamating Protestantism, Catholicism, and Judaism into a sort of theological Brady Bunch. Proponents of state-sponsored Judeo-Christianity also point out that adherents of faiths that fall under that heading have been in this country for many generations and have, consequently, played a major role in its development. In response, foes of state-sponsored prayer assert that neither historical longevity nor demographic status justifies using the machinery of the state to promote any particular religious tradition. Teaching about the Founders' religion and its role in the history of this nation, they declare, is quite different from suggesting that the government should encourage contemporary American children to practice that faith as a matter of patriotism or national identity. It is this disagreement over the designation of a common American religious tradition, more than any other issue, that fuels ongoing conflicts that go far beyond specific prayers or practices to the fundamental principles governing religious expression in the public schools. The equal-access approach has united many people, including some who used to favor government-sponsored prayer and others who once opposed all prayer in the schools; but as the boundaries of this common ground expand, the activists who remain outside its perimeter are becoming increasingly alienated and marginalized.

IN THE END IS THE BEGINNING

The intractable persistence of arguments over religion in public schools understandably frustrates people who wish it could all be *settled,* by which they mean resolved in a way that they would find acceptable. But what satisfies one person will alienate another, so that the only ways to end the debate are either wildly unlikely—one side totally converts all its opponents—or deeply undesirable—one orthodoxy dominates to such an extent that all but the most intrepid foes are cowed into silence. Thus, despite the intense criticism leveled at public officials and courts for failing to find a definitive answer to the school-prayer debate, the real problem lies with the demand itself. It is a rare person who would seek to brush teeth so that they need never be brushed again, or feed a dog so that it *stays* fed, or mow the lawn once and for all. By their nature, teeth, dogs, and lawns are not amenable to such summary treatment, but must be maintained rather than solved. Indeed, any alternative to ongoing maintenance would entail their destruction. The same is true of religious liberty; dealing with diverse religious views in a free society is a matter of social or cultural maintenance, not once-and-for-all solutions. Not only does any resolution based on a particular viewpoint inevitably energize its opponents, but as social and cultural conditions change—and, sooner or later, they do—the times, places, and circumstances in which a given policy remains viable become increasingly narrow.

Although conflicts over governmentally supported expressions of religion are commonly associated with religious diversity, even cultures that are strongly dominated by one religious tradition eventually find themselves beset by sects and schisms, giving rise to the same kinds of struggles that might otherwise occur between different groups. It is difficult to escape the conviction that each person is aware of an interior truth that is subjectively experienced as self-evident: a particular view of God or at least goodness, and of society and what it should be. The tendency to hold such convictions, to join with like-minded allies, and to grapple with the holders of other views thus appears to be an inescapable element of human society, even if the specific controversies through which it manifests itself are perceived (or misperceived) as being capable of definitive resolution. Perhaps this dynamic may ultimately be leading toward the revelation or emergence of some transcendent and universally shared spiritual truth that will revolutionize human understanding—a consideration that belongs more to the realm of theology or metaphysics than to the political and legal world of which this book treats. But even in the terms of that mundane world, it is clear that when religion, for all its sacred character, becomes entwined with public policy, it partakes of the nature of politics; and as Prime Minister Benjamin Disraeli had occasion to observe almost a century and a half ago, "Finality is not the language of politics" (Speech to the House of Commons, February 28, 1859).

Appendix

The information provided here is based on each group's description of itself; its critics would no doubt offer a different characterization. Additional information may be found on each group's website.

Although religious denominations routinely engage in lobbying activities, they are not classified here as "advocacy groups." For instance, the Catholic League for Religious and Civil Rights appears on this list, but the U.S. Catholic Conference does not, because the former is an advocacy group with a distinctively Catholic orientation whereas the latter represents the American Church itself. Similarly, the Baptist Joint Committee on Public Affairs is included, but the Southern Baptist Convention is not.

This list does not include organizations that appear only once in the book and are adequately described in the relevant chapter, nor does it cover ephemeral or long-defunct groups.

- **American Center for Law and Justice:** "Law firm founded by Pat Robertson to represent Christians in church–state cases" (*www.aclj.org*).
- **American Civil Liberties Union:** Works "in courts, legislatures, and communities to defend and preserve the individual rights and liberties guaranteed to all people in this country by the Constitution and laws of the United States" (*www.aclu.org*). Each state has one or more ACLU affiliates, and it is these affiliates that file the kinds of lawsuits discussed in this book; examples include ACLU—Delaware (*www.aclu-de.org*) and the New York Civil Liberties Union (*www.nyclu.org/about.html*).
- **American Family Association:** A Mississippi-based organization founded by Reverend Donald Wildmon, AFA promotes efforts to "change the culture to reflect Biblical truth and traditional values" (*www.afa.net*).

- **American Federation of Teachers:** A union that "represents one million teachers, school support staff, higher education faculty and staff, health care professionals, and state and municipal employees" (*www.aft.org*).
- **American Jewish Congress:** Works to "protect fundamental constitutional freedoms and American democratic institutions, particularly the civil and religious rights and liberties of all Americans and the separation of church and state" (*www.ajcongress.org*).
- **Americans United for Separation of Church and State:** Established as Protestants and Other Americans United..., this group "brings together Americans of many faiths and political viewpoints to defend church–state separation" (*www.au.org*).
- **Anti-Defamation League:** Originally the Anti-Defamation League of B'nai B'rith, this group seeks "to fight anti-Semitism and bigotry, and promote respect among diverse groups in America and the world" (*www.adl.org*).
- **Baptist Joint Committee on Public Affairs:** "The mission of the Baptist Joint Committee is to defend and extend God-given religious liberty for all, bringing a uniquely Baptist witness to the principle that religion must be freely exercised, neither advanced nor inhibited by government" (*www.bjcpa.org*).
- **Catholic League for Religious and Civil Rights:** "Defends the right of Catholics—lay and clergy alike—to participate in American public life without defamation or discrimination.... [And] works to safeguard both the religious freedom rights and the free speech rights of Catholics whenever and wherever they are threatened" (*www.catholicleague.org*).
- **Cato Institute:** "A non-profit public policy research foundation.... [It is] named for Cato's Letters, a series of libertarian pamphlets that helped lay the philosophical foundation for the American Revolution" (*www.cato.org*).
- **Christian Coalition:** "Founded in 1989 by Pat Robertson to give Christians a voice in government [and to] represent the pro-family point of view before local councils, school boards, state legislatures and Congress" (*www.cc.org*).
- **Christian Legal Society:** "A national non-denominational membership organization of attorneys, judges, law professors, and law students, working in association with others, to follow Jesus' command 'to do justice with the love of God'" (*www.clsnet.org*).
- **Concerned Women for America:** "The vision of CWA is for women and like-minded men, from all walks of life, to come together and restore the family to its traditional purpose and thereby allow each member of the

family to realize their God-given potential and be more responsible citizens" (*www.cwfa.org*).

- **Coral Ridge Ministries:** "A television, radio, and print outreach which is touching the lives of millions—nationwide and overseas. CRM's three-fold mission is to evangelize, nurture Christian growth through biblical instruction, and act in obedience to the Cultural Mandate by applying the truth of Scripture to all of life, including civic affairs" (*www.coralridge.org*).

- **Eagle Forum:** Designed "to enable conservative and pro-family men and women to participate in the process of self-government and public policy making so that America will continue to be a land of individual liberty, respect for family integrity, public and private virtue, and private enterprise" (*www.eagleforum.org*).

- **First Amendment Center:** An independent affiliate of the Freedom Forum, this group is "a nonpartisan foundation dedicated to free press, free speech and free spirit for all people" (*www.freedomforum.org/templates/document.asp?documentID=3928*).

- **Free Congress Foundation:** The group's "main focus is on the Culture War. Will America return to the culture that made it great, our traditional, Judeo-Christian, Western culture? Or will we continue the long slide into the cultural and moral decay of political correctness? If we do, America, once the greatest nation on earth, will become no less than a third world country" (*www.freecongress.org*).

- **Lambda Legal Defense and Education Fund:** "A national organization committed to achieving full recognition of the civil rights of lesbians, gay men and people with HIV/AIDS through impact litigation, education and public policy work" (*www.thebody.com/lambda/lambda.html*).

- **Liberty Lobby:** "A pressure group for patriotism—a lobby to fight the organized, special-interest lobbies (both foreign and domestic) that proliferate in the nation's capital" (*www.spotlight.org*).

- **Moral Majority:** "U.S. political action group composed of conservative, fundamentalist Christians.... the group played a significant role in the 1980 elections through its strong support of conservative candidates. It lobbied for prayer and the teaching of creationism in public schools, while opposing the Equal Rights Amendment...homosexual rights, abortion, and the U.S.-Soviet SALT treaties.... The Moral Majority was dissolved in 1989" (*www.encyclopedia.com/html/e/e-moralmajo.asp*).

- **National Association for the Advancement of Colored People:** This group defines its focus as "the protection and enhancement of the civil rights of African Americans and other minorities" (*www.naacp.org*).

- **National Association of Evangelicals:** "The mission ... is to extend the kingdom of God through a fellowship of member denominations, churches, organizations, and individuals, demonstrating the unity of the body of Christ by standing for Biblical truth, speaking with a representative voice, and serving the evangelical community through united action, cooperative ministry, and strategic planning" (*www.nae.net*).
- **National Community Relations Advisory Council:** In its brief to the Supreme Court in *Abington v. Schempp,* this group described itself as "a policy-forming and coordinating body for national and local Jewish organizations concerned with community relations." Its constituent organizations were the Synagogue Council of America, the American Jewish Congress, the Jewish Labor Committee, the Jewish War Veterans of the United States, and 57 local Jewish Community Councils. No website could be found.
- **National Council of the Churches of Christ in the U.S.A.:** "The leading organization in the movement for ecumenical cooperation among Christians in the United States," the NCC is made up of thirty-six Protestant, Anglican, and Orthodox Christian denominations. The organization "works for peace and justice in the United States, addressing issues ranging from poverty and racism, to the environment, family ministries, and much more. It serves churches through a wide variety of educational ministries. And it coordinates the production of national network television and cable TV programming of religious interest" (*www.ncccusa.org*).
- **National Education Association:** "America's oldest and largest organization committed to advancing the cause of public education. . . . NEA proudly claims more than 2.6 million members who work at every level of education" (*www.nea.org*).
- **National Parent Teacher Association:** "A not-for-profit association of parents, educators, students, and other citizens active in their schools and communities, PTA is a leader in reminding our nation of its obligations to children" (*www.pta.org/index.asp*).
- **National School Boards Association:** "Engages in a public relations program designed to increase public awareness of NSBA, the state school board associations, local school boards and issues directly affecting public elementary and secondary education" (*www.nsba.org*).
- **People for the American Way:** "Organizes and mobilizes Americans to

fight for fairness, justice, civil rights and the freedoms guaranteed by the Constitution" (*www.pfaw.org*).

- **Rutherford Institute:** Does "vital legal work in courtrooms around America [for] parents whose rights are violated, churches whose doors are unlawfully shut, women who endure sexual harassment, schoolchildren whose rights to religious free expression and due process are curbed, and many other people in need of legal service" (*www.rutherford.org*).

- **Synagogue Council of America:** In its brief in *Abington v. Schempp*, this group described itself as "a co-ordinating body representing the three divisions of Jewish religious life: Orthodox, Conservative and Reform." Its members included associations of rabbis and congregations, such as the Rabbinical Council of America and the Union of American Hebrew Congregations. No website could be found.

- **Traditional Values Coalition:** "The largest non-denominational, grassroots church lobby in America [whose] membership of over 43,000 churches bridges racial and socio-economic barriers and includes most Christian denominations" (*http://64.55.184.74/tvc1/index.php*).

- **Wallbuilders:** "Dedicated to the restoration of the moral and religious foundation on which America was built" (*http://ssl.catalog.com/~wall/IntroductiontoWB*).

Notes

CHAPTER ONE: CRUCIBLE

1. Hood also demanded satisfaction for an episode that had occurred the previous year, when Zachary was in kindergarten. In response to an assignment to draw a Thanksgiving poster to be displayed in the hallway outside the classroom, he drew a picture of Jesus. School officials first included all the children's drawings in the display, then took Zachary's down, then put it back up in a less conspicuous position among the other posters. The federal district court dismissed that claim, but the Court of Appeals for the Third Circuit ordered that Hood be given a chance to amend some flaws found in her complaint. As of June 2003, no subsequent decisions had been filed.

CHAPTER FIVE: STALIN AND SCHOOL PRAYER

1. Any individual, group, or organization that is not a party in a lawsuit but will be affected by the outcome may request a court's permission to present its views in an amicus curiae (friend of the court) brief. If the brief is submitted on behalf of more than one entity, the plural is "amici curiae." In this instance, two Jewish organizations petitioned for leave to submit an amici brief because, among other things, the children of minority faiths are affected by the way in which school prayer is handled. Descriptions of these organizations, as well as the other advocacy groups mentioned in this book, can be found in the Appendix.

2. Only the majority opinion of the Court is legally binding, but any justice is free to write a separate, nonbinding opinion of his or her own, or to sign on to an opinion written by another justice. Concurring opinions, also called concurrences, are written by justices who agree with the majority decision but wish to emphasize a particular point or to express additional views that the majority of the Court may not share. Dissenting opinions, also called dissents, are written by justices who desire to explain why they disagree with the majority decision.

CHAPTER SIX: THE MYTH OF MADALYN MURRAY O'HAIR

1. Additional early scholarly studies on responses to *Engel* and *Abington* are summarized in Boles, 1967.

CHAPTER SEVEN: PICNIC WITH A TIGER

1. Alternatively, constitutional amendments could be initiated by a constitutional convention called by Congress at the request of two-thirds of the state legislatures, but that has never happened. Any such amendment would have to be ratified by three-quarters of the states.
2. The words "Protestants and Other" have since been deleted from the group's title.
3. The words "of B'nai B'rith" have since been deleted from the group's title.

CHAPTER EIGHT: BEWARE OF THE LEOPARD

1. Federal cases are tried in whichever federal district court has jurisdiction over the relevant geographical area; each state has one or more federal district courts. On appeal, the case goes to the circuit court of appeals that has jurisdiction over that state. There are eleven such courts of appeals and one for the District of Columbia. *Stein* was decided by the Court of Appeals for the Second Circuit, which deals with cases from New York, Vermont, and Connecticut. Any decision of a circuit court is binding in all the states it covers but not in any other state. A map showing the circuit courts and the states each one covers can be found at *http://www.law.emory.edu/FEDCTS.*
2. The rules of the Senate, although complicated, can be understood by a normal human being within the average lifespan. The logic of the House rules does not appear to be terrestrial in origin.

CHAPTER NINE: FULL COURT PRESS

1. Some proponents of this legislation call it "court-checking" or "court-curbing"—terms that intentionally suggest disciplining an unruly dog that wants to leave its mark anywhere and everywhere. Other advocates of the practice, however, proudly employ the term "court-stripping." Because "court-stripping" is widely used by both sides, and because "court-checking" and "court-curbing" are broader terms that also cover such approaches as judicial impeachment and term limits, "court-stripping" is used here as the best way to describe attempts to remove certain topics from the jurisdiction of the federal courts.

CHAPTER TEN: THE REST IS SILENCE

1. In 1979, the Massachusetts legislature once again amended the law, this time to permit vocal prayer. When that version was struck down in *Kent v. Commissioner of Education,* 380 Mass. 235 (1980), the legislature established a period of "reverent silence." The current version of the law, enacted in 1985, provides for a minute of silence "for personal thoughts," with no reference to prayer or meditation.
2. Current New Mexico law states, "Students in the public schools may voluntarily engage in student-initiated moments of silent meditation" (N.M. Stat. Ann. § 22–27–3 [1995]).
3. Rodney K. Smith's *Public Prayer and the Constitution* (1987) provides a particularly articulate and thoughtful treatment of this originalist approach to the Constitution with respect to school prayer, addressing several of the specific legislative proposals

discussed in Chapters Nine through Twelve. A broader and similarly excellent treatment of these issues by an anti-originalist author may be found in Peter Irons's *Brennan vs. Rehnquist: The Battle for the Constitution* (1994).

4. Warren A. Nord, in *Religion and American Education: Rethinking a National Dilemma* (1995), analyzes this case within the context of the tension between conservative Christianity and various kinds of humanism. Having examined the challenged texts, he concludes that even if secular humanism is not a religion, the texts violated governmental neutrality between religion and nonreligion because they "promote secular over religious ways of making sense of the world" (p. 179). An extended discussion of this case also appears in my 1992 book, *What Johnny Shouldn't Read: Textbook Censorship in America.*

CHAPTER ELEVEN: CAUTION! PARADIGMS MAY SHIFT

1. The First Amendment states: "Congress shall make no law respecting an *establishment* of religion, or prohibiting the *free exercise* thereof; or abridging the freedom of *speech,* or of the press, or the right of the people peaceably to assemble, and to petition the Government for a redress of grievances" (emphasis added).

2. Following its success with regard to school prayer, the phrase "equal access" has been used with increasing frequency in other contexts to suggest that the desired outcome would set a certain class of persons or a particular type of action on a par with another, rather than granting privileged status to either. The term has, for instance, been used in reference to voting rights, health care, participation in political campaigns, and the ability to influence legislation.

3. Jarmin described Christian Voice as "a national lobby with a membership of over 300,000 evangelical Christians" ("Voluntary School Prayer Constitutional Amendment," p. 242).

CHAPTER TWELVE: PERKINS'S LAST STAND

1. Lott was elected to the Senate in 1988 and later served as majority leader.

2. Mack was elected to the Senate in 1988.

CHAPTER THIRTEEN: MISSISSIPPI LEARNING

1. In 1981, the Court of Appeals for the Fifth Circuit had struck down a somewhat similar law in *Karen B. v. Treen*. At issue was a Louisiana statute authorizing school officials to allow teachers to ask whether any student wished to lead a prayer that could be no more than five minutes in length. If no student volunteered, the teacher could lead a prayer. The Fifth Circuit's decision was summarily affirmed by the Supreme Court in 1982. Similarly, *Chandler v. James* (later *Chandler v. Siegelman*) challenged an Alabama statute that was almost identical to its Mississippi counterpart; this case is discussed in Chapter Fourteen.

2. The lawsuit also addressed the distribution of Gideon Bibles to fifth-graders, classroom prayers led by some teachers, and a history teacher's use of religious materials, but the main issues were loudspeaker prayer and Bible classes.

CHAPTER FOURTEEN: THE SCHOOL AND THE RABBI

1. The decision in *Lemon v. Kurtzman* covered two cases, one from Pennsylvania and one from Rhode Island. Attorney Henry Sawyer III, who had represented the Schempps in *Abington v. Schempp*, acted on behalf of Pennsylvania plaintiffs who opposed public funding for religious education. Leo Pfeffer, who had argued against school prayer in *Chamberlin v. Dade County* and testified at several congressional hearings in opposition to a constitutional amendment, played a similar role in the Rhode Island case.

2. Other plaintiffs sued neighboring Talladega County, where school officials changed their policies and were dismissed from the case at an early stage.

CHAPTER FIFTEEN: ZEN AND THE ART OF CONSTITUTION MAINTENANCE

1. The Religious Freedom Restoration Act provided that the government cannot refuse to waive any requirement that inadvertently burdens someone's ability to practice his or her religion unless the denial is justified by a compelling state interest. Thus, if a Sikh were ordered to remove his turban in a courtroom only because it is the custom for men to uncover their heads indoors, he could challenge that order under RFRA if he wished to retain his turban for religious reasons. This legislation, which President William Clinton signed in 1993, was struck down by the Supreme Court in *Boerne v. Flores* (1997).

2. In October 2002, a revised version of the Joint Statement was published under the title *A Shared Vision: Religious Liberty in the 21st Century*. Endorsed by only five comparatively like-minded groups—the American Jewish Committee, Baptist Joint Committee on Public Affairs, Interfaith Alliance Foundation, National Council of Churches, and Religious Action Center of Reform Judaism—it offers a more separationist interpretation of current law. It may be found on the website of the Baptist Joint Committee (*www.bjcpa.org*).

Works Cited

Adams, Douglas. *The Hitchhiker's Guide to the Galaxy.* New York: Pocket Books, 1979.

Address of the Catholic Lay Citizens, of the City and County of Philadelphia, to Their Fellow-Citizens, in Reply to the Presentment of the Grand Jury of the Court of Quarter Sessions of May Term 1844, in Regard to the Causes of the Late Riots in Philadelphia. Philadelphia: M. Fithian, 1844.

Alley, Robert S. *School Prayer: The Court, the Congress, and the First Amendment.* Buffalo, N.Y.: Prometheus Books, 1994.

———. *Without a Prayer: Religious Expression in Public Schools.* Amherst, N.Y.: Prometheus Books, 1996.

"Amending the Pledge of Allegiance to the Flag of the United States." Committee on the Judiciary of the U.S. House of Representatives, 83d Congress (1954), 2d Session, Report No. 1693.

American Jewish Congress, et al. "Religion in the Public Schools: A Joint Statement of Current Law" (1995).

Asbury, Herbert. *The Gangs of New York: An Informal History of the Underworld.* New York: Thunder's Mouth Press, 2001 (originally published in New York by Alfred A. Knopf [1928]).

Baptist Joint Committee on Public Affairs, et al. *The Equal Access Act and the Public Schools: Questions and Answers* (n.d.).

Beaney, William M., and Edward N. Beiser. "Prayer and Politics: The Impact of *Engel* and *Schempp* on the Political Process." In Robert Sikorski, ed. *Prayer in Public Schools and the Constitution, 1961–1992.* Vol. 1. New York: Garland Publishing, 1993, pp. 411–39 (originally published in the *Journal of Public Law* 13 [1964]: 475–503).

The Bible in the Public Schools. Introduction by Robert G. McCloskey. New York: Da Capo Press, 1967 (originally published in Cincinnati, Ohio, by Robert Clarke & Co. [1870]).

Billington, Ray Allen. *The Protestant Crusade, 1800–1860: A Study of the Origins of American Nativism.* New York: Macmillan, 1938.

Binney, Charles C. *The Life of Horace Binney, with Selections from His Letters.* Philadelphia: Lippincott, 1903.

Boles, Donald E. *The Bible, Religion, and the Public Schools*. Ames, Iowa: Iowa State University Press, 1961.

————. *The Two Swords: Commentaries and Cases in Religion and Education*. Ames: Iowa State University Press, 1967.

Bourne, William O. *History of the Public School Society of the City of New York, with Portraits of the Presidents of the Society*. New York: W. Wood, 1870.

Brann, Henry. *Most Reverend John Hughes, First Archbishop of New York*. New York: Dodd, Mead, 1892.

Burrows, Edwin G., and Mike Wallace. *Gotham: A History of New York City to 1898*. New York: Oxford University Press, 1999.

Center for Law and Religious Freedom of the Christian Legal Society. *A Guide to the Equal Access Act*. Revised edition. Annandale, Va.: 1993.

"Congress, the Court, and the Constitution." Hearing Before the Subcommittee on the Constitution of the Committee on the Judiciary of the U.S. House of Representatives, January 29, 1998.

"Constitutional Restraints Upon the Judiciary." Hearings Before the Subcommittee on the Constitution of the Committee on the Judiciary of the U.S. Senate, May 20, 21, and June 22, 1981.

DelFattore, Joan. *What Johnny Shouldn't Read: Textbook Censorship in America*. New Haven: Yale University Press, 1992.

Dolbeare, Kenneth M., and Phillip E. Hammond. *The School Prayer Decisions: From Court Policy to Local Practice*. Chicago: University of Chicago Press, 1971.

Dudley, Mark E. *Engel v. Vitale (1962): Religion in the Schools*. New York: Twenty-First Century Books, 1995.

Dunn, William. *What Happened to Religious Education? The Decline of Religious Teaching in the Public Elementary School, 1776–1861*. Baltimore: Johns Hopkins University Press, 1958.

English Bible, Translated Out of the Original Tongues by the Commandment of King James the First, Anno 1611. Vol. 1. London: David Nutt, 1903.

"Equal Access: A First Amendment Question." Hearings Before the Committee on the Judiciary of the U.S. Senate, April 28 and August 3, 1983.

Feldberg, Michael. *The Philadelphia Riots of 1844: A Study of Ethnic Conflict*. Contributions in American History, No. 43. Westport, Conn.: Greenwood Press, 1975.

Fenwick, Lynda B. *Should the Children Pray? A Historical, Judicial, and Political Examination of Public School Prayer*. Waco, Tex.: Markham Press Fund of Baylor University Press, 1989.

Fleming, William S. *God in Our Public Schools*. 2d edition. Pittsburgh: National Reform Association, 1944.

Formicola, Jo Renée, and Hubert Morken, eds. *Everson Revisited: Religion, Education, and Law at the Crossroads*. New York: Rowman & Littlefield Publishers, 1997.

Fraser, James W. *Between Church and State: Religion and Public Education in a Multicultural America*. New York: St. Martins Griffin, 1999.

Friendly, Fred W., and Martha J. H. Elliott. *The Constitution: That Delicate Balance*. New York: Random House, 1984.

Full and Complete Account of the Late Awful Riots in Philadelphia. Philadelphia: J. B. Perry, 1844.

Hassard, John R. G. *Life of John Hughes, First Archbishop of New York.* New York: Arno Press and the *New York Times,* 1969 (originally published in New York by D. Appleton and Co. [1866]).

"Hearings on the Equal Access Act." Hearings Before the Subcommittee on Elementary, Secondary, and Vocational Education of the Committee on Education and Labor of the U.S. House of Representatives, June 16, October 18, 19, 20, 1983.

Hertzke, Allen D. *Representing God in Washington: The Role of Religious Lobbies in the American Polity.* Knoxville: University of Tennessee Press, 1988.

Important and Interesting Debate on the Claim of the Catholics to a Portion of the Common School Fund; with the Arguments of Counsel, Before the Board of Aldermen of the City of New-York, on Thursday and Friday, the 29th and 30th of October, 1840. Specially Reported by R. Sutton, Professional Short-Hand Writer. 2d edition. Published by the Proprietor of the New-York Freeman's Journal, 1840.

Irons, Peter. *Brennan vs. Rehnquist: The Battle for the Constitution.* New York: Alfred A. Knopf, 1994.

Jackson, Joseph. *Encyclopedia of Philadelphia.* Vol. 1. Harrisburg, Penn.: The National Historical Association, 1931.

Johnson, Alvin W., and Frank H. Yost. *Separation of Church and State in the United States.* Minneapolis: University of Minnesota Press, 1948.

"Judicial Activism: Defining the Problem and Its Impact." Hearings before the Subcommittee on the Constitution, Federalism, and Property Rights of the Committee on the Judiciary of the U.S. Senate, June 11, July 15, 29, 1997.

"Judicial Misconduct and Discipline." Hearing before the Subcommittee on Courts and Intellectual Property of the Committee on the Judiciary of the U.S. House of Representatives, May 15, 1997.

"Judicial Reform Act of 1997." Hearing before the Subcommittee on Courts and Intellectual Property of the Committee on the Judiciary of the U.S. House of Representatives, May 14, 1997.

Kaestle, Carl F. *The Evolution of an Urban School System: New York City, 1750–1850.* Cambridge: Harvard University Press, 1973.

———. *Pillars of the Republic: Common Schools and American Society, 1780–1860.* American Century Series. New York: Hill and Wang, 1983.

Kirlin, Joseph L. J. *Catholicity in Philadelphia from the Earliest Missionaries Down to the Present Time.* Philadelphia: John Joseph McVey, 1909.

Lannie, Vincent P. *Public Money and Parochial Education: Bishop Hughes, Governor Seward, and the New York School Controversy.* Cleveland, Ohio: Press of Case Western Reserve University, 1968.

Laubach, John H. *School Prayers: Congress, the Courts, and the Public.* Washington, D.C.: Public Affairs Press, 1969.

Laycock, Douglas. "Equal Access and Moments of Silence: The Equal Status of Religious Speech by Private Speakers." *Northwestern University Law Review* 81 (1986): 1–67.

Lord, Robert H., John E. Sexton, and Edward T. Harrington, *History of the Archdiocese of Boston in the Various Stages of Its Development, 1604–1943.* Vol. II. New York: Sheed and Ward, 1944.

McCollum, Vashti. *One Woman's Fight.* Garden City, New York: Doubleday, 1951.

Moen, Matthew C. *The Christian Right and Congress.* Tuscaloosa: University of Alabama Press, 1989.

Morris, Irving. "Of Power and Prayer." *Delaware Lawyer* (Fall 1986), pp. 8–15.

Murray, William J. *Let Us Pray: A Plea for Prayer in Our Schools.* New York: W. Morrow, 1995.

Nord, Warren A. *Religion and American Education: Rethinking a National Dilemma.* Chapel Hill: University of North Carolina Press, 1995.

Oberholtzer, Ellis P. *Philadelphia: A History of the City and Its People.* Vol. 2. Philadelphia: Clarke, 1912.

O'Connor, Thomas H. *Fitzpatrick's Boston, 1846–1866: John Bernard Fitzpatrick, Third Bishop of Boston.* Boston: Northeastern University Press, 1984.

O'Hair, Madalyn Murray. *An Atheist Epic: The Complete Unexpurgated Story of How Bible and Prayers Were Removed from the Public Schools of the United States.* Austin, Tex.: American Atheist Press, 1989.

O'Shea, John J. *The Two Kenricks.* Philadelphia: John Joseph McVey, 1904.

"Prayer in Public Schools and Buildings—Federal Court Jurisdiction." Hearings Before the Subcommittee on Courts, Civil Liberties, and the Administration of Justice of the Committee on the Judiciary of U.S. House of Representatives, July 29, 30, August 19, 21, September 9, 1980.

"Prayers in Public Schools and Other Matters." Hearing before the Committee on the Judiciary of the U.S. Senate, July 26, 1962.

"Proposed Constitutional Amendment to Permit Voluntary Prayer." Hearings Before the Committee on the Judiciary of the U.S. Senate, July 29, August 18, September 16, 1982.

Ravitch, Diane. *The Great School Wars: New York City, 1805–1973. A History of the Public Schools as Battlefield of Social Change.* New York: Basic Books, 1974.

Ravitch, Diane, and Joseph P. Viteritti, eds. *Making Good Citizens: Education and Civil Society.* New Haven: Yale University Press, 2001.

Ravitch, Frank S. *School Prayer and Discrimination: The Civil Rights of Religious Minorities and Dissenters.* Boston: Northeastern University Press, 1999.

"Religious Liberty." Hearings Before the Committee on the Judiciary of the U.S. Senate, September 12, October 20 and 25, 1995.

"Religious Speech Protection Act." Hearing Before the Subcommittee on Elementary, Secondary, and Vocational Education of the Committee on Education and Labor of the U.S. House of Representatives, March 28, 1984.

Report of the Select Committee of the Board of Education, to Which Was Referred a Communication from the Trustees of the Fourth Ward, in Relation to the Sectarian Character of Certain Books in Use in the Schools of That Ward. New York: Levi D. Slamm, 1843.

Report of the Trial of McLaurin F. Cooke, Sub-Master of the Eliot School, of the City of Boston, for An Assault and Battery upon Thomas J. Wall, a Pupil in That School, with the Arguments of Counsel, and the Opinion of the Court Reported in Full. Boston: A.M. Lawrence & Co., 1859.

Sandburg, Carl. *Abraham Lincoln.* Vol. 3. New York: Scribner's, 1926.

Scharf, J. Thomas, and Thompson Westcott. *History of Philadelphia, 1609–1884.* Philadelphia: L. H. Everts, 1884.

"School Prayer." Hearings Before the Subcommittee on Constitutional Amendments of the Committee on the Judiciary of the U.S. Senate, August 1, 2, 3, 4, 5, 8, 1966.

"School Prayer Constitutional Amendment." Committee on the Judiciary of the U.S. Senate, 98th Congress (1984), 2d Session, Report No. 98–347.

"School Prayers: Proposed Amendments to the Constitution Relating to Prayers and Bible Reading in the Public Schools." Hearings before the Committee on the Judiciary of the U.S. House of Representatives, April 22, 23, 24, 28, 29, 30; May 1, 6, 7, 8, 13, 14, 15, 20, 21, 27, 28; June 3, 1964.

Shaw, Richard. *Dagger John: The Unquiet Life and Times of Archbishop John Hughes of New York.* New York: Paulist Press, 1977.

Shea, John G. *A History of the Catholic Church within the Limits of the United States, from the First Attempted Colonization to the Present Time.* Vol. 4. New York: John G. Shea, 1892.

Sherrow, Victoria. *Separation of Church and State.* New York: F. Watts, 1992.

Smith, Rodney K. *Public Prayer and the Constitution: A Case Study in Constitutional Interpretation.* Wilmington, Del.: Scholarly Resources, 1987.

Spear, Samuel Thayer. *Religion and the State, or, The Bible and the Public Schools.* New York: Dodd, Mead, 1876.

"Statutory Limitations on Federal Jurisdiction." Hearings Before the Subcommittee on Courts, Civil Liberties, and the Administration of Justice of the Committee on the Judiciary of the U.S. House of Representatives, June 3, July 16, 23, 1981.

Story, Joseph. *Commentaries on the Constitution of the United States.* Reprinted with an introduction by Ronald D. Rotunda and John E. Nowak. Durham, N.C.: Carolina Academic Press, 1987 (originally published in Cambridge, Mass., by Charles Folsom [1833]).

"Voluntary School Prayer Amendment." Committee on the Judiciary of the U.S. Senate, 98th Congress (1984), 2d Session, Report No. 98–348.

"Voluntary School Prayer Constitutional Amendment." Hearings Before the Subcommittee on the Constitution of the Committee on the Judiciary of the U.S. Senate, April 29, May 2, June 27, 1983.

Warren, Rita, with Dick Schneider. *Mom, They Won't Let Us Pray.* Old Tappan, N.J.: Chosen Books, 1975.

Way, H. Frank. "Survey Research on Judicial Decisions: The Prayer and Bible Reading Cases." In Robert Sikorski, ed. *Prayer in Public Schools and the Constitution, 1961–1992.* Vol. 1. New York: Garland Publishing, 1993, pp. 457–73 (originally published in the *Western Political Quarterly* 21 (1968): 189–205).

Index